2nd edition

Teaching Children and Youth with Behavior Disorders

THOMAS M. SHEA
Southern Illinois University at Edwardsville

ANNE M. BAUER
University of Cincinnati

PRENTICE-HALL, INC., Englewood Cliffs, New Jersey 07632

Library of Congress Cataloging-in-Publication Data

Shea, Thomas M. (date)
   Teaching children and youth with behavior disorders.

   Bibliography: p.
   Includes index.
   1. Problem children—Education—United States.
2. Mentally ill children—Education—United States.
3. Individualized instruction. I. Bauer, Anne M.
II. Title.
LC4802.S43 1987   371.93′0973   86-5065
ISBN 0-13-891888-0

Editorial/production supervision and
  interior design: **Marjorie Borden**
Cover design: **Wanda Lubelska Design**
Manufacturing buyer: **John Hall**

To
Dolores, Kevin, and Keith
  and
Riley and Demian

LC
4802
.S43
1987

ISBN 0-13-891888-0   01

Prentice-Hall International (UK) Limited, *London*
Prentice-Hall of Australia Pty. Limited, *Sydney*
Prentice-Hall Canada Inc., *Toronto*
Prentice-Hall Hispanoamericana, S.A., *Mexico*
Prentice-Hall of India Private Limited, *New Delhi*
Prentice-Hall of Japan, Inc., *Tokyo*
Prentice-Hall of Southeast Asia Pte. Ltd., *Singapore*
Editora Prentice-Hall do Brasil, Ltda., *Rio de Janeiro*

Contents

Preface

A special educator of students with behavior disorders related the following incident that occurred during an individual instructional session with Carl, a fourteen-year-old student.

> Carl and I had been working on a mathematics lesson for about 15 minutes. During this time Carl remained calm, cool, and collected, effectively ignoring all my attempts to motivate him and engage him in the problems at hand.
>
> Finally, in a state of utter exasperation, I said, "Come on, Carl. Let's get with it. It wouldn't hurt you to be a little more cooperative, here."
>
> Carl looked at me with astonishment and said, "Mrs. Foley, no one ever told you that teaching kids like me was going to be easy."

Carl is right. Working with children and youth with behavior disorders is a difficult, frustrating, and complex job. It requires special educators who are dedicated to their profession, concerned about the students with whom they work, and able and willing to give of themselves. However, it is significant work from which a special educator can derive much satisfaction and joy. In our work with children and youth with behavior disorders, there are no magical techniques or miraculous cures.

As Smith and McGinnis (1982) suggest, there is no single approach that provides the special educator with the strategies needed to deal with the variety of problems exhibited by students with behavior disorders. Kavale and Hirshoren (1980) continue on the same note when they say that teacher education programs "should provide students with the opportunity to explore elements from a number of theoretical models by producing a comprehensive functional training program incorporating a variety of theoretical approaches and techniques" (p. 154). Through the application of an ecological framework, this text strives to provide special educators with the many theoretical perspectives, interventions, strategies, and decision-making skills they need to effectively help students with behavior disorders and their parents.

Part I introduces the reader to the problems and characteristics of the children and youth about whom this book is written. Current definitions, and an ecological framework designed to facilitate the special educator's analysis and understanding of the problems of children and youth with behavior disorders, are presented. The section concludes with a discussion of behavior characteristics frequently exhibited by children and youth with behavior disorders.

Part II focuses the reader's attention on assessment, identification, and the Individualized Education Plan, and placement. Services needed by children and youth with behavior disorders are presented. Behavioral assessment is offered as a method for determining the student's present level of functioning as a basis for program planning.

Part III addresses instruction and models of teaching. This section includes techniques for developing appropriate instructional plans and explores the parameters of the instructional environment. Models of teaching and the selection of strategies for teaching students with behavior disorders are discussed.

Part IV is an extensive review of management and instructional interventions, and their application. Behavior management is defined, and several guideines for the application of any intervention are provided. Psychodynamic-psychoeducational, behavioral, biophysical, and environmental interventions are reviewed. The importance of involving parents in the education of the child with behavior disorders and techniques for parent-special educator involvement is addressed. The problems, characteristics, and service needs unique to secondary students with behavior disorders are also discussed.

This text is a synthesis of the contributions of hundreds of special educators, researchers, authors, parents, and students. We have attempted to acknowledge their contributions with extensive references at the end of the book. To any person we have neglected, we extend an apology. The oversight is unintentional.

Finally, special thanks to Dolores Shea and Riley Humler, our best friends and partners, and to Kevin, Keith, and Demian, for their patience and encouragement.

Thomas M. Shea
Anne M. Bauer

1

An Introduction to Children and Youth with Behavior Disorders

INTRODUCTION

On February 5, 1963, John F. Kennedy, thirty-fifth President of the United States, delivered to Congress and the nation a message that was to significantly impact on the education of children and youth with behavior disorders. His message included several proposals designed to facilitate a national effort on behalf of individuals with mental illness and mental retardation.

This national effort initiated the development of a new philosophy of service for children and youths with behavior disorders. The education of exceptional children became not a goodwill gesture but a matter of justice (Gilhool, 1973). PL 88-164, passed in 1963, foreshadowed a series of legislative actions that impacted upon the education of exceptional children. Of particular significance is Public Law 94-142 (The Education for All Handicapped Children Act), which mandates a *free, appropriate, public education for all handicapped children.*

Congress emphasized the key elements of Public Law (PL) 94-142 with the words *free, appropriate, public,* and *all.* Congress intended that *all* handicapped children receive an education regardless of their race, religion, sex, or the uniqueness of their disability. They are to receive an education that is *appropriate* to their individual needs. This education is to be *free* (without cost) to the child or his or her parents or guardian. Finally, the handicapped child's *free, appropriate* education is to be provided by the *public* school system rather than in private schools or institutional settings.

1

Practitioners of special education willingly accepted the mandates of PL 88-164 and PL 94-142, and have made significant progress in the education of children and youth with behavior disorders since 1963.

In this text, many facets of the development of special education for children and youths with behavior disorders are discussed. Included are many proposals and recommendations designed to assist in the efforts of special educators to provide a truly free, appropriate public education for all children and youths with behavior disorders.

In this chapter, an effort is made to differentiate between the behavior problems indigenous to normal child growth and development and those characteristic of children and young persons with behavior disorders. The problem of defining behavior disorders, as well as several related variables such as prevalence, persistence, sex, age, and intelligence, are discussed. The second portion of the chapter is devoted to a review of the major premises of four traditional theoretical perspectives of the etiology of behavior disorders.

OBJECTIVES

After completing this chapter, you will be able to—

1. describe the differences between the developmental problems of normal children and the problems of children and youth with behavior disorders;
2. discuss the elements of a definition;
3. describe several definitions of behavior disorders;
4. contrast behavior disorders and pseudobehavior disorders;
5. discuss several important variables to be considered when applying a definition of behavior disorders;
6. describe the major premises of the four major theoretical perspectives of the etiology of behavior disorders.

A CASE FOR CONSIDERATION

The teacher was sitting on a stool, facing four elementary-school students across a kidney-shaped table. She was presenting flash cards of the day's reading vocabulary. The students were holding the word cards they had correctly read.

When it was John's turn, he continued to gaze out the window, though the teacher repeated his name twice. She gently moved his head toward her, saying, "John, it's time to read." John read the word in a high-pitched parrotlike voice, and was given the card to hold. He immediately returned to gazing out of the window. Michael, spinning a word card while waiting his turn, tried to grab the card the teacher was holding, saying, "It's my turn. Give me the card." The teacher replied, "Hands down. Then you may have your turn." Michael continued to grab for the card, saying, "Give me my turn. He's got more cards than me. I got to get more cards." The teacher repeated, "Michael, hands down. Then you may have your turn." Michael dropped his hands, read the word, and grabbed the card.

Linda, the third student, was tapping her pencil and swinging her feet while waiting her turn. The teacher said, "Your turn, Linda. Pencil down." Linda put the pencil down, read the word, and took the card. Kevin, the last child at the table, was then shown a card. "It's 'put,'" he stated. The teacher replied, "No, Kevin, the word is 'pot.'" Kevin shouted, "I said 'pot.' Give me the card." The teacher presented him with another flash card. "Give me the card. Can't you hear? Give me the _____ card." Kevin grabbed John's cards, tore them in two, and threw them at the teacher.

This sketch describes the behavior of four very different children. One child is withdrawn, another verbally aggressive. A third student seems more active than children of the same age, and a fourth frequently destroys materials and is verbally and physically aggressive. Their one commonality appears to be placement in a special-education program for the behavior-disordered. Yet the teacher is responsible for meeting the individual behavioral and instructional needs of each student. The first several objectives of this chapter involve a discussion of the characteristics shared by children and youth with behavior disorders.

OBJECTIVE ONE: *To describe the differences between the developmental problems of normal children and the problems of children and youth with behavior disorders.*

Baker and Stullken, writing in 1938, stated, "All children are at times problems" (p. 37). Ten years later, Rubenstein (1948) reiterated that in the diagnosis of a behavior disorder we must make the difficult comparison of the "unlikeness" of the child to normal standards of childhood that are themselves frequently problematic. Children and youth with behavior disorders do not have a "monopoly" on problem behaviors; problem behaviors indicative of behavior disorders are commonly found among normal children (Hewett & Taylor, 1980).

Children perceived as "normal" have periods during which, under certain environmental conditions, they could be classified as behavior-disordered. It is normal (not unusual) for human beings to have periods that are characterized by poor decision making, inadequate learning of acceptable behavior, crisis, conflict, depression, and stress. At these times the individual manifests socially unacceptable behaviors similar to the behaviors exhibited by those classified as behavior-disordered.

MacFarlane, Allen, and Honzik (1954) reported the findings of a longitudinal study of the developmental problems of normal children. The researchers selected every third child born in Berkeley, California, between January 1, 1928 and June 30, 1929, or a total of 252 boys and girls. They analyzed four developmental problem categories: (1) biological functioning and control (eneuresis, insufficient appetite); (2) motor manifestations (thumb-sucking, overactivity, nail-biting); (3) social standards (negativism, lying); and (4) personality patterns (overdependence, excessive reserve). At each of fourteen age levels between the twenty-first month and fourteenth year, one third or more of the followed children exhibited behavior problems in at least one of the categories. This study and later ones (Johnson, Wahl, Martin, & Johansson, 1973; Werry & Quay, 1971) indicate that behavior problems are a common manifestation of the growth and development patterns of normal children.

The range and reliability of normal behavior is problematic when defining behavior disorders (Kauffman, 1981). A broad range of behaviors are accepted as normal. Behavior problems of normal children may be transient, age-specific, and developmentally common problems that do not persist over an extended period. The differences in the behavior of "normal" children and youth and those with behavior disorders are identified by differences in the frequency, degree, duration of behaviors, and symptom clustering rather than in the kind of behavior (Hewett & Taylor, 1980; Kauffman, 1985). More specifically, the differences are quantitative rather than qualitative. Identifying children and youths with behavior disorders involves comparing them to the nebulous and indeterminate standards of normal (Kauffman, 1985). Thus, it appears that individuals generally perceived as "normal" could be mistakenly diagnosed and labeled abnormal or deviant at certain developmental stages and under certain environmental conditions.

OBJECTIVE TWO: *To describe the elements of a definition.*

The definitions of behavior disorders in use today are hardly more reliable than those used during the nineteenth century (Kauffman, 1976). Historically, definitions of behavior disorders have relied primarily on clinical judgment (McGinnis, Kiraly, & Smith, 1984). This is essentially true of the vast majority of the definitions used presently in the literature. The definition a special educator accepts is important, because it reflects how that individual conceptualizes the problem and selects interventions to help these children and youth. Definitions are applied to determine "who" will be served "how."

Wood (1982) suggested that a useful definition or description of disordered or disturbed behavior contains six elements—four related to the definition itself and two to its application. The first element is the "disturber," who is seen as the focus of the problem. This is followed by the "problem behavior" element, which asks how the problem behavior is described. The third element in a definition is the "setting," or where the behavior occurs. The fourth is the "disturbed" element, or who perceives the behavior as a problem.

One element that refers to the application of the definition is "operationalizing"; that is, through what operations and by whom is the definition used to differentiate children and youth with behavior disorders from other nondisturbed and exceptional children and youth or to assess their needs? The final element in a definition is its "utility" as a basis for planning activities for labeled or identified individuals.

If these six elements are not sufficiently addressed in a definition, Wood suggests that those discussing behavior disorders should not assume they are communicating with one another. In all probability, each person involved in the discussion is functioning under a personal definition that may differ from other individuals'.

In the next section, several definitions or descriptions of those students classified as behavior-disordered are presented. The reader is encouraged to apply Wood's elements of a good description of disordered/disturbed behavior while studying and discussing the definitions.

OBJECTIVE THREE: *To describe several definitions of behavior disorders.*

The problem of the multitude of definitions has been an enduring one; in 1938 Baker and Stullken wrote of the confusion in terminology concerning behavior disorders. This confusion is compounded by the "realization that the norms, rules, and professional appraisal of the extent to which particular behaviors deviate from the norms are matters of subjective judgement" (Kauffman, 1981, p. 14). Each of the definitions discussed here appears to be determined in part by (1) the discipline of its author(s) (physician, attorney, psychiatrist, psychologist, educator); (2) the author's theoretical perspective (behavioral, psychodynamic, biophysical); and (3) the purpose for writing the definition. As Kauffman (1981) indicated, individuals who disagree about behavior disorders at a conceptual or philosophical level are unlikely to agree on a particular definition. Inconsistencies are not found simply in definitions, but rather exist in the views of the world from which the definition is derived (Rhodes & Paul, 1978).

According to Reinert (1972), the phrase *emotionally disturbed* appeared, without a precise definition, in the professional literature in approximately 1900. This term has been superseded since the beginning of the century by a variety of labels designed to clarify its intent. Among the most widely used and recognized are *socially maladjusted, seriously emotionally disturbed, mentally ill, predelinquent, delinquent, emotionally handicapped, socially handicapped, children in conflict* and *behavior-disordered.*

One of the first widely accepted definitions of emotional disturbances in children was offered by Lambert and Bower (1961a). This definition is the basis for the definition of children identified as "seriously emotionally disturbed" in PL 94-142. In this law, that term means:

(i) . . . a condition exhibiting one or more of the following characteristics over a long period of time and to a marked degree, which adversely affects educational performance.

(a) An inability to learn which cannot be explained by intellectual, sensory, and health factors;

(b) An ability to build or maintain satisfactory interpersonal relationships with peers and teachers;

(c) inappropriate types of behavior or feelings under normal circumstances;

(d) A general pervasive mood of unhappiness or depression; or

(e) a tendency to develop physical symptoms or fears associated with personal or school problems.

(ii) The term includes children who are schizophrenic or autistic.* The term does not include children who are socially maladjusted unless it is determined that they are seriously emotionally disturbed (*Federal Register, 42* (163), August 23, 1977, 42,478).

The major difference between the Lambert and Bower definition and that included in Public Law 94-142 is the exclusionary clause and the use of the term *seriously emotionally disturbed* rather than *emotionally handicapped.*

This definition has been criticized as too vague and too broad (Hewett & Taylor, 1980). Although the preceding definition is the federal one, a study by Epstein, Cullinan, and Sabatino (1977) indicated than only six of the thirty-three states responding used the term *seriously emotionally disturbed*. State definitions have also been criticized as vague and ambiguous, varying greatly from one state to another and in some cases contradicting one another.

Grosenick and Huntze (1979) suggested applying the term *behavior-disordered* rather than *emotionally disturbed* to this category of children. Behavior-disordered is preferred because it is generally considered broader in scope and conceptually inclusive of a variety of problem behaviors that warrant professional attention. *Behavior-disordered* appears to be not only more useful, but more comprehensive. The term *emotionally disturbed* communicates a psychodynamic perspective and stresses behavior as a manifestation of disturbed thoughts and feelings. In a 1984 position

---

*On January 16, 1981, the Office of Special Education, U. S. Department of Education, published a technical change in the regulations of PL 94-142 that removed autism from the category of "seriously emotionally disturbed" and listed it as a separate subcategory under "other health impaired."

paper, the Council for Children with Behavioral Disorders indicated that the use of behavior disorders would divorce legal terminology from causation and be less stigmatizing to the children. The term emotionally disturbed is seen as negative and stigmatizing by teachers and parents (Long, 1983). Feldman, Kinnison, Jay, and Harth (1983) maintained that the difference between behavior disorders and emotional disturbance is more than a semantic one. "Behaviorally disordered" children are favored over "emotionally disturbed" ones in both educational and social access. Behavior-disordered children are perceived more positively by both preservice and in-service regular educators.

There is as little agreement on what is to be included in the definitions as there is on the terminology to be used. Paul and Epanchin (1982) indicate that definitions should relate to some theoretical formulation; be interdisciplinary; incorporate cultural pluralism; avoid blaming children, parents, or social situations as responsible for the disturbance; and facilitate the identification and measurement of the disorder.

Algozzine, Schmid, and Connors (1978) take a different perspective in their discussion of definitions. They maintain that an operational definition is needed that includes a measurable index of the alternative educational environments that were attempted with the child, a measurable indication of the amount of behavioral deviation, a component concerning behavioral interference, and a measurable exclusion etiology. Here is their definition:

> The emotionally disturbed child is the student who, after receiving supportive educational assistance and counseling available to all students, still exhibits persistent and consistent severe to very severe behavioral disabilities which interfere with productive learning processes. This is the student whose inability to achieve adequate academic progress and/or satisfactory interpersonal relationships cannot be attributed primarily to physical, sensory, or intellectual deficits (p. 49).

F. Wood (1982) expresses some concern with operational definitions such as the preceding. He maintains that operational definitions of concepts such as emotional disturbances and behavior disorders can never be "true" because of the complexity of the concept that they are attempting to describe. He maintains that the question of benefiting individuals needing services must supersede the precision of the definition.

The issue of definition is further clouded by the variety of purposes for which definitions exist. Cullinan and Epstein (1982) indicate that there are at least three purposes for defining behavior disorders: research, authoritative, and administrative. Research definitions clarify the external validity of an investigation by clarifying the population to which the study's results are applicable. Authoritative definitions serve as position statements for specific theoretical perspectives. Administrative definitions, such as the federal definition discussed previously, appear in rules, regulations, and governmental pronouncements published to facilitate the provision of services and distribution of funds.

To demonstrate the range of definitions that occurs for these three purposes, two research, two administrative, and four authoritative definitions (from the psychodynamic, biophysical, behavioral, and environmental points of view) follow.

Research definitions of behavior disorders vary from very specific to very broad. For example, in a study by Morrow and Presswood (1984), the subject was precisely defined as "diagnosed (DSM-III) as having schizophrenia, disorganized type, and a mixed specific developmental disorder." Thus, by precisely defining the subject of the study, and then implementing a treatment technique, the researchers allow the reader to infer that the technique would probably be appropriate for use with other individuals diagnosed in the same precise category.

A broad research definition is used by McGinnis, Kiraly, and Smith (1984), who gave their sample as "elementary school students identified as behaviorally disordered (excluding autistic students)." This includes a much broader range of students, and thus the research is more difficult to replicate and apply to other students similarly identified.

Administrative definitions vary between governmental units and with the purpose of the rules and regulations being written. Though the federal government uses the adaptation of Lambert and Bower's definition (1961a) previously discussed, other governmental agencies use different definitions. For example, in Florida, the term to describe behavior-disordered students is *emotionally handicapped*, and is defined as

> one who after receiving supportive educational assistance and counseling services available to all students, still exhibits persistent and consistent severe behavioral disabilities which consequently disrupt the student's own learning process. This is the student whose inability to achieve adequate academic progress or satisfactory interpersonal relationships cannot be attributed primarily to physical, sensory, or intellectual deficits (Florida, 1979b).

This definition is similar to that presented by Algozzine and associates (1978).

In Colorado, however, the term for these students is *significant identifiable emotional or behavioral disorder,* and is defined as follows:

> Social or behavioral functioning such that the child cannot be adequately and/ or safely educated in the regular school program. The following are characteristics of emotional/behavioral disorders when they are exhibited at a rate higher than that which other children exhibit, are exhibited in almost all settings within the total environment, including school, home, and community, and have been evident for a period of time. One or more of the following characteristics will indicate a significant identifiable emotional or behavioral disorder:

Behavior which is dangerous to the child himself and/or others.

Behavior which seriously interferes with the child's learning or that of his classmates.

Inability to retain academic information.

Significantly limited self-control.

Lack of positive and sustained interpersonal relationships.

Persistent physical complaints related to stress and/or anxiety.

Pervasive moods of anxiety or depression.

Persistent patterns of bizarre and/or exaggerated behavior reactions to routine environment.

Extended periods of time with observable withdrawal that has no apparent positive coping aspect (Benson and Cessna, 1980).

These two very different definitions may delineate two different groups of children.

Similar differences occur in authoritative definitions. To exemplify these differences, four theoretical definitions are presented. These definitions are representative of the traditional perspectives of behavior disorders: psychodynamic, biophysical, environmental, and behavioral.

Psychodynamic definitions emerged from Freud's psychoanalytical perspective, and focus on an individual's resolution of or failure to resolve crises faced at particular stages of development. The Joint Commission on Mental Health provides a psychodynamic definition:

> An emotionally disturbed child is one whose progressive personality development is interfered with or arrested by a variety of factors so that he shows impairment in the capacity expected of him for his age and endowment: (1) for reasonably accurate perception of the world around him; (2) for impulse control; (3) for satisfying and satisfactory relations with others; (4) for learning; or (5) for any combination of these (1969, p. 253).

This view contrasts strongly with the definition offered by Rimland (1969), who assumes a biological basis for behavior disorders. He defines a biogenic behavior disorder as "a severe behavior disorder that results solely from the effects of the physical-chemical environment" (p. 706). Russ (1972), on the other hand, defines behavior disorders from the behavioral perspective: "as a learned behavior, it develops and is maintained like all other behaviors."

Hewett and Taylor (1980) represent the environmental perspective with their statement: "When we single out an individual child as being emotionally disturbed or exhibiting a behavior disorder, we are using descriptive terms that really mean there is not a good fit—a discordance—between the child and his or her own environment" (p. 79).

All definitions proposed for behavior disorders must be applied with care. McGinnis, Kiraly, and Smith (1984) maintain that multiple sources of information must be used before a child is classified as behavior-disordered because the child's deviance may be biased by the opinion of the observers, based on unwarranted inferences about behavioral difficulties and determined by the availability of placements. In a study of the sources of data used by public-school personnel to make special education eligibility decisions, they found that in only 24.2 percent of the cases were three or more sources of information on behavior disorders present before a decision was made. The most noted source of behavioral data was a paragraph summarizing the student's behavior; that is, a general statement by those present at the decision-making meeting.

OBJECTIVE FOUR: *To contrast behavior disorders and pseudobehavior disorders.*

The most frequent source of information for the diagnosis of children and youth with behavior disorders is a summary of the student's behavior (McGinnis, Kiraly, & Smith, 1984). Redl (1965, p. v) stated that "it makes a great difference whether we talk about the 'emotionally disturbed child' or about behavior which indicates a 'state of emotional disturbance.'" F. Wood (1981) presented a six-step model which traces the progression of a child's "disturbing" behavior from the point of teacher awareness of the behavior through the process of labeling the child as behaviorally disordered or emotionally disturbed. This model is depicted in Figure 1-1.

As can be seen in the model, after being attracted to the student's behavior, the teacher decides whether the behavior is pleasing or disturbing, and, if the latter, whether or not it is disturbing enough to take action. After deciding to take action, the teacher labels the disturbing behavior *disordered*, and finally the label *behaviorally disordered* or *emotionally disturbed* is applied. The process is based on the teacher's perceptions of the behavior as a major criterion for labeling.

Kauffman (1981) indicates that a behavior may be disordered in one situation and context and not in another simply because of differences in behavioral expectations. In this way, there are differences between disturbing and disturbed behaviors. Disturbing behaviors are those that are situation-specific, occurring in a certain place, at a certain time, and in the presence of certain individuals. Disturbed behaviors occur in multiple settings, and are part of the usual behavior patterns of the specific student. For example, a student who becomes angry with a substitute teacher and tears his spelling test is demonstrating a disturbing behavior. He may never demonstrate such a behavior to his regular teacher or even another substitute teacher. A student, however, who frequently tears up tests and refuses to respond to adult interaction at school, in the home, and in the community is demonstrating disturbed behaviors. His behavior is not

FIGURE 1-1   How Teachers Influence the Labeling of Student Behavior as Behaviorally Disordered/Emotionally Disturbed

Step 1: Teacher's attention is attracted to the behavior of a student.

Step 2: Teacher decides whether behavior is pleasing or disturbing. (Continue if teacher finds student behavior disturbing)

Step 3: Is teacher disturbed sufficiently to take some action to change or stop the disturbing behavior? (Continue only if teacher finds behavior sufficiently disturbing to take action. This can be the result of accumulated instances of being disturbed. If teacher is not sufficiently disturbed to take action, his or her awareness of the disturbing behavior usually begins to lessen.)

Step 4: Teacher wishes to take some action to bring an end to the disturbance. What alternatives exist? A salient factor to be considered is the interpersonal power characteristics of the situation. Based on appraisal of social and political factors, the teacher may decide to do nothing, to act immediately, to seek alliances with others who will support taking action to stop or change the student's behavior, or to escape from the situation through transfer or resignation. (Continue if teacher's decision is to take action, alone or in alliance with others.)

Step 5: Teacher's first action is to have student's disturbing behavior labeled publicly as disordered, disruptive, or problematic. Often, at the same time, an additional label suggesting the perceived severity of the problem is attached by the labelers: mild, moderate, severe. (Continue if labelers wish to make or can make inferences about the causes of the disordered behavior.)

Step 6: Teacher (by now usually acting in alliance with social workers, psychiatrists, psychologists, and others who lend political authority to the labeling process) infers that the student's disturbing behavior is a function of past learning and present environmental factors. Preferred label: *behaviorally disordered*. Preferred interventions: behavioral.

And/or

Teacher infers that the student's disturbing behavior is a function of past experiences and present inner emotional state. Preferred label: *emotionally disturbed*. Preferred intervention: psychodynamic.

From F. Wood (ed.), *Perspective for a New Decade* (Reston, VA: Council for Exceptional Children, 1981), p. 52.

dependent on a specific person, place, and time. Disturbing behaviors, though they are stressful for the individuals concerned, are not necessarily symptomatic of emotional disturbance.

Algozzine (1980) further explores the contrast between disturbed and disturbing behaviors. He indicates that children are perceived as problems based on the extent to which their behavior differs from their teachers' (or others') desires. He states that

> it *is not simply* the level and type of behavior that a child exhibits which may result in being identified as "disturbed," but the fact that that particular set of characteristics which make him/her an individual results in differential reactions (or degrees of disturbingness and intolerance) from others within the child's ecosystem (p. 112).

In his study of nineteen regular and nineteen special-education teachers, he found that regular education teachers found certain behaviors more disturbing than did special educators, though both groups were most distressed by socially defiant behaviors.

Another example of a pseudobehavior disorder is that of hyperresilient behavior. Redl (1965) described hyperresilient children and youth as

> youngsters who are perfectly healthy—as normal, clinically speaking, as anyone might wish a youngster to be. In fact, being normal and healthy, they have a sharp nose for situations which are putrid, for life experiences which are sickening, for teacher and parent behavior which is downright impossible on any count (p. vi).

Rather than being symptomatic of a behavior disorder or emotional disturbance, hyperresilient behaviors are a defense or adjustment mechanism applied by the child in an effort to live in a state of relative comfort in an unacceptable or unaccepting environment. These defensive behaviors are characterized by either overt aggression, used to keep others away, or withdrawal, used to prevent others from entering into the child's life-space. In a positive, exciting, and accepting environment little or no therapeutic intervention is necessary to assist these children. Generally, within a matter of days or weeks, the child settles into the environment and becomes productive. Special educators frequently question why the child is in a special class. They indicate that the child is "normal," "okay," or their "best child."

Psychonoxious or "brat" behaviors (Knoblock, 1983) refers to those behaviors that are mildly irritating and attention-getting. Generally, these behaviors do not severely impact upon the student's classroom performance. "Brat" behaviors are usually situation-specific, of very brief duration, and indicative of a "mood" or stage of development.

Iatrogenic behaviors are those caused by the interventions or treatment that the individual receives. In medicine, for example, a rash that develops from an injection would be considered an iatrogenic disorder. In the same way, children may demonstrate behavior disorders that are a result of the way in which they are assessed, labeled, taught, or treated. Algozzine (1980) suggests that teachers "'identify' a great many children as problems and that they may accept a narrow range of behaviors as a basis for defining deviance" (p. 112–113). Hobbs (1966) indicated that "there is a real possibility that hospitals make children sick. The antiseptic atmosphere, the crepe soles and white coat, the tension, the expectancy of illness may confirm a child's worst fears about himself, firmly setting his aberrant behavior" (p. 1105).

Caution must be used when applying the term *behavior disorders* to students who demonstrate disturbing, hyperresilient, psychonoxious, or iatrogenic behaviors. Rather than being indicative of a disorder, such behaviors may represent an intolerance and a lack of acceptance of minimal behavioral differences by others.

OBJECTIVE FIVE: *To discuss several important variables to be considered when applying a definition of behavior disorders.*

These variables include prevalence; background variables such as age, sex, socioeconomic status, and intelligence; and classification variables.

Prevalence

Early studies of behavior problems identified large numbers of students as having adjustment or behavior difficulties. Kauffman (1976) indicated that prior to 1900, determining the prevalence of children and youths experiencing behavior problems is difficult, because of reviewers' inaccuracies and distortions of the literature, inattention to historical documents, an inordinate emphasis on the negative and bizarre, and unwarranted concern with the moral etiology of exceptionality.

In a study using teachers' rating of the adjustment problems of children ages six to twelve years, Wickman (1928) concluded that 7 percent of the children in his sample were seriously maladjusted and 42 percent demonstrated mild adjustment problems. Hildreth, also in 1928, found that 7 to 8 percent of a sample of kindergarten-through-twelfth-grade students were identified as maladjusted by school personnel. In a review of sixty-five studies, Baker and Stullken (1938) reported a range of 1.2 to 6.9 percent of the school-age population having behavior problems.

More recent studies estimate the incidence of behavior disorders from 1 to 35 percent of the population (Huntze & Grosenick, 1980). Though 2 percent of the school-age population is generally agreed to be a conservative and minimally expected prevalence, only two of the fifty states actually serve 2 percent of the population. Huntze and Grosenick report that nationally, only 0.56 percent of students are counted as having behavior disorders, leaving an estimated 1.44 percent of the school population in need of identification and services. In a more recent study, Maroney

(1983) reported that the percentage of the total school population (ages five through seventeen served, ranges from 0.01 percent in the District of Columbia to 1.83 percent in Utah.

Huntze and Grosenick (1980) suggest several possible reasons for discrepancies in prevalence estimates. These include differences reported between urban and rural educational districts, the definitional problems previously discussed that may cause variance in the number of students reported in the different states, and limited fiscal resources, which may limit the number of students reported as behaviorally disordered by various educational units. However, 2 percent is the generally accepted estimate of the prevalence of behavior disorders among school-age children and is the one presently used by the United States Office of Special Education.

Background Variables

Age and sex.   Behavior disorders do not respect either age or sex. Boys and girls of all ages may have behavior disorders. Research results generally suggest that there is a three-, four-, or five-to-one ratio of boys to girls who are behavior-disordered. In their investigation of public-school classes for emotionally handicapped students, Morse and associates (1964) found a sex ratio of 5 boys to 1 girl. As a conclusion of their analysis of several research reports, Clarizio and McCoy (1976) reported that "information on sex differences in maladjustment indicates an approximate sex ratio of 3 boys to 1 girl" (p. 126). These ratios may be affected to some degree by societal and/or parental expectations for boys and girls: Boys are expected to be outgoing and aggressive, whereas girls are expected to be more reserved and quiet. Such ratios will, in all probability, change as traditional sex roles continue to blur.

In their early review of the literature, Baker and Stullken (1938) reported that two-thirds of the students described as behaviorally disordered were ten to fifteen years old. Gilbert (1957) found that boys outnumbered girls four to one with respect to aggressive, acting-out problems and three to one for academic problems, with the most problem referrals occurring between the ages of six and ten years. Bower (1961) found the lowest incidence of emotional disturbance in the early primary grades and a higher occurrence in the elementary- and junior-high-school grades. In their study of public school programs for the emotionally handicapped, Morse, Cutler, and Fink (1964) found 75 percent of the children to be in the upper-elementary-school grades and junior high school.

Edelbrock (1984) compared reports on the Child Behavior Checklist of fifty boys and fifty girls, "normal" and disturbed, at each age from four through sixteen years. He found that 84 of the 118 behavior problems on the checklist demonstrated significant age effects. Girls were found to manifest more "internalizing" problems, whereas boys showed more "externalizing." From these data, Edelbrock developed a description of behavior problem syndromes exhibited by boys and girls at various ages. These behavior clusters are summarized in Figure 1-2.

FIGURE 1-2   Behavioral Problem Syndromes Derived for Boys and Girls Aged 4–5, 6–11, and 12–16

INTERNALIZING	MIXED	EXTERNALIZING
Boys 4–5		
1. Social Withdrawal	5. Sex Problems	6. Schizoid
2. Depressed		7. Aggressive
3. Immature		8. Delinquent
4. Somatic Complaints		
Girls 4–5		
1. Somatic Complaints	5. Obese	6. Aggressive
2. Depressed		7. Sex Problems
3. Schizoid		8. Hyperactive
4. Social Withdrawal		
Boys 6–11		
1. Schizoid	6. Social Withdrawal	7. Hyperactive
2. Depressed		8. Aggressive
3. Uncommunicative		9. Delinquent
4. Obsessive-Compulsive		
5. Somatic Complaints		
Girls 6–11		
1. Depressed		6. Sex Problems
2. Social Withdrawal		7. Delinquent
3. Somatic Complaints		8. Aggressive
4. Schizoid-Obsessive		9. Cruel
5. Hyperactive		
Boys 12–16		
1. Somatic Complaints	6. Hostile-Withdrawal	7. Delinquent
2. Schizoid		8. Aggressive
3. Uncommunicative		9. Hyperactive
4. Immature		
5. Obsessive-Compulsive		
Girls 12–16		
1. Anxious-Obsessive	5. Immature-Hyperactive	6. Delinquent
2. Somatic Complaints		7. Aggressive
3. Schizoid		8. Cruel
4. Depressed, Withdrawal		

From C. Edelbrock, "Developmental Considerations," in T.H. Ollendick & M. Hersen (eds.), *Child Behavioral Assessment Principles and Procedures* (N.Y.: Pergamon Press, 1984), p. 33. Reprinted with permission of C. Edelbrock and Pergamon Press.

Intelligence and achievement.   Although the intelligence quotient is generally agreed to be a reliable predictor of school success and achievement, caution must be used in interpreting the IQs of children and youth with behavior disorders. In their sample of 298 children attending public-school classes for the emotionally handicapped, Morse and associates (1964) found "more children at the higher levels of intelligence than would be expected in a normal distribution" (p. 35). These researchers concluded that intellectual retardation was not a significant factor in the disturbed children's classification and placement.

Achievement is a significant factor in behavior disorders, though it is difficult to discern the cause-and-effect relationship between these factors. Hobbs (1966) indicated that "underachievement in school is the single most common characteristic of emotionally disturbed children" (p. 1110).

In their study of classes for the emotionally handicapped, Morse and associates derived reading quotients for 154 children. They found 55 percent of the sample functioning below the level expected for their mental age and 45 percent functioning above it. These researchers also investigated present and former teachers' perceptions of emotionally handicapped children's academic retardation. Former teachers perceived no retardation among 21 percent of the sample; present teachers perceived retardation among 30 percent. Although the degree of retardation was unspecified, former teachers perceived academic retardation among 52 percent of the sample, and present teachers among 44 percent.

In a four-year study of 198 emotionally handicapped students, Stennett (1966) compared the educational progress of nonhandicapped with that of emotionally handicapped boys and girls. He found that, generally, the further the emotionally handicapped children progress in school without service, the further they are educationally behind nonhandicapped peers. This educational retardation was more pronounced in boys than girls.

Leone (1984) found that even among adolescents who had successfully graduated from a program for youth with behavior disorders, a significant deficit in academic skills was evident.

Children and youth with behavior disorders may also differ from other children in their cognitive strategies. Emotionally disturbed children have been found to be more impulsive than normal children of similar age (Finch & Montgomery, 1973). Emotionally disturbed children were found to use more hypothesis-scanning questions in an apparent attempt to guess correct solutions.

Socioeconomic status and other related variables.   Long (1983) found that, overall, school systems with more financial resources detected more emotionally disturbed children. Districts with higher prevalence rates were those in which special-education directors expressed more positive attitudes toward programming for emotionally disturbed children. In addition, districts with active community groups tended to identify more behaviorally disordered students.

Long (1983) concluded that children from poorer school districts and districts with a high proportion of minority group students appear to be the least adequately served.

Classification

The classification of children and youth with behavior disorders once they have been identified is a recurrent problem, which has been met with a wide range of potential solutions. In 1938, Baker and Stullken found that two groups of behavior-disordered children emerged—the "conduct" group (delinquent or predelinquent behavior) and the "personality" group (maladjusted or psychoneurotic). Algozzine, Schmid, and Connors (1978) indicated that there are Type I, or regular emotionally disturbed children, usually found in the regular public school setting and responsive to environmental-intervention strategies; and Type II, or clinically emotionally disturbed, children who are problems at school and home, have organic inadequacies, usually require therapeutic services, and are not as responsive to environmental interventions.

Grosenick and Huntze (1979) identified two groups of children, a mild/moderate group, requiring mild to moderately intense intervention and a moderate degree of control from outside regular education; and a severe group, requiring a high degree of control from specialized personnel outside regular education and whose interventions are extremely intense.

In a study designed to ascertain if there was a real distinction between mild, moderate, and severe groups, teachers were asked to rate twenty-three behavioral characteristics as mild, moderate, or severe (Olson, Algozzine, & Schmid, 1980). Five behaviors were rated by at least 50 percent of the teachers as being indicative of mild behavior disorders. The mildly disordered students were felt to require only brief interventions, able to respond to help from the school counselor, demonstrated academic problems not unlike those of their peers, demonstrated infrequent rates of behavioral disturbances, and were able to profit from regular class placement with support- or crisis-teacher assistance. The five behaviors indicative of the severely disordered group include residential centers seen as the best placement, a diagnosis of autism or schizophrenia, a lack of social interest, multiple handicaps, and problems more likely to be genetically or organically based. No consensus was found on characteristics for the moderate group.

A four-cluster classification system was proposed by Quay (1978). In this system, students are identified as having conduct disorders (behaviors that are clearly at variance with societal expectations in almost all situations and are aversive to adults and children), personality disorders (subjective distress with behaviors having a much less negative impact on the child's environment), inadequacy-immaturity (characterized by preoccupation, short attention span, clumsiness, and confusion), and socialized or sub-cultural delinquency (adopted patterns of behavior reinforced by peers and by the subculture that has provided their socialization experiences). This classification system is presented and discussed in detail in Chapter 2.

The Diagnostic and Statistical Manual of Mental Disorders of the American Psychiatric Association, third edition (referred to as the DSM III, 1980) provides a complex system for categorizing behavior disorders. This is a classification system based on the clinical expertise of hundreds of mental-health practitioners. It includes seventeen major diagnostic categories, including one specifically for infants, children, and adolescents. Within this category ten major syndromes and forty-five subsyndromes are presented. Each diagnostic syndrome is described in detail. Figure 1-3 is representative of a diagnostic description in the DSM III.

Because of ambiguity and confusion with the definitions of behavior disorders, public-school personnel have begun to look at the DSM III diagnostic procedures more carefully. Special educators are urged to become familiar with the DSM III (Forness & Cantwell, 1982).

OBJECTIVE SIX: *To describe the major premises of four traditional perspectives of the etiology of behavior disorders in children.*

Human behavior is complex, and there are several different and definitive scientific and quasi-scientific ways to understand it (Paul & Epanchin, 1982). All human beings have a perspective, or point of view, through which they interpret the world. This personal and unique perspective includes the individual perception of self and personal actions as well as a perception of others and their actions and places, objects, and events that make up the world.

An individual's perspective of human nature is critical, because it is that element that channels, harnesses, and gives energy form and direction. Consequently, it influences the quality of that individual's actions (Rhodes, 1972).

This personal perspective is not an esoteric, abstract theory that can be set aside and stored in the deep recesses of the mind to care for itself. It is expressed in our behavior. It is a critical human attribute to be developed, harnessed, directed, and modified. It is an integral factor in professional decision making. Our perspective should be meaningful and applicable to our actions in behalf of children and youth with behavior disorders.

FIGURE 1-3. Sample Category from DSM-III

Diagnostic Criteria for Attention Deficit Disorder with Hyperactivity

The child displays, for his or her mental and chronological age, signs of developmentally inappropriate inattention, impulsivity, and hyperactivity. The signs must be reported by adults in the child's environment, such as parents and teachers. Because the symptoms are typically variable, they may not be observed directly by the clinician. When the reports of teachers and parents conflict, primary consideration should be given to the teacher reports because of greater familiarity with age-appropriate norms. Symptoms typically worsen in situations that require self-application, as in the classroom. Signs of the disorder may be absent when the child is in a new or one-on-one situation.

The number of symptoms specified is for children between the ages of eight and ten, the peak age range for referral. In younger children, more severe forms of the symptoms and a greater number of symptoms are usually present. The opposite is true of older children.

A. **Inattention.** At least three of the following:
   (1) often fails to finish things he or she starts
   (2) often doesn't seem to listen
   (3) easily distracted
   (4) has difficulty concentrating on schoolwork or other tasks requiring sustained attention
   (5) has difficulty sticking to a play activity

B. **Impulsivity.** At least three of the following:
   (1) often acts before thinking
   (2) shifts excessively from one activity to another
   (3) has difficulty organizing work (this not being due to cognitive impairment)
   (4) needs a lot of supervision
   (5) frequently calls out in class
   (6) has difficulty awaiting turn in games or group situations

C. **Hyperactivity.** At least two of the following:
   (1) runs about or climbs on things excessivley
   (2) has difficulty sitting still or fidgets excessively
   (3) has difficulty staying seated
   (4) moves about excessively during sleep
   (5) is always "on the go" or acts as if "driven by a motor"

D. Onset before the age of seven

E. Duration of at least six months

F. Not due to Schizophrenia, Affective Disorder, or Severe or Profound Mental Retardation

---

From *Diagnostic and Statistical Manual of Mental Disorders,* 3rd ed. (Washington, D.C.: American Psychiatric Association, 1980), pp. 43-44. Used with permission.

A CASE FOR CONSIDERATION

A group of four college students studying to be special educators were observing with their instructor a class of children with severe behavior disorders through a one-way mirror. Their objective was to observe the behavior of six-year-old John, who had been recently enrolled in the class.

The group observed John's behavior for ten minutes and then closed the curtain of the observation window to discuss and evaluate their observations. After a brief discussion, they reached consensus on the behavior they observed:

1. John entered the classroom, slammed the door, took off his coat and hat, and dropped them on the floor.
2. John ran to the toy box, picked up a truck, ran it over the tops of a desk and a bookcase, and threw it on the floor.
3. John picked up a doll that was near the toy box, banged it several times on the floor, and threw it at the teacher's aide.
4. John ran around the room three times. While running, he bumped into two children.
5. John stopped near the sand table and twirled around on his toes, with his hands fully extended above his head, six or seven times before running to the sink.
6. John stopped in front of the sink and turned on both faucets. He looked into the sink and remained in this position for the final four minutes of the observation period.

After the college students reached consensus on the behavior John exhibited in the classroom during the ten-minute observation period, the instructor asked each student to discuss the reason for this behavior. The following are summaries of the students' personal perspectives:

STUDENT 1:   John behaves as he does because he had not learned to act appropriately in the classroom situation. He has evidently been rewarded for similar behavior by the teacher in the past. She reinforced his behavior during our observation by attempting to stop him.

(Student 1 is enrolled in experimental-psychology and behavior-modification courses this semester.)

STUDENT 2:   John is obviously hyperactive as a result of brain damage. He should be administered appropriate symptom-control medication.

(Student 2 is an ex-premed student who transferred into special education this semester.)

STUDENT 3:   John behaves the way he does because he is emotionally driven. The behavior is his way of expressing hostility and frustration. This behavior is beneficial for John, and he should be encouraged to continue expressing himself.

(Student 3 is enrolled in courses in Freudian psychoanalytic theory and practice.)

STUDENT 4:   John behaves as he does because of the classroom environment. It is noisy, confusing, cluttered, and lacks organization. He is only imitating what he sees others doing in the classroom. John needs an uncluttered, orderly, structured classroom environment.

(Student 4 is an ex-sociology major who recently transferred to special education.)

Each of the students in the foregoing example interpreted John's behavior from a perspective that evolved from their personal formal and informal learning and experiences. The pespectives of the four students represent only a few of the many viewpoints possible.

The various theories of psychology, the study of human behavior, applied in the education of children and youth with behavior disorders are based in part on the individual theorist's perspective of the principles underlying human conduct and thought.

In the field of psychology, there are several perspectives on human behavior: the psychodynamic, behavioral, humanistic, transpersonal, and so on. In an effort to analyze, organize, and synthesize the psychological perspectives applicable to the education of children and youth with behavior disorders, Rhodes and Paul (1978) suggested the following points of view: behavioral, psychoneurological, sociological, ecological, countertheoretical, and existential. Three of these perspectives as well as the psychodynamic one are reviewed in this section. They are applied to various topics throughout the remainder of the text in relation to interventions and programs.

The Psychodynamic Perspective

The psychodynamic perspective involves a diversified group of theories that have in common the belief in the existence of a dynamic intrapsychic life. However, they vary greatly in their stress on the impact of the environment on behavior, instinctual drive energizing psychic life, and the functions of the components of the personality (Munroe, 1955; Roberts, 1975). The special educator with a psychodynamic perspective sees the causes of behavior as being within the individual. Behavior is determined by a dynamic intrapsychic life.

As a consequence of efforts to apply psychodynamic theories to educational processes for children and youths with behavior disorders, educators developed the psychoeducational method of classroom management and instruction. Significant contributions to this process have been made by Axline (1947), Baruch (1952), Bettelheim (1950), Glasser (1965), Morse (1965), Redl and Wineman (1951, 1952), and others.

In the classroom, emphasis is placed on (1) developing a mentally healthy atmosphere, (2) accepting the child and the pathological condition without reservation, (3) encouraging and assisting the child in learning, beginning at a level and under circumstances in which the child can perform successfully. Assuming the role of educational therapist, the teacher accepts, tolerates, and interprets the child's behavior (Walker & Shea, 1984, p. 8).

The psychodynamic perspective no longer dominates programs for the education of children and youth with behavior disorders, as was the situation in the 1960s. However, it remains a dominant force in contemporary society in popular literature, child-care books, movies, novels, television shows, and casual conversations.

The Biophysical Perspective

The biophysical perspective places emphasis on organic origins of behavior. The proponents of this perspective postulate a direct relationship between physical defects, malfunctions, and illnesses, and the behavior exhibited by the individual.

Although not the dominant theory of causation in the education of children and youth with behavior disorders, the biophysical perspective does have proponents among professionals and parents concerned with severely emotionally disturbed, learning-disabled, perceptually handicapped, and developmentally disabled children and youth. The special educator with a biophysical perspective is concerned with changing or compensating for the individual's malfunctioning organic mechanisms or processes that are causing the behavior.

Some proponents of this theoretical perspective believe that the individual's external environment is unimportant to the behavior problem (Rimland, 1969). Others accept the importance of the external environment and believe that this is the factor that triggers an inherent organic predisposition within the individual organism (Rosenthal, 1963).

Schroeder and Schroeder (1982) noted two groups of biophysical theories related to behavior disorders in children and youth. These are the biological-defect and developmental theories. Biological-defect theories include genetic theories (Wilson, 1975), temperament theory (Thomas & Chess, 1977), neuropsychopharmacological theories (Lipton, DiMascio, & Killam, 1978), nutritional-disorder theory (Rutter, 1980; Sankar, 1979), and neurological-dysfunction theory (Rutter, Tizard, & Whitmore, 1970).

Development theories include the Doman-Delacato theory of neurological organization (Delacato, 1966), Kephart's perceptual motor learning theory (Dunsing & Kephart, 1965), Getman's physiology of readiness theory (1963), Ayres's theory of sensory integration (1979), and Frostig's developmental theory (1968).

Several curative and preventive interventions have been developed to mitigate or modify the effects of biophysical factors. Among these are prenatal and postnatal health care, proper nutrition and diet, megavitamin and similar therapies, general and specific physical examinations, symptom-control medications, and genetic counseling. These interventions are discussed in Chapter 10.

A summary of this perspective as it applies in the educational setting is provided by Hewett (1968):

> The primary goal of the sensory-neurological strategy is to discover the child's sensory and neurologically based deficit, often through extensive observation and diagnostic testing. Once these deficits are uncovered, the child is viewed as a learner who must be trained to accurately perceive and comprehend stimuli and to demonstrate motor efficiency before he is given complex learning tasks (p. 24).

The special educator who is influenced by the biophysical perspective emphasizes order and routine in the classroom, daily schedules, the frequent repetition of learning tasks and their sequential presentation, and a reduction or elimination of extraneous environmental stimuli.

The Behavioral Perspective

The behavioral perspective is the predominant theory taught in American colleges and universities today (Kavale & Hirshoren, 1980).

The statement "What you do is influenced by what follows what you do" (Sarason, Glaser, & Fargo, 1972, p. 10) summarizes the behavioral perspective. Whereas the biophysical and psychodynamic perspectives are concerned primarily with *why* individuals behave as they do and how intra-human factors affect the individual's behavior, the behaviorist is concerned primarily with *what* behaviors an individual exhibits that are appropriate and inappropriate and what interventions can be designed and imposed to change these behaviors (Walker & Shea, 1984).

For the special educator with a behavioral perspective, behavior is defined as all human acts that are observable and measurable, excluding chemical and physiological processes (Roberts, 1975). The cause of human behavior is perceived as outside of the individual in the environment. Special educators using the behavioral model assume that behavior (appropriate and inappropriate) is the consequence of the lawful application of the principles of reinforcement.

The behavior modifier believes that behavior is controlled by the individual's impinging environmental stimuli (Kameya, 1972). Behavior is changed by the manipulation of these stimuli.

The procedures for applying behavior modification in the special-educational setting require the teacher to (1) observe and clarify the behavior to be changed; (2) select and present a potent reinforcer at the appropriate time; (3) design and impose, with consistency, an intervention based on the principles of reinforcement; and (4) monitor and evaluate the effectiveness of the interventions.

There are a variety of specific behavior-modification interventions that may be applied to change behaviors. These interventions are presented in detail in Chapter 9.

The goal for behavior modification in the special education of children and youth with behavior disorders is summarized by Hewett (1968) in this way:

> The basic goal for the behavior modifier is the identification of maladaptive behaviors which interfere with learning and assisting the child in developing more adaptive behavior. Every child is considered a candidate for learning something regardless of this degree of psychopathology and other problems. This "something" may only represent a starting point (e.g., chair sitting) and be but a small part of the eventual "something" the teacher hopes to accomplish (e.g., reading), but care will be taken to insure its mastery before more complex goals are introduced. The child's behavior is viewed in the broadest possible context without rigid adherence to a priority ranking of behavioral goals on the basis of inferences regarding emotional conflicts or brain dysfunctions (p. 34).

The Environmental Perspective

As it applies to the education of children and youths with behavior disorders, the environmental perspective explores the reciprocal relationships between the child or group and others (individuals, groups), "objects," and events in the environment.

Environmental theorists maintain that isolating a child's behavior from the environment in which it occurs denies the phenomenal nature of that behavior (Rhodes & Paul, 1978). From this perspective, "we assume that the child is an inseparable part of a small social system, an ecological unit, made up of the child, his family, his school, his neighborhood, and community" (Hobbs, 1966, p. 1108). Reactions of others in the child's ecosystem affect the way in which the child acts (Algozzine, 1980).

Unlike the other perspectives, the environmental perspective emphasizes the child's problem as being a product of a "particular collective in a particular environment or place at a particular time in history" (Rhodes & Paul, 1978). The problem of a behavior disorder has as much to do with the child's environment as with the child as an individual.

The labeling of children and youth who deviate from the norms and rules of the community as having behavior disorders has long been a concern of special educators, who fear the effects of labeling and its implications on the child's behavior and on expectations of the child. Labels may generate a tolerance for deviant behaviors that only perpetuate those behaviors (Algozzine, Mercer, & Countermine, 1977).

Labeling theory emphasizes that an individual does not become a deviant by breaking rules; the individual must be labeled a deviant before the social expectations defining the particular form of deviancy are activated. When an individual is officially labeled as deviant, he or she assumes the role expectations assigned to that particular form of deviance in an effort to conform to the expectations of society. This theoretical perspective is closely related to Parsons's (1951) concept of the sick role. He proposed four societal expectations that encourage persons labeled "sick" to assume this role:

1. The sick person is relieved of his normal role obligations.
2. Because he is sick, the person is not morally responsible for his condition.
3. The sick person must express his desire to return to normal functioning.
4. The sick person must seek technically competent help from appropriate caretakers (psychiatrists, psychologists, special educators).

Reviewed by Wagner (1972), a variety of interventions have evolved out of ecological theories. Many of these interventions are reviewed in some detail in Chapter 10; a few are given here to acquaint the reader with their general composition and diversity.

> *Remediation interventions.* In these cases, the child is instructed in the social and interpersonal survival skills for appropriate functioning in the environment.
> *School-community interventions.* These interventions are essentially special education, counseling, therapy, cocurricular activities, and referral services designed to modify the school's environment in a manner responsive to the child's needs.
> *Artificial-community interventions.* These involve the development of specialized communities designed specifically for the benefit of its members.
> *Family-environment interventions.* These interventions see the child's problem as resulting from the family, and take the form of family therapy, parent therapy, maternal care, and foster care.
> *School-environment interventions.* The focus here is on modifying the school environment in response to the needs of the individual.

In programs for children and youths with behavior disorders, application of the environmental theory is characterized by (1) an awareness of the impact of the environment on the group and/or individual and the monitoring and manipulation of the environment for the benefit of the individual and/or group, and (2) an awareness of the dynamic reciprocal relationships that exist between the group and/or individual and the environment, and monitoring and manipulating these relationships for the benefit of the individual and/or group.

SUMMARY

In this chapter, the reader was introduced to children and youth with behavior disorders. Reasons for defining behavior disorders and several current definitions of this group of children and youth were discussed. The important variables impacting on the identification of children and youth with behavior disorders were reviewed. The second part of the chapter was devoted to a description of the major premises of four theoretical perspectives on behavior disorders. The last of these approaches, the environmental perspective, is discussed in detail in Chapter 2.

REVIEW QUESTIONS

1. Discuss the present and future impact of Public Law 94-142 on the lives of individuals with exceptionalities.
2. Discuss the meanings and implications of the phrase "a free, appropriate public education for all handicapped children."
3. Discuss the difference between the terms *emotional disturbance* and *behavior disorders*. What are the possible implications of using each term?
4. Evaluate the definition of behavior disorders used in your state or province. How does it compare with those presented in this chapter? Evaluate it using Wood's six elements of a definition.
5. Discuss several reasons for the difficulty in determining the prevalence of behavior disorders.
6. Discuss the implications of intelligence and achievement for programs serving children and youths with behavior disorders.
7. Why is it essential that special educators develop a personal perspective with regard to the causes of behavior disorders?
8. Compare and contrast the service implications of the behavioral, biophysical, environmental, and psychodynamic theories of behavior. (*Note:* Do not restrict your research to the material presented in the text; study several of the works cited in the references for this chapter.)

APPLICATION ACTIVITY

As you know from reading this chapter, children present both "disturbed" and "disturbing" behaviors. Read each of the following examples. Consider the differences between the behaviors that are simply disturbing and those that are disturbed which is characteristic of a behavior disorder. Indicate whether each behavior is disturbed or disturbing.

John taps his pencil on his desk constantly while he is doing work at his seat. Miguel scratches himself on the arms and face at home, school, and in the community whenever he is interrupted during an activity.

May giggles in the hall when the seventh-grade boys leave their classroom.

Chantelle keeps a string wrapped around her left wrist at all times and becomes aggressive when an attempt is made to remove it.

Whenever Ms. Wong is on playground duty, Franklin does not participate in team games; he remains close to her. When other staff members are supervising, however, he plays with the other children.

Reggie becomes very quiet whenever the principal visits the classroom.

Jenny curses on the playground, but uses appropriate language in class.

What are the clues that allow you to determine which behaviors are disturbing and which are disturbed?

2

An Integrated Perspective on Behavior Disorders

Behavior disorders in children and youth are complex phenomena that may be viewed from the psychodynamic–psycho-educational, behavioral, biophysical, and environmental contexts within which they occur. Their complexity and the diversity of the theoretical perspectives from which they are viewed precludes simple diagnosis and treatment. However, through the application of an integrated, ecological framework, it may be possible to coordinate the extant perspectives into a manageable assessment-intervention model.

In this chapter, the limitations inherent in applying a single theoretical perspective in the education of children and youth with behavior disorders are discussed. Next, a model designed to integrate the perspectives discussed in Chapter 1 is presented. This presentation is followed by discussion of several philosophical and personal characteristics of special educators that affect their perceptions and thus their instruction of children and youth with behavior disorders. The chapter concludes with a detailed description of the characteristics frequently exhibited by children and youths with behavior disorders.

OBJECTIVES

After completing this chapter, you will be able to—

1. identify the limitations inherent in the application of a single theoretical perspective in the education of children and youth with behavior disorders;

28

2. apply an ecological framework to the education of children and youth with behavior disorders that integrates the four traditional perspectives;
3. describe several characteristics of special educators that affect decision making with regard to children and youth with behavior disorders;
4. describe the behavioral characteristics frequently exhibited by children and youth with behavior disorders.

A CASE FOR CONSIDERATION

"I've had it with him," Mrs. Jones stated. "The only thing Charles does in his free time is sit and read. And he reads about the strangest things! For three weeks, all he read about was dinosaurs. Now it's computers. All the other kids are out riding bikes, playing ball, or just playing. I've told Charles that if he doesn't get out, I'm taking away his library card. His brother and two sisters are terrific at sports. They're never home, what with practice, games, and going to their friends' houses. My husband is the children's coach, and he's really upset with Charles."

"I'm sorry, Mrs. Jones," said Mrs. Palikowski, Charles's fourth-grade teacher. "Here at school we don't see Charles as a problem. He has several good friends who have the same interests and read as much as he does. It's true he's not the star, but he does hold his own in physical education. We will fill out an evaluation request if you wish, but frankly, Mr. Riley, the resource-room teacher, and I don't believe that Charles needs special education."

Is Charles a child with a behavior disorder? His mother views his interests and reading as deviant. It is possible that in his family, competitive physical activities are viewed as essential, and because Charles enjoys passive activities he is viewed as "abnormal." Yet, in the classroom, his "abnormal" behavior is encouraged and rewarded. To determine if a child's behavior is normal or abnormal, it must be viewed in context. When special educators view a child's behavior from a single point of view, they may be limiting their ability to help the child or youth.

OBJECTIVE ONE: *To identify the limitations inherent in the applications of a single perspective in the education of children and youth with behavior disorders.*

Interventions are selected and applied in part as a result of the special educator's perspective on behavior disorders. Special educators are typically trained in the behavioral perspective in colleges and universities, though when actually engaged in teaching they have demonstrated a more practical approach, using interventions that work even if they are not theoretically pure (Kavale & Hirshoren, 1980). Though usually only one theoretical perspective is formally taught in special-education training programs, there is general agreement that no single approach provides the broad perspective and many strategies needed to address the varied problems of children and youths with behavior disorders (Apter, 1977; Rich, 1978; Smith & McGinnis, 1982).

One traditional perspective on behavior disorders to which special educators are frequently exposed is the child-pathology model. According to it, the problem is within the child, and consequently, the child is perceived as dysfunctional.

A classic example of the child-pathology model is the medical model used by proponents of the biophysical perspective. In the medical model, it is assumed that the cause of the illness can be isolated, identified, and treated, and that the cause is specific, tangible, and singular. There is general agreement among those applying the medical model as to what constitutes a given illness and how it is to be classified. The outcome of the illness is generally known and predictable. Treatment is frequently specific.

Proponents of this model assume that a behavior disorder is symptomatic of an underlying biophysical pathology, and the function of the professional is to identify the cause of the behavior, classify it, and treat it.

Although somewhat broader in scope, in a strict sense, the behavioral model is a pathology model. According to Hallahan and Kaufman (1982), proponents of the behavioral model view disordered behavior as maladaptive, to be taken at face value, evaluated, and modified. The behavior modifer need only determine what specific behavior is troublesome, objectively and accurately record its occurrence, and arrange environmental events to instate, reinstate, remove, accelerate, or decelerate it. No attempt is made to find an underlying cause of the problem or to classify the disorder according to its etiology. The "real" problem is assumed to be the behavior itself; the behavior is not seen as a symptom of an underlying pathology, and one need not be concerned about symptom substitution. Behavior pathology is seen as the product of environmental events that shape specific responses in the individual; consequently, rearrangement of the environment is necessary, and is sufficient to change the problem. Special educators applying the behavioral model concentrate their efforts on the environmental arrangements needed to produce the desired responses in the children.

Professionals applying either the medical or behavioral model exclusively tend to respond only to those segments of the child's total life-space that are within the limited purview of their model and expertise. The individual professional's perception may be further limited by the fact that there is generally little coordination with other professionals who perceive the disordered behavior from a different perspective. Consequently, contradictory efforts on behalf of the child may occur. Such inefficient programming may result in a child's failing to respond to intervention. The child-pathology model is an example of the limitations imposed on treatment when a single perspective with regard to behavior disorders in children and youths is applied.

According to Forness (1981), practitioners with an ecological perspective have begun to replace the more traditional practitioners in the education of children and youth with behavior disorders. From the ecological perspective, rather than being seen as rooted within the child or in the environment exclusively, a behavior disorder is seen as a result of the interaction between the child, the child's idiosyncratic behaviors, and the unique environments in which the child functions. Ecological practitioners suggest that traditional practitioners may "miss" educationally and socially-emotionally relevant variables affecting functioning by their adherence to a single perspective.

OBJECTIVE TWO: *To apply an ecological framework to integrate the extant perspectives of behavior disorders with the education of children and youth with behavior disorders.*

Before discussing the ecological framework applied in the model to be presented, some technical terms are defined to facilitate communications.

Ecology is the interrelationship of humans with the environment, and involves reciprocal association (Thomas & Marshall, 1977). It is all the surroundings of a behavior (Scott, 1980). From the ecological perspective, it is assumed that a child is an inseparable part of the ecological unit, which is composed of the child, the school, the neighborhood, and the community.

Development is the continual adaptation of the child and environment to each other. It is a progressive accommodation that takes place throughout the life span between growing individuals and their changing environments. It is based on "the person's evolving conception of the ecological environment and his relationship to it, as well as the person's growing capacity to discover, sustain, or alter its properties" (Bronfenbrenner, 1979, p. 9). Thomas and Marshall (1977), relating this continual adaptation or development to the role of the special educator, stated:

> "The environment seldom adapts, and never completely to the specific needs of an individual with a handicap. Therefore, the ultimate purpose of any special education program is to assist that individual in adapting to the environment to his maximum capacity" (p. 16).

Behavior is the expression of the dynamic relationships between the individual and the environment (Marmor & Pumpian-Mindlin, 1950). Behavior occurs in a setting that includes specific time, place, and object "props" as well as the previously established pattern of behavior (Scott, 1980). Understanding behavior exceeds the simple observation of behavior by one or two persons. It requires an examination of the systems of interaction surrounding the behavior and is not limited to a single setting. In addition, it must take into account those aspects of the environment beyond the immediate situation in which the individual is functioning that may impact on behavior (Bronfenbrenner, 1977).

Congruence is the "match" or "goodness of fit" between the individual and the environment. Thurman (1977) suggests that individuals whom we judge to be normal are operating in an ecology that is congruent: The individual's behavior is in harmony with the norms of the environment. Thurman maintains that when there is no congruence, the individual is viewed as either deviant (being out of harmony with norms) or incompetent (lacking necessary behaviors). Congruence between the individual and the environment results in a maximum competence and acceptance.

In order to maintain a balanced classroom ecology or congruence, children must behave in ways that are in harmony with teachers' expectations (Mour, 1977).

The framework proposed here includes several interrelated ecological contexts. Those that affect the individual's development and behavior are the microsystem, mesosystem, exosystem, and macrosystem (Belsky, 1980; Bronfenbrenner, 1979). An additional system, the ontogenic (Belsky, 1980), which influences the individual's behavior and development, is included in the framework. The ontogenic system is concerned with the individual's impact on his or her personal development and behavior. The five systems are discussed next and presented in Figure 2-1.

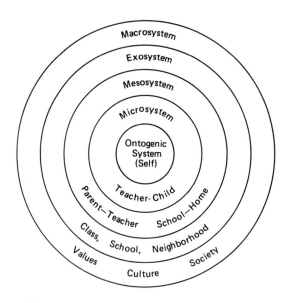

FIGURE 2-1 The Five Systems of the Integrative Framework

The microsystem. This system includes interrelationships within the immediate setting in which the individual is functioning, such as the teacher-student and child-child relationships in the instructional setting. Both child and teacher are actors and reactors in this setting (Carroll, 1974). Their interrelationship is a crucial element in determining *if* the child or young person is to be considered disturbed. Algozzine (1980) suggests that it is not simply the level and type of behaviors that the child exhibits that result in identification as disturbed, but the reactions of others in the microsystem to the behavior. In an educational setting, the most frequent and significant "reactor" to the child's behavior is the teacher.

Some teachers have been found to be more tolerant of certain "disturbed" behaviors in children than others (Curran & Algozzine, 1980). Consequently, they are less likely to label a child as disturbed. Educational programming for children and youths with behavior disorders begins with an analysis of the teacher-student relationship as it occurs in the microsystem. This important relationship is discussed in Chapter 5.

The mesosystem. The mesosystem is the interrelationship between the settings in which the individual is actually functioning. It is a system of microsystems. The mesosystem includes the interrelationships among the several settings in which the developing individual is functioning at a particular point in life. For children and youths with behavior disorders, the mesosystem may include the relationships among home, school, church, and community, for example. Included in the child's mesosystem is parental involvement, which is discussed in Chapter 12. The adolescent's mesosystem includes work-study and other community-based programs, discussed in Chapter 13.

The exosystem. The exosystem is the larger social system in which the microsystem and mesosystem are imbedded. It includes both formal and informal social structures, such as the home, school, law-enforcement, recreational, political, and transportation systems. Although the individual may not actively participate in these systems or be directly affected by them, they do influence the individual's microsystem and mesosystem, and thus, indirectly, the individual. The special educator of children and youths with behavior disorders must view these disorders not only in the context of microsystem and mesosystem, but in that of the exosystem (Paul & Epanchin, 1982). Besides providing the special educator with insight into the behavior disorder, the exosystem provides clues with regard to appropriate interventions. It can provide support structures such as friends, counselors, parents, and relatives who can contribute to interventions. Understanding the exosystem permits the special educator to explore the extent of environmental change needed to facilitate positive changes in the student's behaviors. As Hobbs (1966) indicated, abandoning "cures" and defining the problem of teaching as doing what we can to make differences in the ways in which the social system works *for* the young person with behavior disorders will impact most positively for that young person. The exosystem is discussed in detail in Chapter 7.

The macrosystem. This system includes the overriding cultural beliefs and values, as well as the general perceptions, of the social institutions common to a particular culture or subculture in which the child is functioning (Bronfenbrenner, 1979). The beliefs, values, and attitudes of the macrosystem directly and indirectly influence the child's or young person's behavior. Relevant areas in the macrosystem include the general perspective of the teacher, the educational system, the social role of the student, family styles, and community values (Riegel, 1975). Some generalized patterns that may impact upon the child or young person with behavior disorders include the social stigma of being labeled behavior-disordered and society's perceptions of (1) the teacher's role (2) the special education program, and (3) the school in general, especially in terms of the education of children and youth with behavior disorders. The theoretical perspectives discussed in Chapter 1 and their related interventions, which are discussed in chapters 8, 9, and 10, contribute to the macrosystem.

The ontogenic system. The ontogenic system includes the individual's personality, skills, abilities, and competencies. Each student exhibits intra-individual factors for coping in the environment. For example, students with high resistance to stress are usually perceived as being stable, while those with low resistance are usually perceived as unstable. Children are, in part, constituted of the beliefs and concepts they have about themselves. As Gatlin (1980) stated:

> . . . in the face of social contingencies over which people have only limited control, a social reality which people can consciously control only in relatively minor ways, they struggle both to fit and to resist the demands made on the form and content of their personal lives. Some lose, many are disfigured in the struggle, but always in their family life people attempt to satisfy their needs as best they understand them, while attempting to maintain some sense of personal and social integrity and keeping in mind the desire for the respect of those who matter most to them. They do this often with the realization that they are not completely in control of the forces they must control to be really satisfied, yet recognizing that they cannot await the kind of changes that are necessary before they could live the kinds of lives they would like to (p. 252).

The characteristics of children and youth with behavior disorders discussed in the second section of this chapter and the diagnostic evaluation and assessment processes discussed in Chapter 3 focus attention on the ontogenic system.

These five systems provide the ecological contexts within which special educators should respond to the needs of children and youth with behavior disorders. The systems are interdependent, and the nature of this interdependence is dynamic (Kurdek, 1981). Consequently, it is difficult to determine which specific system or systems should be the focus of interventions at a particular point in time. For example, a child's lack of independence (ontogenic factors) may be complicated by the impact of an inadequate school program (an exosystem factor) or a personal conflict with the teacher (a microsystem factor). However, by applying an ecological framework such as the one proposed, the special educator can generate hypotheses concerning the processes at work in the behavior disorder and systematically plan and apply potentially effective interventions.

Swap (1974) discussed the application of ecological-contexts theory in an essay on improving congruence between teacher and student. She stated that with increased "goodness of fit" between teacher and student, the incidence of disruptive classroom behaviors may be significantly decreased. Rich (1978) suggests that rather than arbitrarily applying a set of interventions presumed to be effective, the special educator who is applying the congruence or "matching model" can more readily determine those strategies and teaching styles that may be most effective for achieving specific objectives with specific children. By attending to the interrelationships among the five contexts, the special educator may be more successful in developing interventions appropriate for each individual student.

Kauffman (1982) presented a series of hypotheses that relate to an integrated approach to behavior disorders several of which are similar to that proposed here. He indicates that:

> Behavior, environment, and person variables are reciprocally determined, though the reciprocal influences they exert on one another are a matter of degree. In the microsystem, for example, either the teacher or the student may have a greater influence on their interactions at a specific point in time.
>
> In both assessment and intervention, the particular behaviors, environmental variables, and the degree of reciprocal influence among these factors must be specified. Through using the five systems discussed earlier, the special educator is provided a structure for clarifying relevant environmental variables for analysis.
>
> Environmental variables are the only avenue for direct intervention when attempting to alter levels of development, except to the extent that this development or the intervention is self-directed.

OBJECTIVE THREE: *To describe several characteristics of special educators that impact on decision making with regard to children and youth with behavior disorders.*

The "goodness of fit" between teacher and child involves matching teacher characteristics, styles, values, and goals with those of the child or youth person with behavior disorders. To serve a child with behavior disorders, the special educators must possess or learn the skills and strategies needed to effectively intervene on behalf of the child. Rather than searching for *the* technique and *the* strategy that is effective for all children and youth with behavior disorders, special educators need to search out and develop a repertoire of techniques and strategies (Rich, 1978) and then "match" them to the child's needs. To make a "match" that is beneficial to the child involves a series of teaching decisions (Brophy & Evertson, 1976):

> . . . effective teaching is not simply a matter of implementing a small number of "basic" teaching skills. Instead, effective teaching requires the ability to implement a very large number of diagnostic, instructional, managerial, and therapeutic skills, tailoring behavior in specific contexts and situations to the specific needs of the moment. Effective teachers not only must be able to do a large number of things; they also must be able to recognize which of the many things they know how to do applies at a given moment and be able to follow through by performing the behavior effectively. In short, effective teaching involves the orchestration of a large number of factors, continually shifting teaching behavior to respond to continually shifting needs (p. 139).

Special educators make many decisions to respond to the "continually shifting needs" of children and youth with behavior disorders. The five-system ecological framework can be applied in the decision-making process. Characteristics of special educators that influence decisions about students and interventions can be related to each of the systems.

Decisions in the ontogenic system are affected by the professional and personal characteristics of the special educator. Decision making is affected by the educator's life experiences, values and standards, philosophy of human nature, perspective on the education of children and youth with behavior disorders, and teaching and behavior-management skills. In addition, decisions are affected by the special educator's personal needs. For example, a teacher with a strong need for social order in the classroom may be less tolerant toward students who challenge that order than a teacher with less of a need for it.

Awareness of the ontogenic system encourages special educators to reflect on their personal development, experiences, values, needs, and philosophy. Personal reflection assists the special educator in determining whether a student is demonstrating disturbing behaviors or a behavior disorder. Decisions related to the ontogenic system address the question: "Is there a problem with the student's behavior?"

The microsystem is concerned with interactions between the child or youth with behavior disorders and the special educator in a specific instructional setting. Teaching decisions are affected by tolerance for diversity among their students (Curran & Algozzine, 1980). Two general sets of teachers' behaviors are in effect in the microsystem: productive behaviors, which foster and promote creativity, experimentation, and learning (that is, continued efforts to understand each student, willingness to share, fair treatment, listening, trusting, and respecting students); and counter-productive behaviors (forcing students to submit to the teacher's will, control by punishment or threat of punishment, shaming or belittling students, authoritarianism) (Mour, 1977).

Decisions related to the microsystem address the question: "What is the nature of the problem?" The teacher must decide if the behavior is indicative of a disturbance or is simply disturbing. Again, problems are not seen as either the child's or the special educator's, but their relationship in a common microsystem (Algozzine, 1980).

The mesosystem involves the interrelationships of microsystems in which a child participates. In decision making, the teacher addresses the question: "Who will be involved in the intervention?" For example, an intervention may necessitate parental involvement, collaboration with regular educators, and the services of school-based or community-agency personnel to meet the needs of children and youth with behavior disorders.

The exosystem is the larger social system in which the microsystem is embedded; this includes the special-education program (school program, support or related services) in which the child or young person with a behavior disorder is placed. In the exosystem, the teacher's individuality impacts on the classroom climate, goals of the program, and the selection of interventions. The classroom may be managed externally, by means of direct dominance of the teacher; or internally, through indirect, reflective management by the teacher (Rich, 1978). Class and individual goals may vary from concrete, functional goals and lists of specific skills to be completed within a discrete period of time to abstract, global goals of improved behavior. Strategies may vary from behavior modification to humanistic education. In the exosystem, the question is: "What are the interventions that are available to address the needs of this student?"

The macrosystem is related to the accepted cultural and subcultural beliefs, values, and attitudes surrounding behavior disorders and the education of children and youths with behavior disorders. Special educators' perspectives on behavior disorders (psychodynamic, biophysical, environmental, or behavioral), influence decisions about what interventions can best meet the child's needs and their potential effectiveness. Decisions in the macrosystem are affected by the philosophy and values of the school and community. For example, Long (1983) found that school districts in which there were active community groups supporting children and youth with behavior disorders tended to identify more students for special-education services. Districts in which special-education directors expressed more positive attitudes toward programming for emotionally disturbed children also demonstrated a higher prevalence of such students.

The relationships between the five ecological systems, teaching decisions, and attributes of teachers are summarized in Figure 2-2.

FIGURE 2-2   Teaching Decisions and Teacher Attributes

SYSTEM	DECISION	TEACHERS' ATTRIBUTES
Ontogenic	Is there a problem?	Personal values Philosophy of human nature Philosophy of education Personal needs

Microsystem	What is the nature of the problem?	Tolerance for diversity
		Teaching behaviors
		  Productive behaviors
		  Counter-productive behaviors

Mesosystem	Who will be involved in the intervention?	Ability to coordinate team members Communication skills Ability to involve parents

Exosystem	What interventions are available?	Classroom climate
		  External management
		  Internal management
		Goals
		  Concrete
		  Abstract
		Strategies
		  Instructional
		  Managerial

Macrosystem	What intervention best meets the child's needs?	Perspectives
		  Behavioral
		  Biophysical
		  Psychodynamic
		  Environmental
		Values of the school
		Values of the community

Increased awareness of each system in the integrative framework enables the special educator to further integrate efforts to match the needs of students with behavior disorders to appropriate, successful interventions. As Forness (1981) suggests, effective teaching involves observing students' reactions to treatment and making conscious teaching decisions to modify those treatments as necessary in response to students' needs.

OBJECTIVE FOUR: *To describe the behavior characteristics frequently exhibited by children and youth with behavior disorders.*

As discussed in the previous section, special educators bring to the teaching environment several personal attributes that impact on their decisions about children and youth with behavior disorders. Similarly, the latter bring to the teaching environment a variety of behavioral characteristics that affect their decisions and the decisions the special educator makes about them and interventions selected and implemented to assist them. In this section, the behavior characteristics frequently exhibited by children and youth with behavior disorders are discussed. Throughout the discussion, it must be remembered that no two children with behavior disorders are exactly alike. It must also be remembered that the behavior characteristics of these children differ significantly in terms of the frequency, intensity, and duration with which they are exhibited.

The work of Quay and his associates (1964, 1965, 1966, 1975, 1977, 1978, 1979) and Peterson (1961, 1964) and Peterson and associates (1959, 1961) is used to organize the discussion of student characteristics in this section. Quay's work is based on that of Peterson and associates, who investigated the feasibility of applying factor analytic methods to classify the behavior problems of children and youths with behavior disorders. In a study of 831 kindergarten and elementary-school children, using teachers' ratings of fifty-eight behaviors, Peterson et al. (1961) found two factors: Conduct Problem and Personality Problem. In a subsequent study of 259 seventh graders and 259 eighth graders using teachers' ratings, a third factor, Inadequacy-Immaturity, emerged (Quay & Quay, 1965). Later studies indicated four major constellations of behavior disorders: conduct disorders, personality disorders (anxiety-withdrawal), inadequacy-immaturity, and socialized aggression (subcultural delinquent) (Quay, 1977). These factors or clusters and the behavior characteristics they include are presented in Figure 2-3.

Conduct Disorders

The conduct disorder cluster represents behaviors that clearly differ from school and community expectations in almost all situations. These behaviors are aversive to both teachers and other children or young persons. Students demonstrating conduct disorders are not responsive to internal controls or the usual social controls (Quay, 1977). Several of the behaviors included in the conduct-disordered cluster are described next.

Aggression includes fighting and assaultive behaviors; destruction of personal or others' property; dominating others, bullying, and threatening; temper tantrums and verbal aggression and profanity. Decisions concerning whether or not a particular child is aggressive depends on several considerations: (a) the individual's intention, (b) the intensity of the aggressive behavior, and (c) the reaction of the person or group toward

FIGURE 2-3   Behavior Clusters and Characteristics

CONDUCT DISORDER

Physical aggression
Temper tantrums
Disobedience
Destructiveness
Impertinence, acting"smart"
Uncooperativeness, resistance
Disruptiveness, disturbing
   others
Negativity
Restlessness, boisterousness,
   noisiness
Irritability
Attention-getting behaviors
Domination, threatening
Hyperactivity
Dishonesty
Verbal aggressiveness
Jealousy
Argumentativeness
Irresponsibility
Stealing
Distractibility
Blaming others
Pouting, sulking
Selfishness

SOCIALIZED AGGRESSION

(Subcultural delinquency)
Loyal to delinquents
Group stealing

Gang membership
Violating curfew
Truancy (home and school)
"Bad" companions

PERSONALITY DISORDERS

(Anxiety-Withdrawal)
Anxiety, fear, tension
Shyness, timidity
Withdrawal, seclusion
Depression, sadness
Hypersensitivity
Self-consciousness
Inferiority
Lacking self-confidence
Reticence, secretiveness
Easily flustered, cries easily
Aloofness

INADEQUACY-IMMATURITY

Poor task completion
Messiness, sloppiness
Inattentiveness
Poor attention span
Poor physical coordination
Preoccupation, daydreaming
Passivity, lacking initiative
Sluggishness, drowsiness
Boredom, general lack of
   interest

(Adapted from Quay, 1979.)

whom the behavior is directed (Bandura, 1973). In addition, the characteristics of the person (the special educator, for example) observing the
aggression and the individual being aggressive must be considered. It
should be remembered that all aggression is not deviant; appropriate
aggression is prized and encouraged in society. Aggression may be either
physical or verbal, and directed against either self or others.

The control or management of aggression, both physical and verbal,
is perhaps the most difficult problem confronting the special educator.
Exhibited inappropriately, aggression has a direct negative effect on the
members of the group. Extreme physical aggression in the school setting
cannot be ignored. Aggression generates aggression or withdrawal by

others, thus inhibiting their functioning. External control must be initiated when physical aggression may cause harm to the self, others, or property. Verbal aggression is generally less threatening to others than physical aggression; however, in extreme forms it must be externally controlled.

Noncompliance includes disobedience and defiance, impertinence, resistance and inconsiderate behavior, and negativism. Disobedience is action contrary to the directions of an authority figure. Negativism is extreme and consistent verbal opposition and/or resistance to the suggestions, advice, and directions of others.

Disruptive behaviors may include interrupting, disrupting, and boisterousness. Disruptive behaviors are actions that interfere with the activities of others. In the classroom setting, disruptive behaviors include inappropriate talking, laughing, clapping, foot stamping, shouting, singing, whistling, and other behaviors that interrupt ongoing activities. Also included in this classification is a lack of cooperation during an activity and the use of vulgarity and sarcasm.

Inattentive behaviors include restlessness and distractibility. Inattentiveness is the inability to focus on a perceived stimulus situation for sufficient time to purposefully engage in a task. This behavior includes (a) not attending to a task, (b) not attending to the teacher's directions, and (c) wandering about the immediate environment touching and inspecting item after item without apparent purpose. The inattentive child often appears to be preoccupied or daydreaming.

Hyperactivity is heightened, persistent, sustained physical action. It is characterized by disorganization, disruption, and unpredictability. It is apparently nongoal-directed. Hyperactive children overreact to the stimuli in their environment. Their behavior is frequently described as restless, jittery, nervous, impulsive, and disinhibited. Teachers report that children exhibiting hyperactive behavior are "in constant motion" or "unable to stay still."

Attention-seeking behavior is action (verbal or nonverbal) that the child or young person uses to gain the attention of others and is inappropriate for the environment in which the child is functioning. Attention-seeking behaviors include shouting, boisterousness, clowning, showing off, running away, and having the last word in any verbal exchange. Other attention seekers are more subtle, and engage in foot tapping, finger snapping, hand waving, shyness, tattling, and whining. The attention-seeking child is often confused with the hyperactive child. However, it is generally found that, unlike the hyperactive child, the attention seeker's level of activity decreases rapidly immediately after attention is received.

According to Quay (1979), other behaviors common among students demonstrating conduct disorders are irritability, dishonesty, irresponsibility, selfishness, and stealing.

Personality Disorders (Anxiety-Withdrawal)

Quay's second behavior cluster is personality disorders (anxiety-withdrawal). The behaviors characteristic of a personality disorder contrast sharply with those of conduct disorders. Behaviors in the personality-disorder cluster represent a retreat from the social environment in which the child is functioning, rather than an aggressive or hostile response to it. Students with personality disorders may demonstrate social withdrawal, shyness, anxiety, crying, hypersensitivity, chronic sadness, worrying, timidity, lack of self-confidence, and inability to enjoy themselves. These children are frequently not diagnosed because their behaviors are less easily observed and less disturbing in the classroom.

Anxiety   is exhibited in observable behavior indicative of apprehensiveness, tension, and uneasiness. This behavior may be the result of anticipating a danger whose source is unknown or unrecognized by the individual. Anxious children and youths are frequently described as fearful, fidgety, shy, and withdrawn. They appear not to be productively involved in the environment. They may be equally anxious about success and failure. They have difficulty meeting new friends and bidding farewell to old ones, as well as beginning new and ending familiar activities. If their anxiety increases to a higher level, they may become immobilized, for all practical purposes.

Feelings of inferiority and worthlessness   Many children and youths in this cluster perceive themselves as inadequate, inferior, and unacceptable. These individuals lack self-confidence, fear the unfamiliar, express feelings of inferiority, are hypersensitive to criticism, resist independent functioning, and are reluctant to attempt activities. They are frequently immobilized when confronted with "new" or "different" problems and situations.

Withdrawal   is the act of emotionally leaving or escaping from a life situation that, in the individual's perception, may cause personal conflict or discomfort. Withdrawing behaviors include isolation, preoccupation, daydreaming, drowsiness, shyness, fear, depression, and anxiety. The child's affect is described as "flat" or "unresponsive."

According to Quay (1979), children and youths with personality disorders may also appear to be aloof and easily flustered. They may seem self-conscious and easily embarrassed.

Inadequacy-Immaturity

Quay's third behavior cluster is inadequacy-immaturity. The behaviors exhibited by inadequate/immature children are inappropriate in terms of developmental expectations for children their age. Behaviors in this cluster include preoccupation, short attention spans, clumsiness, passivity, daydreaming, sluggishness, drowsiness, excessive giggling, masturbation, and lack of perseverance.

Passive-suggestible behaviors are actions that the individual exhibits, with little apparent forethought, at the request of others or to please others. The passive-suggestible child or young person is frequently described as "irresponsible," "easily led," and a "follower." The passive-suggestible child uses others as an excuse for personal actions and lack of action. Behavior may be positive or negative, productive or nonproductive. These children appear to lack skill in solving problems and making decisions.

Social immaturity is defined here as age-inappropriate behavior; that is, a child or young person exhibits behavior that is typical of children of a younger chronological age. The behavior is most observable when the child is in unfamiliar or stressful situations. The social-response mechanisms the child has available for immediate use are limited, thus requiring the child to use less-mature responses. This immature behavior causes others to describe the child as "a baby" "a sissy" or "immature." Socially immature children characteristically prefer the company of younger or older children and adults to peers. They select toys, games, and activities below their age level. Occasionally, in familiar, nonstressful situations, they will exhibit pseudo-adult behaviors.

Socialized Aggression (Subcultural Delinquent)

The children and youths classified in this cluster, according to Quay, generally live in urban areas. The behaviors in this cluster include gang activities, cooperative stealing, habitual truancy, being accepted by and identifying with a delinquent subgroup, and participating in the street culture. These youths adopt behaviors that are reinforced by their peers. The delinquent subculture in which they function effectively provides their socialization experiences.

Characteristics Related to School Achievement

Cullinan, Epstein, and Kauffman (1984) have explored the characteristics of children and youths with behavior disorders to answer the question, "What constitutes a behavior disorder in school?" Using Quay's system of analysis, they determined that the most pervasive differences between children and youths with behavior disorders and other children and youths are "unhappiness, sadness, or depression" and "poor school work." They indicate that the picture is of "unhappy youngsters who are behavioral misfits at school, likely to cause the consternation of teachers, and almost certain to be avoided by their peers" (p. 18). Students with behavior disorders were scored as a problem at a higher frequency on every item of the Behavior Problem Checklist than were their nonhandicapped peers. They demonstrated a "dislike for school" and "anxiety-physical complaints" significantly more frequently than the nonhandicapped. Forty to 60 percent of the children and youths with behavior disorders were considered "odd," as opposed to only 8 to 20 percent of the nonhandicapped individuals. Three times as many children and youths with behavior disorders were depressed.

Poor achievement in school is characteristic of all children and youth with behavior disorders (Hobbs, 1966). Whelan, DeSaman, and Fortmeyer (1984) attempted to determine whether poor achievement preceded adjustment, or the reverse. They found that in elementary-school students, positive feelings appeared to result in achievement on academic tasks. Secondary-school students were found to link internal feelings of self-worth with the successful completion of tasks: when performance was good, positive feelings resulted. These findings indicate that successful instructional experiences are essential for children and youth with behavior disorders.

In addition to those described by Quay, children and youth with behavior disorders may demonstrate other behaviors that impact on their school achievement. These include:

1. *Inflexibility*, characterized by a limitation in the number of adjustment mechanisms the individual has available for use and in the quality with which the individual applies the available mechanisms (compulsiveness, aloofness, restricted interests, inhibition, and overcriticalness of self and personal productions).
2. *Deficiencies in awareness of cause-and-effect relationships*, involving a lack of awareness on the part of the child or youth of the dependencies between personal actions and the consequences of those actions.
3. *Impulsivity*, characterized by near-instantaneous response to environmental stimuli.
4. *Perseveration*, the tendency to continue an action after it is no longer appropriate for the task at hand.

SUMMARY

In this chapter, an integrated approach to meeting the needs of children and youth with behavior disorders is proposed. By applying the ecological framework described by Bronfenbrenner (1977, 1979), a "matching" or "goodness of fit" model for making teaching decisions was presented. Several characteristics of special educators that influence decision making and the need for a well-defined personal philosophy are discussed. The chapter concluded with a detailed presentation of behavioral characteristics frequently exhibited by children and youth with behavior disorders. Quay's classification categories were applied to organize the discussion of these characteristics.

REVIEW QUESTIONS

1. List several limitations inherent in the application of a single theoretical perspective in the education of children and youth with behavior disorders.
2. Using the integrative ecological framework, describe several variables associated with the following contexts that impact on the behavior of a child or young person with behavior disorders:
   microsystem
   mesosystem
   exosystem
   macrosystem
3. Review the teaching decisions discussed in the chapter (see Figure 2-2). Applying two different perspectives, discuss how the responses to the following questions will differ:
   Is there a problem?
   What is the nature of the problem?
   Who should be involved in the intervention?
   What interventions are available for implementation to assist the child?
4. Research the relationship between achievement and adjustment with regard to children and youth with behavior disorders.
5. Review the research on Quay's four clusters of behavioral characteristics of children and youth.

APPLICATION ACTIVITIES

1. Teaching decisions are based on the contexts in which behavior occurs. Review the case of a student with whom you are familiar (or one of the cases in Appendix B). Describe the variables in each of the systems that impact on the individual's behavior. Describe the ways in which your consideration of the context of behaviors impact on your teaching decisions.

   Would your teaching decisions be different for another child? What are some of the unique considerations concerning the behavior of this individual?
2. As discussed in this chapter, the special educator's personal attributes impact on decisions concerning children and youth with behavior disorders. To make conscious decisions to increase the "match" or "goodness of fit" between individual students and their treatments, special educators must be aware of their personal attributes.

SYSTEM	IMPACT ON BEHAVIOR	IMPACT ON TEACHING DECISION
Ontogenic System		
Microsystem		
Exosystem		
Mesosystem		
Macrosystem		

In the following application activity, you are to address several of the attributes considered essential to effective decision making with regard to teaching children and youth with behavior disorders. You will discover, as you attempt to respond to the questions, that there are no short, simple answers.

Respond to each of the questions from the perspective of *your* personal feelings.

THE ONTOGENIC SYSTEM

What are some of my personal values that I consider essential to my being and would be unwilling to change (for example, independence, honesty, leadership, integrity)?

What do I believe is the essence of human nature? Are individuals in control of their behavior? Are people basically good? Neutral? Weak? Strong?

What is the role of education? Does education form or facilitate development? Does education give answers or assist individuals in finding answers?

What are my personal needs? Why do I choose to teach? Do I need to have children need me? Do I wish to give of myself? Do I wish to control others?

THE MICROSYSTEM

How do I feel about children who are different?

What behaviors or characteristics of children do I find most annoying? How much diversity can I tolerate in the classroom?

Am I or will I be a teacher who listens? Who respects others? Do I control students or help them control themselves? Who is "in charge" in my classroom?

THE EXOSYSTEM

Is the classroom managed externally or internally? Do I dominate the classroom? Is the class operated in an authoritarian or a democratic way?

Do I have specific concrete goals? Do I just seek general improvement? With which strategies am I most comfortable?

THE MESOSYSTEM

How do I feel about involving parents? Community agencies? Related services?

What are my strengths in working with parents? My weaknesses?

What are my strengths in working with community agencies and related services? My weaknesses?

THE MACROSYSTEM

What is my perspective on behavior disorders?

How will I evaluate the effectiveness of interventions?

What are the values of the school in which I work (or will work)?

What are the values of the community?

3

Screening, Evaluation, and the Individualized Educational Program

The specific ecological context discussed in this chapter is the ontogenic system, the unique characteristics of each individual. Other contexts (the microsystem and mesosystem) are discussed as they relate to the application of behavioral, ecological, and functional assessment techniques. The role of teacher is stressed throughout the chapter, because the teacher is often the first to encounter children who need help (Long, Morse, & Newman, 1980). It is generally agreed that teachers have sufficient information about their students from daily interaction with them to make highly accurate professional predictions about the course of a student's school career (Bower, 1980). In addition, the application of the results of evaluations is stressed, because it is our position that the youngster's standing on *particular* dimensions is far more important than any general label.

OBJECTIVES

After completing this chapter, you will be able to—

1. describe the screening and referral, diagnostic evaluation, and placement process;
2. identify effective screening instruments by the application of a set of criteria;
3. describe the roles of members of the interdisciplinary team in the diagnostic-evaluation process;

4. identify the safeguards for evaluation mandated by Public Law 94-142;
5. identify the content of the Individualized Education Plan and its role in placement;
6. describe the steps in developing the Individualized Educational Plan;
7. define behavioral assessment from an ecological perspective;
8. identify the techniques applied in behavioral assessment;
9. describe ecological and functional assessment methods for programming for children and youth with behavior disorders.

A CASE FOR CONSIDERATION

Though it was late October, five-year-old Amy had not yet settled down in her kindergarten classroom. She wandered about the room during group and individual work periods. Amy had to be physically placed in her chair by the teacher when directed to sit. If another child was playing with a toy that Amy wanted, she would grab the child by the hair and pull the toy from the child's grasp. If the class schedule was changed because of a late bus or an assembly, Amy would become very upset, cry, throw chairs, and throw herself on the floor.

Mr. Velasquez, the kindergarten teacher, was quite concerned about Amy's inability to follow class rules and the physical danger she might cause to herself and her classmates. He requested a meeting with Ms. Hallal, the school's special-services consultant. Together, Mr. Velasquez and Ms. Hallal completed a screening instrument indicating that Amy was demonstrating aggressive and noncompliant behaviors with greater frequency, intensity, and for a longer period of time than her classmates. The consultant conducted a structured interview with the teacher to determine the management techniques used in the classroom, specifically those used to try to manage Amy's behaviors. The interview showed that Mr. Velasquez consistently applied a variety of positive behavior interventions with Amy, with little success. Teacher and consultant agreed that Amy's problems needed further study. Mr. Velasquez and Ms. Hallal developed the following plan of action:

> Amy's parents would be invited to school for a conference with the teacher. Though Mr. Velasquez had been working closely with them, further information and permission to evaluate Amy was needed.
>
> If Amy's parents agreed to an evaluation, it would be formally requested by the teacher, Mr. Velasquez and Ms. Hallal would collect educational and behavioral data for presentation to the evaluation team.
>
> After collecting appropriate data, the members of the team would meet and discuss their findings. Amy's parents, Mr. Velasquez, and Ms. Hallal would attend this meeting. Amy's characteristics would be compared with those generally agreed upon in the district for eligibility for special services. During the meeting, the team would make an effort to diagnose Amy's problem.

Goals and objectives would be written for Amy. The team would reach a consensus on the services needed to help Amy attain those goals and objectives.

Next, an appropriate placement would be agreed upon. At the conclusion of the meeting, an individualized Education Plan, a complete document, would describe Amy's program and placement.

As a result of her teacher's concern about her functioning in kindergarten, Amy was screened, evaluated, diagnosed, and placed in an appropriate special education service. The screening and referral, diagnostic evaluation, placement, and Individualized Education Program processes, similar to those applied in Amy's case, are discussed in detail in the remainder of this chapter.

OBJECTIVE ONE: *To describe the screening and referral, diagnostic evaluation, and placement processes.*

Screening and Referral

There are two processes whereby a child or youth is identified; that is, called to the attention of school authorities as potentially in need of special services. These processes are screening and referral.

Screening is the process of identifying students who, at least on the basis of first-level study, deserve further study. The further study should result in classifying a child as having no problem; a transitory problem; a problem that is a response to social or academic stresses in school that could be altered; or a problem that is evident in school, home, and neighborhood (Long, Morse, & Newman, 1980).

Screening differentiates *potentially* exceptional, high-risk, or vulnerable children from the total school, class, district, or community population. The results of screening do not classify or label the child as exceptional.

Lambert and Bower (1961a) describe four purposes of screening. It more adequately identifies children with problems early in their school careers, and helps those children receive additional study and, if appropriate, services. Screening increases teachers' awareness of disabilities and coping skills. Through screening, educational adjustments are also provided to students who need them.

Students may also be identified for further study through a referral process. A referral may be from school personnel, parents, doctors, community agency personnel, or another service.

School referral is a two-step process. First, information is collected from all individuals who currently interact with the child in the school. The classroom teacher, for example, may be requested to assist in completing a rating scale or checklist, or to complete information sheets such as that provided in Figure 3-1. The second step in the referral process is to invite the parents for a conference, at which school concerns are explained and parents are asked for permission to evaluate the child.

FIGURE 3-1 Sample School Referral Form

```
                    School _____

                    Date referral initiated _____

Student's name _____

Sex _____        Date of birth _____   Age _____

Primary language _____

Name of parent(s) or guardian primarily responsible for

child _____   Telephone _____

Address _____

Name and affiliation of person initiating referral (if
other than parent or guardian) _____

1. What behaviors caused you to consider referring this
   student?  (Be as specific and complete as possible.)
   _____

   _____


2. Parent Contact

      What information relating to this referral resulted
   from parent contact?  Be as specific as possible.  If you
   have an ongoing relationship with the child or parent,
   attach log of contacts.)
   _____

   _____


3. Medical Information
      Pertinent medical history _____

      _____

      _____

      Is the student receiving any medication?  If yes, what?

      _____

      _____

      Prescribing physician _____

4. Information from Student's Cumulative Records
      A. Vision screening _____

         Hearing screening _____

         Speech and language screening _____
```

B. Test Scores

Achievement tests _____

Intelligence tests _____

Others (please specify) _____

C. Attendance over Past Year

5. Interventions Applied Thus Far to Assist the Student

   A. Curriculum modifications _____

   B. Schedule changes _____

   C. Teaching strategies _____

   D. Counseling _____

   E. Family assistance and conferences _____

   F. Outside agency services _____

   G. Staff/administrative conferences _____

   H. Other (specify) _____

6. Attach any of the following information that is available:

   A. Behavior rating scale and/or checklist;

   B. Behavior observations over a three-week period (if observational data is not presently available, collect it on the referral behavior which you described in #1);

   C. Behavior observations from outside source;

   D. Samples of academic work (include examples from several academic areas if possible);

   E. Relevant anecdotal records;

   F. Parent permission (if it has already been obtained).

Teacher's signature and date _____

Principal's signature and date _____

(Adapted from Florida Department of Education, 1979a.)

Benson and Cessna (1980) describe the school referral process as "two pronged." First, the student's behavior is studied in terms of its frequency and intensity. This information is recorded by the teacher on a form such as the "Social or Behavioral Functioning" form in Figure 3-2. The second "prong" focuses on the actions the school has taken thus far to assist the student. More specifically, what interventions have school personnel made to help the child? The "School Intervention Checklist" in Figure 3-3 can be used to record this information. The information on both of these forms is used when making a decision to evaluate, not evaluate, or continue to study the referred child.

FIGURE 3-2 Social or Behavioral Functioning Checklist

Definition: Social or behavioral functioning that differs to such an extent that the child cannot be adequately or safely educated in the regular school program, signifying the need for interventions and/or placement.

Directions: Each area (1-8) is considered and rated by the interdisciplinary team in terms of intensity and frequency.

For example: A severe behavior that occurs often would receive a numerical rating of 12. Scores are recorded in the appropriate column.

FREQUENCY

	Never	At Times	Often	Frequent	Constant
INTENSITY					
Adequate	1	2	3	4	5
Mild	6	7	8	9	10
Moderate	11	12	13	14	15
Severe	16	17	18	19	20
Profound	21	22	23	24	25

Social or Behavioral Functioning	Total Possible	Score
1. Dangerous to self and others	25	_____
2. Interferes with own or other's learning	25	_____
3. Limited self-control	25	_____
4. Lack of positive and/or sustained relationships	25	_____
5. Physical complaints related to stress and/or anxiety	25	_____
6. Pervasive anxiety or depression	25	_____
7. Bizarre or exaggerated behavioral reactions to routine environment	25	_____
8. Extended periods of withdrawal having no apparent coping aspect	25	_____
Total	200	_____

Staffing decision for placement _____

DESCRIPTIONS OF BEHAVIORS

1. Dangerous to Self or Others
   Physical aggression to persons or property
   Self-abusive behaviors
   Physical resistance, hostility

2. Interferes with Own or Others' Learning
   Verbally disruptive
   Inattentive
   Inappropriate movement
   Tantrums
   Attention-seeking behaviors
   Noncompliance
   Truancy

3. Limited Self-control
   Easily frustrated
   Tantrums
   Wanders about room
   Inappropriate verbalization or noises
   Physical or verbal aggressions
   Denial and blaming
   Crying
   Profanity

4. Lack of Positive and/or Sustained Relationships
   Few or no friends
   Changes friends frequently
   Avoids participation with others
   Often hurts others during interactions
   Plays alone
   Places self in position for physical/verbal abuse
   Chooses older or younger friends

5. Physical Complaints Related to Stress and/or Anxiety
   Often ill
   Reports illnesses or pains
   Uses physical complaints to avoid stress
   Seems tired; lack of energy
   Soils or wets self
   Frequent trips to restroom

6. Pervasive Anxiety or Depression
   Seeks constant reassurance
   Nervous mannerisms
   Avoids eye contact
   Persistent negativism
   Tends to overstudy or not finish task
   Fearful
   Preoccupied with disaster, death, disease
   Mood swings
   Sad, tearful
   Sleeping or eating disorders

7. Bizarre and/or Exaggerated Behavioral Reactions to
   Routine Environment
     Self-stimulation
     Ritualistic behaviors
     Immature language
     Repetitive behaviors
     Noncontextual language
     Emotional outbursts
     Severe reactions to change
     Inappropriate sexual behavior
8. Extended Periods of Withdrawal with no Apparent
   Positive Coping Aspect
     Poor eye contact
     Physical withdrawal from touch
     Lethargy
     Limited affect
     Self-isolation
     Daydreaming

(Adapted from Benson & Cessna, 1980.)

Diagnostic Evaluation

Diagnostic evaluation is the process of studying a child or youth to determine the nature of the problem, if in fact there is one. Generally, because of the nature of the screening process, children and youth are identified as potentially vulnerable who are not. During the diagnostic evaluation process, some of these children are found to be normal or demonstrating transient, situational, or mild problems. As a consequence, diagnostic evaluation for the purpose of providing special education is discontinued and the child is referred to the appropriate service provider within the school; that is, counselor, remedial teacher, and so on.

The purpose of diagnostic evaluation is—

1. to determine if the child or youth has a behavioral and/or learning problem;
2. to determine the nature of the problem; and
3. to study the problem from a multidisciplinary perspective.

It should also be recognized that, in traditional terms, diagnosis and treatment are not entirely separate processes. The adult continually discovers new aspects of the child's world in a diagnosis, and the adult's sharing of and reaction to the child's problems are an integral part of the treatment. Diagnosis is progressive, often specific in focus, and existential in appearance, and prescriptive planning must be flexible, open, and always progressing (Long, Morse, & Newman, 1980, p. 91).

FIGURE 3-3 School Intervention Checklist

STUDENT'S NAME _____ SCHOOL _____ DATE _____

Please indicate which interventions have been tried with this student. Comment on the effectiveness of the techniques tried.

TECHNIQUE	TRIED YES/NO	DATES BEGIN/END	PERSONS INVOLVED*	COMMENTS
1. Time out				
2. Contingency reinforcement				
3. Contracting				
4. Observational time-out				
5. School counseling				
6. Nonschool/agency counseling				
7. Home-School Behavior Management programs				
8. Nonschool/agency family therapy				
9. Parent conferences				
10. Environmental change/preventive planning				
11. Teacher-child conferencing				
12. Special services consultation				
13. Principal intervention				
14. Rule delineation				
15. Schedule change				
16. Instructor change				
17. Others (be specific)				

*List all personnel currently involved in planning and implementing this intervention.

(Adapted from Benson & Cessna, 1980.)

Diagnostic evaluation involves the use of a variety of scales, inventories, observations, and tests, which are discussed in detail later in this chapter. Evaluation concludes with the writing of an Individualized Education Program for the child and placement for services.

Placement

A placement decision with regard to a specific child is made by an interdisciplinary team, composed of the child's parents and several school personnel familiar with the child's functioning and diagnostic data. During the interdisciplinary-team meeting, the members determine if the available diagnostic evaluation data meet the criteria for a diagnosis of behavioral disorders or some other exceptionality. If eligibility is confirmed, the committee writes educational goals and objectives, determines the service needs, and recommends an appropriate placement for the child.

When making a placement decision, the interdisciplinary team engages in the following activities:

1. Reviews all information available on the child and the environments in which the child is functioning.
2. Seeks parental evaluation of the information and determines if additional information is needed before placement can be recommended.
3. Analyzes the student's academic and behavioral strengths, weaknesses, and learning style to use as the basis of his or her educational goals and objectives.
4. Considers the placement alternatives in view of the student's educational goals, objectives, and learning style.
5. Reviews the placement selected with regard to its restriction on the child's freedom and responsivity to the child's individual needs.

OBJECTIVE TWO: *To identify effective screening instruments by the application of a set of criteria.*

The Teacher and Screening

Screening generally refers to "quick, valid measurement activities that are administered systematically to large groups of children" (Paul & Epanchin, 1982, p. 89). There are two main types of screening: community and school.

Community screening attempts to solicit referrals from agencies and individuals in the community. This is usually done through correspondence with local doctors, day-care centers, preschools, nonpublic schools, mental-health agencies, community agencies, and family and children's services. Local media are also used to alert the community to services available for children and youth with behavior disorders.

School screening relies heavily on the classroom teacher. With the possible exception of a child or young person's parents, the classroom teacher is the most likely individual in the child's life to recognize that he or she appears to differ from normal children. The teacher has an intimate knowledge of the child and is in close personal contact with him or her throughout the school year.

Teachers' judgments of children have been found to be important variables in any screening process. In an extensive research study of procedures for identifying emotionally handicapped children in California, Bower (1960) concluded that "teachers' judgments of emotional disturbance were very much like the judgments of clinicians" (p. 62). Bower's sources of data were reading achievement, arithmetic achievement, intelligence, sociometric status, teachers' ratings of behaviors, and others. Maes (1966), using similar data, found that teachers' ratings and intelligence (as measured by the California Test of Mental Maturity Short Form) were as effective as Bower's for screening purposes. Harth and Glavin (1971) applied an abbreviated form of Lambert and Bower's in-school screening technique. They concluded that teacher rating is one valid technique for screening emotionally disturbed children.

Cosper and Erickson (1984) drew similar conclusions regarding teachers' abilities to use direct-observation techniques. This study demonstrated that teachers' ratings can be considered valid criteria for initial identification or screening.

The teacher may be the most valuable source of data on high-risk or potentially deviant children. "Teachers work with the children daily and know more about them than any diagnostician can find out in one brief diagnostic session" (Koppitz, 1977, p. 13).

Selecting Screening Procedures

Marcus, Fox, and Brown (1982) assert: "It is important that a useable set of behavioral criteria, mutually agreed upon by professionals of all disciplines involved in the education and treatment of children, be established" (p. 255). It is important to remember that screening is used only to identify children appropriate for further study. Screening is not used for diagnostic purposes or to determine if a child needs special education.

Lambert and Bower (1961b) suggested several criteria for large-scale screening processes:

1. The teacher should have adequate information to complete the process without assistance.
2. The procedure should not require extensive training or supervision.
3. The results of the procedure should be *tentative identification* of children with emotional problems—leading the teacher to *referral* for evaluation.
4. The procedure should not encourage the teacher to diagnose emotional problems, to draw conclusions about their causes, or to label or categorize children.
5. The procedure should honor confidentiality.

6. The procedure should be nonthreatening to the child.
7. The procedure should be inexpensive.

These criteria are recommended for the evaluation of any screening procedures used to identify children and youth with behavior disorders for the purpose of referring them for further study. Several screening techniques used to identify children at high risk for behavior disorders are presented in Appendix A.

OBJECTIVE THREE: *To describe the roles of members of the interdisciplinary team in the diagnostic evaluation process.*

Diagnostic evaluation is the process of studying selected children or youth to determine the nature of the deviation that is present if, in fact, there is one.

The strategies used in a diagnostic evaluation depend in part on the student's age and the purpose of the evaluation (Koppitz, 1977). Older students are generally referred for remedial or therapeutic help for existing problems. Younger students are referred to prevent problems or to minimalize existing ones. In addition, the selection of specific diagnostic evaluation strategies depends on the perspective and basic assumptions concerning behavior disorders held by the diagnosticians involved.

Koppitz (1977) suggests that care should be taken during diagnostic evaluation because the child's most obvious problems are not always his or her most serious problem. She further suggests that diagnostic evaluation data be obtained from at least five different sources. First, the child is to be observed in various school settings (classroom, playground, and so on). The second source of information is the teacher, whose information about the child is "indispensable." Information should also be obtained from the child's cumulative school records and from the parents. The final data should be obtained by testing and interviewing the child.

The Federal Rules and Regulations for the implementation of Public Law 94-142 state that "no single procedure shall be the sole criteria for determining an appropriate educational program for a child" (Federal Register, 1977, p. 42,497). Yet minimal information is often used for diagnostic evaluation and placement purposes. During a twenty-one-month period, McGinnis, Kiraly, and Smith (1984) reviewed the school records of forty-five elementary school students identified as behaviorally disordered and found little documentation in the files for those functional areas most clearly related to the child's behavior disorder. The most frequent source of data on the child's behavior disorder was a description of his or her behavior. The next most frequently found source of information was a family/environmental history. The information available on the child's behavior disorder was based on subjective rather than objective data.

Similar findings were reported by Smith, Frank, and Snider (1984), who concluded that

> the identification of children as behaviorally disordered in this sample, to a great extent, was based on traditional measures of academic and intellectual assessment, even though different professional groups appear to believe that such information is the least valuable for such a task (p. 30).

Diagnosis in all cases is tentative at best. Diagnostic evaluation of children and youth is particularly difficult because:

1. children have limited language skills; thus, other communications media must be used during diagnosis (play, projective techniques, observation, and the like).
2. children have limited experiential backgrounds to call on in their efforts to express and solve problems.
3. children have different developmental rates within and between sexes; thus, the diagnostician must determine where a child is developmentally and compare the "assumed normal behavior" for the child's developmental stage with the "present behavior."
4. consideration must be given to the relative instability of children's personalities during their years of rapid growth and development.
5. consideration must be given to the effects of the child's culture and subculture on his or her personality and behaviors.

Concerned with the increasing number of children (and adults) being diagnosed as mentally ill, White (1961) states that "a child (or any person) should be considered innocent of psychological problems until proven guilty" (p. 75). She proposed ten essential questions that should be answered by all members of the interdisciplinary team engaged in diagnostic evaluation.

1. What evidence is there that a problem exists?
2. What is the child's learning ability?
3. What is the child's socioeconomic status?
4. What is the child's cultural background?
5. What is the child's social role with peers?
6. What is the child's physical health?
7. Is the child passing through a normal developmental phase?
8. Is the child reacting to some subtle conditions in the school environment?
9. Is the child reacting to some subtle conditions at home?
10. Is the child simply "different"?

The responses to these questions require the diagnostic team to view the child or young person developmentally, physically, intellectually, culturally, and experientially. They require that the team not take the existence of a problem for granted simply because the child has been referred for evaluation. The members of the team are required to seek the locus of the problem if a problem does in fact exist, not only in the child but among his peers, in the school, and in the home.

White's guidelines remind the diagnostician that not all aggression, withdrawal, introspection, or underachievement is indicative of a behavioral disorder. Individuals should not be diagnosed as behavior disordered simply on the basis of their uniqueness as people. White's guidelines recognize that each individual is unique and has a right to be different.

The Interdisciplinary Team

Since the implementation of Public Law 94-142, the jurisdictional disputes among mental health professionals are less overt concerning which professional group is responsible for diagnosis and treatment of children and youths with behavior disorders.

Educators have traditionally described children in terms of their behaviors, whereas mental health workers have tended to look at them in terms of dynamic psychological processes (Marcus, Fox, & Brown, 1982). Special educators as well as professionals in medicine, psychology, and the social services may react negatively to others who give the appearance of encroaching on their expertise. Ideally, areas of professional expertise should be complementary to one another when analyzed relative to a child's total possible service needs.

The various professionals serving children and youth with behavior disorders, and their diagnostic functions, are:

1. *The regular classroom educator,* who may contribute descriptive information about the child's (a) behavior in learning and social situations in school, (b) social status, (c) learning style, and (d) estimated achievement level. The role of regular educators in team decision making was studied by Ysseldyke, Algozzine, and Allen (1982), who found that the average amount of participation by regular educators was 27 percent. The majority of teachers' comments dealt with classroom data (43 percent) or with data described as subjective or irrelevant (47 percent). This study seemed to indicate that teachers have just begun to tap the potential contributions their presence can make to the diagnostic-evaluation team.

2. *The special educator,* who may collect and present to the team systematically obtained observation on the child or youth, ask questions of other team members from an educational perspective, and contribute educational findings to the discussion.

3. *The parents,* who have a greater store of knowledge, understanding, and feelings about the child than does any professional member of the diagnostic-evaluation team.

4. *The physician,* who may conduct a physical examination; refer the individual for further examination; recommend medical interventions that are, in his or

her professional judgment, needed to facilitate the child's rehabilitation; and monitor and evaluate the effectiveness of medical interventions in cooperation with the others on the team. Other members of the medical profession the physician may call on for assistance include the pediatrician, the neurologist, the hearing and vision specialists, and the nurse.

5. *The psychologist,* who is responsible for collecting and presenting diagnostic information about the student's cognitive, academic, and personality characteristics. The psychologist may also contribute diagnostic information about the individual's vocational interests, values and standards, aptitudes, and psychomotor abilities. In addition to standardized tests and inventories, the psychologist interviews the child, parents, and teacher; and employs projective and sociometric techniques, as well as direct observation for diagnostic purposes.

6. *The psychiatrist,* who presents to the team reports on character and adaptational diagnoses derived from psychiatric interviews. This information includes the psychiatrist's judgments with regard to treatment and prognosis.

7. *The social worker,* who develops and presents to the team a comprehensive social history of the child or young person.

8. *The speech and language pathologist,* who contributes information to the team on the child's language development, cognitive processes, and speech and articulation.

9. *Other members of the team,* who may include the school counselor, the school administrator, vision specialist, hearing specialist, occupational therapist, physical therapist, recreation therapist, and law-enforcement and correctional personnel. The specific roles and functions of these professionals depend on the needs of the child or youth and the team.

CASE STUDIES

The interdisciplinary team generates two documents: a case-study report and an Individualized Education Plan. The typical case study prepared for the child or young person with behavior disorders may include reports on a physical examination (including vision, hearing, and speech), neurological examination, psychological evaluation, psychiatric interview, family evaluation (including internal and external family functioning), review of the child's preschool and school history, and an educational assessment (Shea, 1968). The specific contents of the case study vary with the child, the presenting problem, and the membership of the diagnostic team.

Kaufman and Reynolds (1984) proposed that an effective case-study report—

1. answer the referral question;
2. describe the behavior as a basis for interpretations and inferences;
3. describe the uniqueness of the individual;
4. be written in a clear, precise, straightforward manner;

5. use standard English, avoiding slang, jargon, and technical terms;
6. synthesize and integrate information, avoiding a test-by-test recital of results, emphasizing the child;
7. provide recommendations that are explicit, specific, and adaptable to the particular setting.

They also urged that the report be completed and distributed quickly.

OBJECTIVE FOUR: *To identify the safeguards for evaluation mandated by Public Law 94-142.*

The Federal Register (1977) states:

Testing and evaluation materials and procedures used for the purposes of evaluation and placement of handicapped children must be selected and administered so as not to be racially or culturally discriminatory (121a.530).

Evaluation procedures: State and local educational agencies shall insure at a minimum, that:

a. Tests and other evaluation materials:
   1. are provided and administered in the child's native language or other mode of communication, unless it is clearly not feasible to do so;
   2. have been validated for the specific purpose for which they are used; and
   3. are administered by trained personnel in conformance with the instructions provided by their producer;
b. Tests and other evaluation materials include those tailored to assess specific areas of educational need and not merely those which are designed to provide a single general intelligence quotient;
c. Tests are selected and administered so as best to ensure that when a test is administered to a child with impaired sensory, manual, or speaking skills, results accurately reflect the child's aptitude or achievement level or whatever other factors the test purports to measure, rather than reflecting the child's impaired sensory, manual, or speaking skills (except where those skills are the factors which the test purports to measure);
d. No single procedure is used as the sole criterion for determining an appropriate educational program for a child; and
e. The evaluation is made by a multidisciplinary team or group of persons, including at least one teacher or other specialist with knowledge in the area of suspected disability;
f. The child is assessed in all areas related to the suspected disability, including where appropriate, health, vision, hearing, social and emotional status, general intelligence, academic performance, communicative status, and motor abilities (121a.532).

OBJECTIVE FIVE: *To identify the content of the Individualized Education Plan (IEP) and its function in placement for service.*

Nelson and Greenough (1983) stated:

> Regardless of a pupil's diagnostic label, the starting point for special education intervention is the IEP. At this level, knowing whether the student has been diagnosed as autistic, dyslexic, moderately retarded, or even deaf-blind is of little use (p. 15).

The second document that the interdisciplinary team prepares, the Individualized Education Plan, is critical to the provision of effective special education services for the child or youth with behavior disorders. It is developed on the basis of the diagnostic evaluation or case-study information discussed in the previous section. The Individualized Education Plan includes two activities: (1) the IEP meeting and (2) the IEP document, which is a written record of the meeting. The IEP meeting is conducted to—

> provide a communication system for parents and school personnel to jointly decide the student's needs, required services and possible outcomes;
>
> provide an opportunity for resolving differences between the parents and the school's perceptions of the student's needs, first through the meeting and then through the procedural protections available;
>
> set forth in writing a commitment of the services to be provided;
>
> provide an evaluation system for determining the student's progress toward the described goals and objectives (Federal Register, 1981). (p. 5461)

The written Individualized Education Plan includes:

> 1. A statement of the child's present levels of performance;
> 2. A statement of annual goals, including short-term instructional objectives;
> 3. A statement of the specific education and related services to be provided to the child, and the extent to which the child will be able to participate in regular educational programs;
> 4. The projected dates for initiation of the services and the anticipated duration of services;
> 5. Appropriate objective criteria and evaluation procedures and schedules for determining, on at least an annual basis, whether the short-term instructional objectives are being achieved (Federal Register, 1977, 121a.346).

The writing of Individualized Education Plans is discussed in detail in Chapter 5. In the next section, the steps in the IEP development process are discussed.

OBJECTIVE SIX: To identify the steps in Individualized Education Plan development:

By systematically progressing through the following nine steps, an IEP can be developed.

1. Collect information on the child's present level of functioning.
2. Organize this information according to curriculum areas; that is, behaviors, communication skills, self-help skills, social skills, reading, mathematics, cognitive skills, and so on.
3. Indicate which areas of functioning appear to be of greatest significance to efforts to facilitate the child's return to as normal an educational program as possible.
4. Specify annual goals: what do you want the student to be able to do in each functional area after one year of programming?
5. Specify the short-term objectives: What do you want the student to be able to do in each functional area after three to five months of instruction?
6. Describe the related services needed to facilitate the annual goals and short-term objectives.
7. Select the placement that is potentially most responsive to the student's needs in the least restrictive environment.
8. Identify procedures to be implemented to evaluate the attainment of the goals and objectives.
9. Project a date for reviewing the IEP.

If a student with behavior disorders is programmed in the regular classroom, the regular education teacher should be involved in the IEP development process. A study by Pugach (1982), however, found that regular teacher involvement in IEP development most often occurs indirectly, through conferring with the special educator and providing information. Only 52 percent of the regular educators in the study had attended the most recent IEP meeting for the students in their class. A majority of the teachers were not systematically involved in developing IEPs for students for whom they had major instructional responsibility.

OBJECTIVE SEVEN: *To define behavioral assessment from an ecological perspective.*

In special education, assessment is useful only if it facilitates effective and efficient decision making with regard to the individual student's placement and service or treatment (Helton, 1984). In addition to its application in the initial placement of a student in the appropriate program, assessment is essential to making programming decisions throughout the student's program. When compared to traditional assessment procedures, behavioral assessment, proposed next, offers a functional and practical approach to the placement and programming of a child or youth with behavior disorders.

There are several differences between the traditional and the behavioral approaches to assessment. Traditional assessment focuses on understanding what is responsible for the child's present level of functioning. Behavioral assessment is an "exploratory, hypothesis-testing process in which a range of specific procedures are used in order to understand a given child . . . and to formulate specific intervention strategies" (Ollendick & Hersen, 1984, p. 6).

In behavioral assessment, behavior is accepted at face value, while in the traditional approach, behavior is seen as a symptom of an underlying cause. Behavioral assessment differs from traditional assessment in terms of the inferences made with regard to the causes of behavior, assumptions with regard to the effect of situational variables on the behavior, and the use of data in the development and evaluation of treatment (Nelson & Hayes, 1979). Behaviors are viewed as "predominantly under the control of contemporaneous environmental and organismic variables rather than determined by underlying mechanisms and inferred personality traits" (Mash, 1979, p. 24). The differences between behavioral and traditional assessment are further summarized in Figure 3-4.

OBJECTIVE EIGHT: *To identify techniques applied in behavioral assessment. These techniques include (a) interviewing, (b) checklists and rating scales, (c) self-reporting instrument, (d) peer-sociometric forms, (e) self-monitoring procedures, (f) observation, and (g) intellectual and academic assessment.*

Behavioral interviewing Haynes and Wilson (1979) describe the behavioral interview as structured interactions between individuals that gather current and historical information about the student's, parents', or regular educator's concerns and goals. Behavioral interviews identify factors that maintain or provoke the problem behaviors and identify reinforcers to which the child may respond. Through these interviews, the potential for change in the student, parent, or regular educator is assessed. Parental informed consent for further assessment, placement, or evaluation of the student can also be acquired in behavioral interviews.

The special educator may find it necessary to interview several persons in order to develop a clear picture of the student and the contexts in which he or she is functioning. Gross (1984) contends that the special educator is the professional person most likely to interview the parent and the student. The special educator should make an effort to obtain information about demographics, parent-child interactions, frequency and duration of behaviors, strengths to be used in developing appropriate behaviors, reinforcers, and the potential for change. The child may communicate perceptions of the reason for referral and family and peer interactions.

FIGURE 3-4   Differences between Traditional and Behavioral Assessment

	BEHAVIORAL	TRADITIONAL
Assumptions		
Personality	Personality constructs used to summarize behavior patterns, if at all	Personality is a reflection of states and traits
Causes of behavior	Behaviors maintained by environment	Within the individual
Implications		
Role of behavior	Sample of person's repertoire in a situation	Indicates underlying causes
Role of history	Unimportant, except for retrospective baselines	Crucial: present is a product of past
Behavior	Specific to situation	Consistent across time and settings
Data	To describe target behaviors and maintaining conditions	To describe personality functioning
	To select treatment	To diagnose and classify
	To evaluate and revise treatment	To predict
Level of Inference		
Assessment	Low Direct	Medium—high Indirect
Timing of assessment	Ongoing, constant	To diagnose, to posttest
Scope of assessment	Specifics; i.e., behaviors, contexts	Global measure of individual

From P.H. Bornstein, M.T. Bornstein, & B. Dawson, "Integrated assessment and treatment," in T.H. Ollendick & M. Henson (eds.), *Child Behavioral Assessment: Principles and Procedures* (N.Y.: Pergamon Press, 1984). Reprinted with permission of the authors and Pergamon Press.

Behavioral assessment interviews may be unstructured or structured. In the unstructured interview, minimum constraints are imposed on the topics and the sequence of topics discussed. In the structured interview, the topic and sequence of topics for discussion follow a predetermined format.

Wahler and Cormier (1970) developed an unstructured interview technique for use with students, parents, and regular educators. The interview is conducted to determine the specific behavior of concern and the contexts in which the behavior occurs. Prior to the interview itself, those interviewed are required to complete the "Child Home Behavior Checklist" (Figure 3-5) or the "Child Community Behavior Checklist" (Figure 3-6) and bring this information to the interview for discussion. During the interview, the special educator determines social contingencies that main-

FIGURE 3-5   Child Home Behavior Checklist

The following checklist allows you to describe your child's behavior in various home situations. In each of the boxes across the top, list one of your child's behaviors that concerns you. The situations are listed in the column at the left. Review each situation in the column and decide if one or more of the behaviors of concern occur in that situation. Check those that fit best (if any).

BEHAVIORS THAT CONCERN YOU

Morning: Awakening			
Dressing			
Breakfast			
Bathroom			
Leaving for school			
Play in house			
Television			
Afternoon: Lunch			
Bathroom			
Play in house			
Chores/homework			
Television			
Evening: Parent(s) home from work			
Dinner			
Bathroom			
Play in house			
Company			
Preparation for bed			

From R.G. Wahler & W.H. Cormier, "The Ecological Interview: A First Step in Out-patient Child Behavior Therapy," *Journal of Behavioral Therapy and Experimental Psychiatry*, (1970) 1, 279-89. Reprinted with permission of the authors and Pergamon Press.

FIGURE 3-6 Child Community Behavior Checklist

This checklist will help you describe your child's behavior in the community. The situations are listed in the columns at left and behaviors are listed across the top. Review each situation in the column and decide if one or more of the behaviors in the row describes your child. Check the behaviors which fit your child (if any).

	Inattentive	Hits/ fights	Noncompliant	Withdraws	Follows directions
In the yard					
In neighbor's yard					
Shopping					
Park/playground					
Church/Sunday school					
In car/bus					

From R.G. Wahler & W.H. Cormier, "The Ecological Interview: A First Step in Out-patient Child Behavior Therapy," *Journal of Behavior Experimental Psychiatry* (1970), 1, 279-89. Reprinted with permission of the authors and Pergamon Press.

tain the problem behaviors, the person or persons providing these contingencies, and how they are provided. Information from the checklists and interview are used to design interventions.

Holland (1970) suggests a structured interview format to obtain the information needed to design interventions. This interview is conducted by a systematic progression through the process presented in Figure 3-7. The structured interview is recommended by Holland for application with parents and educators.

Behavioral checklists and rating scales. Behavioral checklists and rating scales are instruments completed by adults in reference to a student's behavior or characteristics (McMahon, 1984). These behavioral-assessment instruments have three common characteristics: (1) the informant, most frequently the parent and teacher; (2) the scope of comprehensiveness of

FIGURE 3-7 Structured Interview Format

1. Establish general goals and complaints.
2. Reduce the general goals and complaints to a list of behaviors.
3. Rank the list, and select one behavior on which to concentrate intervention efforts.
4. Specify the behavior as it is currently occurring.
5. Specify the desired behavior.
6. Describe a possible step-by-step strategy to proceed to the desired behavior
7. List positive and negative reinforcers that may bring about the behavior changes.
8. Discuss what reinforcers may be withheld.
9. Establish what interventions are preferred.
10. Discuss the situation in which the desired behavior should occur.
11. Discuss the situations in which the undesired behavior should not occur.
12. Discuss the situations that increase the likelihood of the desired behavior.
13. Discuss how positive techniques may be applied.
14. Discuss how negative techniques may be applied.
15. Discuss how withholding reinforcers may be applied.
16. Discuss how removing positive reinforcers may be used.
17. Discuss the use of time-out.
18. Discuss patterning rewards.
19. Discuss varying reinforcers.
20. Discuss applying two or more procedures simultaneously.
21. Verbally rehearse the program.

(Adapted from Holland, 1970.)

the behaviors and population; and (3) the structure, ranging from a few behaviors assessed or observed or not observed, to several dozen behaviors assessed on a multiple-point scale.

Common behavioral checklists and rating scales are included in Appendix A.

A teacher-made rating scale is useful for evaluating the behavioral changes in individual children and youth. Finch, Deardorff, and Montgomery (1974) describe three advantages of individually tailored rating scales. The first advantage is that the behavioral description on which the individual is to be rated is designed to apply specifically to that individual. In addition, the exact language used by the individual who will be using the scale is employed. The final advantage is the ease with which these scales are constructed.

To develop an individual rating scale, the special educator obtains descriptions of the child's behavior from persons familiar with it. These descriptions are then grouped into categories. The level of behavior within each category is then assigned a value of 1 to 5, from most inappropriate to most appropriate. An example of an individually tailored rating scale is provided in Figure 3-8.

Self-report instruments.   The use of self-report instruments is limited in educational programming for children and youth with behavior disorders (Finch & Rogers, 1984). However, the two instruments described next have been applied with students with behavior disorders.

Birleson (1980) developed a self-rating scale for depressive disorders in childhood. This instrument is designed as a series of statements about which the child agrees or disagrees. The instrument was shown to have

FIGURE 3-8   Individually Tailored Behavior Rating Scale

FIGHTING

1. *Physical aggression:* hitting, kicking, biting, destroying property.
2. *Aggressive threats and gestures:* threatening physical aggression, daring others to fight verbally or by "staring down," urging others to fight.
3. *Aggressive threats and gestures with some friendly behavior:* cooperative play; smiling and laughing with others occurring with the same approximate frequency as aggressive threats and gestures.
4. *Friendly behavior:* no physical aggression; approximately three times as many friendly behaviors as aggressive threats and gestures.
5. *Initiating friendly behavior;* initiates at least half of the friendly gestures that occur.

(Adapted from Finch, Deardorff, & Montgomery, 1974.)

high internal consistency, factorial validity, and satisfactory stability. Sample items of those included in this scale are:

1. I look forward to things as much as I used to.
2. I find it very hard to keep my mind on my schoolwork.
3. I get very tired.
4. I find it very hard to sit still.
5. I feel like crying. (Birleson, 1980, p. 82)

Reynolds and Richmond (1978) developed the "What I Think and Feel" instrument for children in grades one through twelve. This instrument includes twenty-eight anxiety items and nine lie items. The average third-grader was found to have little difficulty reading the items on the instrument. Sample items from this scale include:

1. I have trouble making up my mind.
2. I get nervous when things do not go the right way for me.
3. Others seem to do things easier than I can.
4. I like everyone I know [lie item].
5. Often I have trouble getting my breath (Reynolds & Richmond, 1978, p. 274.)

Peer-sociometric forms.   These instruments provide information about how well a child is liked or disliked by peers. Peers are asked to make written or verbal responses to questions about playmates, best friends, or activities. Hops and Lewin (1984) describe three types of sociometric instruments. The first is restricted nomination, in which children choose a set number of classmates in a given situation. The social scores from these measures demonstrate the level of popularity or acceptance of students based on the percentage of positive nominations.

The second type of sociometric instrument is the rating scale. These instruments employ Likert-type scales on which students are asked to circle their preferences for playing or working with each child in the group. An advantage of this format is that each child is rated by every other child in the group.

The final type of sociometric instrument is paired comparison. In this format, all children choose between every pair of children in the classroom excluding themselves. The length of time necessary to administer this instrument usually precludes its use.

Caution must be used when implementing sociometric procedures. Children may be unable to differentiate between "real friends" and "wishful friends." The use of sociometric instruments is limited to defining children who may be at risk for problems in socially interacting with their peers.

Self-monitoring procedures.   Self-monitoring procedures permit an individual to self-observe and then systematically self-record the occurrence of a specific behavior (Shapiro, 1984). Self-monitoring procedures can be applied by students to assess academic performance, activity preferences, and disruptive behavior (Pacquin, 1978).

When self-monitoring is applied, the student is given a sheet of lined paper separated into the days of the week, academic periods or another time frame. The student is then told which behaviors will be rewarded. In one study, a student awarded herself stars for correct responses (Pacquin, 1978). In another, check marks were given for appropriate responses (Cohen, Polsgrove, Rieth, & Heinen, 1981). In both studies, self-monitoring increased correct responding.

Shapiro (1984) noted two weaknesses in the use of self-monitoring techniques. First, self-monitoring is susceptible to reactivity; that is, a behavior changes simply because the student is becoming more aware of personal behavior. In addition, the accuracy of self-graphing is also a concern, and occasional reliability checks with reinforcement for accuracy may be needed.

Direct observation.   Direct observation is "the process by which human observers, using operational definitions as their guide, record the overt motor and/or verbal behaviors of other humans" (Barton & Ascione, 1984, p. 167). Barton and Ascione indicate that direct observation has several advantages when working with exceptional students. They contend that the age of the student may preclude the use of other assessment strategies, specifically those that require a verbal response. In addition, the use of objective definitions imply that responses are observed without inferences about the behaviors. The face validity of direct observation is strong, as is its sensitivity as a measure of interventional effectiveness. The use of direct observation establishes a data base from which hypotheses about the variables controlling the behaviors can be generated. Finally, direct observation can serve as an objective basis on which to decide if a behavioral problem warrants treatment or if treatment changes are clinically significant.

To develop a direct observation system, Barton and Ascione suggest the following steps:

1. Select the behavior to be observed.
2. Objectively define the behavior to avoid ambiguous and idiosyncratic meanings.
3. Determine whether you will use molecular or molar response categories; that is, whether you will group or not group behaviors.

Specific data collection techniques used with direct observation will be discussed in Chapter 5.

Barton and Ascione also indicate that two issues emerge when using direct observation. First, practical issues include observer training and monitoring, the data-collection system, and how much data should be collected. The second concern is an ethical one, and concerns the individual's right to inspect the information.

Intellectual and academic assessment.   Both formal and informal procedures are used for intellectual and academic assessment. Formal procedures usually refer to standardized, commercially available tests, which measure the student's performance as compared to a group, rather than individual mastery. Informal procedures are those that measure the student's performance in response to the environment.

The most frequently used formal assessment instrument is the Wechsler Intelligence Scale for Children—Revised. Other frequently used instruments are the Bender Visual-Motor Gestalt Test and the Wide Range Achievement Test (Ysseldyke, Regan, Thurlow, & Schwartz, 1981). The results of these tests have limited use in the everyday programming for children and youths with behavior disorders. Procedures that assess behavior in the student's environment are recommended (Stainback & Stainback, 1980).

Informal assessment techniques are those that focus on the demands of the student's environment. Mandell and Gold (1984) describe the following informal assessment techniques:

1. Criterion-referenced tests, which compare a student's performance with the material to be mastered
2. Task analysis, which assists the special educator to break an activity into its component parts to identify the problem areas for the student
3. Work-sample analysis, which allows the special educator to determine the student's procedural errors
4. Observation
5. Checklists and rating scales
6. Interviews

Through the use of informal assessment techniques, a clear picture of the student's functioning in response to the IEP may be attained. The use of informal assessment techniques is further discussed in Chapter 5.

OBJECTIVE NINE: *To describe ecological and functional assessment methods for programming children and youth with behavior disorders.*

Ecological assessment.   Prieto and Rutherford (1977) described an ecological assessment model in which the classroom is considered an eco-system. The teacher assesses each of the child's "niches" as positive or negative and then examines the role the child plays in that niche. To conduct an ecological assessment, the special educator follows these steps:

1. Develop a hypothesis as to whether the student's niche is positive or negative.

2. Determine the number of positive and negative roles the student plays in the classroom.
3. Decide if the original hypothesis concerning the student's niche is confirmed.
4. Objectively state the problem.
5. Begin to collect data related to the problem involved. Data are collected concerning the antecedents of the behavior, the behavior itself, and the consequences of the behavior.

Ecological assessment focuses attention on the antecedents and consequences of student's behaviors. Through developing a precise picture of the behavior and its antecedents and consequences, the special educator can plan interventions to change the behavior.

Functional assessment.   Strain, Sainto, and Maheady (1984) suggest the use of functional assessment with severely handicapped learners. They suggest that the standardization procedures available for traditional assessment instruments are inappropriate for application with severely involved students. These instruments do not indicate whether a student cannot perform the task at hand or will not perform it. Special educators should follow these steps when conducting functional assessment:

1. Describe the elements of the student's behavior that interfere with the instruction; specifically, whether the student demonstrates:
   a. self-stimulatory or self-injurious behavior
   b. short attention span
   c. aggression toward others or property
   d. prolonged tantrums or seizures
   e. general noncompliance or inattention
2. Describe how the behaviors that interfere with instruction can be reduced through determining the motivation mechanisms behind the behavior; specifically, whether the behavior occurs to:
   a. Provide the student with positive reinforcement.
   b. Allow the student to escape unpreferred tasks.
   c. Provide the student with preferred sensory stimulation.
3. Determine what seems to motivate the student to attend and perform.
4. Determine the level of assistance necessary for the child to execute the tasks not finished independently.

By completing this assessment, the special educator may be more able to arrange the classroom environment to improve the student's functioning.

SUMMARY

In this chapter, several systems for assessing the students with behavior disorders were discussed; that is, screening; diagnostic evaluation; and behavioral, ecological, and functional assessment.

By means of screening procedures, students are identified for diagnostic evaluation. Diagnostic evaluation is the process of determining the nature of a student's problem (if one exists). During the process of constructing an Individualized Education Plan, an appropriate plan is developed and then the student is placed for service.

The content and steps in developing an IEP were discussed. The first step of the IEP process is determining the student's present level of functioning. This task is accomplished by applying behavioral, ecological, and functional assessment techniques. Behavioral assessment procedures were judged to be more effective than traditional assessment procedures when determining the functional level of children and youth with behavior disorders. In addition, ecological and functional assessment techniques were proposed as useful when a special educator wished to assess a specific behavior problem.

In the following chapter, making decisions with regard to placement and placement options, based on the information derived through evaluation, is described.

REVIEW QUESTIONS

1. Discuss the definition, purposes, characteristics, and reliability of the screening process.
2. Discuss the definition, purposes, characteristics, and reliability of the diagnostic-evaluation process.
3. Compare and contrast screening and diagnostic evaluation.
4. What are the roles and functions of the special educator in the screening process?
5. Describe the safeguards for evaluation mandated by Public Law 94-142. Give an example of the violation of each of these safeguards.
6. Research and discuss the role and functions of one member of the interdisciplinary team. Consider this individual's functions as both a professional and team member.
7. Contrast traditional and behavioral assessment. Develop a rationale for the use of behavioral assessment with children and youth with behavior disorders.
8. Why are parents important members of the interdisciplinary team? What is the probable effect of parents as active team members on the professional members? On the parents themselves? On the child?
9. Select one of the techniques used in behavioral assessment. Use the professional literature to explore the technique you selected.

APPLICATION ACTIVITY—ECOLOGICAL ASSESSMENT

Ecological assessment techniques make relevant data available to the special educator and increase his or her options for intervention (Prieto & Rutherford, 1977).

In this activity, you will complete an ecological assessment of an individual with whom you are familiar or taken from Appendix B. As you work through the steps described, contrast this method with other assessment techniques described in this chapter.

1. Review the information that you have on the student. Is the student's overall "niche" or place in the classroom system positive or negative?
2. Describe as positive or negative the roles the student demonstrates in each of the following environments:

   Interactions with teacher
   Interactions with peers
   Interactions with other adults
   Subject areas (list):
   a.
   b.
   c.
   d.
   e.
   Manipulation of materials
3. Is your original hypothesis regarding the student's niche upheld (yes or no)? (Refer to your response to #1).
4. If the original hypothesis is upheld, what are possible antecedents and consequences of the behavior?

In this activity, you will practice completing an "Ecological Baseline Card" (Prieto & Rutherford, 1977) on an individual in your environment. This "ecological baseline" is the activity that was simulated in Step 4 of the preceding application activity.

1. Briefly observe an individual in your environment. Describe a behavior that you will document on the ecological baseline chart.
2. Observe this individual long enough to observe the behavior's occurrence at least five times.
3. Complete the following ecological baseline:

Antecedents to Behavior	Statement of Behavior	Consequences of Behavior

Amount of time observed:
Time when behavior typically occurs:
Place where behavior typically occurs:
How often or for how long does behavior occur?
What is the implication of this information for interventions?

4

Services

Special educators of children and youth with behavior disorders cannot function in a vacuum. They must interact positively and productively with parents, professionals, and paraprofessionals if the child or youth is to be effectively served. Bell, reflecting on his profession, states that "the teacher is continually being impacted upon not only by the students' needs, but also by the large environmental influences within which the teacher teaches" (1979, p. 169). He believes that being a special educator involves relating to other personnel, being a team member. Special educators "need to be able to conceptualize and describe in operational terms what their jobs are, and how their jobs relate with those of the other personnel around them" (p. 170).

In this chapter, the role of the members of the educational and related services team are presented. In addition, working successfully with other professionals through consultation and teaming are discussed. The chapter concludes with discussions of the termination of special-education services and the mainstreaming of the child or young person with behavior disorders into the regular education program.

OBJECTIVES

After completing this chapter, you will be able to—

1. describe the service options or placement alternatives typically available in the public schools to children and youth with behavior disorders;

2. describe the least restrictive environmental imperative and the safeguards applied to assure appropriate placement;
3. identify roles of members of the educational and related service team;
4. identify the basic components of the consultation and teaming processes;
5. describe criteria for the termination of special-education services to children and youth with behavior disorders.

A CASE FOR CONSIDERATION

"I don't know how you spend your day," said Ms. Jenson, the sixth-grade teacher. "You only have eighteen students. I have thirty-one, and they stay with me all day."

"I keep busy," replied Ms. Reilly as she turned to leave for the resource room. As she walked along the hall, she wondered, "Just exactly how do I spend my day?" The next morning, she began to log "a day in the life of a resource-room teacher in a public middle school."

8:10 Unlocked the room.

8:10–8:20 Waited for a student to pick up his new "Daily Report to Principal" form. Signed several reports and letters.

8:20–8:25 Met with a fourth- and a sixth-grade teacher individually, to determine the assignments their students would need to complete that day in the resource room.

8:25 Stopped in hall to help the fifth-grade teacher break up a fight between two boys.

8:27 Accompanied the teacher and the combatants to the principal's office; principal was with parent. The fifth-grade teacher said he would wait with the students.

8:30–9:20 Three students scheduled to attend the resource room came in with a note asking if they could watch a movie with their language arts class. One student arrived with her social-studies assignment and text; read the day's assignment with her and answered questions about the content. Principal called to find out why a student he referred to special education was not receiving services. Told him the parents have not given permission to evaluate the student.

9:25–10:15 Went to the language arts room to watch the movie with the students; had to know content of movie because worksheets for the next week's assignment are based on the film.

10:10–10:20 Met with student who received in-school suspension because of inappropriate behavior in the hall. Discussed the school rules and contingencies.

10:20–10:30 Met with psychologist about test protocols. Psychologist brought the incorrect forms; will bring the correct ones tomorrow.

10:30–11:10 Three students scheduled to attend did not arrive. While on the way to find them, the principal called me to make an appointment for a conference with parents.

11:15–12:10 Worked in classroom with students in social studies, drawing maps of Africa.

12:15–1:10   Three students scheduled to attend did not arrive. Three students not scheduled asked to come in for help with history; reported that they were sent by their teacher. Two students came in for help with mathematics assignments.

1:15–2:05   Student scheduled to work on language arts did not arrive. Principal came in to ask me to accompany a group of students to Symphony Hall tomorrow. Student not scheduled arrived and asked for help in science.

2:10–3:00   Four students did not come to their scheduled session because of a guest speaker in the classroom. Two students arrived for scheduled reading help.

2:50   Special education supervisor came to confer on a new student.

3:10   Closed room and began preparation for tomorrow.

4:15   Locked room.

That evening Ms. Reilly reviewed the log. It was certainly a busy day. She had missed lunch and a planning period. The log indicated that she spent at least as much time with other staff members and serving as a liaison as she did actually teaching students.

In this chapter, skills relative to running effective special education programs and consulting with other professionals are discussed.

OBJECTIVE ONE: To describe the service options or placement alternatives typically available in the public school to children and youth with behavior disorders.

Placement decisions have perhaps more impact on the student's educational career than diagnosis, assessment, or treatment. Donnellan (1984) suggests that in making these decisions, the special educator apply the "Criterion of the Least Dangerous Assumption." This indicates that, in the absence of conclusive data, educational decisions should be based on assumptions that, if correct, will have the least dangerous effect on the student. She describes two factors that must be given consideration when making placement decisions. The first is the amount of time students will be mainstreamed. The least dangerous assumption is that the student will be able to succeed when placed with nonhandicapped individuals throughout the school day, and the most dangerous assumption is that the student will require segregated training throughout the day. Special educators must determine how frequently and what kind of interaction must be available to the student to maximize his or her ability to function effectively. The second factor is the nature of the placement strategy itself. The most dangerous assumption is that each diagnostic category designates an automatic placement, and the least dangerous assumption is that placement is an individual issue. In this case, it is assumed that it is safer to make a placement decision independent of the student's diagnostic classification.

Making decisions that have the least dangerous impact on the child's educational future may create "advocacy dilemmas." Frith (1981) describes these dilemmas as conflicts that arise when a professional must decide whether to advocate actively for a child when to do so would contradict the stated or implied position of his or her employer. Special educators may be pressured to make placement decisions that, while not the most beneficial to the child, are the most convenient or economical from the point of view of the school system. In such situations, as professionals, special educators must decide whether their responsibility to students supersedes their responsibility to their employer.

McDowell and Brown (1978) suggest that prior to assigning a child or youth to a particular placement, professionals should consider and respond to the following questions:

How will the placement affect the child?

How will the child's behavior affect the other children in the program?

How will the child's behavior affect the teacher's interactions with all the children in the program, including the child being considered for placement?

These questions should be addressed in the order in which they are presented; if carefully considered, they will facilitate special educators' efforts to apply Donnellan's criterion of the least dangerous assumption.

One of the goals of the interdisciplinary team, as mandated by Public Law 94-142, is the making of decisions with regard to the placement of the child or youth with behavior disorders. Placement decisions are facilitated when each member of the team has a clear understanding of his or her responsibility. Fenton, Yoshida, Maxwell, and Kaufman (1979) suggested that when team members are unaware of their responsibility to make a placement decision, they do not engage in those activities appropriate to making such a decision. Their research suggests that placement decisions are orderly, efficient, and fast-paced to the extent that the team members understand their responsibility to place the child in the most appropriate service options. After surveying 1428 placement-team members, Fenton and associates found that only about one third were cognizant of their responsibilities for placement and program appropriateness. In addition, only one fourth of those surveyed understood their responsibilities regarding eligibility, diagnosis, and evaluations. Team members' awareness of their responsibilities for making the various mandated decisions varied with the individual. Members were found to recognize duties differently according to their perceptions of their role on the team and their professional functions.

Concerned with the factors that influenced interdisciplinary-team members during the decision-making process, Holland (1980), in an interview study, found that there are several variables that impact on team decision making. He reports that "many subtle though nonetheless forceful" factors impact on team decision-making processes. These, in order of impact, include parental pressures, the availability of programs and resources in the school district; the student's sex and race; the vested interests of social agencies and advocacy groups; the interests of the teacher and/or principal; the physical, social, emotional, and academic abilities and behaviors of the student; and the geographic proximity of services.

Those surveyed by Holland suggested that decision making could be improved by—

> more effective communication among school personnel;
> increased time, staff, and program alternatives;
> improved staff development;
> increased in-service training appropriate for classroom teachers and others thrust into decision-making roles.

Sydney and Minner (1983) found that the placement decisions of special education teachers are influenced by the presence of information on the referred student's siblings. They warn that while attempting to facilitate educational decisions by collecting and reviewing a great deal of data, some teachers may be inappropriately influenced by some of that data.

Awareness of the factors already discussed, which may influence decision making, will facilitate the special educator's efforts to make both appropriate and objective decisions based on the individual child's specific strengths, weaknesses, and needs. In an effort to increase objective decision making by the interdisciplinary team, Benson and Cessna (1980) have developed a list of suggestions for use in team meetings. These are presented in Figure 4-1.

Deno (1970) presented what is probably the most discussed and applied continuum of placements in the field of special education. The tapered design indicates the considerable difference in the numbers involved at the different levels, and calls attention to the fact that the system serves as a diagnostic filter. The most specialized facilities are likely to be needed by the fewest children on a long-term basis. The organizational model can be applied to the development of special educational services for all types of disability. Deno's "cascade" of special-education services (Figure 4-2) includes seven levels ranging from the least restrictive to the most restrictive services.

> *Level 1*: Children are placed in regular classes. This group includes exceptional children and youths able to function in regular class accommodations with or without medical or counseling support therapies.

FIGURE 4-1   Suggestions for Staffings

Staffings should focus on student needs, not only the identification of a handicapping condition.

Assign a facilitator to chair the staffing.

Delineate everyone's role before discussing the case (including parents).

Construct an agenda and stick to it!

Give a copy of the staffing agenda to all staffing team members before beginning.

Approximately 1/3 of the staffing should be spent discussing assessment information and student profile, 2/3 of the time should be spent determining student needs and developing the student's program.

Assessment results should be presented in short summary statements and always stated in terms of impact on education, not simply scores or normative results.

The facilitator should direct, listen, question, confirm, and summarize.

The other staffing team members should contribute at appropriate times in as brief and succinct manner as possible.

Staffings are not counseling sessions for parents or teachers. Counseling should occur before or after staffings. However, this does not mean that parents or teachers should not be listened to and nurtured.

Set starting and ending times and stick to these times (usually 45–90 minutes). Staffing length should be appropriate to the needs of each individual case.

Limit participants to essential team members.

Staffings should focus on problem solving and program development, not only finding an appropriate placement.

Avoid reading traditional evaluation reports and try using more informal worksheets which briefly summarize assessment results, child's needs, and services to meet those needs (not people or rooms).

Sometimes having one team member (usually the facilitator) meet with parents prior to the staffing to explain procedures, roles, etc., helps parents feel more comfortable and shorten staffing time.

The facilitator should take notes to summarize and enhance facilitator's role. A person other than the facilitator should be assigned to fill out forms.

Select appropriate team members and design an agenda prior to the staffing.

Avoid the usage of technical/professional language.

Designate appropriate follow-up roles and responsibilities.

Assessment results and conclusions should be presented clearly, directly, and objectively.

When appropriate, invite the students to the staffing.

(From Benson & Cessna, 1980, pp. 46–47.)

> *Level 2*: Children attend regular class and are provided with supplementary instructional services; that is, tutoring, resource-room services, crisis-teacher services.
>
> *Level 3*: Children attend part-time special class and part-time regular class.

FIGURE 4-2 Cascade System of Special Education Services

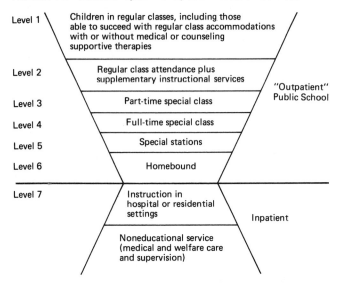

Level 4: Children attend full-time special class.

Level 5: Children attend special day schools.

Level 6: Children remain at home and receive instruction from a homebound teacher.

Levels 1 through 6 are considered "outpatient" programs and are governed by the school system. Seventy-five to 95 percent of identified behavior-disordered students are served within the public schools (Huntze & Grosenick, 1980). "Inpatient," or Level 7, services are governed by community mental health and welfare agencies. These services include instruction in hospital or residential settings and noneducational services such as medical and welfare care and supervision.

This cascade is characterized by flexibility and adaptability in the placement of students for service. It is primarily designed to facilitate the "tailoring" of services to individual needs.

Regular class placement.   According to Paul and Epanchin (1982), the regular education teacher and placement in the regular classroom may assist the child or youth with behavior disorders in four ways: (a) preventing behavior disorders by limiting the academic and social frustrations for students with behavior disorders or at high risk for behavior disorders (b) assisting them during periods of confusion, isolation, boredom, and noncompliance that occur daily in the classroom, (c) referral, and (d) implementing portions of a student's Individualized Education Plan and coordinating services for students with behavior disorders who are placed in their classroom.

Supplementary instructional services. At this level, the student may be receiving services from a consulting, crisis, and/or supportive teacher or be assigned to a resource room for service.

The consulting teacher (Christie, McKenzie, & Burdett, 1972) offers indirect services to students through their regular teacher. The teachers receive consultation services in behavior-management techniques and instructional methods designed to facilitate the child's successful functioning in the regular classroom. In-service training may be provided to individual teachers who have referred students through consultation or in workshops and formal courses.

The helping teacher or crisis teacher (Morse, 1976) provides both direct and indirect services to students with behavior disorders who are placed in regular classrooms. In addition to providing crisis-intervention services to students and consultation services to teachers, the helping teacher may relieve regular educators of their normal duties for a period of time to enable them to work with students with behavior disorders. The helping teacher applies problem-solving techniques to prevent further behavior disorders and assist students to cope in the regular school program.

The resource room. As an instructional-assistance strategy, the resource room is more restrictive than either the consulting- or helping-teacher strategies. Students placed in resource room services are instructed in the regular classroom part time and in a resource room part time. The amount of time the individual spends in the regular class depends on the child's ability to function productively in that setting. The student may be assigned to the regular classroom for those curricular and cocurricular activities in which successful participation is anticipated.

Wiederholt, Hammill, and Brown (1978) present the following advantages of the noncategorical resource room:

1. Students can benefit from specific resource support while remaining integrated with their friends and age-mates in the school.
2. The resource teacher has an opportunity to help more children than does a full-time special class teacher. This is especially true when the resource teacher provides indirect services to children with mild or moderate problems by consulting extensively with their teachers.
3. Resource programs are less expensive to operate than special self-contained classes.
4. Because young children with mild, though developing problems can be accommodated, later severe disorders may be prevented.

5. Flexible scheduling means that remediation can be applied entirely in the classrooms by the regular teacher with some resource support or in another room by the resource program personnel when necessary; also, the schedule can be quickly altered to meet the children's changing situations and needs.

6. Since the resource program will absorb most of the handicapped children in the schools, the self-contained special education classes will increasingly become instructional settings for truly and relatively severely handicapped students, the children for whom the classes were originally developed.

7. Because of the resource teacher's broad experience with many children exhibiting different educational and behavioral problems, he/she may in time become an in-house consultant to the school.

8. Because the noncategorical approach avoids labeling and segregation, it minimizes the stigma that might be associated with receiving special help.

9. Since many elementary schools are large enough to accommodate one or more noncategorical resource teachers, most students can receive help in their neighborhood school; thus, the necessity of busing handicapped children across the town or county to a school that houses an appropriately labeled class or resource program is eliminated or at least reduced.

10. Because placement in the resource program is an individual school matter involving the principal, the teachers, and the parents, no appreciable time lapse need occur between the teacher's referral and the initiation of special services for the child.

11. In the noncategorical alternative, medical and psychological work-ups are done only at the school's specific request rather than on a generalized screening for placement basis; thus, the school psychologist is freed to do the work that he/she was trained to do instead of being relegated to the role of psychometrist.*

On the basis of an extensive review of the literature, Speece and Mandell (1980) developed a list of twenty-six support services provided by the resource program. Two hundred twenty-eight regular educators rated these services in terms of (1) the importance of the service to the successful mainstreaming of the student and (2) the frequency with which the service is provided. Only two services, remedial instruction in the resource room and informal student-progress meetings, were provided with regularity. The results of this study are summarized in Figure 4-3.

The special class.   Students with behavior disorders may be placed full or part time in the special class. Huntze and Grosenick (1980) indicated that usually eight students are assigned to a classroom for children or youth with behavior disorders. They reported that states that provide guidelines usually specify that five to ten students may be assigned to a special class without a paraprofessional.

Special classes vary in terms of how much they adhere to a "program," the relative emphasis placed on behavior and affective goals, and the mix

*From J.L. Wiederholt, D.D. Hammill, & V. Brow, *The Resource Teacher: A Guide to Effective Practices* (Boston: Allyn & Bacon, 1978), pp. 10-11. Used by permission.

FIGURE 4-3 Percentage Ratings of Importance and Frequency of Support Services to Regular Educators

	% RATED AS IMPORTANT	% RATED AS FREQUENT	% RATED AS INFREQUENT
1. attends parent conferences	74.2	6.6	93.4
2. meets informally to discuss student progress	74.2	86.2	13.8
3. provides remedial instruction in the resource room	67.0	73.0	27.0
4. provides information on behavioral characteristics	54.5	43.7	56.3
5. provides academic assessment	53.9	25.8	74.2
6. schedules meetings to evaluate student progress	52.7	32.9	67.1
7. provides materials for classroom use	52.1	34.2	65.8
8. suggests materials for classroom use	52.1	35.3	64.7
9. provides written reports of students' activities and progress	51.5	20.4	79.6
10. helps evaluate instructional techniques	49.7	36.0	64.0
11. aids in education programming for nonhandicapped	48.5	25.8	74.2
12. offers classroom-management techniques	46.7	37.1	62.9
13. helps adapt instructional techniques for classroom use	46.7	36.0	64.0
14. schedules meetings for planning	41.9	29.4	70.6

15. demonstrates use of materials	39.5	33.0	67.0
16. explains purpose and procedure for IEP	28.8	9.0	91.0
17. provides techniques to evaluate student progress	28.2	10.8	89.2
18. asks for assistance in writing IEP	27.0	10.1	89.9
19. observes students in classroom	24.6	8.9	91.1
20. provides ideas to facilitate peer acceptance	24.0	12.6	87.4
21. plans in-service to explain instructional techniques	22.2	4.2	95.8
22. plans in-service to explain LD/IBD (learning disabilities/ behavior disorders) characteristics	21.6	5.3	94.7
23. trains peers' tutors	16.2	12.0	88.0
24. suggests classroom-environment modification	13.8	4.2	95.8
25. helps with class trips and parties	12.6	6.0	94.0
26. teaches handicapped/ nonhandicapped students in regular class	10.8	3.0	97.0

(Adapted from Speece & Mandell, 1980.)

of therapy and instruction provided by the teacher (Paul & Epanchin, 1982). A child is usually placed in special class because of an inability to function productively in a less restrictive environment without personal difficulty and without disrupting the normal school regimen.

The special school.   The special school is designed to serve children and youth with severe behavior disorders who cannot function in a regular school setting without extraordinary personal difficulty and/or disruption of the normal school regimen.

The special school is generally located in a physical facility separate from the regular elementary or secondary school. It usually contains several classes. It is often staffed by an interdisciplinary team including special educators, crisis teachers, psychologists, social workers, recreation therapists, and psychiatrists. Its supportive systems (transportation, food, and administrative services) are usually separate from those of the regular school.

Homebound programs. The child or youth with a severe behavior disorder may be assigned for a brief period of time to a homebound program. This is usually done only when a more appropriate placement is not immediately available. In this placement, the child is visited by an instructor daily, twice a week, or weekly, depending on the rules governing this service in the state and local school district. The homebound instructor offers instruction in the child's areas of greatest need.

OBJECTIVE TWO: *To describe the least restrictive environmental imperative and the safeguards applied to assure appropriate placement.*

The child's placement should be the final decision made by the interdisciplinary team responsible for the Individualized Education Program (Wehman & McLaughlin, 1981). Ethically and appropriately, placement can only be determined after the team has reviewed the student's goals and objectives and decided on the services required to meet those goals and objectives. The placement decision is also made with consideration given to the least restrictive environment in which the child can succeed. The child or youth with behavior disorders cannot be segregated from regular education students more than is necessary to meet his or her goals and objectives.

Public Law 94-142 requires that the states develop procedures assuring that—

> 1. To the maximum extent appropriate, handicapped children, including children in public or private institutions or other care facilities, are educated with children who are not handicapped; and
> 2. Special classes, separate schooling, or other removal of handicapped children from the regular educational environment occurs only when the nature or severity of the handicap is such that education in regular classes with the use of supplementary aids and services cannot be achieved satisfactorily (Federal Register, 1977, 121.550).

Those involved in making placement decisions must give consideration to two essential points: Can the placement under consideration meet the student's individual needs? Does the placement provide the maximum integration of the child or youth with behavior disorders with nonhandicapped individuals while still providing an environment in which the child or youth can function successfully?

OBJECTIVE THREE: To identify the roles of members of the educational and related-services team.

With the exception of the parent, the special educator is probably the primary agent of change in the life of a child or youth with behavior disorders. Although other professionals can and do make significant contributions to planning and implementing the child's Individualized Educational Program, their impact is restricted as a consequence of the limited time and attention they can devote to an individual child. Conversely, the impact of these allied professionals can be significantly enhanced when their expertise and recommendations are expressed or implemented through the teacher. Together, the teacher and other professionals form the educational and related-services team, whose purpose it is to meet the needs of the child or young person with behavior disorders.

Ethically, when writing an IEP, you may not give consideration to existing school programs, financial exigencies, or the child's or parents' social or cultural background. If services are required, they must be included. There are many "related services" listed in Public Law 94-142 that may be beneficial to a child or youth with behavior disorders.

> Transportation and such developmental, corrective, and other supportive services as are required to assist a handicapped child to benefit from special education and includes speech pathology and audiology, psychological services, physical and occupational therapy, recreation, early identification and assessment of disabilities in children, counseling services, and medical services for diagnostic and evaluation purposes. The term also includes school health services, social work services in schools, and parent counseling and training (Federal Register, 1977, 131a.13).

Very few school districts have the professional personnel available to provide the entire range of services listed in Public Law 94-142. Unfortunately, when a service is not available within a district, the child's need is usually not addressed (Huntze & Grosenick, 1980).

The team interacting with a child or youth with behavior disorders may include, among others, the regular educator, the special educator, a psychologist or psychiatrist, the social worker, the parents, the speech and language therapist, and occupational and physical therapists. The services provided by these team members are briefly described next.

The regular educator.   Regular educators frequently initiate the provision of services to children and youths with behavior disorders through the referral process. The regular educator may implement portions of a student's Individualized Education Plan and coordinate services for the students with behavior disorders in the regular classroom. In addition, the regular educator communicates with the special educator concerning the academic, social, and behavioral progress of the student.

The special educator.   The special educator may fill a wide range of roles, depending on the intensity of services received by the child or young person with behavior disorders. The amount of direct programming received by the child from the special educator may range from none (as in the case of the helping teacher or when the student receives consultative services) to the child's entire educational program. The special educator usually coordinates the student's Individualized Education Program.

The psychologist or psychiatrist.   The psychologist, psychiatrist, and trained counselor can provide several direct and indirect services to benefit the child or youth with behavior disorders. Among these are the diagnostic and assessment services discussed previously, and individual and group psychotherapy, parent therapy, and family therapy.

The provision of psychotherapy for children by the schools is a controversial issue. Grosenick, Huntze, Kochan, Peterson, Robertshaw, and Wood (1982) indicate that the controversy is at two levels: (a) whether or not psychotherapy is required to assist the child or young person to benefit from special education, and (b) if the child or young person does need psychotherapy, is it a service that Public Law 94-142 requires the local school district to provide? Grosenick and associates describe several problems that are created by the inclusion of psychotherapy as a related service:

> Paying a psychotherapist or psychiatrist is a significant financial burden for a school district.
>
> Community mental-health agencies that currently pay the psychotherapist would pass the cost of the service on to the public-school system.
>
> Private insurance agencies would stop paying for the service.
>
> Psychotherapeutic and psychiatric services are essential health services and may not, in fact, be considered a legitimate educational service.

On the other hand, Grosenick and associates maintain that for children and youth with behavior disorders, it is frequently impossible to separate the child's emotional and educational needs. They also maintain that cost should not be a primary consideration in meeting the needs of such children.

The roles of psychologist, psychiatrist, psychotherapist, and counselor frequently overlap. The amount and type of overlap in service provided by these professionals is largely a function of the individual professional's training and experience.

The social worker.   The social worker serves as a liaison between the educational team and the family, and school and community agencies. The social worker is the team member who reaches into the community to obtain information and services for the child and family. Social workers may also, if appropriately trained, provide counseling services to children and their families.

The parents.   Parents are essential members of the service team. They are partners with the teacher in the child's educational and related service program. Parents have a greater store of knowledge and understanding of and concern for their child than any other member of the team. The importance of parents to the effectiveness of special education programs is discussed in Chapter 11.

The speech and language therapist.   The speech and language therapist may provide services either directly to the student or indirectly in cooperation with the teacher. The speech therapist provides services concerned with both the remediation of speech problems and the development of language and communication skills.

The occupational and physical therapists.   Occupational and physical therapists are recent additions to the interdisciplinary team serving children and youth with behavior disorders. Noie (1983) indicated that the need for therapy as a related service depends on the extent of each child's exceptionality. Occupational and physical therapy services may take the form of direct service or consultation. The service functions of the teacher and therapist overlap. The neurological and medical training of the therapist may provide the special educator with insight into successful teaching strategies.

OBJECTIVE FOUR: *To identify the basic components of the consultation and teaming processes.*

Special educators, as described in the first section of this chapter, provide educational services to children and youths with behavior disorders in several different instructional settings. Regardless of the particular setting, however, they must work cooperatively with others; that is, parents, allied professionals, and paraprofessionals. Speece and Mandell (1980) stated that:

> no longer can training programs emphasize the development of skills that focus solely on teaching the handicapped child. Rather, the program scope must be broadened to teach special educators how to interact effectively with colleagues from other disciplines by developing their consultation skills (p. 53).

According to Kerr and Nelson (1983), generalization and maintenance of behavior changes may not occur if the special educator does not include others in the child's program. They indicate that to effectively remediate a behavior problem, those persons who previously perceived the problem as such must see it as improved. To adequately meet the needs of children and youth with behavior disorders, special educators need the skills necessary to consult with those individuals responsible for serving them, including regular educators.

Consulting with Regular Educators

Consultation is "indirect services to students through direct work with their teachers or parents" (Lilly & Givens-Ogle, 1981). A key phrase of the definition is "working with," making both parties equal participants in the process. Conoley, Apter, and Conoley (1981) warn:

> Consultation should be seen, therefore, not as the more knowledgeable consultor giving answers to a puzzled consultee. Rather, it must be viewed as a collaborative problem solving process during which the consultant facilitates the creative coping skills of the consultee and learns from the consultee about the unique aspects of the problem and the consultee's situation (p. 113).

Conoley and associates suggested that though regular educators may, at times, press the consultant to provide direct services to a child, the provision of such service may be self-defeating; that is, students receiving limited direct services may not improve as rapidly as those consistently receiving appropriate services from their regular teacher in consultation with the special educator. In addition, the provision of direct services by the consultant makes the prevention of behavior problems in the classroom more difficult, and encourages the "expert" trap with "magical cures" for behavior disorders sought by the regular teacher.

Consultants serve the important purpose of training and motivating teachers to attempt new approaches with the children in their classrooms (Nelson & Stevens, 1981). Heron and Catera (1980) found that changes in students' performances only occurred after the consultant and teacher cooperatively planned and evaluated specific management strategies. Consultation was most successful when—

1. the consultant was able to analyze the environment in which the child was experiencing difficulty and to ascertain the regular teacher's willingness to implement a cooperatively developed intervention plan;
2. the regular educator was allowed to express opinions as to whether or how long an intervention should be implemented;
3. the consultant was able to suggest more than one solution;
4. the regular educators collected data and arranged for reliability checks on the interventions applied;
5. the consultant taught classroom-appropriate behaviors to the students outside the classroom and then "transplanted" the techniques that maintained those behaviors into the classroom.

Special educators should remember that regular educators have many responsibilities in the classroom in addition to meeting the needs of the children and youth with behavior disorders.

The particular types of interventions suggested by the consultant influence the success of those interventions. In a survey study involving 180 preservice and student teachers, Witt, Elliott, and Martens (1984) found that for regular educators, the amount of teacher time, the severity of the behavior problem, and the type of intervention suggested were the salient dimensions used by regular educators to evaluate an intervention. Those surveyed found positive interventions more acceptable than negative ones. They suggested that interventions that took less teacher time were more acceptable than those requiring greater amounts of time.

There are several strategies that the special educator may employ to ensure the success of the consultation process. Our review of the literature (Conoley, Apter, & Conoley, 1981; Elman & Ginsberg, 1981; Kerr & Nelson, 1982; Montgomery, 1978) suggests grouping consultation strategies into (1) "public-relations" strategies, (2) communication strategies, and (3) reinforcing or motivational strategies.

"Public relations" strategies.   As a collaborator on behalf of children and youths with behavior disorders, the special educator must be aware of the political realities of the school (Kerr & Nelson, 1982). Montgomery (1978) suggests that a teacher's classroom is his or her castle, and that the students about whom special educators consult are not "their" kids. Any visit to a classroom should be made with the permission of the regular educator. The special educator should make a point of communicating positively with the teacher. Respecting the regular educator's privacy is essential.

The following are some specific public-relations strategies that the special educator can employ (Conoley, Apter, & Conoley, 1981; Elman & Ginsberg, 1981; Kerr & Nelson, 1982; Montgomery, 1978):

1. Start programming for students on the first day of school.
2. Assume the lunch, bus, and other duties assigned to all educators in the school; special educators are a part of the staff and should accept the same responsibilities as other professional staff members.
3. Establish proximity with other teachers. Eat and socialize with them, and make an effort to become involved in extracurricular activities with them.
4. Take a genuine interest in the other teachers.
5. Conform to "regularities." Attend evening programs even if it is not required. Offer to help with school plays and programs.
6. Expect a certain amount of discomfort. Montgomery (1978) maintains that successful consultants recognize how irritating they can be to others when attempting to initiate change. As a rule it is necessary to be aggressive enough to stimulate change, but not so aggressive as to be ostracized.

7. Avoid the "missionary spirit." Before attempting a change, make sure the child's or youth's problem really is a problem, and not a philosophical difference between the consultant and other staff members.

Communication strategies. Many professionals providing services to children are not effective communicators. Kerr and Nelson (1983) suggest that whenever approaching another professional (or when you are approached), an attempt should be made to clarify the purpose of the communication and the mutual responsibilities involved in the problem under consideration. Strategies for increasing and maintaining effective communication include (Conoley, Apter, & Conoley, 1981; Elman & Ginsberg, 1981; Montgomery, 1978) the following:

1. Be accessible.
2. Listen.
3. Avoid special education and psychological jargon.
4. Deal frankly with any anxiety, frustration, or anger expressed by the teacher.
5. Foster the consultee's self-respect and ensure and maintain confidentiality.
6. Practice "one-downsmanship." Channel the credit for change to other professionals.

Reinforcing or motivating strategies. People interact with individuals who reinforce their interactions. When consulting with regular educators, the special educator should be a model of empathy, tolerance, and acceptance. Special educators should communicate to the regular teacher appreciation for the assistance being given the child or young person by that individual and their confidence that the interventions will be successful. Specific motivational strategies include (Conoley, Apter, & Conoley, 1981; Elman & Ginsberg, 1981):

1. "Being an expert is not so smart" (Montgomery, 1978 p. 111). Communicate that problems are solved *together*, and that special educators can learn from regular ones.
2. Communicate that teaching is a complex process, and that if one technique is not acceptable or effective, then another may be selected and implemented.
3. Sincerely praise the efforts of the regular educator.

In addition to regular educators, special educators must team with other professionals—that is, psychologists, social workers, and so forth—on behalf of children and youth with behavior disorders. According to Huntze and Grosenick (1980), there is a lack of viable interdisciplinary collaboration. Among the deterrents to collaboration are geographic location, whereby professionals are frequently assigned to several schools or programs, and "turf protection," in which individuals guard their professional territory. To avoid these two problems, McCormick and Goldman (1979) suggest applying a "transdisciplinary model."

Unlike the interdisciplinary-team model, described previously, the transdisciplinary-team model includes a communication system designed to reduce compartmentalization and fragmentation of service and responsibility. The responsibility for the child's or youth's service is assigned to one or two team members, with the others available for consultation and direct assistance (McCormick & Goldman, 1979). The interdisciplinary and transdisciplinary approaches are contrasted in Figure 4-4.

Lyon and Lyon (1980) describe three components of a transdisciplinary approach: (1) a joint-team approach (2) continuous staff development, and (3) "role release." Professionals are relatively familiar with teaming and staff development; however, the effective implementation of role release requires an adjustment in professional attitudes and activities.

Role release.   According to Lyon and Lyon (1980), role release refers to sharing between two or more members of a team on three levels. First,

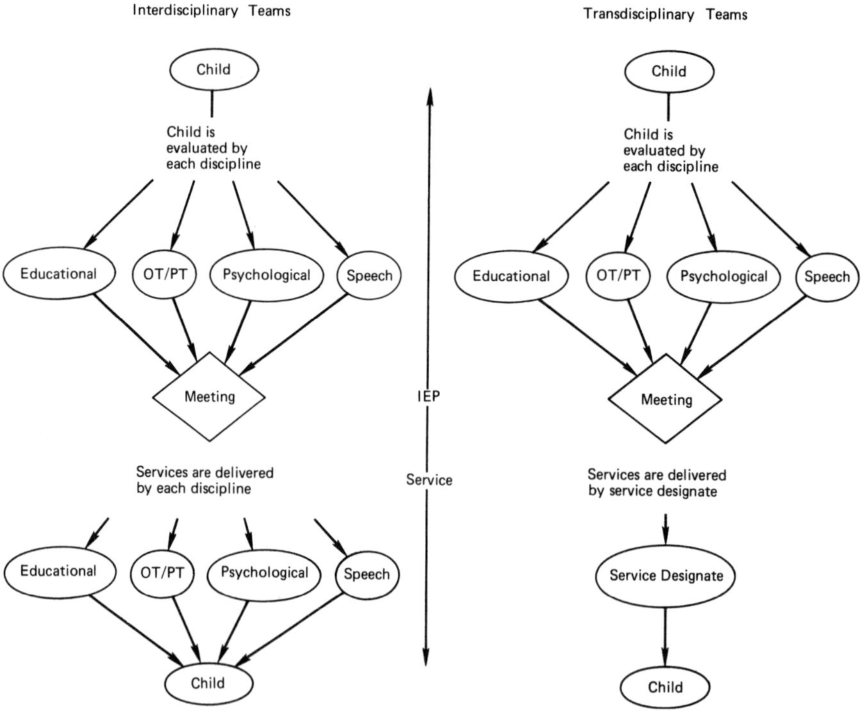

FIGURE 4-4   Interdisciplinary and Transdisciplinary Teams

all team members share general information regarding their individual expertise, duties, and responsibilities. Second, each team member teaches other team members to make specific teaching decisions within his or her area of expertise. Finally, the professional shares performance competencies; that is, trains others to perform specific skills within the individual's area of expertise.

Role release can be facilitated by applying one of two models. The first is "educational synthesizer." The teacher is the actual implementer of programs, with other team members providing training, skill development, and information. The other model, "generic role release," assumes that all team members regularly teach, care for, and interact with the child or young person throughout the day.

In the role of educational synthesizer, special educators must be aware of their personal and professional limitations (Kerr & Nelson, 1982). For example, special educators do not possess the professional authority to perform counseling; however, when the role-release model is implemented; they may conduct group meetings and individual conferences. Special educators can accept the role of intervention implementer when treatment is prescribed and supervised by others with the needed expertise.

OBJECTIVE FIVE: *To describe criteria for the termination of special-education services to children and youth with behavior disorders.*

Children and youth with behavior disorders increase their adaptive behaviors as a result of programming. Because of these successes, special-education services change in intensity as the student progresses. Successful "termination of services," mainstreaming, or "phasing out" must be planned. In this section, strategies to facilitate the termination of services are discussed.

Brown (1984) indicates that in successful mainstreaming, the expectations of the regular classroom teacher must be "overmatched"; that is, the mainstreaming program must exceed the teacher's expectations. When terminating special education services, the special educator should make four assumptions:

1. Some schools', classrooms', or teachers' expectations about the child or youth with behavior disorders can be changed.
2. Some student behavior can be changed.
3. Some classrooms or programs may simply be too problematic for children and youth with behavior disorders.
4. Many support services and strategies are available to decrease the "mismatch" between the student and the program.

One technique that Brown suggests is instructing students in "teacher-pleasing behavior" in order to minimize the mismatch between child and program.

A systematic plan for phasing out or mainstreaming a child or young person with behavior disorders should be developed. The plan includes preliminary, planning, implementation, and evaluation activities.

Preliminary activities.   Preliminary activities set the stage for phasing the student into regular education. During these activities, the special educator shares materials with regular educators in the potential placement. The special educator emphasizes the positive abilities of the student and, if possible, cooperates in the planning of field trips or activities that informally increase interaction with the regular teacher.

Tymitz-Wolf (1984), in reviewing the literature concerning preparation for mainstreaming, concluded that traditionally, readiness for termination of special education services has been assessed through standardized tests. However, she maintains that multifactored assessment, in both academic and social areas, provides better understanding of the student's readiness.

An important preliminary activity for the special educator seeking a less restrictive educational environment for a student includes studying the nature of potential programs and classrooms. An analysis of the contextual and environmental variables within the regular education classroom is helpful in predicting success in the mainstream (Brown, 1982). Careful analysis of the educational environments available will assist in "overmatching" students and programs. By being aware of the specifics of an educational setting, special educators can direct their instruction toward behaviors and skills necessary for success in the classroom or program. A classroom-assessment form, developed from the literature (Brown, 1984; Gallagher, 1979; Salend and Vigilianti, 1982), is presented in Figure 4-5.

By completing this assessment, the special educator can analyze the requirements of the environment. The types of tasks required of the student are explored so that more specific training can take place.

Planning activities.   Formal planning to terminate special education services takes place at the Individualized Education Plan meeting. During the meeting, the team discusses goals and objectives to be met in the new instructional environment and the related services needed to insure student success. Special educators must demonstrate progress, while communicating problems and adaptation needs that remain. The new placement must be rationalized and accepted. Specific techniques to continue to meet the needs of the student must be discussed.

If at all possible, the regular educators involved in the mainstreaming should attend the IEP meeting. Minner, Knutson, and Minner (1981) sug-

FIGURE 4-5 Analyzing Potential Instructional Environments For Mainstreaming

```
INSTRUCTIONAL MATERIALS AND SUPPORT PERSONNEL

1. Textbooks used _____

   Grade levels _____

2. Supplementary instruction materials used _____

   _____

   Grade levels _____

3. Media used:

   _____ television          _____ record player

   _____ films               _____ audio tapes

   _____ overhead projector  _____ slides/film strips

   _____ computer            _____ blackboard

   _____ other

4. Personnel available:

   _____ aide                _____ volunteer

   _____ peer tutor          _____ others

SUBJECT MATTTER PRESENTATION

1. Format:

   _____ lecture             _____ individualized

   _____ small group

   _____ large group         _____ language level

2. Student responses:

   _____ note taking         _____ copying from the board

   _____ reading aloud       _____ independent work

   _____ participation       _____ requesting assistance

   Kinds of directions given _____

   Number of directions given _____

3. Student evaluation and feedback:

   Frequency of evaluation _____

   Manner of evaluation _____

   Grades _____

   Test types:

   _____ essay               _____ true/false

   _____ fill-in             _____ oral
```

_____ recall   _____ analysis

_____ other

Homework:

    Type _____

    Frequency _____

    Amount _____

    Contingency _____

Extra credit work _____

CLASSROOM MANAGEMENT

    Stated rules _____

    Unstated rules _____

    Positive consequences _____

    Negative consequences _____

    Reinforcement _____

    Routines _____

SOCIAL INTERACTIONS

    Student interaction:

    _____ no interaction _____ cooperative _____ competitive

    Norms:

        Dress _____

        Appearance _____

        Interests _____

        Tolerance for differences _____

        Sub-groups _____

        Unique characteristics _____

    Effect of teacher's personality on class _____

PHYSICAL DESIGN

    Barriers _____

    Design for academics _____

    Design for socialization _____

ANALYSIS OF SAMPLE ASSIGNMENTS REQUIRED IN THE CLASSROOM

SOURCE OF TASK:

    _____ instruction _____ commercial sequence _____ fun

    Purpose _____

    Format _____

    Directions _____

Language _____

Teacher's attitude toward assisting students _____

Time allowed _____

Number of units _____

Evaluation _____

Feedback _____

Follow up _____

POSSIBLE ADAPTATIONS FROM OBSERVATIONS AND TASK ANALYSIS

Teacher variables:

Change environment _____

Clarify expectations _____

Modify materials _____

Modify assignments _____

Modify organization _____

Modify instruction _____

Notebook/notetaker _____

Student variables:

Teacher pleasing behaviors _____

Knowledge of product format _____

Aids to memory _____

Means of checking and verifying _____

Time management _____

Physical conditions _____

Self-monitoring-self reinforcement _____

Product revision _____

Test-taking strategies _____

Study skills _____

gest that attendance can be facilitated by a "roving substitute" employed by the school district, who works in the classroom for regular educators when necessary. A second strategy is the "teaching-period exchange," in which teachers cooperatively cover one another's rooms during lunch, planning, and conference periods, to allow for participation in IEPs.

Implementation activities. To successfully implement mainstreaming, a gradual phasing-out period may be needed. The special educator should select, with the regular educator, initial activities during which the student will probably find success in the regular class. Activities to increase the acceptance of the student with behavior disorders by regular-education students and soliciting "helpers" may assist the effort. During implementation, the special educator must be available to provide daily feedback and keep parents, students, and the principal informed.

It is important to confer with the mainstreamed student throughout the process. Tymitz-Wolf (1984) suggested that in light of the lack of research information with regard to social and emotional adjustment in the mainstream, it is important to make an effort to understand the student's perceptions of the process. In a study of mainstreamed educable mentally handicapped students, she described a range of worries the student had relative to academic performance, social interactions, and transitions inherent in split placement. The percentage of responses of these students with regard to their worries are described in Figure 4-6.

Evaluation activities.　Phasing-out plans and their implementation should be evaluated throughout the process and during the IEP conference. Revisions in the plan are made as necessary. Further analyses of the instructional environments may be necessary to allow for continued planning.

SUMMARY

In this chapter, services for children and youth with behavior disorders are described. The variables that should be considered in making the best possible placement decisions, including the least-restrictive environmental imperative, are discussed. The roles of members of the educational and related-services team are described.

Strategies for successful consultation and teaming are presented. The concepts of role release and the teacher as an educational synthesizer are presented as potentially effective methods for coordinating the services for children and youths with behavior disorders. The chapter concludes with a discussion of several strategies for terminating special education services to a child or youth with behavior disorders.

REVIEW QUESTIONS

1. Why is a broad range of related services needed to effectively service children and youth with behavior disorders?
2. Why is a continuum of educational services required for the effective treatment of children and youth with behavior disorders?
3. In an interview with the appropriate educational administrators, attempt to

FIGURE 4-6 Distributions of Percent Responses by Item in Order of Descending Rank

RESPONSES BY MORE THAN 70% OF THE STUDENTS	
I worry about having a (girl) (boy) from the new class to sit with at lunch/on the bus.	97.5
I worry about getting good grades on my daily work in the new class.	92.5
I worry about having to answer out loud.	92.5
I worry about being the only one from (a special-education class) in my new class.	82.5
I worry about being sent back to (the special-education class) when I get punished.	82.5
I worry about the new teacher sending me back to special education.	82.5
I worry about being chosen to play on the playground/at recess.	80
I worry about being liked as much by (special education teacher).	77.5
I worry about which teacher is the boss.	77.5
I worry about being called names.	77.5
I worry about being asked to go to parties.	75
I worry about still being liked as much by the kids in my old class.	75
I worry about being liked by the new teacher.	74.5
I worry about being made fun of by the other kids.	72.5
I worry about having to ask for a lot of help.	72.5
I worry about having a girlfriend/boyfriend.	72.5
I worry about finishing my work on time.	72.5
I worry about making my parent(s) mad/sad about how I'm doing.	72.5
I worry about being picked by the other kids to play on a team in PE.	70

(Adapted from Tymitz-Wolf, 1984.)

determine the range of special and regular educational services available to children and youth with behavior disorders in your community. How do the services available in your community compare with the range of services presented in this chapter?

4. Describe some variables that may impact upon placement decisions for children and youth with behavior disorders.

5. What is the least restrictive environmental imperative? What are some of the difficulties in fully implementing this principle?

6. Describe the advantages and disadvantages of the resource room.

7. List the roles that may be assumed by the special educator serving as a resource-room or support teacher.
8. Describe the role-release approach to teaming. What are the advantages of this model? What are some of its potential problems?
9. Contrast the interdisciplinary and transdisciplinary team models.

APPLICATION ACTIVITIES

1. You are a special educator assigned to a resource room for children with behavior disorders in a public middle school. To be as responsive as possible to the needs of the teachers and students, you are planning public-relations, communication, and reinforcement activities. Describe at least three specific activities in which you might engage in each of these areas.
   Public relations:
   Example: volunteered to sponsor cheerleaders.
   Communication:
   Examples: Scheduled open house—doughnuts and coffee.
   Scheduled daily "open-door period," during which teachers may come in and discuss concerns.
   Reinforcement activities:
   Example: designed "Happygrams" for "good things" teachers may do.
2. As a resource-room teacher, you must be aware of the kinds of tasks required of the students by regular teachers. To increase your awareness of the demands on students, analyze two assignments from regular education, using the format provided below.

   SOURCE OF TASK:
   _____ instruction   _____ commercial sequence   _____ fun

   PURPOSE:

   FORMAT:

   DIRECTIONS:

   LANGUAGE LEVEL:

   TEACHER'S ATTITUDE TOWARD ASSISTANCE:

   TIME ALLOWED:

NUMBER OF UNITS:

EVALUATION:

FEEDBACK:

FOLLOW-UP:

5

Making Decisions About Instruction

"There are no absolutely right teachers, methods, or environments" (Apter, 1977, p. 372). Though this statement may appear to be a negative overgeneralization, it is essentially correct. No special educator of children and youth with behavior disorders can successfully meet student needs by following preordained systems or procedures. Each school day is filled with new and unique behavioral and instructional problems, which continually challenge the special educator's ability to respond effectively to student needs.

In this chapter, teaching is presented as a problem-solving process. Specific strategies are described to address the programming problems inherent in the formulation of effective Individualized Education plans. Problem-solving strategies designed to assist the special educator's efforts to develop appropriate goals and objectives for the student are presented. The use of data-collection procedures to facilitate the solving of teaching problems is discussed.

OBJECTIVES

After completing this chapter, you will be able to—

1. Describe the instructional decision making process;
2. Develop appropriate instructional goals and objectives for children and youth with behavior disorders;

3. Translate IEP goals and objectives into daily instructional plans for students with behavior disorders;
4. Apply data-collection procedures to the solving of daily teaching problems.

A CASE FOR CONSIDERATION

Six-year-old Joseph had completed one semester while receiving consultative and supportive services from a resource room teacher. Though an individualized education plan had been written and resource room placement was made, the aggressive behaviors for which Joseph was originally referred had steadily increased. Ms. Nolan, the resource room teacher, decided to reconvene the transdisciplinary team to reevaluate Joseph's IEP and placement.

Ms. Nolan requested Mr. Stuart, Joseph's kindergarten teacher, to report on the programming currently being implemented in his classroom. Mr. Stuart indicated that Joseph was consistently praised and received points for keeping his hands to himself, and was removed from the group for two minutes after each act of hitting, biting, or scratching. The team evaluated the charts that Mr. Stuart kept on Joseph's behavior. Joseph seemed to be most aggressive during the mornings; after juice break, his aggressive behaviors decreased. Mondays and Fridays were particularly difficult for Joseph, and his aggression was frequent. Mr. Stuart mentioned that if Joseph was given a few crackers or a piece of fruit at the beginning of the school day, he was less aggressive.

A conference call was made to Mrs. Franzini, Joseph's mother. She was unable to attend the meeting because of her work schedule. During the conference call, Mrs. Franzini said she relied on Joseph's older sister to get him ready for the school bus in the morning. However, she had Tuesdays and Wednesdays off, and on those days prepared breakfast for Joseph and his sister and spent some time with them before they left for school. Mrs. Franzini mentioned that Joseph's sister was frequently rushed in the mornings and often sent Joseph to school without breakfast.

The team considered all the information provided by Ms. Nolan, Mr. Stuart, and Mrs. Franzini, and developed a series of hypotheses concerning Joseph's aggression. Each of the hypotheses was then linked to a specific intervention strategy. The hypotheses and strategies included the following:

Hypothesis: Exclusion from the group to decrease aggression is not effective. *Strategy*: Implement an isolation time-out procedure to decrease the aggressive behavior.
Hypothesis: Structure available in the kindergarten classroom is not decreasing the aggressive behavior. *Strategy*: Place Joseph in a self-contained classroom for young children with behavior disorders, to decrease the aggression, then mainstream him into the kindergarten.

Hypothesis: Joseph arrives at school upset and hungry. *Strategy*: Suggest to Mrs. Franzini that Joseph be given breakfast before school every day.

Hypothesis: Joseph arrives at school upset and hungry. *Strategy*: Determine Joseph's eligibility for the school breakfast program.

After reviewing each of the hypotheses, the team decided to maintain Joseph in kindergarten and work with Mrs. Franzini to ensure that he received breakfast daily. Notes would be kept on whether or not he had received breakfast in the morning. The family's eligibility for the school breakfast program would be investigated. The current behavior management strategy of exclusion would be continued, and data would be collected on Joseph's behavior.

In Joseph's case, teaching was approached as a problem-solving process. Joseph was demonstrating an inappropriate behavior. The transdisciplinary team generated and weighed a series of hypotheses to address his problem and decided to implement the least restrictive intervention. Rather than assuming that Joseph required more restrictive programming, they followed the criterion of the "least dangerous assumption" (Donnellan, 1984). They determined that the least dangerous assumption in this case was that Joseph's increased aggression was related to being hungry and upset in the mornings, rather than to the failure of his current educational program.

OBJECTIVE ONE: *To describe instructional decision making.*

Poplin (1979) stated that "each day, new questions haunt the special educator" (p. 1). Teaching children and youths with behavior disorders is a daily challenge. The special educator is continuously confronted with teaching problems that must be solved if the students' needs are to be addressed effectively. The special educator must also solve a variety of curriculum problems. Poplin warns that "we do not know what we are teaching." The special educator must address the problem of what areas of instruction to pursue that will best facilitate the return of the child or youth to regular education. To accomplish this task, the special educator determines what factors are perceived by regular educators as impeding and facilitating the implementation of classroom interventions (Witt, Elliott, & Martens, 1984). Special educators should have a repertoire of strategies available to meet behavioral and instructional problems with which they are confronted on a daily basis.

The application of problem-solving strategies to teaching problems has been demonstrated to facilitate student growth. Slowitschek, Lewis, Shores, and Ezzell (1980) explored the use of problem-solving strategies by special educators in a state psychiatric hospital for adolescents with behavior disorders. They trained teachers to solve instructional problems by applying trend- and error-analysis techniques, so that student performance could be continually monitored and remediation procedures modified and implemented as needed to facilitate learning. The strategies were found to aid teachers in problem solving, as reflected in student performance. Four out of five students substantially increased their rate of correct responses and decreased their rate of incorrect ones during the study.

Students benefit when teaching is conducted as a problem-solving activity. Problem-solving strategies are applicable to students' behavioral and educational performances. The first step in teaching as problem solving is to define the problem. Defining a teaching problem involves analyzing errors, performing an ecological assessment, consulting others familiar with the problem situation, and administering formal and informal assessment instruments.

After defining the problem, the special educator develops several hypotheses concerning probable causes of the problem. Next, each hypothesis is linked to an intervention strategy that may be implemented to solve the problem. The case of Joseph that opened this chapter is an example of teaching as a problem-solving process.

In the remainder of the chapter, the problem-solving approach is applied to determine *what to teach* and *how to teach it.*

OBJECTIVE TWO: *To develop appropriate instructional goals and objectives for children and youth with behavior disorders.*

Perhaps the greatest challenge confronting the special educator is determining what to teach the child or youth with behavior disorders. Unlike regular educators, who have the advantage of published curricula, basal texts, and standardized instructional materials to give them a sense of structure and security, special educators—by the nature of their assignment and the children with whom they work—do not (Poplin, 1979). According to Poplin, special educators need to be competent in—

1. planning daily instructional activities that reflect a wide range of goals and objectives;
2. solving problems on the spot when those goals and objectives are not being met;
3. evaluating and selecting materials to meet those goals and objectives;
4. continually evaluating student progress and mastery of those goals and objectives.

Unless appropriate goals and objectives have been developed for a student, the special educator's effectiveness in the foregoing activities is limited. More specifically, teaching effectiveness is based on the appropriateness of the student's goals and objectives.

Tymitz-Wolf (1982) describes several problems frequently confronted by special educators when writing IEP goals and objectives. First, available assessment data are often incomplete. Without an accurate and complete description of the student's present level of functioning, it is impossible to develop goals and objectives that respond to the student's needs and can be realistically completed within a one-year IEP program. Second, available assessment data in many cases are unusable for instructional purposes. They may include irrelevant information or terminology and test sophistication beyond the special educator's ability to interpret the results for instructional purposes. As a consequence of these inadequacies, initial assessment data may be of scant practical assistance in the writing of an instructional program.

As discussed in Chapter 3, a behavioral assessment approach is useful and practical for programming purposes. Regardless of the specific assessment approach used, however, the special educator is responsible for writing individual student goals and objectives. These goals and objectives must be based on the individual student's needs as described in his or her present level of functioning.

Goals.   A goal is a statement of what a student is expected to achieve by a particular date in the school year (Deno, Mirkin, & Wesson, 1984). IEP goals are generally written on an annual basis.

Short-term objectives.   Appropriate short-term objectives are critical to the ultimate effectiveness of the student's instructional plan (Larson & Poplin, 1980). A well-conceived and written short-term objective contains a) the activity in which the student will engage or the observable behavior the student will exhibit, b) the special conditions for the performance of the activity or exhibition of the behavior, and c) the criteria for successful completion of the objective.

Tymitz-Wolf (1982) describes three common pitfalls in the writing of short-term objectives:

1. The objective is simply a restatement of an annual goal, requiring the child to perform the same behavior stated in the goal but in a limited (watered-down) fashion.
2. The objective is incomplete.
3. The objective is a description of a specific activity rather than the process involved.

Tymitz-Wolf designed a checklist for the evaluation of goals and objectives, which is presented in Figure 5-1.

FIGURE 5-1   Checklist for Evaluation of Goals and Objectives

1.   Does the goal statement refer to target areas of deficit? or:
     Have I written a goal which is unrelated to remediation needs described in present level of performance and assessment information?
2.   Given the assessment data, is it probable that this goal could be achieved in a year (i.e., annual period for the IEP)? or:
     Is the goal so broad that it may take two or more years to accomplish?
3.   Does the goal contain observable terms with an identified target area for remediation? or:
     Have I used words which fail to accurately describe the problem area or direction I am taking?
4.   Have goals been written for each area of deficit? or:
     Do I have dangling data (data which indicates a need for remediation but has been overlooked)?
5.   Is the scope of the objective appropriate? or:
     Have I written any objectives that encompass the entire year, thus making them annual goals?
6.   Do the objectives describe a subskill of the goal? or:
     Have I failed to determine the hierarchy needed to teach the skill?
     —Did I simply rephrase the goal statement?
     —Did I describe a terminal skill, but only less of it?
7.   Are the objectives presented in sequential order? or:
     Have I listed the objectives in random order, unrelated to the way the skill would logically be taught?
8.   Do the objectives show a progression through the skill to meet the goal? or:
     Do the objectives emphasize only one phase of a particular skill?
9.   Does the objective contain an appropriately stated condition? or:
     Have I failed to describe the exact circumstances under which the behavior is to occur?
     —Have I described irrelevant or extraneous materials?
     —Does the condition refer to an isolated classroom activity?
10. Does the objective contain an appropriately stated performance using observable terms? or:
     Is the mode of performance (e.g., oral) different from the desired goal (e.g., written)?
11. Does the objective contain an appropriately stated standard? or:
     Is the standard unrelated to the assessment information and level of performance?
     —Am I using the performance statement as a standard?
     —Am I using percentages when the behavior requires alternative ways to measure?
     —Have I chosen arbitrary percentages?

In the preceding discussion, only the mechanics of writing instructional goals and objectives were discussed. Their appropriateness as a reflection of the needs of the child or young person with behavior disorders was not addressed. In the discussion that follows, two models are presented to facilitate the special educator's efforts to accomplish this important task. The first model is suggested for students requiring intensive programming in basic skills. This is the functional curriculum approach of Guess and Noonan (1982) and Sailor and Guess (1983). The second model, for students requiring less intensive interventions and receiving a major part of their education in the mainstream, is the curriculum-modification approach, as suggested by Edwards (1980).

The Functional Curriculum

Guess and Noonan (1982) state that the typical curriculum for students receiving intensive training in the basic skills generally takes one of two approaches: the developmental/cognitive or the remedial/behavioral.

Developmental theory assumes that children move through various developmental levels, and that success with skills at each level is required for achievement at the next higher level. The remedial/behavioral curriculum suggests that special educators need not be concerned with the order in which a child should learn skills, but with those skills that would improve the child's ability to interact effectively in the environment.

Both the developmental/cognitive and the remedial/behavioral approaches fail to address the special needs of children and youth with behavior disorders. The developmental/cognitive curriculum addresses the problem of instruction in nonfunctional and non-age-appropriate skills. The remedial/behavioral approach does not address the problem of generalization and "slavish adherence to strict behavioral technology," which "carries the danger of blocking discovery of other important concepts in teaching" (Guess & Noonan, 1982, p. 6).

To meet the individual needs of students for whom both of these approaches are inappropriate, Holvoet, Guess, Mulligan, and Brown (1980) suggest a functional curriculum, utilizing an Individualized Curriculum Sequence to meet the unique needs of exceptional students.

The major element in this approach is the functional response. This produces an immediate, motivating effect for the individual that is natural to the student's environment (Guess, Horner, Utley, Holvoet, Maxon, Tucker, & Warren, 1978).

In the functional curriculum, goals and objectives are determined by an environmental assessment. Falvey, Ferrara-Parrish, Johnson, Pumpian, Schroeder, and Brown (1979) suggest that the environmental assessment to be used as the basis of goals and objectives requires:

1. Selecting a specific environment in which the student is or will function; for example, school, home, workshop.

2. Dividing the environment into relevant areas or subenvironments; for example, dividing the school into classroom, restroom, hallways, playground, lunchroom.

3. Delineating activities occurring in each subenvironment; for example, in the classroom, group work, study time, recitation, requesting assistance, and so on.

4. Specifying the skills involved in the activity; for example, group work in the classroom includes remaining in a seat, attending to discussions, following the teacher's directions, or raising a hand to get the teacher's attention.

Sailor and Guess (1983) suggest using a matrix to determine appropriate functional skills. An example of a completed matrix is presented in Figure 5-2.

Brown, Nietupski, and Hamre-Nietupski (1976) recommended that the special educator respond to the following six questions to determine the appropriateness of functional curriculum objectives.

1. Why should this skill be taught?
2. Is the skill necessary to prepare the student to function in a less restrictive environment?
3. Could the student function if he or she did not acquire the skill?
4. Is there a different skill that will allow students access to less restrictive environments more quickly and more efficiently?
5. Will the skill reduce or restrict the student's functioning in a less restrictive environment?
6. Are the skills, materials, tasks, and level of competency required similar to those encountered in the proposed less restrictive environments?

The functional curriculum approach has several advantages for a child or young person with behavior disorders who requires intensive intervention. The skills and behaviors addressed in this approach are those that impact most on the student's actual functioning; for instance, rather than learning color recognition, a child may be taught to remain in his or her seat and to attend to the teacher's directions; or rather than learning skills specific to a particular subject matter, an adolescent may be taught to ask for teacher assistance, interact productively with peers and teachers, and so on.

In summary, the functional curriculum approach directly addresses the problem of teaching the child or youth with behavior disorders those skills that will effectively and efficiently improve the student's functioning in the environment.

Curriculum Modification.   Edwards (1980) suggested a curriculum-modification approach to develop goals and objectives for children and youth with behavior disorders. This approach is most appropriate for students placed in the regular classroom for a major part of their educational programs. The curriculum-modification approach is based on the premise

Environment	Subenvironments	Activities	Skills
School	Classroom	"Working"	In seat Complete tasks Follow directions Attend to teacher Hands to self Request assistance
		Language group	Sharing experiences Taking turns Attending to others Answering questions
	Lunchroom	Lunch line	Hands to self Following directions Taking care of own possessions Carrying tray

FIGURE 5-2 Matrix for Determining Goals and Objectives

114

that an increase in academic functioning results in decreased behavior problems. Consequently, it is primarily a strategy to increase the student's mastery of academic tasks.

Edwards maintains that his approach is a "modified curricular approach" rather than an "individualized" instructional approach, because its major objective is to provide methods that enable students with behavior disorders to proceed through materials and content areas at the same pace as other children. The procedures applied to develop a modified curriculum are:

1. Formulating objectives—the special educator consults with regular educators with regard to the broad instructional goals within each academic area
2. Adapting content—modifying content by seeking other textbooks that approximate the content covered or using taped materials
3. Providing immediate corrective feedback through immediate return of a short daily quiz
4. Reinforcing through self-graphing activities
5. Modifying existing workbook materials

Motivation is crucial to the effectiveness of the curriculum-modification approach. Students are reinforced for both attention to task and accuracy.

Edwards compared the efficacy of the modified curriculum approach to a traditional instructional approach with twenty-three fourth-grade students with behavior disorders. Four classrooms were randomly assigned to either the modified or the traditional curriculum approach. Results indicated that students receiving the modified curricular approach scored significantly higher on periodic quizzes and summative tests. In addition, the modified-curriculum group demonstrated greater on task behavior and fewer incidents of deviant behaviors than the traditional curriculum group.

Edwards contends that special educators, in cooperation with regular educators, can design educational interventions that will increase the academic performance and decrease the inappropriate behaviors of children and youth with behavior disorders.

OBJECTIVE THREE: *To translate IEP goals and objectives into a daily instructional plan for students with behavior disorders.*

Although an IEP provides a set of educational goals and objectives for the student, it does not include the daily instructional plans needed for the actual delivery of instruction (Sailor & Guess, 1983). In addition, the typical "lesson plan" format used by educators is generally insufficient to meet the programming needs and priorities of children and youth with behavior disorders.

The following plan is an adaptation of an approach suggested by Sailor and Guess and is modified specifically to respond to the needs of children and youth with behavior disorders. It requires the special educator to systematically and logically engage in teaching as a problem-solving process. This requires the educator to complete a series of specific activities and note their results on various forms. These forms, discussed next, include a program plan cover form, an instructional-strategy form, and a data collection form.

The cover form, when properly completed, enables the special educator to monitor the student's progress on short-term objectives. Each IEP objective is listed on the cover form. Also included on the form is the date on which the intervention was implemented, the data collection system applied to determine the effectiveness of the intervention, the date the intervention was terminated, and other pertinent information. The cover form serves as a frequent reminder to the special educator of the student's short-term objectives and his or her progress toward those objectives. A sample cover form is provided in Figure 5-3.

After completing the cover form, the special educator completes an instructional strategy and a data-collection form for each short-term objective. Instructional techniques, reinforcement methods, materials, and data-collection procedures are described on the instructional-strategy form. A data-collection form is completed daily on each student's progress on the interventions described on the instructional-strategy form, with one such form completed for each student objective. Sample instructional strategy and data-collection sheets are presented in figures 5-4 and 5-5. Data-collection procedures are discussed in detail in the next section.

Each day, the teacher consults the program plan to evaluate the student's daily progress toward his or her short-term objectives. If the special educator notes any deviations from the anticipated progress, the program plan is then used as the basis for problem solving. Using the program plan for problem solving is discussed in the following section.

OBJECTIVE FOUR: *To apply data-collection procedures to the solving of daily teaching problems.*

There are no "bad" students, only "bad programs" (Kerr & Nelson, 1983). Even though special educators carefully develop appropriate goals and objectives for their students, problems frequently arise during the instructional process. To remain aware of students' progress toward these goals and objectives, special educators must have available procedures designed to document change in student behavior. Such documentation is referred to as data collection, or the gathering of facts to facilitate problem solving.

FIGURE 5-3 Cover Form

Student *Joseph Franzini*

Objectives*	Date Begun	Date Terminated	Data System	Comments
Keeps hands to self during morning group, < 2 aggressions per period	9-3-86		frequency counts taken daily	
Remains in seat throughout snacktime — leaves seat no more than 1 time	10-15-86		frequency counts taken daily	
Completes tasks with no more than 2 reminders to "keep working"	10-2-86	10-31-86	frequency counts taken daily	tasks were no more than 5-7 minutes long
Works consistently on a task for 10 minutes with no cues	11-1-86		duration taken daily	

*to be copied from the student's Individualized Educational Plan

FIGURE 5-4 Instructional Strategy Form

Student _Joseph Frazini_   Date _11-1-86_

Objective _Joseph will keep his hands to himself during morning group with no more than 2 aggressions per period for 3 consecutive school days._

INSTRUCTIONAL STRATEGY:

    Joseph will be removed from the group for 2 minutes each time he hits, bites, or scratches. He will receive praise for keeping his hands to himself, and a star for each five minutes of "hands to self." When Joseph hits, he will be cued "The rule is, 'Keep your hands to yourself,'" and he will be removed.

CONTINGENCIES:

Removal for aggression.

Stars on chart for each 5 minutes without aggressive behavior. Three stars will purchase an extra carton of milk during snack.

MATERIALS:

    Stars
    Chart
    Milk

DATA COLLECTION:

    Number of times Joseph is removed is graphed daily.

FIGURE 5-5 Data Collection Form

Student _Joseph Franzini_ _____ Date Initiated _9-30-86_
Objective _Joseph will keep his hands to himself during
morning group with no more than 2 aggressions per
period for 3 consecutive school days._

FREQUENCY OF BEHAVIOR

15	15	15	15	15	15	15	15	15	15	15	15	15	15	
14	14	14	14	14	14	14	14	14	14	14	14	14	14	
13	13	13	13	13	13	13	13	13	13	13	13	13	13	
12	12	12	12	12	12	12	12	12	12	12	12	12	12	
11	11	11	11	11	11	11	11	11	11	11	11	11	11	
10	10	10	10	10	10	10	10	10	10	10	10	10	10	
9	9	9	9	9	9	9	9	9	9	9	9	9	9	
8	8	8	8	8	8	8	8	8	8	8	8	8	8	
7	7	7	7	7	7	7	7	7	7	7	7	7	7	
6	6	6	6	6	6	6	6	6	6	6	6	6	6	
5	5	5	5	5	5	5	5	5	5	5	5	5	5	
4	4	4	4	4	4	4	4	4	4	4	4	4	4	
3	3	3	3	3	3	3	3	3	3	3	3	3	3	*Criteria*
2	2	2	2	2	2	2	2	2	2	2	2	2	2	
1	1	1	1	1	1	1	1	1	1	1	1	1	1	
0	0	0	0	0	0	0	0	0	0	0	0	0	0	

DATES

Directions:
    Indicate behavior counted _number of times Joseph is
removed during morning group_
    Enter date or time period

    Cross out one number each time the behavior occurs on
each date. Circle the total number of times the behavior
occurs. Connect circles to form graph.

Although it is crucial to the solving of teaching problems, some special educators object to the systematic collection of data in the classroom. They state that the process is too time-consuming, the data collected aren't helpful, and administrative or parental support for collecting data is not given (Kerr & Nelson, 1983). Some special educators feel that collecting data violates the teacher's role (Scott & Goetz, 1980). They suggest that students view the teacher as inaccessible when he or she assumes the role of observer during data-collection periods.

Special educators frequently become frustrated with data collection. This is especially true when they attempt to collect more data than can be used effectively (Lund, Schnaps, & Bijou, 1983). Collecting data on nonessential behaviors is a waste of teaching time (Kerr & Nelson, 1983).

However, data collection has several advantages when prudently applied. To arrange the most effective learning opportunities for students, special educators need continual and immediate information on student performance (Fabry & Cone, 1980). Data collection helps solve instructional problems by providing the special educator with opportunities to obtain valuable feedback applicable to program development. On a more practical basis, data collection provides a concrete means of accountability and a common basis for discussion of individual students' progress and programs. When behavioral or instructional changes are small, data collection can provide reinforcement for the teacher, parent, and child (Lund & associates, 1983). The special educator's observational skills may improve as a result of data-collection activities (Scott & Goetz, 1980). Although admittedly time-consuming, data collection is helpful by reducing the possibility that a special educator will pursue an intervention strategy having little or no effect on student performance (Scott & Goetz, 1980).

Several guidelines have been suggested for selecting or designing effective data collection systems. But in general, the system should be inexpensive, simple to teach to others (parents and paraprofessionals), and unobtrusive in the teaching situation (Deno, Mirkin, & Wesson, 1984). It should be manageable and a natural, integral part of the program; data should be easily collected while teaching. The system should provide for the collection of usable data only, and should offer a simple means for efficiently displaying data in a meaningful form (Lund & associates, 1983). In summary, data collection should be realistic, systematic, objective, and an integral component of the teaching plan (Fitzgerald, 1982).

Developing a Data Collection System

The most important part of developing a data-collection system is the selection of a measurement strategy. To select an appropriate strategy, the special educator reviews each short-term objective and determines the measurable characteristic of the behavior that is its focus. Kerr and Nelson (1983) suggest that:

1. the data-collection system be as direct and sensitive a measure as possible.
2. the behaviors should be recorded where they occur.
3. the behaviors should be defined carefully, and only responses that meet the definition should be recorded.
4. the behaviors should be recorded on a daily basis. Special educators should collect at least three to five days of baseline data on a behavior before implementing an intervention.
5. only as many behaviors as can be reasonably managed should be observed.

Fitzgerald (1982) suggests that for some behaviors, periodic data collection through a pretest-posttest system may suffice. Pretest-posttest options include behavior-rating scales, self-rating scales, and sociometric instruments. Academic changes may be documented through the use of standardized and informal assessment instruments. The special educator may wish to develop and periodically administer an instructor-made academic or behavioral checklist to monitor progress. Although it documents changes over time, in many cases the pretest-posttest format is not adequate for solving daily instructional problems. To have information applicable to the formulation of hypotheses and the solving of instructional problems, the special educator must generate data that document the processes whereby the student did or did not attain the short-term objectives.

Special educators may document the instructional process through (a) event recording (the frequency or number of times the behavior occurs), (b) duration recording (the amount of time during which the behavior occurs), or (c) level-of-assistance recording (the amount of support the student needs to successfully exhibit the behavior. These forms of data collection provide ample information for instructional problem solving.

Event recording procedures are used when the issue is the number of times a behavior occurs. In this case, the behavior is discrete, and its duration is not pertinent to the objective. Examples of events that may be recorded are the number of correct responses, the number of verbalizations during group discussions, the number of times the student initiates social interaction with another student during free play, verbalization, and initiating playing.

Duration recording procedures are used when the issue is the amount of time a behavior occurs. In this case, the short-term objective is concerned with increasing or decreasing the amount of time the behavior is exhibited. Examples of duration recording are length of a temper tantrum, amount of time out of seat, and amount of time attending to task.

Levels of assistance data procedures are used to record the kind and amount of support a student needs to successfully complete a step, activity, or objective. According to Poplin (1979), a student may respond independently or may require one of three levels of assistance: priming, prompting, or cuing. Priming is total assistance, in which the teacher either physically primes (for example, hand-over-hand letter formation while writing) or verbally primes (reading each word aloud before the student reads it) a response. Prompting, the second level of assistance, involves the teacher's either physically or verbally starting the task for the child or assisting in the completion of the task. Cuing involves a verbal or physical signal to the child to exhibit or not exhibit the behavior. By recording the amount of support the student requires to successfully complete a task, the special educator has available a means of determining the child's level of performance and changes in performance.

Data may be used not only to evaluate students' performance and the effectiveness of the instructional process, but to communicate students' progress to parents, regular educators, and support personnel.

Generally, data collection is a two-step process: (1) recording data and (2) putting it in graph form (Fabry & Cone, 1980). Both steps are important. Data that are collected and not graphed are of limited value for the purpose of communication. Fabry and Cone suggest using self-graphing techniques to minimize the time devoted to preparing graphs. Each of the data-recording procedures presented next includes a self-graphing procedure.

Event recording.   Fabry and Cone (1980) suggested a self-graphing procedure to maintain trial-by-trial response data on student performance. In this system, the special educator begins with a blank grid with the appropriate number of boxes for the number of response opportunities to be offered to the student. Correct responses are accumulated upward from the bottom of the grid. Incorrect responses are accumulated downward from the top of the grid (see Figure 5-6). After the number of opportunities for responses are completed, the special educator draws a bold line across the top of the highest cell of the last correct response. Graphing is completed by connecting the lines. An advantage of this system is that it can be applied to any behaviors using a trial or event format.

In this example, the student is required to correctly identify numbers presented on cards by the special educator. The child has ten opportunities daily. On day one, the child responded correctly three times and incorrectly seven times. On days two and three, the rates were four correct and six incorrect, and on the fifth day, five correct, five incorrect.

Another collection system responding to the event format and using a self-graphing procedure is presented in Figure 5-7. To employ this system, the special educator lists the correct responses in data columns moving from left to right on the form. If a student responds correctly, a slash is placed through the cell corresponding with the appropriate trial. At the end of the lesson, the total number of correct responses is recorded by circling the appropriate number in the lower half of the daily column. As the series of lessons progress, the circles are connected to form a graph.

When the total number of trials is not essential to the short-term objective or the special educator simply wants to record the number of responses, the graphing system in Figure 5-8 can be applied. In this system, the total number of responses is circled for each day or time period. The circles are then connected to form the graph.

Duration recording.   A system similar to that presented in Figure 5-8 may be used for collecting and graphing duration data. In this format, the special educator circles the amount of time consumed by the behavior, task,

FIGURE 5-6 Blank Grid Trial Graphing System

3	3	5	3														
5	5	6	5														
7	7	7	7														
8	8	8	8														
10	9	9	10														
9	10	10	9														
6	6	4	6														
4	4	3	4														
2	2	2	2														
1	1	1	1														

Day 1   Day 2   Day 3   Day 4

Stimuli: What's this number?
Last day of data:

Trial	Correct Response	Student's Response
1	3	3
2	1	1
3	7	1
4	2	2
5	8	6
6	4	4
7	10	1
8	5	2
9	6	6
10	9	6

or incident. The circles are then connected to form a graph. This system is depicted in Figure 5-9.

Level-of-assistance recording.   Level-of-assistance recording enables the special educator to determine objectively the amount of support a student needs in order to successfully complete a specific task or behavior.

FIGURE 5-7 Trial Specific Frequency Graph

Student _Joseph Franzini_

Objective _Joseph will recognize numbers 1-10 with no cues for 3 consecutive school days._

Trial Responses		10-1	10-2	10-3	10-4	10-5	10-8	10-9
					Dates			
A	1	1̸5	1̸5	1̸5	1̸5	1̸5	1̸5	1̸5
B	4	14	1̸4	1̸4	1̸4	1̸4	14	1̸4
C	2	1̸3	13	1̸3	1̸3	1̸3	1̸3	1̸3
D	7	12	12	12	12	1̸2	12	12
E	9	11	11	11	11	11	11	11
F	6	10	10	10	10	1̸0	1̸0	1̸0
G	3	9̸	9̸	9	9̸	9̸	9̸	9̸
H	5	8	8	8	8	8	8	8
I	8	7	7̸	7̸	7	⑦	7̸	7̸
J	10	6	6	6̸	6	6̸	⑥	⑥
K		5	5	⑤	5	5	5	5
L		4	④	4	④	4	4	4
M		③	3	3	3	3	3	3
N		2	2	2	2	2	2	2
O		1	1	1	1	1	1	1
P		0	0	0	0	0	0	0

Directions: Place slash (/) over number in dated column for correct response.

At the end of the lesson, circle number in column which corresponds to total correct responses for day.

Connect total daily response numbers to make graph.

124

FIGURE 5-8 Data Collection Form

Student _Joseph Franzini_ ____ Date Initiated _10-15_
Objective _Joseph remains in seat throughout snack time, leaving his seat no more than 1 time each period._

FREQUENCY OF BEHAVIOR

15	15	15	15	15	15	15	15	15	15	15	15	15	15
14	14	14	14	14	14	14	14	14	14	14	14	14	14
13	13	13	13	13	13	13	13	13	13	13	13	13	13
12	12	12	12	12	12	12	12	12	12	12	12	12	12
11	11	11	11	11	11	11	11	11	11	11	11	11	11
10	10	10	10	10	10	10	10	10	10	10	10	10	10
9	9	9	9	9	9	9	9	9	9	9	9	9	9
8	8	8	8	8	8	8	8	8	8	8	8	8	8
7	7	⑦	7	7	7	7	7	7	7	7	7	7	7
⑥	6	6	6	6	6	6	6	6	6	6	6	6	6
5	⑤	5	⑤	5	5	5	5	5	5	5	5	5	5
4	4	4	4	④	4	4	4	4	4	4	4	4	4
3	3	3	3	3	③	③	3	3	3	3	3	3	3
2	2	2	2	2	2	2	2	2	2	2	2	2	2 criteria
1	1	1	1	1	1	1	1	1	1	1	1	1	1
0	0	0	0	0	0	0	0	0	0	0	0	0	0
10-15	10-16	10-17	10-18	10-19	10-22	10-23							

Dates

Directions:
     Indicate behavior counted _number of times Joseph leaves his seat during snack time_

     Enter date or time period

     Cross out one number each time the behavior occurs on each date. Circle the total number of times the behavior occurs. Connect circles to form graph.

A form for collecting level-of-assistance data is presented in Figure 5-10. To use this system, the special educator first writes a description of the tasks, activities, or behaviors to be assessed, in the column titled "objectives." Next, the special educator instructs the student and records the amount of assistance required to ensure his or her success in the task, activity, or behavior. Next, the date is written at the top of the appropriate column under the level of assistance. The letter *A* and the numbers 0–3 correspond to the levels of assistance noted on the bottom of Figure 5-10. As the student completes the activity, the special educator determines the level of assistance needed and circles the appropriate letter or number. The circles are then connected to form the graph.

FIGURE 5-9 Data Collection Form

Student _Joseph Franzini_ _____ Date Initiated _11-1-86_

Objective _Joseph will work independently at a task for 10 minutes._

DURATION OF BEHAVIOR IN MINUTES

15	15	15	15	15	15	15	15	15	15	15	15	15	15	
14	14	14	14	14	14	14	14	14	14	14	14	14	14	
13	13	13	13	13	13	13	13	13	13	13	13	13	13	
12	12	12	12	12	12	12	12	12	12	12	12	12	12	
11	11	11	11	11	11	11	11	11	11	11	11	11	11 criteria
10	10	10	10	10	10	10	10	10	10	10	10	10	10	
9	9	9	9	9	9	9	9	9	9	9	9	9	9	
8	8	8	8	8	8	8	8	8	8	8	8	8	8	
7	7	7	7	7	7	⑦	7	7	7	7	7	7	7	
6	6	6	6	⑥	6	6	6	6	6	6	6	6	6	
5	5	⑤	5	5	⑤	5	5	5	5	5	5	5	5	
④	④	4	4	4	4	4	4	4	4	4	4	4	4	
3	3	3	③	3	3	3	3	3	3	3	3	3	3	
2	2	2	2	2	2	2	2	2	2	2	2	2	2	
1	1	1	1	1	1	1	1	1	1	1	1	1	1	
0	0	0	0	0	0	0	0	0	0	0	0	0	0	
11-1	11-2	11-3	11-4	11-5	11-8	11-9								

Dates

Directions:

Indicate behavior counted _amount of time Joseph works independently (with no cues or reminders)_

Enter date or time period

Cross out one number each time the behavior occurs on each date. Circle the total number of times the behavior occurs. Connect circles to form graph.

There are more traditional systems for data recording that are useful to the special educator when assessing some behaviors. Examples of traditional graphing systems for duration and frequency data are presented in figures 5-11 and 5-12. These traditional systems are presented in detail in the discussion of behavioral techniques in Chapter 9.

FIGURE 5-10   Level of Assistance Data Collection Form

Student: *Joseph Franzini* _____ Date Initiated *10-1-86*
School: *Don Allen Elementary* _____
Special Education Teacher *Ms. Nolen* _____
Regular Education Teacher *Mr. Stuart* _____
Objectives: *Joseph will follow 3 playground rules*
independently. _____

Dates

Objectives	Level of Assistance							
	10-1	*10-2*	*10-3*	*10-5*	*10-8*	*10-9*		
Joseph initiates 1 appropriate social interaction with a peer	3	3	3	3	3	3	3	3
	2	②—	—②	2	②—	—②	—②	2
	①	1	1	①	1	1	1	1
	0	0	0	0	0	0	0	0
	A	A	A	A	A	A	A	A
Joseph responds to playground monitors directive to "line up"	3	3	3	3	3	3	③	3
	2	2	2	2	②—	—②	2	2
	1	1	1	①	1	1	1	1
	0	0	⓪	0	0	0	0	0
	Ⓐ—	—Ⓐ	A	A	A	A	A	A
Joseph uses playground equipment appropriately (sits on swings rather than flinging them, goes down slide on seat, etc.)	3	3	3	3	3	3	3	3
	2	2	②—	—2	②—	—②	—②	2
	①—	—①	1	①	1	1	1	1
	0	0	0	0	0	0	0	0
	A	A	A	A	A	A	A	A

Rating code:
    3 - completes the objective independently and successfully.
    2 - requires one verbal reminder to successfully complete objective.
    1 - requries direct supervision and handshaping to complete objective successfully.
    0 - physical assistance required.
    A - unable to successfully complete objective (i.e., had to be removed, refusal, tantrum, etc.).

FIGURE 5-11 Traditional Duration Graphing

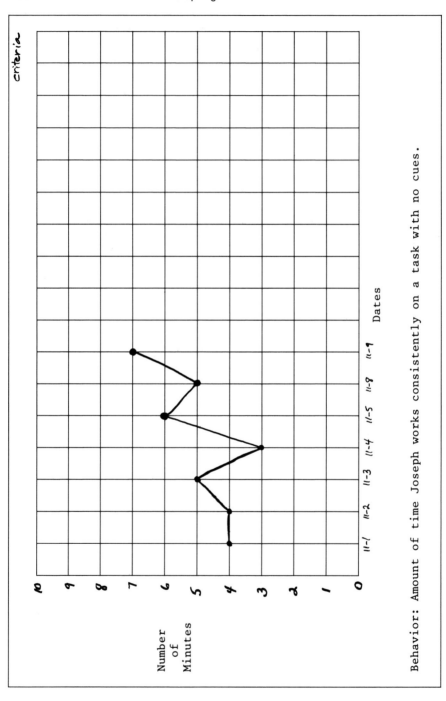

Behavior: Amount of time Joseph works consistently on a task with no cues.

FIGURE 5-12 Traditional Frequency Graphing

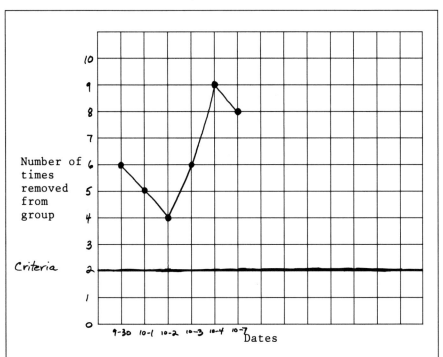

Behavior: Joseph keeps his hands to himself during morning groups with less than two aggressions per group period. Number of times Joseph must be removed from group is recorded.

How to Use Data-Collection Systems

Before implementing an intervention to address a short-term objective, it is necessary to collect baseline data. These are data collected on a behavior as it naturally occurs before an intervention is implemented. They are used as the basis for determining the effectiveness of the intervention. It is generally recommended that baseline data be collected for a minimum of three to five days before an intervention is initiated to change the behavior.

In addition to "eyeing" intervention data and comparing them to the baseline data for the evaluation purposes, Haring, Liberty, and White (1980) urge special educators to apply decision-making rules to intervention data for evaluation. Their research indicated that mildly handicapped students whose teachers consistently applied decision rules to solve instructional problems demonstrated greater progress than students whose teachers do not. The decision-making rules, suggested by Haring and associates, are applicable when—

1. a program is designed to teach a new behavior or improve performance on an old behavior;
2. consistent instructional procedures are applied;
3. a minimum of ten opportunities is provided the student during each instructional session;
4. a standard of performance is defined that includes accuracy, time, and conditions;
5. data are collected and charted during each instructional session.

Decisions are made by constructing a learning picture from the student's performance data. The steps for constructing a learning picture are the following:

1. Determine the six most recent data points. (See Figure 5-13a and 5-13b.)
2. Looking at the first three points, place a plus sign (+) at the intersection of the second-highest point and the second day of data. Looking at the second three data points, place a plus sign at the intersection of the second-highest point and the fifth day of data. (See Figure 5-13b.)
3. Draw a line through the two pluses. This line is called an anticipated-performance line. Continue this line to the ends of the graph. (See Figure 5-13c.)
4. Draw a line from the intersection of the prediction line and criteria line to the bottom of the graph. This line will intersect with the date when criteria should be met. (See Figure 5-13d.)
5. Compare the anticipated performance rate with the actual performance rate.

A learning picture enables the special educator to draw conclusions concerning the effectiveness of the instruction. Haring and associates describe four possible changes the special educator may make to improve instructional effectiveness: change antecedents, change consequences, return to the previous step in the instructional sequence, or increase compliance.

Antecedent changes are appropriate when student performance (number of correct responses) decreases or stays at the same level. Among the antecedent changes the special educator may implement are to provide more precise directions, provide demonstrations, change the level of assistance, and modify instructional materials.

Consequence changes are appropriate when student performance (number of correct and incorrect responses) stays the same or decreases. Changing the reinforcer may be necessary to accelerate performance.

A return to a previous step in the instructional sequence may be required when the number of correct responses stays the same and the number of errors increases. When the number of correct performances decreases rapidly, student compliance may be the problem. When this

FIGURE 5-13 Applying Decision Rules

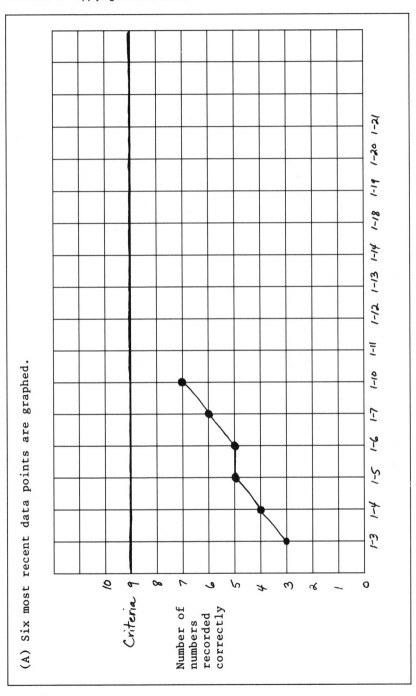

(A) Six most recent data points are graphed.

FIGURE 5-13 Applying Decision Rules (continued)

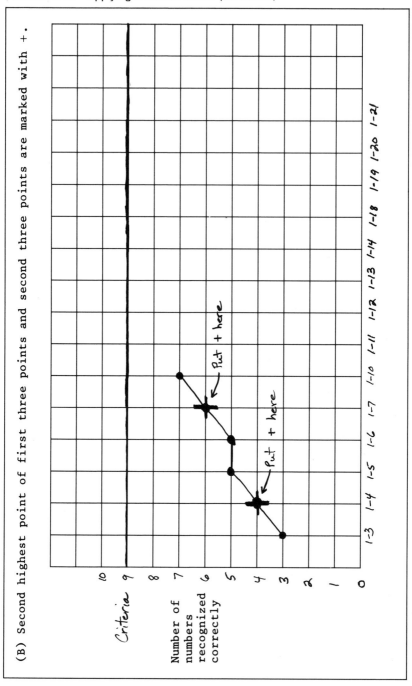

(B) Second highest point of first three points and second three points are marked with +.

FIGURE 5-13 Applying Decision Rules (continued)

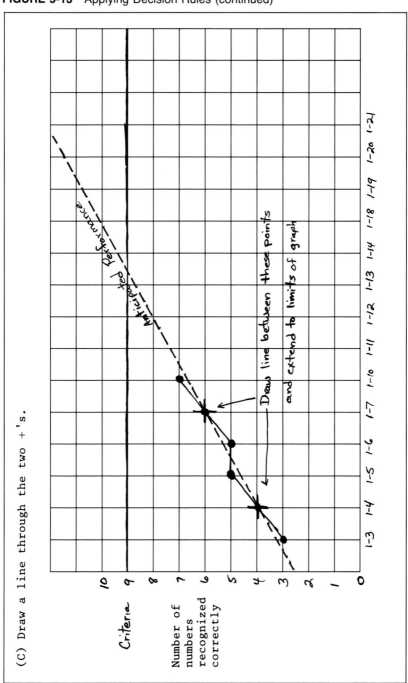

(C) Draw a line through the two +'s.

FIGURE 5-13 Applying Decision Rules (continued)

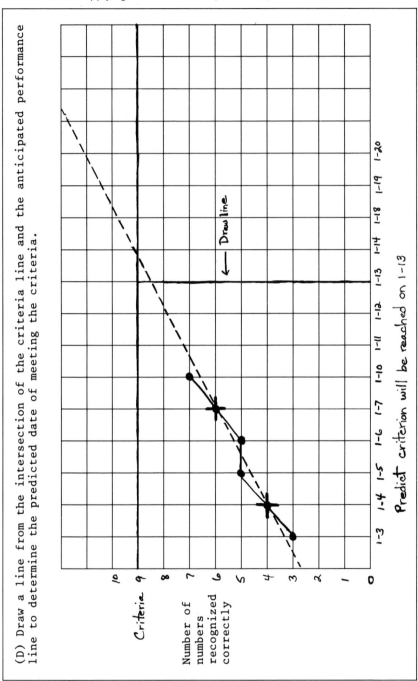

(D) Draw a line from the intersection of the criteria line and the anticipated performance line to determine the predicted date of meeting the criteria.

occurs, a change in the directions given to the student may accelerate performance. In some instances, progressing to a more difficult skill level may increase compliance. Other techniques for increasing compliance and, as a consequence, improving performance include changing motivating consequences, changing reinforcement schedules, or instituting a response cost system.

Even when a special educator chooses not to apply the decision-making rules such as those described, he or she must respond to students' unacceptable performance by implementing instructional changes. Lund, Schnaps, and Bijou (1983) suggest options that may apply when student performance on an instructional program is unacceptable. The special educator may change to another instructional program or alter reinforcers, materials, and cues. Checking the error patterns and returning to a previous instructional level or simplifying the task may be appropriate. Assessing the student's readiness skills may be necessary. The program may simply need to be terminated and replaced with a more appropriate program.

Data-collection and analysis procedures make the special educator sensitive to students' instructional needs and enable them to address those needs appropriately.

SUMMARY

In this chapter, teaching is presented as a problem-solving process. Two strategies were presented to facilitate the selection of goals and objectives for children and youth with behavior disorders: the functional curriculum approach (Guess & Noonan, 1982) and the modified curriculum approach (Edwards, 1980).

It was suggested that although the IEP includes goals and objectives that a student is to complete within a year, these are generally not very useful for the planning, conducting, and evaluating of daily instructional activities. To overcome this shortcoming, a plan is proposed to facilitate instruction of children and youth with behavior disorders on a day-to-day basis. Data-collection techniques and instructional decision-making strategies were presented.

REVIEW QUESTIONS

1. Select a child with whom you are familiar (or select a case from Appendix B). What are some possible hypotheses you can make regarding this student's current level of performance? What are the teaching problems that need to be

addressed? What are some interventions that may be applied to solve the teaching problems?

2. Review the common problems confronting the special educator when writing short-term objectives (Tymitz-Wolf, 1982). Write three short-term objectives for a student with whom you are familiar (or take a case from Appendix B). Evaluate these objectives, using the checklist in Figure 5-1.

3. Contrast goals and objectives. Are they the same? How do they differ?

4. Contrast the developmental and remedial approaches. What are the advantages of each approach? The disadvantages?

5. Review the steps involved in the modified curriculum strategy (Edwards, 1980). For each step in the modified curriculum process, give an example of a cooperative activity you would undertake with a regular educator.

6. Discuss the positive aspects of data collection in the special-education setting for children and youths with behavior disorders. What are some of the concerns special educators frequently express about data collection? Do you agree? Disagree? Why?

7. List three behaviors that you would assess using (1) frequency data, (2) duration data, and (3) level-of-assistance data. Which of the data-collection systems presented in the chapter would you use to collect data for each behavior you listed in response to the first part of this question?

APPLICATION ACTIVITIES

1. Complete the following environmental-assessment matrix.

Environment	Subenvironment	Activities	Skills
School	Hall	Waiting for bus	
	Playground	Lining up to return to class	
Home	Dining room	Dinner	

2. In this application activity you will use the Haring, Liberty, and White (1980) decision-analysis rules. Complete each step to determine the appropriate instructional decisions for Josie.

Josie is an eight-year-old girl who does not participate in group activities. One of her instructional objectives is to participate verbally in two daily class meetings. The criterion to be met for this objective is that Josie will verbally participate at least twelve times during the two class meetings combined. Her participation data for twelve consecutive school days are:

Day	Verbalizations
1	2
2	3
3	2
4	4
5	5
6	4
7	6
8	5
9	5
10	8
11	5
12	7

a. Plot these data on the graph on p. 138.
b. Find the midpoint of the first three data points by adding the three data points and dividing by two. Plot this point over the second data point in the graph you completed above.
c. Find the midpoint for the second three data points, and plot this point over the fifth data point.
d. Draw the prediction line that intersects the midpoints you made and extend it to the point where it crosses the criteria line.
e. Draw a line to the date line from the intersection of the prediction line and the criteria line. This is the predicted time at which the student will meet the criteria on the instructional program. This prediction line is made on the student's performance during the first six days. Now you have developed your prediction date for the completion of the program. Continue to plot Josie's data. Is her performance following the prediction? If not, what could be happening in this child's program?
  i. Is the instructional objective too difficult?
  ii. Is the setting in which it is being taught conducive to learning?
  iii. Is the timing of the program affecting instruction?
  iv. Is the reinforcement for the program affecting instruction?
  v. Does the student need additional prompts, materials, cues, and the like, in order to complete the objective?
  vi. Is the instructional technique appropriate?
  vii. Are the materials appropriate and motivating?
  viii. What other variables may you wish to consider?

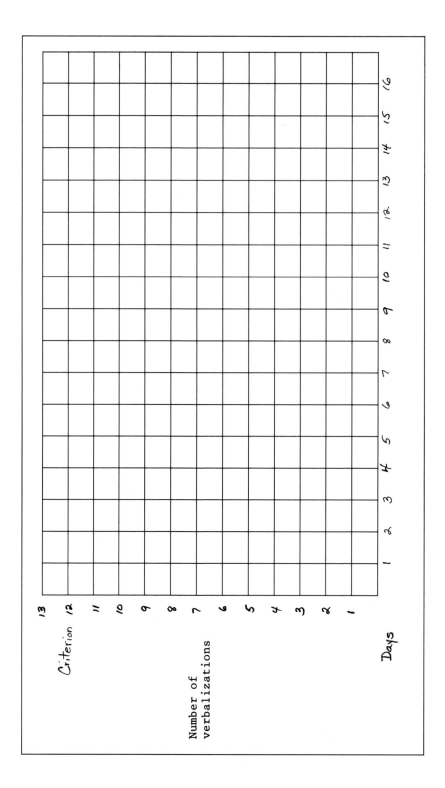

6

The Instructional Environment

Bell (1979), in a discussion of his commitment to teaching children and youth with behavior disorders, remarked that within the first five days of teaching, he was required to perform a variety of tasks for which teacher training had ill-prepared him. Although competent to teach content to students, he was unprepared for the noninstructional tasks thrust upon him. These included determining the budgetary allotment for materials, writing a job description for a paraprofessional, and scheduling students.

In this chapter, those tasks that are prerequisite for effective and efficient programming from the first day of class to the end of the school year are described. Consideration is given to constructing effective instructional schedules, making decisions on grouping for instruction, arranging the physical environment, selecting appropriate materials, and adapting materials to meet the needs of individual students.

After completing this chapter, you will be able to—

1. identify the parameters for constructing effective instructional schedules;
2. make decisions concerning grouping students for instruction;
3. arrange a physical environment responsive to students' needs;
4. select appropriate instructional materials;
5. adapt instructional materials to the needs of individual students.

A CASE FOR CONSIDERATION

"But Julia, you just don't understand. If I let one student use a tape recorder to take notes in history class, I'll soon have a classroom full of tape recorders." Dolores Atherton, the middle school social studies teacher, was adamant.

Julia Webster, the resource-room teacher, was surprised by Dolores's comment. She responded, "Well, Dolores, I know it's unusual, but Michelle is trying her best to fit into your class. She enjoys history and really wants to do well in regular class. But with her attention problem, taking notes is difficult. Her tape recorder helps a great deal."

"There has to be another way, Julia," replied Ms. Atherton. "If she needs that much help, maybe she doesn't belong in my history class. Perhaps it is best if she stays with you that period."

"I'm sorry, Dolores," replied Ms. Webster. "I didn't realize you felt so strongly about students using tape recorders. Maybe we can think of something else. Do you have any students who take thorough notes?"

"Of course. There are several capable students in the class."

"Great. Perhaps we can partner Michelle with one of them. I wonder if there's a student who not only takes good notes but would be willing to help her."

"Mary Elizabeth Daniels is a wonderful student. She has a handicapped sister. She's rather shy, and helping Michelle may help her too."

"That's a terrific idea, Dolores," Ms. Webster agreed. "Let's meet with Mary Elizabeth, and talk to her about the kind of help Michelle needs. I'll show her some of the ways Michelle is learning to deal with her problems, such as doing her behavior charts and time-management sheets. As you said, it may help Mary Elizabeth overcome some of her shyness."

"Okay, Julia," replied Ms. Atherton. "But please, don't send her to class with anything like a tape recorder, which will interfere with what I'm doing."

Michelle requires a modification of instructional procedures and materials to succeed in regular class, and especially social studies. Ms. Webster thought she had an ideal way of dealing with Michelle's attention problem. However, in her enthusiasm, she had forgotten to consult with the one person most affected by the proposed interventions—the regular classroom teacher. In this chapter, the selection, adaptation, and application of instructional materials with children and youths with behavior disorders, as well as other facets of an effective teaching environment, are discussed.

OBJECTIVE ONE: *To identify the parameters for constructing effective instructional schedules.*

Special educators frequently comment on the constant "time and materials crunch" with which they work. However, careful scheduling, characterized by consistency and flexibility, can help teachers manage the "crunch."

GENERAL CONSIDERATIONS—ALLOCATED AND ENGAGED TIME

Rosenshine (1977) found that student learning increases when teachers allocate a great deal of time to instruction while maintaining a high level of task engagement. In the development of an effective instructional schedule, these two important variables, allocated time and engaged time, are carefully considered.

Englert (1984) describes allocated time as the amount of time scheduled for a specific subject or activity. Allocated time is measured simply by looking at the daily instructional schedule and calculating how much time is devoted to various subjects and activities. However, simply because a certain amount of time is allocated for a subject does not mean the students are actually engaged in learning that subject. Consequently, special educators must not only allocate sufficient time for instruction, but they must be sure that students are engaged in the scheduled subject during the time allocated for its study.

Research indicates that when scheduling is done with care, the time available for instruction increases (Rosenshine, 1980). The appropriate allocation of time is assured when the special educator follows a well-thought-out, carefully planned schedule; begins and ends activities on time; facilitates transitions from activity to activity; and assigns scheduled activities first priority, rather than engaging in spontaneous, alternative activities (Englert, 1984). Engelman (1982) urges the use of specific transition techniques to decrease transition time and increase teaching time. Special educators may apply the following techniques to facilitate transitions:

Model appropriate transition behaviors

Signal the beginning and ending of activities

Remediate transition problems such as slowness and disruptiveness

Observe the student's performance during transitions and, if he or she is having difficulties, repeat the rules until they are firmly established within the student's behavior pattern

Reinforce quick, quiet transitions

Engelman's transition techniques can be enhanced by "work rules." Good (1983) suggested establishing "work rules" for early finishers, students unable to continue assigned tasks, students requiring additional help, and others. Work rules are communicated to students by teaching and rehearsing new lesson procedures prior to their implementation. Students can be taught how to use new equipment before it is actually applied for instructional purposes. By means of rules and rehearsals, students become aware of what is expected of them, and thus intrusions into teaching time are minimized.

Although sufficient instructional time is necessary if students are to learn, Englert (1984) maintains that instructional time should not be arbitrarily increased without giving consideration to task engagement time. Task engagement should be measured during both direct instruction—that is, during teacher-directed lessons—and during seat work. Seat-work engaged time can be assessed by the special educator as he or she circulates among students. Seat-work tasks should be completed accurately. Seat work should be used for practice, drill, and overlearning of previously learned skills.

Englert developed a self-rating instrument to help special educators improve their instructional organization and scheduling effectiveness. A modification of this scale is presented in Figure 6-1.

GUIDELINES FOR SCHEDULE DEVELOPMENT

Scheduling is a dynamic process. The two kinds of scheduling of greatest concern to the special educator are overall program scheduling and individual student scheduling. In this section, guidelines for developing these schedules are presented.

Gallagher (1979) suggests that scheduling is a continuous, creative activity. She offers scheduling guidelines based on a hierarchy of the phases through which students are assumed to progress during the school year; that is, schedules used during the first part of the school year will differ from those at various times during the remaining weeks and months. Gallagher suggests that during the year, daily planning for individual students gradually evolves into group plans. Instruction that began at an individual level gradually evolves into small- and large-group instruction. Short work periods and limited tasks gradually evolve into longer work periods and more complex tasks. Individual work areas gradually become group work areas. The amount of adaptation in the curriculum and in materials is gradually reduced as flexibility in class periods increases. Teacher supervision and planning is gradually replaced by self-monitoring and student planning. As the year progresses, the time students spend in the special education classroom decreases. Reinforcement becomes intermittent, delayed, and natural.

Gallagher suggests that each student be given a personal daily schedule. This schedule is an "organizer" that alerts the student to the activities that will occur throughout the day. As a consequence, the student wastes

FIGURE 6-1   Self-Rating Scale for Instructional Organization

Rate your performance on each of the competencies below, using the following scale:

(1) Not at all like me   (4) A great deal like me
(2) Somewhat like me   (5) Very much like me
(3) Moderately like me

COMPETENCIES	PERFORMANCE EVALUATION
Allocated Time	
Schedule students into direct instruction and interact with 70% or more of the students each hour	1 2 3 4 5
Spend 80% or more of class time in instructional activities	1 2 3 4 5
Minimize transition time with less than three minutes between a change of students and activities, and 30 seconds between a change of activities only	1 2 3 4 5
Signal students to begin and end activities	1 2 3 4 5
Gain students' attention before beginning a lesson and maintain attention at 90% level	1 2 3 4 5
Prepare students for transitions by stating behavioral expectations	1 2 3 4 5
Engaged Time	
Maintain attention on seatwork at 80% level	1 2 3 4 5
Monitor students' seatwork by scanning	1 2 3 4 5
Circulate among students doing seatwork	1 2 3 4 5
Maintain seatwork accuracy at 90% level	1 2 3 4 5
Communicate the importance and reasons for seatwork	1 2 3 4 5
Relate seatwork to academic goals	1 2 3 4 5
Set and enforce standards for seatwork	1 2 3 4 5
Use tutoring and other supports to increase active responding during seatwork	1 2 3 4 5
Establish work rules	1 2 3 4 5
Review seatwork	1 2 3 4 5
Require students to correct work	1 2 3 4 5
Require students to make up missed or incomplete work	1 2 3 4 5
Give informative feedback	1 2 3 4 5

(Adapted from Englert, 1984.)

little time during the day asking when various activities, lunch, breaks, or special events are going to occur.

Gallagher suggests the following guidelines be applied when developing schedules for children and youth with behavior disorders:

1. Only work that can be finished by the end of the school day should be scheduled.
2. Students should be required to complete one task before beginning another.
3. Time reminders should be provided, via kitchen timers, verbal cues, and other signals to alert students to the schedule. As students' awareness of time increases, these reminders are phased out.
4. When tasks are completed ahead of schedule, no additional work should be assigned. Assigning additional work after the completion of an assigned task does not reinforce future task completion.
5. Establish expectations for the student in advance. Do not introduce spontaneous, unexpected activities.
6. Each student's schedule should include a combination of self- and teacher-monitoring techniques.
7. Provide positive feedback.

THE "HOW-TO" OF SCHEDULE DEVELOPMENT

Creating program and individual schedules is a challenging task. Schedule development is based on the priorities of the individuals within the group. After group priorities have been determined, the special educator must fit available time, personnel, and materials to these priorities. The step-by-step process outlined in Figure 6–2 can be applied to schedule development.

SCHEDULE FORMATS

There are various formats that can be used to design schedules responsive to the needs of children and youths with behavior disorders. Four example formats are presented in this section: the Premack principle, IEP organizer, distributed duties, and learning areas.

The most easily applied format is the schedule based on the Premack principle. This states that behavior that occurs frequently can be used as a reinforcer for less frequently occurring behaviors. This principle is also known as "Grandma's law," which says, "Eat your vegetables and you may have dessert" (Walker & Shea, 1984).

To apply this principle in a schedule, the special educator first marks each scheduled period with a positive (+) and a negative (−) sign. The plus marks denote behaviors that naturally occur at a high frequency, and the minus marks, those that do not. It is suggested that the day begin and end with positive activities. The partial schedule in Figure 6-3 demonstrates the use of the Premack principle.

Development

Step 1: Using each student's Individualized Education Plan as a data base, complete a 3 by 5 card for each goal on each IEP. On the card, write the student's name, current level of functioning on the goal, and the short-term objectives for each goal.

Step 2: Group the students by sorting the cards by levels and goals.

Step 3: Choose a schedule format (see sample formats on pp. 145–47). Reproduce the schedule format selected on a standard-size sheet of paper. In the left-hand column, write the time periods available for scheduling.

Step 4: Write the "given" activities (lunch, recess, physical education, art, music, speech therapy, and other services) on the schedule. Resource room personnel must consider the "givens" imposed on the schedule by other teachers (that is, activities in regular class and specialized instruction). Write times needed for transitions. Be sure to include the time you need, as the teacher, to record data, communicate with other teachers, and prepare materials and oneself for instruction.

Step 5: Write group activities on the schedule. Adjust group activities until there are no conflicts with other schedule activities.

Step 6: Review and discuss the proposed schedule with others serving the student—regular teachers, principal, parents, and related-services personnel.

Step 7: Remember, scheduling is a dynamic process—periodically evaluate and adjust the schedule.

FIGURE 6-2   A Step-by-Step Procedure for Schedule

Manley and Levy (1981) designed a scheduling format called the "IEP Organizer." This format is used to coordinate the IEPs of all students in a classroom, thus eliminating the need for daily lesson plans. The Organizer is a 3-by-4-foot poster board that is affixed to the chalkboard or wall of the classroom. It contains a time schedule, a brief description of each period, and two pockets (approximately four by six inches) for each period. A sample IEP Organizer schedule is depicted in Figure 6-4.

The two pockets are labeled "individual objectives" and "activities." In

FIGURE 6-3   Partial Schedule Demonstrating the Use of the Premack Principle

+	9:00	Selection of free-time activity while waiting for other students to arrive
−	9:10	Students return to seats for quiet activities during attendance, lunch count, "housekeeping activities"
+	9:15	Sharing time
−	9:35	First reading group, independent seat work
+	9:55	Drinks, transition activity to next group
−	10:00	Second reading group, independent seat work
+	10:20	Recess

FIGURE 6-4   Sample IEP Organizer

Time	Activity	Individual Objectives	Activities
9:00	Opening activities	☐	☐
9:30	Reading groups	☐	☐
10:00	Recess	☐	☐
10:15	Reading groups	☐	☐
10:45	Group meeting	☐	☐
11:05	Language development	☐	☐
11:35	Lunch	☐	☐
12:05	Outdoor play	☐	☐
12:20	Activities of daily living	☐	☐
12:50	Math groups	☐	☐
1:20	Math groups	☐	☐
1:50	Social Studies	☐	☐
2:20	Language Arts	☐	☐
2:50	Units	☐	☐
3:00	Group Activity	☐	☐

the objectives pocket, the special educator places a card on which the child's IEP objectives related to the scheduled period are written. The activities pocket contains cards on which are listed group and/or individual activities and materials responsive to the objectives.

As the special educator progresses through the school day, he or she refers to the cards in the pockets to review the students' objectives and activities that may be engaged in in response to the objectives. When a student achieves an objective, the special educator writes on the card the date on which it was completed and files it in the student's folder. The student's next short-term objective, as written in the IEP, is then inserted into the objectives pocket. If several students have a similar objective, they may be included on one card.

Manley and Levy suggested that the organizer increases teachers' awareness of the students' IEP objectives, and is, in effect, a lesson plan. The organizer facilitates continuous evaluation of students' performance. Data-collection charts can be inserted into the objectives pockets, providing even further organization for the special educator.

The distributed-duties schedule (Bauer, 1980) is especially useful for programs in which paraprofessionals, volunteers, and other personnel are available to meet the needs of students. To apply this schedule format, students are grouped homogeneously by functional level and IEP goals and objectives. Next, they are grouped into the same number of groups as there are personnel available to work with them during a particular period of the day. Each person assumes responsibility for a group's instruction during his or her available time periods. Personnel are assigned to groups on a rotating basis. A partial schedule using the distributed-duties format is presented in Figure 6-5.

	Group A			Group B			Group C	
	Jay	Mary	Luis	Tim	Tom	Lisa	Marjorie	Michael
9:00	all students — group meeting							
9:20	sight words	sight words	sight words	reading – distar		speech therapy	Basics	Concepts
9:40	number concepts	number concepts	system 80	math	math	speech therapy	personal hygiene	language master
10:00	activities of daily living		system 80	system 80	math	math	language master	personal hygiene
10:20	all students — recess							
10:40	independent work	system 80	fine motor	language master	handwriting	handwriting	reading	readiness
11:00	system 80	independent work	gross motor	fine motor	language master	independent work	fine motor	fine motor
11:20	Distar – language	Distar – language	language	language arts	language arts	system 80	number concepts	number concepts
11:40	instrumental enrichment	instrumental enrichment	independent work	independent work	system 80	self help	fine motor/gross motor	gross motor
12:00	all students — lunch							

STAFF:

	Ms. Riley	Ms. Nolan	Ms. Keith
Group A	9:00 – 11:40	12:30 – 1:30	1:30 – 3:15
Group B	1:30 – 3:15	9:00 – 12:00	12:00 – 12:30 / 12:30 – 1:30
Group C	12:30 – 1:30	1:30 – 3:15	9:00 – 12:00
Lunch	11:40 – 12:10	12:00 – 12:30	12:30 – 1:00

FIGURE 6-5 Partial Distributed-Duties Schedule

The distributed-duties format is particularly useful in programs in which the students require intensive interventions. The staff member assigned to the group is responsible for all the group's activities. For example, if students must be removed from the group, the assigned staff member removes them, or if students refuse to comply, the staff member assigned to the group is responsible for intervening.

The learning areas format is the final one discussed in this section. In this schedule, instruction in particular content areas occurs in specific locations in the classroom. For example, when studying math, students physically move to a "mathematics area," in which all materials and programs for that subject are located. Other areas may include reading, language, social studies, science, activities of daily living, and a reinforcement area. This format is particularly helpful with young children who are provided with legitimate opportunities to move about during transitions. In addition, students tend to identify specific areas of the room with specific subjects.

Another variable that must be considered when developing any schedule is the length of the activity periods. As a rule, it is more effective to begin with short activity periods and gradually lengthen them than to schedule long activity periods and risk losing students' attention and interest.

THE USE OF PARAPROFESSIONALS AND VOLUNTEERS

Paraprofessionals and volunteers can be of assistance to special educators wishing to maximize both the allocated and engaged time provided to children and youths with behavior disorders. These persons relieve the special educator from many routine but necessary tasks, freeing the teacher to plan, coordinate, and supervise instruction.

School districts typically employ paraprofessionals at two levels—teachers' assistants and teachers' aides (Greer, 1978). The teacher's assistant works under the direct supervision of a special educator, therapist, or other professional staff member. The assistant may provide direct instruction to individuals and small groups. Generally, an assistant is required to have one to two years of college. In some jurisdictions, assistants are required to meet state certification standards for substitute teachers.

The teacher's aide functions under the direct supervision of a special educator or another professional. The aide may take no independent action regarding instruction, and performs predominantly routine tasks. The duties of the assistant and aide are presented in Figure 6-6 (Greer, 1978).

OBJECTIVE TWO: *To make decisions concerning grouping students for instruction.*

Instruction is provided to students in both one-to-one and group settings. Donnellan (1984) suggests that the exclusive use of a one-to-one instructional setting encourages students to interact with a few familiar persons only and to do so in a limited number of specific settings. In addition, programs that rely predominantly on the one-to-one instructional setting generally have inordinate amounts of time during which

FIGURE 6-6 Duties of Assistants and Aides[a]

1. Reinforcing positive behavior*
2. Assisting in instructing large groups
3. Tutoring individual and small groups of children
4. Correcting homework and seat work
5. Checking standardized and informal tests
6. Observing and recording behavior*
7. Collecting materials and preparing displays, teaching centers and similar instructional activities*
8. Assisting children with makeup work as a result of absence from school or class
9. Assisting students with oral and written communication
10. Participating in reading and storytelling activities
11. Assisting with hands-on activities*
12. Assisting with fine and gross motor activities, physical development, and lifetime physical-recreational activities*
13. Providing a model with whom the children can identify*
14. Recording written materials for children who have visual or other learning disabilities*
15. Assisting children with extended-day activities
16. Helping children solve personal conflicts with other children
17. Assisting on instructional field-trip activities*
18. Assisting children with self-care activities*
19. Assisting with feeding and toileting*
20. Working with audiovisual equipment*
21. Assisting the teacher with noninstructional tasks*
22. Assisting in classroom organization and management

[a]an asterisk (*) indicates those duties suitable for teachers' aides.

(From Greer, 1978, p. 4.)

students are not engaged in meaningful activities. In order to adequately address the criterion of the least dangerous assumption, Donnellan suggests using a variety of instructional arrangements to decrease the dependence on one-to-one instruction and as a result increase the amount of time students are engaged in meaningful activities in the classroom.

Brown, Holvoet, Guess, and Mulligan (1980) proposed a decision-making model for planning group instruction. They contend that group instruction has several advantages over one-to-one instruction. First, in a small group, the special educator has increased control over the motivational variables. Materials, cues, and reinforcers provided to other students may increase the response rates and appropriate behaviors of other group members. In addition, in the group, students have opportunities to observe the appropriate behavior of others and modify their behavior accordingly. In groups, peer interaction and peer communication is enhanced. Finally, generalization is facilitated in that materials, cues, and prompts used in groups vary across time.

Three variables are involved when planning group instruction. First, the compatibility of students' needs must be determined. When the students' needs are incompatible, it is difficult to address them in a group. The second consideration is whether the skill to be taught is usually performed in a group or individually. For example, dressing and personal-hygiene skills are inappropriate for group instruction. The third variable is the student's need for training in interpersonal interaction, observation, and communication skills. More specifically, the special educator must determine if the students are capable of profiting from instruction in a group setting.

Brown and associates recommend that decisions with regard to grouping for instruction be made at three levels: structure, content, and individualization. At the structure level, the special educator must determine whether the skills to be taught are intrasequential (students are merely seated together in a group, with no systematic structuring of peer interaction) or intersequential (interactions between students serve as cues, prompts, and reinforcers for others).

At the content level, the special educator must make one of three decisions. The first content decision involves whether or not to use a group even though the students will be presented different programs with different themes. For example, in a group of three students, one child may be working on addition, another on sight words, and the third on shoe-tying. The second decision focuses on using the group to present different programs with the same theme. This is the typical structure in special education. For example, within the general theme of addition, one student may be learning basic addition facts; another, adding with counters; and a third, regrouping. The final content decision involves same program, same themes. In this group, all the students work on the same instructional objective.

The third decision making level is concerned with the individualization of instruction. When making this decision, the learning variables characteristic of the individual students are considered. These may include learning and response modes, the discreteness of task analysis required, and the materials and supports needed for learning. Students may vary in terms of verbal response; for instance; by verbalizing, pointing to pictures, writing a word. Students vary in terms of the steps of the task analysis they require to succeed. Another variable in individualization is the specific objective for instruction. Some students may be working on skill acquisition, while others are working on skill maintenance. The final consideration is individualization of materials. The kind of materials and supports required for each child may vary.

After considering these decision levels, the special educator can make a knowledgeable decision about whether or not to group students for instruction. The therapeutic uses of groups is discussed in Chapter 11. Group-management techniques are reviewed in Chapter 8.

OBJECTIVE THREE: *To arrange a physical environment responsive to students' needs.*

Special education programs are located in a variety of physical settings. Fortunately, the days of the "special room" located in the school basement, next to the boiler room, have for the most part ended. Special educators are often employed by cooperatives or joint agreements rather than by the local district, and consequently are "guests" in the school to which they are assigned. The location of special education facilities is not a high priority in most schools.

Regardless of the specific physical setting in which they must work, there are several variables that special educators can manipulate to make the environment conducive to learning. These include:

Comfort: The room should be an environment in which the students feel free to function. It should be an enjoyable place to work.

Organization: The room should be organized to facilitate both large- and small-group activities as well as individual study.

Communication: Communication among group members may be maximized by eliminating unnecessary physical barriers. With the exception of the time the students devote to individual study, they should be within the special educator's field of vision.

Movement: Learning centers should be located in the room in such a way as to minimize unplanned movement.

Privacy: Each student should be provided with a private area. Desk and locker or storage box are "private property," where students are free to store treasures and work materials. An area of the room should be provided for students who are frustrated or who have lost control over their behavior.

Unexpected visitors should be discouraged. It is distracting to both students and staff to be frequently interrupted by visitors during activities.

Size and shape: A standard-size classroom is recommended for special education. A square or rectangular room is preferable to an oddly shaped or angular room. The square or rectangular room provides structure and definite boundaries for individual and group activities.

Scale: All furnishings except those needed by the special educator and teaching assistant should be scaled to the appropriate size for students.

Color: The color of the room and its furnishings should be warm, which tends to relax the individual, rather than harsh and cold which is distracting.

Accessibility: The materials and equipment in a room are primarily for student use. Though cabinets are recommended for the storage of materials and equipment, these cabinets and the items stored in them should be readily accessible to students.

Usability: All instructional materials and equipment should be usable. Before they are purchased, all materials should be evaluated for ease of operation, safety in the hands of children, and durability. The child or youth with behavior disorders has sufficient difficulty functioning when things are going smoothly, without having to deal with poorly designed materials and equipment.

Clutter: The environment should be devoid of clutter (piles of books, papers, magazines, and records; distracting bulletin boards; and other odds and ends).

Normalization: The classroom appearance should be age-appropriate and resemble a regular education setting as closely as possible.

Though it may seem impossible to consider all these variables, an environment can be designed to meet the needs of students with behavior disorders. The following steps should be taken:

1. Determine the priorities of your students. List the areas that you will need to include in the classroom in response to student priorities. Consider one-to-one, small-group, large-group, and independent work areas.
2. Make a floor plan of the "givens" (blackboards, outlets, closets, bulletin boards, doors, windows, built-in furniture).
3. List available furniture on small cards.
4. Arrange cards on the layout to meet the priorities determined in step 1.
5. "Walk through" the layout as if you were a student. For example, for primary-school children, make sure materials needed are within easy reach.
6. Double-check for pathways and spaces needed for adaptive equipment.
7. Implement the plan, evaluate it, and reorganize it as needed.

A rating form for evaluating the instructional environment is presented in Figure 6-7. This form may be used to address the specifics of the physical environment needed by your students.

FIGURE 6-7 Self-Rating Form for Evaluation of the Instructional Environment

Rate each item, yes, no, or undecided.

	Yes	No	Undecided
Do students appear to be physically comfortable in the classroom?	___	___	___
Are there areas for one-to-one training?	___	___	___
Are there areas for small-group activities?	___	___	___
Are there areas for large-group activities?	___	___	___
Are there areas for individual work?	___	___	___
Are there physical barriers between teachers and students?	___	___	___
Are the colors in the classroom pleasant?	___	___	___
Is the decor age-appropriate?	___	___	___
Does the classroom approximate a regular environment as much as possible?	___	___	___
Are materials arranged by content area?	___	___	___
Is there "clutter" which confuses or distracts students?	___	___	___
Are there specific areas which students may use if they wish to be quiet?	___	___	___
Are there specific areas students may use to "let off steam"?	___	___	___
Are students able to begin, end, and change activities without disrupting others?	___	___	___
Do students have personal, private space?	___	___	___
Is the room clean?	___	___	___
Are the furnishings sufficiently flexible to encourage a variety of groupings?	___	___	___
Are feedback and exemplars provided in the environment? (Mirrors, handwriting samples, reinforcement menus, etc.)	___	___	___
Does the special educator have visual access to all students?	___	___	___

Are there sufficient materials and   ___ ___   ___
   equipment to minimize conflicts
   over property rights?
Is the environment periodically   ___ ___   ___
   modified in response to new
   student needs and to allay
   boredom?
Are there sufficient work areas   ___ ___   ___
   (individual study areas, small
   group, private areas) to minimize
   conflict?

OBJECTIVE FOUR: *To select appropriate instructional materials.*

Special educators are confronted with a multiplicity of instructional materials and aids, ranging from crayons to computers. Faculty lounges and schools' offices are littered with catalogs proclaiming the benefits of the latest in hardware and software.

All decisions on the selection of instructional materials should be made with regard to students' priorities. A review of each student's Individualized Education Plan enables the special educator to determine specifically what content and objectives need to be addressed by the instructional materials selected for a particular student or group of students. Students' ages and levels of functioning, as well as their individual strengths and weaknesses, are considered. In addition, the preferred learning modality, visual or auditory, is considered. In summary, students' objectives, strengths, weaknesses, ages, functional levels, and learning modalities must be given consideration in the instructional-materials selection process.

A MODEL FOR MATERIAL SELECTION

Cohen, Alberto, and Troutman (1979) suggest using an "inquiry model" when selecting instructional materials for exceptional children. The model is composed of three interrelated components: (1) input (curriculum and assessment information), (2) intervention (the educational procedures and materials), and (3) output (the objective). The model is viewed as an "instructional facilitator," linking input information to output responses. Instructional materials are selected to help the student meet his or her instructional objectives. To evaluate whether materials are appropriate for student objectives, four questions must be answered: who, why, what, and how?

Who? refers to the individual or groups the materials are designed to instruct. Materials are designed for individual or group use. If the material is designed for group use, special educators must determine if the material is primarily for use by the teacher or the student. In addition, the number of participants and group procedures to be used with the material must be determined. Prerequisite and requisite skills—that is, the developmental appropriateness of the material for students—must also be determined.

Why? refers to the purpose for which the material is being selected. Materials should be selected only if they address a concept or skill appropriate for the students. The flexibility of the materials for meeting a variety of student goals and objectives should be determined.

What? the structure of the material, is the third variable involved in materials selection. Consideration is given to the format, methodology, and construction of the material. The format may include games, worksheets, manipulatives, and media such as tapes, cassettes, slides, and filmstrips. Methodology considerations focus on whether the material utilizes inductive or deductive learning, the functional interaction of the material, and the modes of learning addressed. *What?* also focuses on whether: the material can be reproduced under copyright laws, the material is attractive and motivating, answer keys are provided, the material is self-contained or requires additional props, the material is durable, replacement parts are available. It also concerns the stimulus intensity and novelty, and what portion of the material is consumable.

The final component of the inquiry model, *How?*, concerns the way the material is used. Three variables must be assessed: management, feedback, and response mode. Management focuses on whether the material is designed to be used independently by the student or with direction from the teacher. Feedback is concerned with whether the materials are self-correcting or must be checked by a teacher. The response mode includes whether responses are oral, written, or in another form. The component generates a series of questions to be addressed by the special educator:

Is the response mode consistent with the needs and abilities of the student(s)?
Are oral responses required that may be disturbing to others?
Is a permanent product needed for record keeping?
Is the response mode motivating?
Is there variety within and between the tasks?
Is a variety of formats and response modes used to facilitate generalization?
Does the material permit fading from artificial to more natural responses?

The inquiry model enables special educators to systematically assess the materials and compare them to the needs of their students. A sample materials-evaluation form based on the foregoing discussion is presented in Figure 6-8.

FIGURE 6-8 Materials-Evaluation Form

Material _____ Copyright date _____

Publisher _____ Cost _____

Subject area _____

Number of participants _____

To guide you in the selection of instructional materials, answer the following questions yes, no, or undecided.

STUDENT CHARACTERISTICS

____ Is the material age-appropriate?

____ Is the material motivating?

____ Is the material relevant?

____ Is the format of the material appealing?

____ Does the material provide feedback?

____ Is the material free of cultural bias?

____ Are the required physical responses manageable?

INSTRUCTIONAL CHARACTERISTICS

____ Are the objectives clearly stated?

____ Are the objectives sequentially organized?

____ Are the directions for use clear?

____ Is the visual mode used for input?

____ Is the auditory mode used for input?

____ Are objects/pictures accurate representations of reality?

____ Are concrete to abstract experiences provided?

____ Do the materials instruct?

____ Do the materials provide enrichment activities?

____ Are frequent review and generalization activities provided?

____ Is transfer to a real environment encouraged?

____ Is instructor assistance required?

____ Are prerequisite skills required?

____ Does the format promote mastery learning?

____ Are mastery activities provided for instructional objectives?

PRAGMATICS

____ Are additional materials at earlier and later levels required to successfully use the material?

____ Is audiovisual equipment required?

____ Is there adequate storage for the materials?

_____ Can consumable and nonconsumable materials be bought separately?

_____ Is an instructor's manual available?

_____ Are the materials durable and reusable?

_____ Are replacement parts available?

_____ Is the time needed to prepare the material for use justifiable in light of the benefit to the student?

_____ Are research reports available to support the effectiveness of the material?

_____ Will the material require modification for application with my students?

_____ Is the cost justifiable?

THE MICROCOMPUTER

Microcomputers and their accompanying instructional software are currently very popular in educational circles. District policies on computer use in special education range from permissive to mandatory. Clements (1985) encouraged educators to apply the following principles to guide microcomputer use with children and youth with behavior disorders.

1. There are situations in which computers can and should be used, especially when use is consistent with student goals and objectives. There are also situations in which computers *should not* be used; this is especially true when they are used to replace the active learning or social experiences needed by students. Computers *should never* be used simply as a means of keeping students busy, as time fillers, or as electronic flash-card holders.

2. The computer is used appropriately when it motivates students to engage in active learning with some control over their educational environment.

3. By means of both experiential and drill activities, microcomputer programming can be beneficial by facilitating the practice of higher-level experiences.

4. Student preference and pleasure should not be the sole basis for curriculum selection. The computer does not exist to "make learning fun."

5. The student's developmental level must be used as a guideline for computer application. Some students simply cannot profit from computer use.

6. Students should be provided with a wide variety of computer programming, ranging from basic skills development to enrichment, and including reinforcement.

7. Computer activities should be an integral part of the overall curriculum.

8. Computers should be used meaningfully to facilitate cognitive, social, affective, and creative growth.

9. Computer use should be consistent with the student's educational program.

10. The computer is a tool. Learning with computer assistance must be viewed as a means of achieving instructional objectives, not an end in itself.

11. The educator's attitude toward, understanding of, and skill with, computers are crucial to successful computer use in the classroom.

These principles, taken as a whole, cast the computer into its most appropriate and effective role in the education of children and youth with behavior disorders; that is, as a potentially superior instructional material.

Pantiel and Petersen (1984) suggest that there are two general patterns for microcomputer application in the classroom: "computers teaching kids" and "kids teaching computers." In computer-assisted instruction, or "computers teaching kids," three activities are appropriate. Students may use computers for drill and practice activities, which require specific responses to specific questions. Tutorials, a second activity, may be used both to introduce new materials and to reinforce previously learned material. The third activity, simulations, is used in the same way educators enact or role-play in the classroom, except that they are presented via computer.

When "kids teach computers," Pantiel and Petersen suggest two activities: teaching students to program and teaching word-processing. Logo is the most popular computer language taught to students at the elementary-school level. BASIC is the language most frequently taught in middle, junior high, and senior high schools. Word-processing programs refine students' typing, revising, storing, retrieving, and printing skills.

Special educators rarely have a choice of the computer hardware available to students. However, software selection is frequently part of the special educator's responsibility. With the variety and multiplicity of software systems on the market, the selection of appropriate software is a difficult task. Clements (1985) offers step-by-step guidelines for the special educator unfamiliar with the instructional use of microcomputers yet responsible for selecting software:

1. Determine the exact goals the program is to address.
2. Review journals and catalogs to locate an appropriate program. Review what is available in the school district.
3. Determine what instructional and technical assistance is made available on the program from the company selling it.
4. Order the program for evaluation. Request copies of all available documentation regarding program use and effectiveness.
5. Obtain the program on approval, if possible. If the program cannot be obtained for evaluation, request demonstration disks or tapes. When the program is available for evaluation:
   a. Work through the program as a successful student, testing the program for innovative responses.
   b. Work through the program as a more "active" student; that is, make mistakes by typing numbers rather than words, hit several keys simultaneously, press the "reset" or "escape" keys, and so on.
   c. Observe and evaluate the performance of students similar to yours using the program.
6. Complete a software evaluation checklist such as that presented in Figure 6-9.

FIGURE 6-9 Software Evaluation Checklist

Name _____

Hardware required _____

    Brand _____

    Memory _____

    Number of disk drives required _____

Is a backup disk provided? _____

Can the disk be copied for backup? _____

Cost _____

Curriculum area _____

Objectives _____

Prerequisite skills _____

Number of students _____

Average time of interaction _____

Answer each of the following questions yes (Y), no (N), or undecided (U).

CONTENT

____ Is the content appropriate to the student's
      curriculum?

____ Are the objectives clearly defined?

____ Are learning activities well designed?

____ Can the program be adapted?

____ Does the student control the rate and sequence?

____ Is appropriate feedback provided?

____ Are graphics and sound appropriate?

PERFORMANCE

____ Is the program easy to use?

____ Are instructions clear?

____ Is input appropriate?

____ Are directions, menus, and on-line help available?

____ Is the program "bug free"?

____ Can students correct mistakes?

____ Does it load quickly?

(Adapted from Clements, 1985.)

OBJECTIVE FIVE: *To adapt instructional materials to the needs of individual students.*

As special educators evaluate and select instructional materials, they become aware of the failures of many materials to respond to the unique needs of children and youth with behavior disorders. On occasion, even the "best" instructional materials must be adapted to respond to the specific unique needs of students. Lambie (1980) offers seven guidelines for adapting materials in response to student needs:

1. Only adapt materials when there is a mismatch between the student's need and the material. Do not assume materials need to be adapted until you have tried them.
2. Keep changes simple. If a particular material requires several complex adaptations, it may be inappropriate for use. A teacher made material may be more appropriate.
3. Evaluate any changes you make in the material. Are they really necessary?
4. Minimize the time required to change materials. Attempt to adapt materials so that they meet the needs of several students.
5. Make sure any supplementary materials generated as a consequence of adaptations are consistent with the original material.
6. Be aware of the strengths and weaknesses of the materials which you are using.
7. Be aware of the student's characteristics.

In the process of selecting and applying instructional materials, there are several variables over which the special educator has direct control (Goodman, 1978). The decision to select the material is frequently made by the special educator, who is also able to control the amount of the material presented to the student at any given time and the complexity of the language used to present it. In addition, the special educator can usually vary the sequence of the material's presentation. Presentation and response modes can be adapted. For example, materials may be taped rather than presented in print, or responses may be oral rather than written. Finally, the special educator may choose to develop learning aids to supplement the material, such as reading or study guides.

Mandell and Gold (1984) suggest several techniques for adapting materials to individual students' needs. These are (1) rewrite materials, (2) prepare study guides, (3) adapt response modes (4) use old materials to supplement or augment new ones (5) modify the presentation format, (6) tape materials, (7) paraphrase directions, and (8) teach strategies specific to the appropriate use of the materials.

Rewrite materials.   A method of adapting materials that is frequently employed by resource room teachers is to rewrite those used by students in the regular education classroom. This may be necessary in some content areas, such as history, when equivalent materials at appropriate reading levels are not available. However, rewriting is a time-consuming process and should be undertaken only when absolutely necessary.

Prepare study guides.   Students may be able to use grade-level materials successfully if provided with a study guide that defines the key terms and outlines the basic concepts. Dexter (1980) suggests using learning-activity packets to help teach specific topics. When developing an activity packet, she suggests that the teacher first task-analyze the instructional objective. Each packet should include a pretest, an introductory section including key terms and an outline of the basic concepts, objectives, directions, appropriate activities, and a posttest. Activities must be sufficiently flexible to respond to the needs of several students. Materials that are self-correcting reduce both the potential for student errors and the time the special educator must devote to supervision (Kohlfeldt, 1976).

Adapt response modes.   Materials vary in terms of the response modes required. Some children and youth with behavior disorders may be unable to respond adequately, as required by the original materials. Consequently, response modes may need to be changed—for example, from a written form to audio tapes.

Use old materials to supplement or augment new ones.   Old texts and workbooks may be used to build a file of practice materials. If they are sorted by instructional objective, students will have available to them a file of materials to augment the original ones.

Modify the presentation format.   Modifying the format of materials may allow students to use them independently. Reducing the number of tasks on a page may sufficiently reduce the distraction inherent in the material to permit a student to complete them successfully. Presenting only part of the material at a time may allow the student to complete it successfully. When instructing with manipulatives such as cuisinaire rods, presenting only a few rods at one time may facilitate student success, whereas distributing full sets of rods may limit success by causing frustration, confusion, and disruption.

Tape materials.   Taped lessons can be used to help students who have reading difficulties. Tapes can also be used to provide information to supplement lessons.

Deschler and Graham (1980) discuss several variables that should be considered when taping materials for exceptional learners. First, consideration should be given to what materials can be usefully taped. Taping an entire textbook or chapter is generally not desirable, because it is so time-consuming and because students with behavior disorders frequently have limited attention spans. The student's regular teacher should be consulted with regard to the specific content of tapes. The special educator may wish to tape material to demonstrate various skills such as differentiating between main and supportive materials within a chapter, using illustrations, and outlining main ideas.

The learning principles applied to developing tapes are similar to those used in other instructional material. Tapes must be logically organized and contain a variety of activities. They must cue the student to important points and include questions designed to facilitate higher-level reasoning. Key terms, concepts, and ideas should be included in the tape for review and practice. Finally, tapes must provide immediate and delayed feedback.

Deschler and Graham encourage using a marking system in original written materials that correlate with the taped material. As the tape is prepared, the special educator codes the written material that will correspond to it. Deschler and Graham suggest a wavy line (~) for paraphrased material, a broken line (---) for material that is omitted, and an asterisk (*) to cue the student to stop the tape to complete an activity.

Paraphrase directions.   To use some materials effectively, a student may only need alternative directions. These may be a simplified translation of the original directions.

Teach strategies specific to the use of the materials.   The special educator may find it necessary to instruct students in the correct use of a specific material. For example, a student must be taught to use a microcomputer before he or she can use it for instructional purposes. Students may need to learn as sight words those terms found in written directions before they can understand the directions and profitably engage in learning the content of the material. Underlining or prompts incorporated into directions may help the student to complete a task successfully.

TEACHER-MADE MATERIALS

At times, no amount of adaptation will allow a student to use some instructional materials successfully. Consequently, special educators find it necessary to make materials to respond to the needs of individual students. Kohlfeldt (1976) suggests several guidelines for the construction of worksheets, games, task cards, tapes, and other instructional materials. First, materials should be flexible and multifunctional. Special educators do not have the time or resources to prepare complex materials that will be used only once or twice by a few children. Second, teacher-made materials should be open to simple adaptations, to increase its use. Third, all teacher-made materials should be of high interest. Fourth, materials should be self-correcting, to save teachers' time and to prevent the students from practicing errors. Finally, Kohlfeldt suggests involving students in materials production.

Though teacher-designed instructional games are frequently used in classrooms for children and youth with behavior disorders, Thiagarajan (1976) warns that such games can overstimulate students and create competition and peer pressure. The actual transfer of the skills practiced in games has not been documented in research. Thiagarajan offers several suggestions for developing games. The materials and equipment should be self-contained and allow for self-checking to reduce the need for supervision. Game materials should be attractive, colorful, and locally and personally relevant. Games should be brief in duration, and the rules should be simple and unembellished. When a game approach to instruction is implemented, several short, simple games are preferable to a single, complex one.

SUMMARY

In this chapter, several essential noninstructional tasks in which special educators must be proficient are discussed. These include constructing effective instructional schedules, arranging the physical classroom environment, and selecting and adapting instructional materials to meet the special needs of children and youths with behavior disorders.

REVIEW QUESTIONS

1. Contrast the meanings of allocated time and engaged time. Are they usually equivalent during the school day? What are some variables that can be manipulated to increase engaged time?
2. Describe the strategies a special educator may apply to increase the efficiency of activity transitions.
3. Gallagher (1979) contends that schedules continually evolve; that is, the schedule for the first part of the school year will differ significantly from schedules used later in the year. Do you agree? Disagree? How does this concept impact on your tasks as a special educator for children and youth with behavior disorders?
4. What is the Premack principle? How would you apply this principle to scheduling for children and youth with behavior disorders?
5. What duties or tasks would you assign to a paraprofessional? Which ones would you share with the paraprofessional? Which are your responsibilities as a teacher?

6. What are some of the advantages of grouping for instruction? When is grouping inappropriate?
7. Describe several variables to be considered when arranging the physical environment in a classroom for children and youth with behavior disorders.
8. Describe the "inquiry model" for materials selection.
9. Review Clements's (1985) principles for the application of microcomputers for instruction. Do you agree with these principles? Disagree? Why?
10. Discuss the following statements: The software selection process does not differ substantially from the process applied for selection of other instructional materials. The decision about whether or not to use the microcomputer does not differ substantially from that regarding the use of other instructional materials.
11. Review the seven techniques special educators may use in adapting materials. Give an example of each.
12. What are the advantages of teacher-made materials? The disadvantages?

APPLICATION ACTIVITIES

Activity One—Making a Schedule

To complete this activity, you must read and study the student descriptions in Appendix B on pp. 358–63. You will need to have available several 3-by-5 cards and 8½-by-11-inch sheets of paper.

Review the descriptions of the students in the elementary school resource room for children with behavior disorders presented in Appendix B. By completing the following steps, develop an initial schedule to address the needs of these students.

STEP 1:   Using each student's Individualized Education Plan as a data base, complete a three-by-five card for each goal on each IEP. On the card, write the student's name, current level of functioning on the goal, and the short-term objectives for each goal.

STEP 2:   Group the students by sorting the cards by levels and goals.

STEP 3:   Choose a schedule format (see the sample formats on pp. 144–48. On a standard-size sheet of paper, reproduce the schedule format selected. In the left-hand column, write the time periods available for scheduling.

STEP 4:   Write the "given" activities (lunch, recess, physical education, art, music, speech therapy, and other services) on the schedule. Resource-room personnel must consider the "givens" imposed on the schedule by other teachers (such as activities in regular class and specialized instruction). Write times needed for transitions. Be sure to include the time you need, as the teacher, to record data, communicate with other teachers, and prepare materials and yourself for instruction.

STEP 5: Write group activities on the schedule. Adjust group activities until there are no conflicts with other scheduled activities.

STEP 6: Review and discuss the proposed schedule with others serving the student: regular teachers, principal, parents, and related-services personnel. Evaluate the potential effectiveness of your schedule by responding to the following questions:

1. Does the schedule provide for transition time?
2. Is the Premack principle applied?
3. Is time allotted for recording data, communicating with other personnel, and preparation of materials?
4. Are all areas addressed for each child?

Activity Two—Arranging the Physical Environment

Review the description in Appendix B of students assigned to the primary self-contained classroom for children and youth with behavior disorders. Using the floor plan depicted here, design a classroom made to respond to the students' instructional needs. Write in the furniture or large materials that you would use.

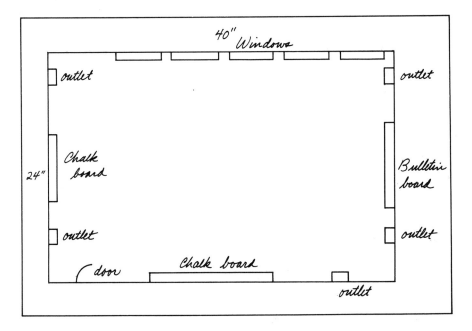

Activity Three—Evaluating Materials

Using one of the students described in Appendix B, select and evaluate one item of instructional material that may be used with that student. Complete the following materials evaluation form.

Material _____ Copyright date _____

Publisher _____ Cost _____

Subject area _____

Number of participants _____

To guide you in the selection of instructional materials, answer the following questions yes, no, or undecided.

STUDENT CHARACTERISTICS

____ Is the material age-appropriate?

____ Is the material motivating?

____ Is the material relevant?

____ Is the format of the material appealing?

____ Does the material provide feedback?

____ Is the material free of cultural bias?

____ Are the required physical responses manageable?

INSTRUCTIONAL CHARACTERISTICS

____ Are the objectives clearly stated?

____ Are the objectives sequentially organized?

____ Are the directions for use clear?

____ Is the visual mode used for input?

____ Is the auditory mode used for input?

____ Are objects/pictures accurate representations of reality?

____ Are concrete to abstract experiences provided?

____ Do the materials instruct?

____ Do the materials provide enrichment activities?

____ Are frequent review and generalization activities provided?

____ Is transfer to a real environment encouraged?

____ Is instructor assistance required?

____ Are prerequisite skills required?

____ Does the format promote mastery learning?

____ Are mastery activities provided for instructional objectives?

PRAGMATICS

_____ Are additional materials at earlier and later levels required to successfully use the material?

_____ Is audiovisual equipment required?

_____ Is there adequate storage for the materials?

_____ Can consumable and nonconsumable materials be bought separately?

_____ Is an instructor's manual available?

_____ Are the materials durable and reusable?

_____ Are replacement parts available?

_____ Is the time needed to prepare the material for use justifiable in light of the benefit to the student?

_____ Are research reports available to support the effectiveness of the material?

_____ Will the material require modification for application with my students?

_____ Is the cost justifiable?

7

Teaching Models

"To teach is to touch someone else's life in progress. To be a teacher is to share human hopes and disappointments with another being" (Yamamoto, 1969, p. viii). Teaching children and youth with behavior disorders is the process of guiding, helping, and supporting them in their efforts to realize their potential and function effectively in the community. Special educators teach so that children or youth with behavior disorders may learn to accept themselves and others and become acceptable to and accepted by others.

This chapter is primarily a selective review of teaching models applied to instruct exceptional children. The models are presented to familiarize the special educator with various methodologies that may be used to teach children and youth with behavior disorders. In addition, an ecological framework for the selection and application of a teaching strategy is presented.

OBJECTIVES

After completing this chapter, you will be able to—

1. describe the impact of a teaching model on the instructional process;
2. differentiate between psychodynamic, biophysical, behavioral, and ecological teaching models;

3. describe an ecological framework for the selection of teaching models for application with children and youths with behavior disorders.

A CASE FOR CONSIDERATION

Ms. Wall dreaded the arrival of the morning buses. Mr. Peden, the principal, had asked her to substitute, and she had agreed to do so before finding out what class she would be assigned to teach. As she walked into the office, the fourth-grade teacher laughed, and said, "Think you'll make it through the whole day in 'that' room?"

The secretary interjected, "Don't worry, Ms. Wall. If you need help, page the office. Mr. Peden and the custodian will come right down."

"What do you mean? What kind of help should I need?" asked Ms. Wall.

"Oh, they get a little rowdy in there sometimes," replied the secretary.

After these comments, Ms. Wall wondered about her decision to accept the day's work substituting in the room for students with behavior disorders.

"You'd better hurry down to the bus—two of your kids are already at each other," said the third-grade teacher as he passed her in the hall. Ms. Wall went down to the bus circle, and found two students assigned to "that" room being physically removed from the bus by the principal. One child's nose was bleeding; the other had scratches on his arms.

Mr. Peden said, "I'm taking these two to the nurse. When she's finished with them, they'll be sent to the room. All I ask is that you keep them in there for the day."

When she arrived in the classroom, Ms. Wall found the record player on, two students dancing, a third rummaging through the teacher's desk, and four others lounging about the room, looking at magazines, or drawing at their desks. She walked over to the record player and turned it off. One of the dancers came over and turned it back on. "Keep it off. It's time for class," Ms. Wall said. "Make me," replied the student. "Okay," replied Ms. Wall, "you can listen to it for a few minutes."

Next, she approached the child going through the teacher's desk. "Does the teacher allow you to look in his desk?" Ms. Wall asked. The young girl stopped, looked at her, and said, "Who's asking?" Ms. Wall said that Mr. Polaski was ill and she was the substitute. The girl listened, paused, then said, "Well, get me a pencil." Ms. Wall took a pencil from the drawer and gave it to the student.

Standing behind the desk, Ms. Wall said in her "firm but friendly teacher" voice: "Okay, everybody, in your seats. I'll find a schedule and we'll get started."

"It's free time," replied one of the students who was drawing. The other students continued their current activities.

"Everybody sit down," Ms. Wall repeated. The two students who were dancing began tugging at each other. "Turn that off and sit down," Ms. Wall said, moving toward the record player. The "dance" became a wrestling match. As the students fell to the floor, the "rummaging" student returned to the teacher's desk, and the two bus combatants arrived in the room, accompanied by the nurse. "Ask Mr. Peden to come up here," Ms. Wall whispered to the nurse. "I'm desperate."

In this case, Ms. Wall entered the classroom unaware of the strategies applied in the teaching and management of children and youth with behavior disorders. Her normal "teacher behaviors" were entirely ineffective for the students in this class.

OBJECTIVE ONE: *To describe the impact of teaching models on the instructional process.*

A teaching model is essentially a plan or framework that is used by the special educator to shape the curriculum, the selection of materials, and to guide instruction (Joyce & Weil, 1980). Joyce and Weil assert that the forms of "good teaching" are many, and that "the evidence to date gives little encouragement to those who would hope that we have identified a single, reliable, multipurpose teaching strategy as the best approach" (p. 8). They make several assumptions about the available teaching models. These are:

1. There are many alternative approaches to teaching.
2. The available models are sufficiently different to impact on the outcomes that result from their use; that is, methods make a difference in terms of what is learned as well as how it is learned.
3. Students react differently to different teaching models, and no two people react in exactly the same way to any particular teaching model.

   The task of the school and the teacher is to equip themselves with a basic variety of teaching models that they can bring into play for different purposes, employ and adapt for different learners, and combine artfully to create classrooms and learning centers of variety and depth (Joyce & Weil, p. 462).

A specific teaching model will emphasize various dimensions of the teaching-learning process. For example, a teaching model based in psycho-dynamic-psychoeducational theory tends to emphasize the child's search for meaning and personal growth, whereas a model based in behavioral theory emphasizes training the child to respond appropriately to specific environmental stimuli. Models differ in terms of the emphasis placed on the personal, social, intellectual, or physical dimensions of the learner and environment. Experiencing a specific model affects the individual in terms of skills, knowledge, and attitudes.

OBJECTIVE TWO: *To differentiate between several psychodynamic, biophysical, behavioral, and ecological teaching models.*

In this section, teaching models are presented from each of the major theoretical perspectives on children and youths with behavior disorders, discussed in Chapter 1: psychodynamic, biophysical, behavioral, and ecological. After studying this selective and limited review, and the pertinent sections of Chapter 1, the student will have the information needed to develop personal teaching models that can be implemented with children and youth with behavior disorders. In all probability, the models the reader develops for implementation will be a synthesis of the best features of those presented here.

PSYCHODYNAMIC MODELS

Two teaching models based in psychodynamic theory are presented in this section: the traditional clinical teaching model described by Berkowitz and Rothman (1960, 1967) and the self-concept model of Purkey and Novak (1984).

Clinical Teaching

Clinical teaching is described by Berkowitz and Rothman as

rooted in the conviction that the children, adolescents, and young adults who are in psychiatric institutions, prisons and treatment centers, or in special classes and special schools are there because they are distressed, disturbed, and in need of treatment. In addition to any psychiatric, psychological or medical services, school and learning are extremely important aspects of the total treatment program available to them. For these youngsters, the process of therapy, and the place of learning, namely the school, become concurrently a place for treatment.*

Clinical teaching procedures are concerned with three major variables: (1) an emotionally disturbed individual, (2) a clinical teacher, and (3) a special education treatment milieu. In clinical teaching, the teacher is not considered to be a psychoanalyst or psychotherapist; that is, a professional who interprets the child's behavior and offers the child opportunities to gain insight into his or her problems. Rather, the clinical teacher is an activist who interacts with children or young people at the ego level, help-

---

*From P.H. Berkowitz & E.P. Rothman (eds.), *Public Education for Disturbed Children in New York City* (Springfield, IL: Charles C. Thomas, 1967), p. 327. Courtesy of Charles C. Thomas, publisher.

ing them live through each hour, each day, each problem, and each crisis as it occurs.

The teacher's behavior toward the child is based on "need-acceptance." Emphasis is placed on the establishment of a positive, and therefore productive, relationship between the child and the teacher. The necessity for establishing such a child-teacher relationship is based in the child's need to learn to accept both the teacher and the educational setting as a prerequisite for successful rehabilitation or reeducation. If the desired relationship is to occur, the teacher must accept the child along with his or her inappropriate behaviors from the first moment of his or her first day in the classroom (Berkowitz & Rothman, 1960).

As an ego-building process, clinical teaching is dependent on experiences that foster the child's individuality, security, and self-respect. It holds, as its prime objective, not the teaching of academic and preacademic skills but the utilization of the child's potential and the resolution of emotional conflicts to facilitate adjustment. The implications for classroom design and operation are many.

> Neither the school nor the teacher should impose arbitrary standards. It is quite common to hear, in reference to educational planning for disturbed children, statements such as: "They *have* to learn to read," "They *have* to learn to write," "They *have* to learn what the group is doing." The teacher's knowing what a child must learn is of little value until the child himself is convinced; moreover, once he recognizes this, he must be emotionally mature enough and his impulses must be controlled enough to permit him to benefit from his convictions.
>
> Clinical teaching cannot be based on "have to." It must be concerned with "how to." How can the emotionally damaged child develop a feeling of well-being, a sense of achievement, and confidence in his ability to stand on his own feet? How can he learn to release his tensions and externalize his anxieties in a socially acceptable manner? (Berkowitz & Rothman, 1967, p. 332-33)

The clinical teacher must not only be accepting of the child and his or her manifest behavior; the teacher must also have an understanding of the forces that motivate that behavior. Thus, observing, analyzing, and interpreting the child's behavior is crucial to successful clinical teaching.

Need-acceptance in the classroom is not synonymous with permissiveness. The behavior of the disturbed child must be controlled and limited. This is true of all children and youth, exceptional and nonexceptional. The disturbed child is not allowed to engage in self-defeating and self-injurious behaviors. Nor is the child allowed to engage in behaviors that are harmful to classmates or teachers. In the classroom, the child learns to accept external control of his or her behavior as the initial step in learning self-control. In the therapeutic classroom, unlike many regular classrooms, all of the rules and regulations that the child is to follow are meaningful in terms of the treatment process. Limitations are never arbitrarily set on a child's behavior. Punishment, if used, is benign and a natural consequence of the child's rule violation.

The program should be sufficiently permissive and flexible

> to ensure that each child is reached on his own level of development. The classroom should present a picture of diverse activities in which the disturbed child can work on his own projects, academic or nonacademic, secure in the knowledge that what he is doing is looked upon with approval and is of value to himself and to the group. The function of the teacher is to provide experiences which the child can meet with growing confidence and success (Berkowitz & Rothman, 1960, p. 118).

Reading, writing, and arithmetic are the core of the disturbed child's academic program. As the child gains skill in these basic subjects, other activities—such as science, social studies, and physical education—are added to the educational program. The child's academic program is conducted in response to the individual's needs. Group work is introduced into the classroom program when feasible from both the behavioral and academic perspectives.

The creative arts are strongly emphasized in clinical teaching. The arts are viewed as a basic component of education for personal social-emotional adjustment. The arts allow the child to externalize emotions in conflict-free activities directed toward individual goals.

During the clinical teaching process, the teacher may choose to be manipulated by the child into assuming various roles. The role the teacher assumes in the relationship with a child at a specific point in the therapeutic process is largely determined by the child's emotional needs at that time.

Self-Concept Model

Invitational education, the self-concept model of teaching, is based on the assumptions that (a) people are able and valuable, (b) teaching is a cooperative activity, and (c) people possess relatively untapped potential that can best be realized through an invitation to develop it by persons who are personally and professionally inviting to others (Purkey & Novak, 1984).

Invitational education is based in the theory that behavior is a product of how people perceive themselves and the situations in which they are involved (Combs, Avila, & Purkey, 1978). Personal perceptions help individuals organize and make sense of their world. The most important perception, in this teaching model, is self-perception or self-concept, which is the view of who we are and how we fit into the world. Self-concept is viewed as a learned, complex system of subjective beliefs about self, which guides the direction of behavior. To apply the invitational teaching model, a special educator blends personal perception, stance, and behavior into teaching practice.

Special educator perception.   Purkey and Novak maintain that the success or failure of a class is likely to result from the teacher's perceptions. The inviting teachers perceive students as able and valuable. Students are seen as being able to make responsible choices. In addition, inviting teachers view themselves and education positively.

Special educator stance.   The inviting stance is intentional (involving commitment and conviction), respectful of students, direct (involving coming together with others in mutually beneficial ways), and responsible.

Special educator behavior.   Once the special educator's stance is established, behaviors are exhibited as a product of that stance. The inviting teacher must invite, yet must ask oneself: "Is this the most appropriate action I can take with this person at this time?" (Purkey & Novak, 1984, p. 48). Concurrent with inviting is accepting, which involves a willingness to risk.

The purpose of invitational education is to help the special educator become a beneficial presence in the lives of students. By applying a positive, perceptual approach, students' successful educational experiences are felt to enhance their coping skills.

Although the clinical teaching and invitational models are based on psychodynamic theory, they contrast sharply. Berkowitz and Rothman view the student as "sick," having a problem that must be cured. Purkey and Novak view the child as a capable and responsible individual who will learn by invitation. These models demonstrate that within a single theoretical perspective, there is great variation.

BIOPHYSICAL PERSPECTIVE

The biophysical teaching models, discussed next, are the traditional environmental-control strategy (Cruickshank, 1967; Strauss & Lehtinen, 1947) (Cruickshank, Bentzen, Ratzeburg, & Tannhauser, 1961) and the mediated learning strategy (Harth, 1982).

Environmental Control

Strauss and Lehtinen's work with brain-injured children was derived from early work with the mentally retarded by Itard and Sequin. Strauss and Lehtinen studied brain-injured children, who were characterized by hyperactivity, impulsivity, emotional liability, short attention span, and distractibility.

In an educational setting, these behaviors interfere with the learning of the child and his or her peers, who are frequently disturbed and distracted by the brain-injured child's unusual behavior. Strauss and Lehtinen posited that brain damage itself could not be treated; consequently, they designed a controlled environment in which the child was to be trained. In this environment, the undamaged portion of the child's brain would be trained to substitute or compensate for its injured portion or portions.

Among the educational provisions recommended by Strauss and Lehtinen for the classroom instruction of brain-injured children are (1) elimination or reduction of extraneous sights and sounds, (2) sparsely furnished, spacious classrooms, (3) desks facing the wall, with partitions between them, (4) the masking or shading of printed matter so that the child can view or attend only to the needed portion, (5) the directing of motor activity into productive channels, and (6) the logical sequencing of learning tasks.

To a considerable extent, the work of Cruickshank and his associates (1961) is an extension, expansion, and application of the premises suggested by Strauss and Lehtinen. The controlled educational environment recommended for brain-injured children by Cruickshank and associates included a structured program with reduced space and environmental stimuli, concurrent with an increase in the stimulus values of the teaching materials.

This educational environment was recommended by Cruickshank (1967) for children with the following characteristics: sensory hyperactivity, motor hyperactivity, dissociation (an inability to distinguish the whole, or Gestalt, relative to the parts), figure-ground reversals, perseveration, and motor immaturity.

Mediated Learning

Mediated learning was developed by Feuerstein (1980) to remediate the cognitive deficits of exceptional students. In his discussion of mediated learning, Harth (1982) contends that the development of cognitive structures in an individual is a function of the organism interacting with the environment. Organismic-environmental interactions leading to learning occur in two ways. First, beginning in early life, there is a direct exposure to sources of stimuli that impact on the organism. Second, an individual engages in mediated learning experiences, in which a mediating agent (or agents) transforms stimuli for the individual. The agent may be a parent, sibling, teacher, or care-giver.

In the mediation process, the child acquires behavior patterns and learning sets that allow him or her to learn by direct exposure to stimuli. With mediation, individuals are able to frame, filter, and schedule direct stimuli themselves.

Feuerstein's theory is unique to the biophysical perspective. The case of the child's ineffective or inappropriate behavior is not seen as the etiology of the problem itself (heredity, organic dysfunctions). Rather, the cause of the child's poor performance is considered an organic problem triggered by a lack of mediated learning experiences that is directly responsible for the cognitive deficit. This lack of mediated learning experience suggests that the child's environment has not been mediated in such a way that he or she can be modified by direct exposure to stimuli. The handicaps that result from a lack of mediated learning experience are presented in Figure 7-1.

FIGURE 7-1   Cognitive Deficits Resulting from a Lack of Mediated Learning Experiences

Deficits at the input level

Blurred and sweeping perceptions; generalizations
Unsystematic and impulsive exploratory behavior
Impaired discrimination
Impaired spatial orientation
Impaired temporal concepts
Impaired conservation; perceptual inconstancy
Imprecise data gathering
Inability to consider two or more sources of information simultaneously

Deficits at the elaboration level

Inability to perceive and define problems
Inability to discriminate relevant and nonrelevant information
Impaired comparative behavior
Narrow mental field
Impaired need for logical evidence
Impaired inferential-hypothetical thinking
Impaired strategies for hypothesis testing
Impaired cognitive elaboration skills

Deficits at the output level

Egocentric communication
Impaired ability to express relationships
Impulsive, guessing responses
Impaired ability to communicate elaborate responses
Acting-out behavior

(Adapted from Harth, 1982.)

Feuerstein's (1980) curriculum, Instrumental Enrichment, is designed to enhance the cognitive structure of the individual by changing his or her cognitive style from that of a dependent to an independent thinker. The teacher uses a "Learning Potential Assessment Device" in a test-teach-retest pattern to develop cognitive functions. The Instrumental Enrichment approach includes five strategies:

1. Regulation of behavior through inhibition and control of impulsivity, in which the teacher uses a time-lapse procedure and cue words such as "stop, think, and listen" to inhibit impulsive responding.
2. Improvement of deficient cognitive functions through the actual teaching of planning and problem-solving skills.
3. Enrichment of the repertoire of mental operations, in which analogies, categorizations, progressions, and seriations are practiced in a structured way.
4. Enrichment of the task-related contentual repertoire, in which specific concepts such as orientation, relationships, and labels are taught and practiced.
5. Creation of reflective, insightful thought processes, in which the individual is urged to reflect on responses and become aware of personal problem-solving behavior.

In mediated learning, teaching is an intentional act, in which the teacher actively points out concepts, sequences, and strategies so that the student becomes aware of the learning process. In addition to teaching individual skills, the teacher implements strategies that transcend the task at hand. Generalization and transfer of learning are stressed. Another characteristic of the Instrumental Enrichment method is the teaching of meaning. Performance on a task is in response to a need, and, as a result, the teacher must create and reinforce the need to perform the task.

Harth suggests that the mediated-learning approach offers possibilities for enhancing the cognitive skills of exceptional learners.

BEHAVIORAL MODELS

The behavior modification model for application with children and youth with behavior disorders is described in detail in Chapter 10. Readers are urged to study the information in that chapter when developing a behavior modification program for classroom use. In this section, the use of behavior modification as a teaching model is discussed.

Homme, Csanyi, Gonzales, and Rechs (1970) proposed contingency contracting as a teaching model to facilitate student learning. To use contingency contracting as an effective teaching model, the teacher makes an agreement with the student whereby rewards are given in return for performing specified work or behavior.

Contracts state: "If you do *x*, then you may do [or get] *y*." In the contract, the amount of work required is specified, the amount of reinforcement is specified, and a time line is agreed upon.

As with all behavioral models, the goal of contingency contracting is self-management. In order to assist students in developing self-management, Homme and associates describe a progression from teacher-controlled to student-controlled contracts. These include teacher control, partial control by the student, equal control by teacher and student, partial control by the teacher, and student-controlled contracts.

In order to implement contingency contracting, Homme and associates suggest a reinforcement area in each classroom. The student's use of this area is stipulated in the contract. Time in the area is monitored by a sign-in/sign-out sheet, with a time clock, or in some other similar manner. Students may be oriented to the program either individually or in a group. Through careful orientation, students are acquainted with the reinforcement area, the menu of available reinforcers, and the nature of contracts.

Contingency contracting has been effectively applied with students by parents and teachers (Bailey, Wolf, & Phillips, 1970; Cantrell, Cantrell, Huddleston, & Woolridge, 1969; Karraker, 1972).

ECOLOGICAL MODELS

The ecological or environmental teaching models of Haring and Phillips (1962) and Hardin (1978) are described in this section.

Haring and Phillips's Thesis

In 1962, Haring and Phillips published the results of a research experiment in the education of emotionally disturbed elementary school children. They researched the effectiveness of a structured classroom environment on disturbed children by contrasting it with two other classroom environments.

The basis of Haring and Phillips's thesis is that children with behavior disorders require specialized environment in order to "recover" and move toward normalization. Two features of their experiment that appear to have had considerable impact on the education of the emotionally disturbed are (1) a shift in treatment focus from the cause of the child's problem to the direct modification of observable behavior and functional abilities and (2) an emphasis on the classroom or learning processes as a form of therapy. They assumed that strategies that enable children to function appropriately in the classroom and make educational progress facilitate their social and emotional adjustment.

The classroom environment recommended by Haring and Phillips is characterized by a reduction of extraneous auditory and visual stimuli, unnecessary physical activities, and group participation. The control exercised over these variables is decreased over time as the child adjusts to the program, develops self-control, and prepares for integration into the regular class.

Although they recognize that the success of any teaching model is greatly dependent on the motivation, interest, and skill of the teacher, Haring and Phillips offer the following guidelines for teaching:

1. Limit subject-matter dilution.
2. Subject matter should focus on concrete rather than abstract concepts.
3. Teaching should begin at the developmental stage at which the child is functioning.
4. The child should be provided with immediate feedback on learning efforts.
5. The child should be alerted to progress or achievement on a daily basis.
6. Subject-matter content should be seen as a means to an end, not an end in itself.

In addition, according to these researchers, the teacher must (1) have clear expectations of the child, (2) follow through on the child's efforts, (3) use logical consequences when misbehavior occurs, (4) reduce personal verbalization, and (5) maintain a firm but kind attitude.

Ecological Assessment and Intervention

Hardin (1978) describes an ecological assessment-intervention strategy for learning disabled students that is applicable to children and youth with behavior disorders.

Hardin defines ecology as "a study of the interactions and interrelationships of living organisms and their environment." Implementing an ecological approach requires both a philosophical commitment to an ecological orientation and a high level of skill in observation, assessment, the interpretation of behavior, and the design of interventions.

To effectively apply Hardin's strategy, each child's uniqueness must first be assessed. Students are assessed in terms of the skills they lack for reintegration into the regular classroom. Assessment is conducted by the application of both informal and traditional instruments.

After assessing the child, the special educator assesses the influences within the school and classroom that may impact on the child. These include the classroom atmosphere, teacher expectancies, the mode and pacing of presentations, and scope and sequence of skills to be mastered. The teacher-learner relationship and learner-peer dynamics are assessed. Teachers must undergo self-assessment to gain insight into the dynamics of the relationship between themselves and individual students.

The final area to be assessed is influence within the home. The parents' perceptions of the child and his or her behavior can be attained through an interview, conference, or home visit.

Hardin maintains that an "ecological assessment is justified only if it leads to ecological intervention" (p. 20). The continuity that should evolve with ecological assessment and intervention is depicted in Figure 7-2.

The data gathered from the environment and all the conditions in which the learner functions results in the identification and clarification of individual needs. From these needs, individual goals and objectives are developed that lead to the selection of teaching strategies. After these are selected, appropriate materials are chosen or designed.

Hardin contends that the use of ecological assessment will inhibit contradictory or confounding techniques that only deter the child from succeeding in the environment. As a result of accurate ecological assessment, interventions can be selected to meet students' needs.

OBJECTIVE THREE: *To describe an ecological framework for the selection of teaching models.*

No single approach to behavior disorders can provide special educators with the strategies needed to deal with the variety of problems exhibited by children and youths with behavior disorders (Smith & McGinnis, 1982). If there is no "right method," "right teacher," or "right environment" (Apter, 1977), then special educators must synthesize a wide range of teaching strategies in response to the needs of these students. In this section, the variables considered when selecting teaching strategies are discussed.

The selection of teaching strategies must be grounded in the contexts in which the student is functioning. Learning and behavioral problems arise as a result of the interaction between a child, his or her repertoire of behaviors, and the contexts in which the child is functioning. Interactions between student and special educator are representative of the match or goodness-of-fit in the context in which the interaction is occurring. In this way, the contexts become the focus for interventions (Forness, 1981). The manipulation of the variables in the context are the only means of direct interventions available to a special educator wishing to enhance the

FIGURE 7-2 An Ecological Schema

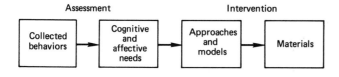

development of the child or youth with behavior disorders (Kauffman, 1982).

When selecting a teaching strategy, the special educator considers five variables. These are (1) the child, (2) the behavior, (3) the contexts relevent to the behavior, (4) the purposes of the intervention, and (5) the characteristics of the intervener. Kerr and Nelson (1983) suggested the use of matrices to assess, prior to implementation, the appropriateness of specific behavior-management interventions for use with children and youth with behavior disorders. A modification of their matrix system, designed to facilitate the assessment of specific teaching strategies for implementation with children and youth with behavior disorders, is presented in this section. Five matrices focusing on the major variables to be considered with assessing the appropriateness of a teaching strategy are presented in Figures 7-4 to 7-8. In each matrix, the strategies being considered are written across the top. Then each variable or characteristic that should be considered when assessing the appropriateness of the strategy is written in the matrix. If a strategy is appropriate from the perspective of a particular variable, an *x* is placed in the corresponding box. The completed matrices provide the special educator with a profile of the strategies being considered for implementation. An example of a completed matrix is provided in Figure 7-3.

The child.   As discussed in Chapter 2, each child develops in nested contexts (microsystem, mesosystem, and so on). In the selection of a teaching strategy, consideration is given to each of the five ecological contexts in which the child develops. The child's age, sex, the nature of the behavior disorder, and the interaction of the contexts in which the child functions are all assessed in deciding upon the appropriateness of a teaching strategy. The specific child-related variables that are considered when determining the appropriateness of a strategy are depicted in the matrix in Figure 7-4 (Carroll, 1974; Gearheart, 1977; Kerr & Nelson, 1983).

The behavior.   There are several behavior variables considered when selecting a teaching strategy. First, the overall number of behaviors needing change is considered. The special educator must order these behaviors by priority and systematically work down the list from the most to the least significant. Next, the frequency, duration, and intensity of the behavior to be changed are considered. Finally, the type of behavior is carefully considered; behaviors that are dangerous to the self and others require more restrictive interventions than benign behaviors. Variables with reference to the nature of the behaviors are presented in Figure 7-5 (Carroll, 1974; (Kerr & Nelson, 1983).

FIGURE 7-3 Example of Child-Variable Matrix

Child: Stuart, ten years old, attends fifth grade in a
regular education setting. Though intellectual assessment
has determined that his ability is well above average, he
is currently receiving C's and D's on his report card. He
self-reports that he dislikes school, that it is "boring,"
and that the teachers require him to do "stupid things"
all day long.

Recently Stuart has become less compliant both at
school and at home. He completes few school tasks, though
he will work at simulation activities on the computer for
extended periods of time. He seems to prefer to be a
member of a group, and refuses to take his turn during
individual activities (i.e., batting during softball,
diving while others are watching, etc.). He enjoys adult
attention, and is very verbal when alone with the teacher.
He is frequently argumentative, and will attempt to
"reason" with those who intervene when he is behaving
inappropriately. He states that he "doesn't have a
problem."

Directions: List the teaching strategies being considered
across the top of the form. List each variable which must
be assessed in the left-hand column. Place an "X" in the
column under the strategy if it appropriately addresses
that characteristic of the child.

STRATEGIES CONSIDERED

Behavior: completes school tasks	Contingency Contract	Mediated Learning	Strauss/ Lehtinen Biophysical Control
Age	X	X	X
Developmental level	X		
Cognitive skills	X	no identified problems	
Level of achievement	X	"	
Preference for large group			
Preference for small group			
Preference for individualization	X		X
Preference for specific personnel	X gives 1:1 time with teacher.		
Preference for learning time A.M. vs P.M. student			not severe enough an attentional problem
Attention span	X	X	
Desire for attention	X		
Desire to change	X may motivate		

Contingency contracting seems to be the most appropriate strategy

182

FIGURE 7-4 Child-Variable Matrix

DIRECTIONS: List the teaching strategies being considered
across the top of the form. List each variable which must
be assessed in the left-hand column. Place an "X" in the
column under the strategy if it appropriately addresses
that characteristic of the child.

STRATEGIES CONSIDERED

Age			
Developmental level			
Cognitive skills			
Level of achievement			
Preference for large group			
Preference for small group			
Preference for individualization			
Preference for specific personnel			
Preference for learning time A.M. vs P.M. student			
Attention span			
Desire for attention			
Desire to change			

The ecologcal contexts.   The environments in which behavior occurs
are important considerations in the selection of a teaching strategy. Strategies that focus on the environments in which the student is functioning
tend to focus on the development of productive and satisfying settings in
which the child can function effectively. In addition, when contexts are
considered, the selection of a model is firmly founded in normalization,
and provides more comprehensive services to the child or youth (Apter,
1977). A special educator can only personally and directly change student
behaviors that are exhibited in contexts in which student and special educator function together. Consequently, the special educator cannot directly
address those behaviors that are specific to contexts outside of the special-
education setting, such as home and community, but does serve as a consultant to those directly interacting with the student in these contexts. Six
variables are assessed within the instructional context. These include facilities, personnel, group, process, time, and resources. These variables are

FIGURE 7-5 Behavior-Variable Matrix

```
DIRECTIONS: List the teaching strategies being considered
across the top of the form.  List each variable which must
be assessed in the left-hand column.  Place an "X" in the
column under the strategy if it appropriately addresses
that facet of the behavior.

Behavior for intervention _____
              STRATEGIES BEING CONSIDERED
```

Frequency _____			
Duration _____			
Intensity _____			
Risk to others _____			
Risk to child _____			
Risk to program _____			
Risk to placement in less restrictive setting _____			
Risk to family interaction _____			
Risk to community interaction _____			

presented in Figure 7-6 (Carroll, 1974; Gearheart, 1977; Kerr & Nelson, 1983).

The implementer.   The individual or individuals implementing the strategy are another important consideration when determining the appropriateness of a teaching strategy. Just as the child or youth with behavior disorders functions within nested contexts, so does the special educator. The characteristics of the special educator responsible for implementing a teaching strategy have a significant effect on its choice. The educator's choice is affected by the strategy's philosophy and personal perspective as well as the individual's ability to implement it. A particular special educator may be unable or find it difficult to consistently apply a strategy with which he or she philosophically disagrees. The educator's training, willingness to implement a specific teaching or management strategy, confidence in its effectiveness, and comfort in implementing it all impact on his or her ability to employ it effectively. The variables considered when assessing the

FIGURE 7-6 Context Variables

DIRECTIONS: List the teaching strategies being considered across the top of the form. List each variable which must be assessed in the left-hand column. Place an "X" in the column under the strategy if it appropriately addresses that facet of the behavior.

STRATEGIES CONSIDERED

Personnel			
Staff availability			
Special training			
Adult-student ratio			
Group			
Peer cooperation			
Peer acceptance			
Climate			
Teacher leadership qualities			
Compliance			
Sensitivity			
Teaching-learning process			
Tasks involved			
Curriculum			
Materials used			
Stimuli mode			
Response mode			
Cognitive level of input			
Rate of input			
Sequence of input			
Time			
Schedule change			
Planning time needed			
Teacher-time ouside of classroom required			

Facilities			
Room arrangement			
Special equipment or furniture			
Private student area			
Individual work area			
Small group work area			
Large group area			
Crisis intervention area			
Resources			
Parent permission			
Parent/caregiver assistance			
Administrative support			
Related services			
State regulations			
District philosophy			

appropriateness of a strategy from the implementer's perspective are presented in Figure 7-7 (Carroll, 1974; Gearheart, 1977; Kerr and Nelson, 1983).

Purpose of teaching.   The purpose for changing the behavior is the final component considered when selecting a teaching strategy. The purpose of all strategies applied in teaching children and youth with behavior disorders is to increase self-discipline and enhance the student's successful functioning in the environment. When consideration is given to the appropriateness of a specific strategy to be implemented for a specific purpose, the variables in Figure 7-8 are assessed (Carroll, 1974; Gearheart, 1977; Kerr & Nelson, 1983).

When a special educator assesses teaching strategies, using the matrix system presented in this section, he or she makes a systematic, cogent decision with regard to its appropriateness.

FIGURE 7-7   Implementer Variables

```
DIRECTIONS: List the teaching strategies being considered
across the top of the form.  Consider each of the
variables in the left-hand column.  Place an "X" in the
column under the strategy if it appropriately addresses
that facet of the implementer.

               STRATEGIES BEING CONSIDERED


Specialized training _____|_____|_____

Willingness to implement ____|_____|_____

Confidence in effectiveness _|_____|_____

Physical stamina _____|_____|_____

Philosophical stamina _____|_____|_____
```

SUMMARY

Teaching models impact on the instruction of children and youth with behavior disorders. In this chapter, several teaching models derived from the context of the four traditional perspectives of behavior disorders presented in Chapter One are discussed. An ecological basis for the selection of teaching models is presented. By using the matrices suggested in the chapter, systematic decisions can be made regarding the selection of appropriate teaching strategies.

The teaching models reviewed in the chapter are selected examples of the many models available for application with children and youth with behavior disorders. It is not feasible to review all of the worthwhile efforts of the many professionals in a single chapter. Regardless of the specific teaching strategy selected for implementation, we, as special educators, must remember that our purpose is to teach. Yamamoto's definition of teaching, quoted at the beginning of this chapter, bears repeating here:

FIGURE 7-8 Purpose Variables

Directions: List each strategy being considered across the
top of the form. Consider each of the variables in the
left-hand column. Place an "X" in the column under the
strategy if it appropriately addresses that variable.

STRATEGIES BEING CONSIDERED

Enhance self-discipline _____|_____|_____

Enhance self-esteem _____|_____|_____

Enhance coping skills _____|_____|_____

Enhance self-confidence _____|_____|_____

Successful interaction
  in special education
  program _____|_____|_____

Successful interaction
  with regular education
  program _____|_____|_____

Successful interaction
  throughout school _____|_____|_____

Successful interaction
  at home _____|_____|_____

Successful interaction
  in community _____|_____|_____

"To be a teacher is to share human hopes and disappointments with another being" (Yamamoto, 1969, p. viii).

REVIEW QUESTIONS

1. Select one of the matrices applied in the teaching-strategy selection process. Carefully study the matrix you have selected. Are there additional variables that should have been included in the matrix? What are they? Why should they be included?

3. Visit one or more programs for children and youth with behavior disorders. During your visit, observe the program in progress and discuss your observations with the special educator. Attempt to clarify and classify the theoretical foundation of the programs as articulated by the teacher. Is it reflected in the program?

APPLICATION ACTIVITIES

Review the following information concerning a child assigned to a self-contained program for elementary-school students with behavior disorders. Using the information provided, complete the following matrix by rating each variable as to whether or not the teaching strategy appropriately addresses that characteristic of the child.

Student: Rebecca, ten years old

Behavioral Concern: general lack of interest in educational materials and activities; prefers to be alone; on the playground walks along the fence; fails to interact with other students; when other students or staff members approach her, Rebecca backs up, cries, chews her fingernails; staff has been unable to identify any consistent rewards of interest to Rebecca.

Cognitive/academic Skills: will perform some academic work with Ms. Wilson, the program paraprofessional; prefers to be left alone to gaze out window; performs at the beginning second-grade level on academic tasks.

	Clinical Teaching	Contingency Contracting	Strauss & Lehtinen
Age			
Developmental level			
Cognitive skills			
Achievement level			
Preference for large group			
Preference for small group			
Preference for individualization			
Preference for learning time			
Attention span			
Desire for attention			
Desire to change			

Which strategy seems to best address Rebecca's personal characteristics?

8

Behavior Management: An Introduction

This chapter is an introduction to the study of the management of children and youth with behavior disorders. The chapter begins with a brief discussion of the relationship between the theoretical perspectives presented in Chapter 1, the behavior management interventions derived from those perspectives, and the outcomes or consequences of applying those interventions to children and youth with behavior disorders. In the discussion, a broad definition of behavior management is provided. This is followed by a discussion of several guidelines for special educators applying the interventions presented in this chapter and in chapters 9, 10, and 11.

In addition, the chapter discusses the differences between classroom-management and individual-management problems. Finally, several suggestions for improving classroom management are provided.

OBJECTIVES

After completing this chapter, you will be able to —

1. discuss the relationship between a theoretical perspective, the interventions derived from it, and the consequences of applying those interventions;
2. define behavior-management interventions;
3. identify and discuss the guidelines for the effective application of behavior-management interventions;

4. discriminate between classroom-management and individual-management problems;
5. identify strategies to improve classroom management.

A CASE FOR CONSIDERATION

The Individual Education Program planning team was in the process of developing social and behavioral goals and objectives for eleven-year-old Donita.

The social worker stated, "Donita's hyperactivity may be partly due to her lack of activity while at home. As a latchkey child, she has to remain in the house until her mother arrives in the evening. Her mother, tired after a long day of work, justifiably tries to occupy Donita with quiet activities until bedtime. School is Donita's only time for action."

The school nurse disagreed: "We know Donita has increased her activity level at school. If we can monitor her diet, perhaps we can regulate her activity level. I would like to know, for example, if she has sugar-sweetened dry cereal for breakfast. We should be able to chart what she has for lunch, and see if we can regulate her behavior a bit by removing some of the sugar and maybe some of the additives. If not, perhaps a medical work-up will be needed to determine if medication would be appropriate."

The school counselor shook his head. "I do think the fact that Donita is a latchkey child is affecting her behavior, but not in the way discussed earlier. Donita's 'need to belong' is not being met. She still may not have resolved the crisis of her father's leaving the home after a difficult divorce. Perhaps we need to find a way to allow Donita to express any unresolved hostility toward her father. I would suggest such activities as creative movement or art. If we can channel her need to express distress, I'm sure her activity level in the classroom will decrease."

"Wait a minute," said the special educator. "Donita is in my room now, and we have already seen a decrease in her activity level. This occurs when we increase positive reinforcement for staying in her seat and completing her work. If we just continue the way we are, I'm sure she will be ready to return to the regular classroom parttime in about three months."

Four professionals, all very concerned about one student, have generated four different hypotheses concerning the nature and resolution of the student's behavior problem. In the next section, the relationship between theoretical perspectives, interventions, and consequences are discussed.

OBJECTIVE ONE: *To discuss the relationship between a theoretical perspective, the interventions derived from it, and the consequences of applying those interventions.*

Ideas > Actions > Outcomes

What we believe about children and youths with behavior disorders affects how we respond to and act toward them (Wood, 1978). The relationship between a theoretical perspective (ideas), the behavior-management interventions (actions) derived from it, and the consequences (outcomes) of applying those interventions is an important consideration in the special educator's selection of specific interventions to be applied to children and youth with behavior disorders.

> In an intervention, ideas, actions, and outcomes are all tied together and greatly affect each other. Ideas, in and of themselves, are inert unless active energy is added to their influence. Active energy, in and of itself, is meaningless and chaotic unless it is directed. In an intervention, the conceptual framework directs and channels the action, by providing an analysis of the nature of the problem which dictates the interventions, and by suggesting the outcome towards which the intervention is directed.
>
> One form of intervention, carried out within two different conceptual frameworks, can have radically different meanings and lead to radically different experiences and outcomes for the participants (Rhodes, 1972, pp. 23–24).

The significance of this quotation as it relates to the education and management of children and youth with behavior disorders cannot be overestimated. As discussed in some detail in Chapter 2, special educators need a well-developed philosophy of human nature (including that of children) and of education and behavior management on which to base their activities with children. For example, the special educator who perceives the child as determined by the environment will approach behavior management from a radically different point of view than the educator who perceives the child as totally or partially determining his or her life or having that life determined by intrapsychic forces.

The various conceptual perspectives applied in the education of children and youth with behavior disorders are discussed in Chapter 1. These perspectives should be thoroughly reviewed and their implications for the management of this population carefully weighted before implementing the behavior-management interventions presented in this chapter and chapters 9, 10, and 11.

OBJECTIVE TWO: *To define behavior-management interventions.*

Behavior management is a complex problem that cannot be approached simplistically, but must be studied, planned, and objectively applied and evaluated, with equal emphasis given to all relevant variables: the individual or groups of individuals whose behavior is to be changed, the behavior to be changed, the context in which the behavior occurs, the special educator applying the intervention, and that individual's purpose for wishing to change the behavior. This rather complex statement recognizes that a specific behavior-management intervention effective with a specific behavior of a specific child in a particular context may be ineffective under another set of circumstances when applied by a different special educator to change a different behavior of a different individual or group of individuals.

In this text, behavior-management interventions are defined as *"all those actions (and conscious inactions) educators engage in to enhance the probability that children and youth, individually and in groups, will develop effective behaviors that are personally self-fulfilling, productive, and socially acceptable"* (Shea, 1978).

OBJECTIVE THREE: *To identify and discuss the guidelines for the effective application of behavior-management interventions.*

Guidelines for Application

These general guidelines for the application of behavior management are presented here primarily to stimulate thought and discussion.

The special educator as model and leader.   Outside the family, the teacher is usually the most important person in the life of the child or young person. No other variable in the school setting appears to have a greater potential therapeutic impact on students' behavior than the interpersonal relationship between teacher and child.

Special education programs for children and youth with behavior disorders can be (and have been) operated successfully under adverse conditions, without adequate facilities, materials, equipment, or funds. However, no program can be successful without personnel (special educators and allied professionals and paraprofessionals) who relate positively and productively to children and youths with behavior disorders.

The effective special educator of these students must be an *authentic* person—a *real* person. There are several personal traits that authentic special educators of children and youth with behavior disorders appear to share. These include:

insight into oneself
self-acceptance, self-appraisal, and self-confidence
love and acceptance of children
an understanding of the behavior of children and youths with behavior disorders
curiosity and a willingness to learn
patience with oneself and others
flexibility
humor

Special educators are models for the children and youths with behavior disorders whom they instruct. For better or worse, these young persons will model at least some of their behavior after their teachers. The value of teachers who are highly skilled and knowledgeable in specific subject areas but lack understanding and acceptance of themselves and students is questionable.

In addition to the personal traits presented here, special educators need specific knowledge and skills if they are to work effectively with children and youth with behavior disorders. These include:

1. Establishing routines for their students
2. Maintaining behavioral limits, without personal emotional involvement
3. Controlling emotionally charged situations
4. Being consistent; tolerating a behavior one day and prohibiting it another is confusing to children
5. Investigating behavioral incidents before acting, rather than taking action on the basis of second- or third-person information and rumors
6. Ignoring behaviors when appropriate
7. Communicating verbally and nonverbally with, not to, students
8. Avoiding personal confrontations with students when it is therapeutically appropriate, and confronting students when therapeutically appropriate
9. Adapting activities for therapeutic purposes, recognizing student disinterest, dislike, or resistance
10. Working as a member of a team for the benefit of each student
11. Appealing to students on a human level when students' actions are personally confusing and discomforting
12. Providing security to students, communicating that they are safe from physical and psychological harm while in their care

Beginning teachers seldom arrive in the classroom with all these skills in addition to instructional competence in subject-matter areas. Such skills are developed through experiences and with the assistance and support of colleagues and supervisors.

Self-discipline

Self-discipline is the desired outcome of all the behavior-management interventions presented in this chapter and chapters 9, 10, and 11. Attaining self-control over one's behavior in a variety of circumstances in association with a variety of individuals and groups is not instantaneous, but is developed over a period of time. During the process of achieving self-control, children with behavior problems, like all children, progress and regress, appearing in control one day and not the next. Progress—maturing, growing, and developing—is often measured by the special educator of children and youth with behavior disorders by the slowly increasing lengths of time between the occurrences of unacceptable behaviors.

The word *discipline* is derived from the word *disciple*, or follower of a master's teaching. This concept contains the idea of learning from a teacher whose example the learner personally desires to model; the best discipline is derived from the respect and understanding of one human being for another. Discipline is cooperative and voluntary, not the simple imposition of restriction by an authority figure (Chetkow, 1964).

In special education, harsh, negative disciplinary techniques are avoided. Children and youth with behavior disorders in all probability have a poor or distorted self-image as a result of repeated failure and negative discipline. Many of these children have psychologically insulated themselves from the effects of failure and negative discipline. Positive interventions leading to self-discipline are needed by these students.

Population and time. Children and youth in programs for the behavior disordered generally have behavior disorders. This fact is all too frequently forgotten by those working with such children. Often students are approached as if their behavior disorders did not exist. Teachers become frustrated with children whose unacceptable behavior does not respond to intervention during the first month of placement. The special educator must be patient and adjust to slow, time-consuming change. Instant "cures" are few in number and difficult to observe when they do occur.

Children and youth with behavior disorders have developed "survival" behaviors over a period of years, which, though unacceptable to others, have been and continue to be more or less successful for them. They cannot (and should not be forced to) relinquish their survival behaviors (coping mechanisms) immediately and begin using "new" (and, from our point of view, more acceptable and productive) ways of behaving. Changing deviant behavior requires time and energy. Teachers must be patient, and focus on growth rather than on the final outcome.

Objectives and goals. Although teachers develop long-term goals for their students, such goals are frequently not a daily concern. These goals provide the needed direction for the overall program for the individual child. They are task analyzed into a series of properly sequenced immediate objectives, which structure daily lessons and activities. The procedures for selecting, writing, implementing, and evaluating goals and objectives for children and youth with behavior disorders is discussed in Chapter 5.

One overriding objective for all children placed in special education programs is a positive learning experience. Though the teacher has many learning tasks for the child, these tasks cannot be so consuming of the child's time and energy that school becomes drudgery. Special educators must avoid the trap of finding out what the student cannot do and then proceeding to have them do it all day, every day. School should provide a positive setting in which a variety of opportunities to learn new skills through academic and nonacademic activities are available.

Empathy, not sympathy.   Children and youth with behavior disorders do not need their teachers' sympathy; sympathy distorts the problem and places the teacher in an emotional set that prevents objective evaluation of the child's behavior. When teachers become deeply involved in a child's problem, they may function in biased ways, reacting on an emotional rather than a cognitive level.

Empathetic rather than sympathetic relationships are necessary. Special educators must be able to assume the child's point of view and attempt to approximate the child's feelings. The capacity to empathize permits the teacher to provide children with direction, guidance, and support when such assistance is needed.

Expectations.   Expectations of children and youth with behavior disorders have been found to impact significantly on their performance (Beez, 1972; Rosenthal & Jacobson, 1966; Rubin & Balow, 1971). This self-fulfilling prophecy means that, to a significant extent, if we believe children are and will continue to be incompetent, the probability is increased that they will function that way. Conversely, if a teacher believes and communicates to children that they will learn, the probability is increased that they will respond to our expectations.

In special education programs for children and youth with behavior disorders, the teacher must maintain high but realistic expectations of students. These expectations are realized in an environment developed around a "can do" attitude. Children are told repeatedly throughout each day: "You can do it," "You know and I know you can do it," "You did it," "Great," "Super," "Beautiful!"

Obviously, such an attitude is meaningless and may be harmful unless the program is designed to ensure that the children or young persons receive the needed support and skill training required to complete a task and attain our expectations.

Freedom and independence.   As a general policy, children and youth with behavior disorders should be encouraged to grow and learn as much as possible without teacher assistance. Within realistic limits, anything children can do for themselves, they should do. The special educator's function is to facilitate, not dominate, the child's activities, and be available to instruct, demonstrate, assist, counsel, and encourage. All young people, if they are to grow, need freedom to explore, investigate, and implement new behaviors without adult interference. Often they will succeed in their efforts; occasionally they will fail and require assistance.

Occasional failure is a part of life. The teacher cannot and should not shelter children and youth with behavior disorders from all failure. At appropriate times, students should be allowed to confront the logical consequences—success and failure—of their actions (Dreikurs & Grey, 1968). The teacher should help the child learn to cope with both success and failure.

Often, complete freedom becomes boring. Children are placed in special education to learn productive skills and behaviors. The teacher is responsible for planning the student's individualized program. To do otherwise would be irresponsible and a disservice to the student. Behavior management and curriculum are partners; one is of little value without the other.

OBJECTIVE FOUR: *To discriminate between classroom management and individual-management problems.*

No single approach to behavior disorders can provide a special educator with the many strategies needed to respond effectively to the variety of problems exhibited by children and youth with behavior disorders (Smith & McGinnis, 1982). Beginning special educators quickly become aware that the philosophical positions taught in college and university classrooms do not always meet the needs of the students they are responsible for serving. Out of frustration, the beginner may adopt a "bag-of-tricks" approach to teaching and management. Such an approach is based on a combination of common sense, "old teachers' tales," and school folklore (Weber, 1977). It is probably true that the bag-of-tricks approach may help the special educator survive for another day, but it has generally been proven to be ineffective in the long run. When teachers operate on the basis of common sense and folklore, they are forced into inconsistency, a characteristic quickly recognized and exploited by children and youth with behavior disorders. In addition, the teacher is forced into a reactive rather than proactive role in the classroom.

All transactions occurring between special educators and students are for the purpose of either instruction or management. Therefore, a particular teaching problem may be instructional, managerial, or a combination of both. In addition, a particular teaching problem may be associated with either a group or an individual. To solve these teaching problems, Weber (1977) encourages the special educator to determine (a) if the problem is instructional, managerial, or a combination of both; (b) if it is a group or individual problem; (c) the instructional or managerial strategy most appropriate for solving it. Then the strategy should be applied.

INDIVIDUAL-MANAGEMENT PROBLEMS

Students perform behaviors because they produce an effect. When dealing with individual-management problems, Neel (1984) suggests determining what effect the child is attempting to produce with the inappropriate behavior, and then teaching an appropriate behavior to help the child accomplish the desired effect. To correct individual-management problems, the special educator follows five steps:

1. Describe the problem—what is the inappropriate or ineffective behavior?
2. Describe the purpose of the behavior—why is the child exhibiting the inappropriate or ineffective behavior?
3. Describe the specific contexts in which the inappropriate or ineffective behavior is exhibited—where does the child exhibit the behavior?
4. Determine a behavior that, if exhibited by the student in the same context, would effectively replace the inappropriate one yet allow the student to have the desired effect—what behavior should the student exhibit to appropriately and effectively accomplish his or her purpose?
5. Describe, if any, the readiness or prerequisite skills needed by the student to engage in the appropriate behavior—what skills must the child learn before he or she can exhibit the appropriate behavior?

After completing this analysis of the behavior, Neels suggests an instructional process that is initiated by determining the function or purpose of the child's inappropriate or ineffective behavior. Next, the special educator selects the context in which instruction will occur. A specific instructional plan is then developed. This includes determining the appropriate behaviors to be taught, the level of support needed by the student to perform the behavior, any companion skills that the student must learn to perform, and the criteria for successful performance. The implementation of this or a similar teaching strategy not only eliminates the inappropriate behavior; it also assures the teaching of an appropriate one.

Dreikurs and Cassel (1972) offer further insight into the functions of individual behavior problems. They describe four kinds of individual-management problems: (a) attention-getting behavior (b) power-seeking behavior, (c) revenge-seeking behavior, and (d) behaviors that are displays of inadequacy. They maintain that students unable to gain status in a socially acceptable manner will seek attention through inappropriate passive or active attention-getting behaviors. The power-seeking child's behavior is characterized by lying, contradicting the teacher, or being openly noncompliant. The revenge-seeking child attains success by hurting others and through retaliation. The inadequate child is usually passive, demonstrating hopelessness and helplessness.

Dreikurs and Cassell suggest that the teacher use self-analysis techniques to determine the purpose of the student's behavior problem. By analyzing one's personal responses to the student's inappropriate behavior, the special educator can frequently discern the cause of the problem. If the special educator feels annoyed, the problem is probably an attention-getting behavior. If the teacher feels defeated or threatened, the behavior is probably power-seeking. A feeling of hurt on the part of the special educator usually implies that the child is engaging in revenge-seeking behavior. If the special educator feels helpless, the child is probably engaging in inadequate behaviors.

GROUP-MANAGEMENT PROBLEMS

Johnson and Bany (1970) describe seven classroom group-management problems that may occur alone or in combination:

1. A lack of classroom group unity, characterized by conflicts between individuals and subgroups.
2. Failure to adhere to behavioral standards and work procedures.
3. Negative reactions to individual students.
4. Class approval of misbehavior (the class clown, for example).
5. Frequent distraction or work stoppage.
6. Acts of protest or resistance.
7. Inability to adjust to change. Classes at times react inappropriately to substitute teachers, changes in routine, and new members.

The special educator who is aware of these management problems can implement programs to prevent their occurrence or to manage such problems if they occur. In the next section, specific strategies to improve classroom management are discussed.

OBJECTIVE FIVE: *To identify strategies to improve classroom management.*

Johnson and Bany (1970) identified three inappropriate management strategies used to manage classroom problems. The first one includes the use of punitive, threatening, and ridiculing behaviors, or sarcasm with students. The second inappropriate strategy for managing behavior is diverting students' attention from problems or simply ignoring them. In essence, both of these strategies result in doing nothing directly to remedy the problem. They often involve removing a student from the group or making one student the scapegoat for the problem.

The third inappropriate strategy is the use of dominating or pressuring practices to force conformity. Teachers who use such tactics frequently command, scold, and reproach students for inappropriate behaviors. They may use a single powerful student to help control the group. The inappropriate management strategies identified by Johnson and Bany do not have a role in the education of children and youths with behavior disorders.

Effective classroom management requires that the special educator attend and respond to two major responsibilities: implementing activities to improve classroom conditions and maintaining the improved conditions (Johnson & Bany, 1970). Four techniques for improving classroom conditions are: (1) foster group unity and cooperation, (2) establish standards of appropriate behavior, (3) implement problem-solving activities, and (4) encourage appropriate group goals, norms, and behaviors.

Classroom unity is enhanced by allowing students opportunities to interact and communicate. By creating an environment accepting of all students and giving them a sense of belonging, the special educator communicates a willingness to share with the students the responsibilities for attaining group goals and responding to group needs.

Classroom conditions can be improved when special educators and students together establish appropriate standards of behavior. First, Johnson and Bany stress involving all members of the group in the process of developing group standards and limits. If effective group management is to occur in a classroom, it must be based on standards of behavior that are acceptable to the group.

Group problem-solving activities can be used to foster positive conditions in the classroom. Group problem solving is discussed in detail in Chapter 11. The fourth technique suggested by Johnson and Bany is fostering appropriate group goals, norms, and behaviors. The special educator can accomplish this by consistently helping the group to replace inappropriate and outmoded goals and behaviors with appropriate and timely ones in response to the new and emerging needs of individuals and the group.

The second major classroom responsibility suggested by Johnson and Bany is maintaining improved classroom conditions once they have been attained. This responsibility can be met in three ways. First, when the class's morale and cohesiveness are threatened, the special educator restores it by enhancing cohesiveness and reducing anxiety and stress in the classroom. Second, when conflict and emotionally charged situations threaten the improved conditions, the special educator must respond promptly. Finally, the special educator can minimize management problems by carefully monitoring group conditions and activities. This includes anticipating problems and engaging in preventative planning.

Newman (1982) suggests four rules for the management of subgroups. First, recognize and direct them. The special educator should be aware of the subgroups within the classroom group, how their members interact with one another, and their purposes. When a special educator is aware of a subgroup's purpose, then he or she can use it as a vehicle for positive accomplishment for both its members and the total classroom group.

Newman's second rule is to recognize and direct the subgroup leaders. Classroom management problems occur when the subgroup leaders' goals differ from those of the teacher and the members of the classroom group. Rather than diffusing, discouraging, or antagonizing subgroup leaders, Newman encourages the special educator to support them, strengthen their leadership roles, and employ the leaders' strengths for the benefit of the entire class.

"Select heterogeneous groupings" is Newman's third rule for subgroup management. When special educators are using small groups selected for particular work tasks, heterogeneous small groups selected from various subgroups may be most productive. Closely related to this rule is Newman's final suggestion to switch groups periodically; that is, to change the membership in small work groups from time to time. These final two rules, when applied with consistency, tend to enhance cooperation and tolerance among all the students in the classroom group.

"Levels systems" are becoming an increasingly common management method in special education programs for children and youths with behavior disorders. A levels system can be used to manage both group and individual behaviors.

A levels system applied by Grumley (1984) in a day treatment setting for students with severe behavior disorders is presented next. The system was implemented to increase students' self-control. It is a structured system that provides students with clearly delineated functional expectations and limits. Both students and special educators are responsible for monitoring the performance and progression of students through the five levels. An individual point system is used to monitor performance. The point system is based on the annual goals and short-term objectives in each student's Individualized Education Plan. Points are earned by the student throughout the day for academic, behavioral, and social behavior. Weekly staff meetings are conducted to review each student's performance and revise goals and objectives. Decisions about level changes (with the exception of advancement to Level II) are made at these meetings.

The system consists of five levels: Entry (Level I), Level II, Level III, Level IV, and Ground Level (a disciplinary level). They are described in Figure 8-1.

Students at Level I and Ground Level are under direct staff supervision throughout the day. Ground level offenses and the time consequences for them are presented in Figure 8-2.

As a student progresses through the system, the number of points that can be earned at the various levels decreases. This is accomplished by increasing the time between reinforcement or reward periods. When a student fails to maintain behavior at his or her present level, a probationary period of one week at a lower level is granted. During the probation period, the student must earn 80 percent of the points available at that level to regain the privileges of the original level.

Although the levels system discussed in this section is designed for students with severe behavior disorders, a similar system can be designed

FIGURE 8-1 Levels Systems

	LEVEL I	LEVEL II	LEVEL III	LEVEL IV	GROUND LEVEL
MINIMUM LENGTH OF STAY	9 Weeks	12 Weeks	15 Weeks	9 Weeks (Transition)	3–5 days
REQUIREMENTS FOR MAINTAINING LEVEL STATUS		80% of possible points (4 out of every 5 days).	80% of possible points (4 out of every 5 days).	Meets individual criteria established by special teacher.	Level I —70% pos.pts. Level II —80% pos.pts. Level III—85% pos.pts. Level IV—90% pos.pts.
REQUIREMENTS FOR ADVANCING TO NEXT LEVEL	90% of possible points (45 out of 60 days). No more than 10 Time Outs.	90% of possible points (60 out of 72 days). No more than 6 Time Outs.	90% of possible points (75 out of 90 days). No more than 5 Time Outs.	Meets individual criteria established by special teacher.	
ACADEMIC EXPECTATIONS	Start assignments on command. During weeks 1–5, on task for 15 min. out of each 1/2 hour. Weeks 6–9, on task for 20 min. out of each 1/2 hr. (not necessarily consecutively)	Start & complete assignments within specified time. On-task behavior: Weeks 1–4, 20 min. Weeks 5–8, 25 min. Weeks 8–12, 30 min.	Start & complete assignments within specified time. Stays on task for 30 minutes at a time.	Meets individual criteria established by special teacher.	Same expectations for level below the one student was on prior to offense resulting in Ground Level placement.
BEHAVIORAL EXPECTATIONS	Discusses individual goals & class rules with teacher daily. Demonstrates effort to achieve them.	Independently states individual goals & class rules daily & demonstrates effort to achieve them.	Independently states individual goals & class rules daily & demonstrates efforts to achieve them. Involved in process of determining individual goals for self.	Meets individual criteria established by special teacher.	States reasons for G.L. placement and alternative strategies. Same expectations for level below the one student was on prior to offense resulting in G.L. placement.

FIGURE 8-1 Levels Systems (continued)

SOCIAL SKILLS EXPECTATIONS	Interacts appropriately with one peer at a time with adult supervision. Accepts compliments apppropriately. Interacts appropriately with adults.	Interacts appropriately with 2 or more peers at a time with adult supervision. Compliments self & others at least once a day. Contributes to discussions in daily class meetings.	Interacts appropriately with two or more peers without adult supervision. Compliments self & others at least twice a day. Verbally encourages peers to interact appropriately. Attempts to solve conflicts before asking for help.	Meets individual criteria established by special teacher.	Same expectations for level below the one student was on prior to offense resulting in Ground Level placement.
PRIVILEGES	Free time in classroom. Special activities determined by teacher.	Unescorted restroom & drink breaks & to and from bus. Setting table for lunch. Special Level II purchases in point store. Using computer during free time. Field trips. Purchasing soft drinks & snacks at specified times. Special activities determined by teacher. Playing Atari once a day with supervision.	Lunch in fast-food restaurant once a week. Running errands within building. Playing Atari in office. Special field trips. Special Level III purchases in point store.	Full-time placement in regular class. After a 9-week transition period, mainstreaming will be considered in staff meeting.	Free time earned at teacher's discretion. Scheduled restroom breaks with direct supervision. Eat lunch at separate table. Privilege of using tape recorder, computer, record player, etc. is revoked.

(Grumely, 1984)

FIGURE 8-2   Ground-Level Offenses and Time Limits

Leaving assigned area:	3 days
Physical abuse of staff or peers:	5 days
Destruction of property:	3 to 5 days
Setting off fire alarm:	3 days
Possession of weapons:	5 days
Possession of drugs:	3 to 5 days

for less severely disturbed children. A levels system allows a special educator to reinforce appropriate behavior in a structure that rewards self-management.

SUMMARY

In this chapter, behavior management has been broadly defined to include all actions and conscious inactions educators engage in to enhance the probability that children and youths, individually and in groups, will develop effective behaviors that are personally self-fulfilling, productive, and socially acceptable (Shea, 1978). Guidelines for the application of behavior management were presented.

A generic discussion of classroom-management and individual management problems was presented. A process for the analysis of these problems was suggested, as were strategies for improving classroom management. Finally, a "levels system" was discussed.

In the following chapters, interventions for children and youth with behavior disorders derived from the four perspectives are described. The review is selective as a result of personal and professional preference for certain interventions over others as a result of past training and experience. Our selectivity is also based on our wish to provide practical guidance and suggestions to special educators working with children and youths with behavior disorders. The reader is encouraged to conduct an in-depth study of the interventions in this section before implementing them with children; the chapter references are a useful starting point for this purpose.

REVIEW QUESTIONS

1. Discuss the following quotation: "In an intervention, ideas, actions, and outcomes are all tied together and greatly affect each other" (Rhodes, 1972, p. 23).
2. Discuss the definition of behavior management presented in this chapter. What is your definition of behavior management?

3. What guidelines should be applied in the implementation of any behavior-management intervention? Are there additional guidelines not presented in this chapter?

4. Observe an educational program for children and youths with behavior disorders. What activities does the special educator conduct to maintain and improve classroom conditions?

APPLICATION ACTIVITY

Several problems observed in a secondary school class for students with behavior disorders are described next. Decide whether each problem is a class- or individual management problem. Describe the function of the behavior and the appropriate behaviors to be taught to serve the same function for the student.

> Maurice consistently calls Ms. Dawson, the program paraprofessional, "Mama." Ms. Dawson becomes embarrassed, and says, "You know my name, Maurice," or "I'm not your mother, Maurice." Maurice uses appropriate names and titles for other adults with whom he interacts.
> Class problem .... Individual problem ....
> Function ....
> Appropriate substitute ....
> The class is divided into two groups, the "doves" and the "hawks." The "doves" take the teacher's side and the "hawks" ridicule the "doves."
> Class problem .... Individual problem ....
> Function ....
> Appropriate substitute ....
> Mary Elizabeth, the only girl attending the resource room during fourth period, sits alone at a table in the back of the room and will not join the group.
> Class problem .... Individual problem ....
> Function ....
> Appropriate substitute ....
> The seventh-period group believes Paul was "unjustly" placed in in-school suspension for three days. The group refuses to work until Paul returns to class.
> Class problem .... Individual problem ....
> Function ....
> Appropriate substitute ....
> Henry refers to Mr. Martinez, the resource-room teacher, as "your honor," "your smartness," "my honorable master," and the like. The rest of the class laughs each time Henry uses a new title and is informally keeping a list of the sobriquets.
> Class problem .... Individual problem ....
> Function ....
> Appropriate substitute ....

Ms. Schulz requests that Marcia rewrite an essay required for her history class. Marcia says, "Take it the way it is or don't take it, lady." Other students say, "Be fair, Ms. Schulz. You know Marcia's really trying."

Class problem .... Individual problem ....
Function ....
Appropriate substitute ....

Michael has been consistently late for third period. Ms. Smithers informs him that, according to the school policy on tardiness, she is writing him a detention slip. Michael says, "You know, Ms. Smithers, tires sometimes go flat on the parking lot for no reason at all."

Class problem .... Individual problem ....
Function ....
Appropriate substitute ....

9

Psychodynamic–Psychoeducational Interventions

In this chapter, the psychodynamic–psycho-educational framework is introduced. This framework is essentially a set of broad operating principles used by special educators applying the psychoeducational model with children and youths with behavior disorders. Counseling, "surface" management strategies, and the expressive media as behavior-management strategies, and the expressive media as behavior-management interventions are discussed. The chapter concludes with a discussion of the self-control curriculum.

OBJECTIVES

After completing this chapter, you will be able to—

1. Describe the psycho educational framework;
2. Describe counseling interventions based on the psychodynamic–psycho educational perspective;
3. Describe interventions for managing surface behavior derived from a psychodynamic–psychoeducational perspective;
4. Describe the use of expressive media as behavioral-management interventions;
5. Discuss the self-control curriculum.

A CASE FOR CONSIDERATION

"It's time for free play," said Ms. Michael. "Remember the rules. Take only one thing off the shelf at a time. Stay on your rug. No one bothers anyone else while playing."

The four students went to the toy shelf. George went immediately for the building blocks. Martha considered a minute, then took the lighted pegboard. Allen picked up the Tinkertoys, replaced them, and decided on the toy garage. Luisa stood back, watching the others select their toys. After waiting several seconds, she grabbed the dollhouse and took it to her rug.

As Ms. Michael visited each student at his or her rug, she asked them to describe their activities. Using active listening, she reflected their feelings and descriptions back to them. When she reached Luisa, however, she paused and observed her for several minutes. She approached the rug slowly and sat down on its edge in front of the little girl.

"Tell me about the dollhouse, Luisa," she began quietly. Luisa sat grasping one of the small dolls, staring into the house. She remained silent.

"I like the way you have the living room set up, Luisa. Can you tell me about it?" Again, Luisa failed to respond. Ms. Michael noticed that one of the dolls was outside the house. "Who's this, Luisa?"

Luisa paused, and said, "The daddy."

"Why is the daddy outside the house?"

Luisa sat quietly, then answered in a hushed voice, "He doesn't live there anymore."

"Who do you have in your hand?"

Luisa answered, "The baby."

"Why are you holding her?"

"She's sad," replied Luisa.

"The baby is sad, so you're holding her," reiterated Ms. Michael.

"The baby's crying, cause Daddy's gone and Momma's at work."

"The baby's sad, so you're helping by holding her."

"Yes," stated Luisa.

"People like making other people feel better," replied Ms. Michael, as she rose to return to another child. Luisa returned to her play.

Ms. Michael was using a free-play technique with her students. During the daily free play period, students were free to interact with a variety of toys and materials. Ms. Michael remained nonjudgmental throughout the period, echoing back to the students their descriptions of their activities and their feelings. Free play is one of the psycho-educational–psychodynamic interventions that will be explored in this chapter.

OBJECTIVE ONE: *To describe the psychoeducational framework.*

An integral part of the psychodynamic–psychoeducational perspective and interventions discussed here and in Chapter 1 is the psychoeducational framework. This is a generic concept that includes a theory, method, and perspective on the education of children and youths with behavior disorders (Long, Morse, & Newman, 1980). Originally, the psychoeducational model was associated with psychoanalytic-psychodynamic strategy (Berkowitz & Rothman, 1960, 1967; Peter, 1965).

To provide the model with substance and direction, Long, Morse, and Newman (1980) offered the following operating principles and beliefs as a basis for special educators wishing to implement the psychoeducational approach:

1. Cognitive and affective processes are in continuous interaction.
2. Accepting the existence of mental illness, our task is to describe the pupil in terms of functioning skills that highlight areas of strength and pinpoint areas of weakness for remediation.
3. The psychoeducational process involves creating a special environment so that initially each pupil can function successfully at his or her present level.
4. Given this specialized environment, each pupil is taught that he or she has the capacity and resources to function appropriately and successfully.
5. Understanding how each pupil perceives, feels, thinks, and behaves in this setting facilitates educational conditions for optimal behavioral change.
6. There are no special times during the school day. Everything that happens to, with, for, and against the pupil is important and can have therapeutic value.
7. Emotionally troubled pupils have learned a vulnerability to many normal developmental tasks and relationships such as competition, sharing, testing, closeness, etc. As teachers, we are responsible for awareness of these areas and for modifying our behavior in appropriate fashion.
8. Emotionally disturbed pupils behave in immature ways during periods of stress. They will lie, fight, run away, regress, and deny the most obvious realities. We can anticipate immature behavior from children in conflict; our hope for change is to expect mature behavior from adults.
9. Pupils in conflict can create their feelings and behaviors in others; aggressive pupils can create counter-aggressive behaviors in others; hyperactive children can create hyperactivity in others; withdrawn pupils can get other children and adults to ignore them; passive-aggressive pupils are effective in getting others to carry their angry feelings for days. If a child succeeds in getting the adult to act out his feelings and behavior, he succeeds in perpetuating his self-fulfilling prophecy of life, which in turn reinforces his defenses against change.
10. Emotionally troubled children have learned to associate adult intervention with adult rejection. One staff goal is to reinterpret adult interventions as an act of protection rather than hostility. The pupil must be told over and over again that adults are here to protect him from real dangers, contagion, psychological depreciation, etc.
11. We are here to listen to what the pupil says, to focus on what he is feeling

12.   We are to expect and accept a normal amount of hostility and disappointment from pupils and colleagues.

13.   Pupils' home and community lives are an important source of health that must be considered by any remedial process. However, if all attempts fail, the school becomes an island of support for pupils.

14.   We must demonstrate that fairness is treating children differently. Although group rules are necessary for organizational purposes, individual expectations are necessary for growth and change.

15.   Crises are excellent times for teachers to teach and/or pupils to learn.

16.   Behavioral limits can be a form of love, i.e. physical restraint can be a therapeutic act of caring for and protecting pupils.

17.   Teaching pupils social and academic skills enhances their capacity to cope with a stressful environment.

18.   Pupils learn through a process of unconscious identification with significant adults in their lives. This means the teacher's personal appearance, attitudes, and behavior are important factors in teaching, which must be evaluated continuously.*

Nichols (1984) proposed several additional premises to clarify the special educator's role in the psychoeducational framework. She suggests that:

1.   Excluding counseling and other therapeutic interventions, which have been traditionally perceived as outside of their realm, limit special educators' potential as child-helpers. In practice, special educators have been actively and profitably conducting psychotherapeutic activities for many years. Being more aware of their activities as psychotherapists, special educators can avail themselves of increased opportunities to improve their skills.

2.   Psycho-educational practice is becoming increasingly refined and has profited from educational technology. Among the refinements that have occurred in the model since it was originally described are working with groups rather than individual children, attempting to improve the quality of children's responses, and actively seeking change. Rather than dealing with the subconscious, the psycho-educator deals with overt behaviors and covert behaviors such as self-talk.

3.   Special educators go beyond being simply classroom managers, and intentionally teach children new thoughts, feelings, and behaviors.

4.   Together, psychologists and special educators can prepare materials and training opportunities so that the special educator is competent at and responsible for incorporating psychological instruction as a central feature of programs for children and youths with behavior disorders.

Intention is the keystone in Nichols's suggestions with regard to the role of the psycho-educator. She maintains that if special educators know what they want students to know and use direct instruction, modeling, and practice as methods of teaching, programs can be developed in response to the special needs of children and youth with behavior disorders. Such

*From *Conflict in the Classroom*, 4th ed., by N. J. Long, W. C. Morse, and R. Newman. © 1980 by Wadsworth, Inc. Reprinted by permission of the publisher.

"intentional psychological instruction" uses as many components of the direct-instruction process as are required to teach cognitive and behavioral skills, while also utilizing counseling techniques to facilitate therapeutic communication with students and thus help them progress.

It is within the context of the preceding discussion and the psychodynamic–psycho-educational perspective presented in Chapter 1 that the behavior-management interventions in the remainder of this chapter gain significance.

Several counseling techniques, "surface" behavior-management interventions, interventions dependent on the expressive media, and group interventions are presented. Special educators, with appropriate training, may implement these interventions with children and youths with behavior disorders. Several important interventions, such as individual and group psychotherapy, directive and nondirective counseling, and family therapy, employed by professionals in the allied mental health disciplines, are not discussed in this chapter.

With the exception of "surface" behavior-management techniques, the interventions discussed in the following four sections are directed toward the cause of the behavior disorders. The techniques are applied primarily to assist children and youth with behavior disorders in their efforts to establish or reestablish intrapsychic equilibrium, alleviate psychological stress, or fulfill personal needs. It is important to retain this perspective throughout the study of psychodynamic–psychoeducational behavior-management interventions and to recognize that the interventions presented are less objectively applied and evaluated than those derived from the behavioral and biophysical perspectives, discussed in chapters 10 and 11.

OBJECTIVE TWO: *To describe counseling interventions based on the psychodynamic–psycho-educational perspective.*

In this section, two psychodynamic–psychoeducational counseling interventions that may be implemented by special educators are discussed. These techniques are life-space interviewing and reality therapy.

Life-space Interviewing

Redl (1959) recommended the life-space interview as a *here-and-now* intervention built around the individual's *direct life experience.* It is applied by an instructor who is perceived by the child to be an important part of the child's life-space. The interviewer has a definite facilitating role and influence on the child's daily life. The life-space interview is used to structure an incident in the child's life so that the problems confronting the child can be solved. The interview is conducted as soon as possible after the occurrence of the behavioral incident and, if possible, in the location in which the incident occurred. The life-space interview may be applied with both individuals and groups.

According to Redl, the life-space interview may be used for one of two purposes—clinical exploitation of life events, and emotional first aid on the spot—although frequently a single interview is conducted for both purposes.

In the first situation, the *clinical exploitation of life events*, the interviewer uses an actual behavioral incident to explore with the child or young person a habitual behavioral characteristic. This is an effort by the interviewer to use the incident to attain a long-range therapeutic goal previously established for the child.

When the life-space interview is employed for the exploitation of life events, the interviewer assists the individual to increase conscious awareness of (a) distorted perceptions of existing realities, (b) habitual inappropriate behavioral characteristics, (c) hidden social and moral values and standards, or (d) reactions to the behaviors and pressures of the group. The interviewer also uses the technique to encourage the individual to adopt more personally productive and socially acceptable means of solving problems.

The special educator can use life-space interviewing to provide a student with *emotional first aid on the spot* in times of stress, to assist the individual over a rough spot in the road in order to continue an ongoing activity. The interview is conducted to (a) reduce the student's frustration level; (b) support the student in emotionally charged situations; (c) restore strained student-special educator communications; (d) reinforce existing behavioral and social limits and realities; and (e) assist the student in efforts to find solutions to everyday problems of living and to emotionally charged incidents, such as fights and arguments.

As in any counseling situation, the application of the life-space interview depends on several variables: the purpose and goal of the interview; the specific context; the training and experience of the interviewer; the child or young person's personal characteristics; the behavior; and the phase of the rehabilitation process.

The use of life-space interviewing as an integral part of the behavior-management program in a special education program is a decision that involves all members of the student's Individualized Education Program planning team. When the technique is selected for implementation, it should be used consistently by all members of the team.

Morse (1980) outlined a series of steps that occur during the life-space interview. Generally, the interview begins as a result of a specific incident in the individual's life-space. The interviewer encourages those involved in the incident to state their personal perceptions of it. At this time the interviewer must determine if this incident is an isolated happening or a significant part of a recurring central issue.

The interviewer listens to those involved in the incident as they reconstruct it. Their feelings and perceptions are accepted without moralizing or attacking. Although these individual perceptions are accepted, the interviewer may suggest alternative perceptions for consideration by the student.

The interview process then moves into a nonjudgmental resolution phase. Many conflicts and confrontations are resolved at this point, and the life-space interview is terminated. However, if the problem is not resolved, the interviewer may offer his or her view of the incident in which the individual (or individuals) finds himself or herself. Finally, the individual and the interviewer develop an acceptable plan to deal with the present problem and similar problems in the future. A sample life-space interview is presented in Figure 9-1.

Two systematic studies have measured the effectiveness of the life-space interview in educational settings. A study conducted by Reilly, Imber, and Cremins (1978) evaluated the use of the interview in the resource-room setting. The interview was found to decrease students' inappropriate behaviors. In addition, it was found to be a practical technique for applica-

FIGURE 9-1 Sample Life-Space Interview

Step	Sample Behaviors and Verbalizations
Instigating event	Student pulls materials from bulletin board, shredding posters, etc.
Testing for depth and spread	"Marcia was calling me stupid. You always catch me. You just don't like me."
Content clarification	"I was mad at Marcia for calling me stupid, so I ripped down the posters."
Enhancing a feeling of acceptance	Teacher: "You felt angry at Marcia. Being called stupid when you're trying your best can make you angry."
Avoiding early value judgments	Teacher: "How do you feel about your decision to show that you were mad at Marcia by tearing down the posters?"
Exploring change possibilities	Teacher: "What is a better way to show you're mad at Marcia and to let me know how you feel?"
Resolution	"I could get away from her when she calls me names . . . I could just ignore her . . . I could tell you about it . . . I could tell her she's making me mad and that she should stop."

tion by special educators. DeMagistris and Imber (1980) evaluated the appropriateness of the interview in a self-contained classroom for eight emotionally disturbed boys in a residential placement. Though their findings have limited application, they were positive: inappropriate behaviors decreased and academic performance improved.

Reality Therapy

In his 1965 and 1969 publications, Glasser offers a distinct departure from the traditional Freudian and neo-Freudian belief that mental health is a state of contentment and mental ill health a state of discontent. From the reality therapy perspective, mental health is the ability to function competently in the environment, whereas mental illness is incompetence.

An individual in need of psychiatric assistance is unable to fulfill his or her own essential psychological needs. The objective of reality therapy is to lead the individual toward competent functioning in the real environment. This technique is designed to help the individual grapple successfully with the tangible and intangible aspects of the real world and as a result fulfill personal needs, which, according to Glasser (1965), are to love and be loved and to feel worthwhile to oneself and others.

In reality therapy, the process of therapy and the process of teaching are identical. The therapist's or special educator's primary objective during the therapeutic process is to teach the mentally ill person responsible behavior. Responsibility is the ability to fulfill one's personal needs in a manner that does not deprive others of their ability to fulfill personal needs.

According to Glasser's thesis, learning to be a responsible person is not a natural developmental process. Individuals are taught to be responsible through involvement with responsible and significant others. This involvement includes love and discipline. Most individuals learn to be responsible in association with loving and disciplining parents and significant others, such as teachers and guardians.

In summary, reality therapy is the process of teaching irresponsible individuals to face existing reality, to function responsibly, and, as a result, to fulfill their personal needs. For mentally ill individuals, the therapeutic process includes involvement with a caring therapist, who accepts the individual while rejecting the individual's inappropriate behavior.

In a special education program for children and youths with behavior disorders, reality therapy's goal is to guide individuals and groups toward a more responsible behavior: mental health. This goal is attained by means of the reality-therapy interview. The special educator using the reality-therapy interview should:

1. Be personal and demonstrate friendship and interest in the individual's welfare.

2. Focus the therapeutic process on the individual's present behavior, not on past behavior. Accept the individual's expressed feelings, but do not probe into unconscious motivation. Ask "what," "how," and "who," rather than "why" questions.

3. Not preach, moralize, or make value judgments about the individual's behavior.

4. Help formulate a practical, cooperative plan to increase the individual's responsible behavior.

5. Encourage the individual to overtly commit him- or herself to the cooperative plan.

6. Not accept excuses for irresponsible behavior. When a plan fails or cannot be implemented, develop another.

7. Not punish the individual for irresponsible behavior. Allow the person to realize the logical consequences of irresponsible behavior unless the consequences are unreasonably harmful.

8. Provide the individual with emotional support and security throughout the therapeutic process.

Reality therapy, because it is primarily verbal in nature, is perhaps most appropriately utilized with upper elementary school children and junior and senior high school youths who are capable of carrying on meaningful verbal transactions.

Although it is primarily an individual technique, Glasser (1969) recommended reality therapy for application with classroom groups. In an effort to reduce the present emphasis in the schools on competition and achievement, Glasser proposed reality therapy meetings to teach decision making, social responsibility, and cooperation. These tasks are accomplished through three types of meetings: social problem-solving, open-ended, and educational-diagnostic. The social problem-solving meeting is focused on individual and group problems in the classroom and school. Open-ended meetings are discussions of any thought-provoking questions related to the members of the group or the group itself. Educational-diagnostic meetings focus on the content of the educational program in which the children are involved in the classroom. Group meetings are further discussed in Chapter 11.

A limited number of studies of the effects of reality therapy with various groups of children have been conducted. In general, these studies lack experimental rigor, and the results have been mixed. Cook (1972; cited in Shearn & Randolph, 1978) reported no significant changes in the positive or negative behaviors of sociometrically underselected adolescents exposed to reality therapy. Hawes (1970; cited in Shearn & Randolph, 1978) reported significant gains in the self-concept of black children in reality therapy. However, Glick (1968; cited in Shearn & Randolph, 1978) reported no significant changes in the self-concept and self-responsibility of emotionally disturbed boys in a residential school. However, significant changes in self-esteem were reported. Scheaf (1972 cited in Shearn & Randolph, 1978) noted no significant changes in the reading achievement of delinquents involved in reality therapy. Shearn and Randolph (1978), using a four-group experimental design, studied the effects of reality therapy on the task-oriented behaviors and self-concept of fourth-grade students; results were not significant. In a follow-up study of adolescents who had successfully left a facility using reality therapy and contingency-management procedures, most of the students were found to be moderately successful young adults; only one of the eighteen subjects returned to the facility, and only four were unemployed two to four years after leaving the program, despite substantial deficits in academic skills (Leone, 1984).

OBJECTIVE THREE: *To describe interventions for managing surface behavior, derived from the psychodynamic–psycho-educational perspective.*

The indirect behavior-management interventions reviewed in this chapter are often criticized as ineffective for the management of inappropriate behaviors that occur frequently in the special education context and may be a threat to the child, group, teacher, program, or property. Using the work of Redl (1959), Long, Morse, and Newman (1980) responded to special educators' needs for techniques designed to manage the "surface" behaviors of children and youth with behavior disorders.

Redl suggested four major alternatives that are available to an educator responsible for managing behavior. These are permitting, tolerating, interfering, and preventing. Permitting, as a behavior-management alternative, involves communicating to a child what behaviors are to be permitted and under what circumstances. Conversely, the alternative communicated is what behaviors are not permissible and under what circumstances.

The effective special educator is tolerant of certain inappropriate behaviors for the therapeutic benefit of the child. For example, the educator may tolerate behaviors that are symptomatic of the child's emotional problem but are not an immediate therapeutic objective. Most certainly, educators will tolerate some inappropriate behaviors that are characteristic of a phase of normal growth and development. Finally, the special educator tolerates behaviors that are a consequence of the child's effort to learn new and more appropriate behaviors.

However, special educators have a responsibility to interfere with behaviors that present a real danger or are psychologically harmful to the child and others. Behaviors that lead to excessive excitement or loss of control and prohibit the continuation of the program must be dealt with. The special educator must interfere with behaviors that spread negativism, lead to conflict with others outside the group, and lead to destruction of property.

Long, Morse, and Newman (1980) have suggested a number of "influence" techniques or "surface" management interventions for use when it is necessary to interfere with behavior. These are:

1. *Planned ignoring.* A teacher often finds it appropriate simply to ignore certain behaviors that, although inappropriate, do not interfere with the child's and group's program and are not primary symptoms of the child's behavior disorder. When a behavior is ignored, it is assumed that because it is not being reinforced, it will decrease.

2. *Signal interference.* Signal-interference techniques are applied to communicate to children by means of a nonverbal gesture that their behavior is inappropriate. Signals may include eye contact, a frown, staring, finger snapping, and so on. Signal interference is especially helpful when it is necessary to communicate to a child without alerting the other members of the group or interfering with an activity.

3. *Proximity control.* Proximity control means interfering with inappropriate behavior by physically moving toward or standing near the misbehaving child. This technique is also useful when a child is experiencing discomfort and frustration. Frequently, the teacher's physical proximity is adequate to provide the child with the security needed to continue the task at hand.

4. *Interest boosting.* Children occasionally become bored and lose interest in an activity. They may be encouraged to continue a task if their teacher exhibits some personal interest in their efforts. This technique requires little more from the teacher than a pat on the back, a word of praise, or a simple question or positive comment about the task.

5. *Tension decontamination through humor.* When activities become tense and children become anxious, a little humor may be appropriate. Humor helps put things in perspective and relaxes the children. Sometimes, program activities are blown out of proportion and become a life-and-death situation in the minds of the children. Humor is never directed at a child or group in a harmful way.

6. *Hurdle lessons.* Sometimes children have a difficult time completing a task. They either can't do it or think they can't. If left entirely to their own resources, they may become disruptive. Hurdle-helping is simply aiding a child with a task. With a little help, the child will probably calm down and reorganize his or her effort.

7. *Restructuring the program.* Children become bored with the same activities day after day; they confront tasks they don't like and occasionally tasks they cannot do. Likewise, teachers become bored with the same activities; they occasionally become overcommitted to a particular activity or a subject. Before the group becomes either disruptive or falls asleep, change—restructuring—is necessary. Restructuring can be as simple as taking a break or as drastic as stopping the lesson and doing another one for a period of time.

8. *Support from routine.* Many children and youths with behavior disorders become uncomfortable in unstructured and permissive environments. Their feelings of security and comfort and their ability to function effectively are enhanced by routines and schedules. They should know the daily who, what, where, when, and how of the program. Changes in routine should be communicated in advance.

9. *Direct appeal to value areas.* Children and young persons with behavior disor-

ders should be viewed as able to control their behavior and respond to a direct appeal from the teacher to stop an inappropriate one. Teachers may appeal to a child's understanding of fairness, authority, the consequences of their behavior, or its effect on others.

10. *Removing seductive objects.* Children carry a wide variety of items to school that are often more interesting than the planned program. Rather than permitting the "temptation," the teacher removes the object in a kind manner and with the understanding that it will be returned to the child at the appropriate time.

11. *Antiseptic bouncing.* When all else fails, it is sometimes necessary to remove a child from a situation in which he or she is either misbehaving or about to misbehave. When antiseptic bouncing is used, the child is taken or asked to go to another setting in which he or she can presumably calm down and regain control. It is communicated to the child that the removal is a helpful act, and not a punishment.

12. *Physical restraint.* On rare occasions, children and youths with behavior disorders lose self-control. They engage in fights or tantrums. If these children are to be prevented from harming themselves, others, or property, they may need to be physically restrained. Such restraint is not a punishment, but is a positive and helpful act designed to comfort the children and help them regain control.

Finally, there is preventative planning, Redl's fourth alternative for behavior management. Prevention is the most effective means of managing behaviors, and requires the special educator to be alert to individual, group, and program needs. It necessitates appropriate materials, equipment, and personnel, and requires limits, routines, and schedules. The most effective behavior management is probably derived from a well-organized, well-conducted program presented by a caring and competent special educator.

OBJECTIVE FOUR: *To describe the use of expressive media behavior-management interventions.*

Expressive media refer to activities that encourage and permit children and youth with behavior disorders to express feelings and emotions through creative activities with minimal constraints.

Expressive media can provide many benefits for the child or young person with a behavior problem. They are not only beneficial in the affective domain, but offer a variety of cognitive and psychomotor learning benefits as well.

If expressive media are to be used as behavior-management techniques, the child must be provided with a variety of opportunities to find media for personal expression. The individual must be provided with consistent, repeated opportunities to express feelings and emotions by means of the chosen media.

Cheney and Morse (1972) have summarized the value of the expressive media for children and youth with behavior disorders:

> This group of interventions supports and develops the child's expressive abilities. Such techniques serve to mobilize the child's internal resources in a number of ways: they facilitate involvement through activity rather than retreat and withdrawal; they provide acceptable channels for cathartic release; they serve as means of both externalizing the child's conflicts and communicating his feelings about them to others (though both the signal and response may be nonverbal and nonconscious and not discussed); and many of the expressive media seem to embody inherent "therapeutic" qualities. For children with verbal inhibitions the whole "language" may be nonverbal (p. 352).

Axline (1947) suggested several principles for play therapy that are applicable by the educator of children and youth with behavior disorders. The therapist must develop a warm relationship, built on accepting the child exactly as he or she is. The therapist establishes a feeling of freedom in the relationship, so that the child feels free to express his or her feelings. The therapist must be sensitive to the feelings of the child and reflect those feelings back to facilitate insight. The relationship is built on respect and a belief that the child can change his or her behavior. The only limits established in this setting are those necessary to assist the child in becoming aware of the responsibility inherent in his or her relationships.

When using the expressive media for therapeutic purposes, the child's or young person's activities should not be prescribed, though some limitations and structure in their application relative to time, place, specific media, and behavioral extremes are necessary.

Minimal limits must be established and communicated to the child either verbally or by demonstrations (Ginott, 1959). These limits involve (a) time, (b) the use of materials and equipment, (c) the location of equipment and materials, (d) the prevention of the destruction of facilities, equipment, and materials, and (e) restrictions to ensure the safety of the child and teacher.

Play therapy and free play. Play therapy, as described by Axline (1947), Baruch (1952), Moustakas (1953), and Solomon (1951), is difficult to initiate in the special education program for children and youth with behavior disorders because of the restrictions inherent in the educational context, the traditional role of the special educator, and lack of training. However, free-play opportunities applying Axline's principles can be offered as a part of the special-education program.

Free-play sessions can be provided for either individuals or groups. If a free-play program is instituted, sessions are provided on a scheduled basis. Play materials and equipment, selected by the teacher, are to be located in a designated area in the classroom. These materials should be basic, so that the child or group can create environments and express feelings.

In a free-play session, the child is invited to play with any of the materials in the play area, and is encouraged to select materials of interest. Activities are restricted only by the limits previously discussed. The special educator's role is generally that of observer and activity facilitator.

Puppetry. Puppets are a medium that may help children with behavior disorders express their feelings and emotions. Some children who cannot communicate with others in a face-to-face relationship may do so through a puppet.

Many respected language development and affective-education programs have successfully used puppetry. Experience in clinical, school, and camp settings has shown that sophisticated puppets and puppet stages are unnecessary. Simple hand puppets, often created by the children and may be personal possessions, are effective (D'Alonzo, 1974).

Puppets may be used to promote social and cultural awareness, to stimulate language communication skills, and in free-play situations (D'Alonzo, 1974). Even the children not involved directly in the puppet show can profit from this activity. They respond and converse with the puppet being manipulated by a teacher or another child. When using puppetry, the special educator should help the child understand that activities are "make-believe" and that it is acceptable to express negative as well as positive emotions. At the conclusion of the session, the teacher helps the child understand the content of the show, interpret it, and seek alternative solutions for the conflicts presented by the puppets.

Role playing and psychodrama. Role playing and psychodrama, developed for therapeutic purposes by Moreno (1946), are potentially valuable interventions. Psychodrama is based on the assumption that individuals may gain greater understanding of their behavior if they act out various aspects of their lives (Newcomer, 1980). It employs dramatization to assist in understanding and resolving interpersonal problems through encouraging the individual to express personal conflicts while using words, movements, and gestures (Creekmore & Maden, 1981).

According to Raths, Harmin, and Simon (1966), role playing can assist an individual in the clarification of feelings and emotions as these relate to reality in three ways. It focuses on real occurrences, which may be reenacted with the participants attending to the feelings aroused, and then changing roles and attending to the feelings aroused by these new roles. Role playing can also focus on significant others and on the processes and feelings occurring in new situations.

Several purposes of drama therapy in the educational setting have been described (Creekmore and Maden, 1981; Necco, Wilson, & Scheidmantel, 1982; Newcomer, 1980). These include—

assisting in finding solutions, making decisions, and assuming responsibility for personal, social, and emotional problems;

assisting in affective education, increasing feelings and emotions, and improving communications skills;

assisting in solving common problems associated with childhood and adolescence;

facilitating the discussion of social and cultural issues;

enchancing group cohesiveness;

experimenting with adult roles;

facilitating the conceptualization of abstract concepts in subject areas such as mathematics, language, and science;

providing entertainment and recreation;

providing teachers with an opportunity to perceive their students situationally and to analyze their personal roles in the educational situation.

Newcomer (1980) urges special educators to implement drama therapy with care. Students should be properly prepared to participate in the program. They should understand its purposes, objectives, and benefits. Rules and restrictions should be carefully explained and discussed prior to implementation. It is especially important that participation be voluntary, that the dramatic presentation be devoid of personal criticism of the participants, and that confrontation be carefully controlled to assure the integrity of the participants.

Movement, dance, and physical activities. As therapeutic activities, movement and dance have the capacity to assist the child or young person to express personal feelings and emotions in an acceptable manner. This can be accomplished in several ways: imitating nature or animals, expressing the feelings of others, and expressing personal feelings in various contexts. In creative movement, the individual can express past, present, and even future feelings and emotions. These activities encourage individuals to externalize their feelings and begin to deal with them.

Movement activities can be conducted with or without music (Hibben & Scheer, 1982). On occasion, voices, hand clapping, foot stamping, environmental sounds, and rhythm instruments are used.

Physical activities have also been used to provide both aerobic activity and a therapeutic restructuring of the environment (Lane, Bonic, & Wallgren-Bonic, 1983). Group "walk-talks" have been demonstrated to produce healthy levels of fatigue and improved peer relationships among adolescents (Lane & associates, 1983). A daily jogging program has also been demonstrated to decrease disruptive behaviors among children with behavior disorders (Allen, 1980).

Music therapy. All individuals are affected by music in some manner. In today's society, we are exposed to mood-modifying music in restaurants, factories, offices, supermarkets, department stores, banks, and so on. This music is designed to affect our behavior—our efficiency, productivity, eating, saving patterns, and spending (Roter, 1981).

In what is perhaps the first definitive work on music for the handicapped, Alvin (1965) suggested that music may help the mental, perceptual, or emotional growth of the child regardless of musical ability. Music may be a nonthreatening means of communication, in which the child has not experienced failure. He states that "music can enable [the handicapped child] to express himself, develop his personality by creating healthy attitudes towards himself and others, and evokes identification at his own emotional level" (p. 37).

In a discussion of the advantages of music as an integral component of the Developmental Therapy curriculum for severely emotionally disturbed children, Wood (1976) suggested that for such children:

> Communication must be established as a basis for trust if there is to be subsequent growth; and of all the ways to communicate, perhaps music is the most universal . . . Whatever form the disturbance takes, and whatever the age of the child, there is a way to reach each child through music in order to begin the gradual movements toward healthier responses (p. vii).

There are several ways to apply music to help children and youths with behavior disorders. These include (Lament, 1978; Purvis and Samet, 1976; Roter, 1981) background music, listening, playing (instruments and rhythm-band activities), singing and chanting, and moving rhythmically.

Michel (1976) suggested that music therapy techniques may be of assistance even if a trained music therapist is not available. Music can be used by the teacher as part of a child's educational intervention, as an adjunct to daily programming, and to teach specific subject matter (Duerksen, 1981). As part of a child's educational intervention, music may be used in the following ways (David & Newcomer, 1980; Ferolo, Rotatori & Fox, 1984; Ferolo, Rotatori, Macklin, & Fox, 1983; Lament, 1978; Thursby, 1977):

> to facilitate cognitive development, through increasing abstract thinking, increasing attending, and providing practice for conceptual skills
>
> to facilitate affective developmental and social skills and encourage social interaction
>
> to increase psychomotor skills, coordination, body image, position in space, movement skills, and auditory and visual discrimination
>
> to assist in the development of self-concept, to develop self-reliance, and to provide an opportunity to be successful
>
> to provide creative experiences, increase expressive skills, and provide an expressive outlet for "blowing off steam"

There are several adjunctive uses of music in the special education setting. (David & Newcomer, 1980; Duerksen, 1981). Music may be used to manage behaviors of individuals and groups, produce a relaxing atmosphere, and may serve as a creative distraction for children and youths with behavior disorders. Musical activities may serve as reinforcement for improved behavior, completion of work, or to motivate students in other ways. Since it is nonverbal, music may serve as both a communicative and an aesthetic outlet for some children and youth with behavior disorders.

Music may also be used to teach subject matter (Duerksen, 1981; Thursby, 1977). It can provide musical settings, backgrounds, and contexts for subject areas. Music may be used to physically structure activities, and may be applied with creative writing, art, and storytelling.

It is important to remember that the goals of music therapy are not to teach specific musical skills and knowledge but to assist the student in reaching nonmusical goals (Duerksen, 1981).

Art therapy.   All productions, from the young child's scribbling to the young adult's realist drawings and paintings, can be perceived as an expression of self. Art as a therapeutic treatment medium is a growth oriented experience that benefits children and youth in many ways: communication, socialization, creativity, self-expression, self-exploration, and manipulation of the environment (Williams & Wood, 1977).

All children and youth, especially those with behavior disorders, should be afforded opportunities to express their feelings and emotions through the arts. Their productions may include pencil drawings and painting with water colors, oils, tempera, and finger paints. Photography may be of assistance to students who are dissatisfied with their attempts to produce creative visual expressions (Minner, 1981). The three-dimensional art forms are more limited because of the nature of the materials, but are nevertheless valuable therapeutic interventions. The child or young person can externalize feelings through the use of clay, plaster, sand, wood, plastic, and other materials. Arts-and-crafts projects are also included here as potentially therapeutic interventions.

Although special educators are generally not trained art therapists, they can apply the discipline's techniques in programs with children and youths with behavior disorders. The special educator must know some basic art techniques and be familiar with popular materials. Such a teacher must communicate to students that their feelings, thoughts, and experiences are worthwhile material for artistic expression and help students set realistic goals for participation. The students and their art productions must be accepted for what they are. The goal of art therapy is the expression of self, not the making of an artist. The special educator must avoid the temptations to either direct student activities or interpret the affective content of their productions (David & Newcomer, 1980).

In the special education program, the goals of art therapy include fostering student growth, promoting interpersonal relationships, and establishing communication through the creative process.

The written word.   It seems logical that children and youths could express feelings and emotions in written communications. By writing, and at times sharing with others that which is written, it is possible to externalize personal conflicts and frustrations (Levinson, 1982).

> The written word is a modality for self-expression, self-exploration, and problem-solving. Through story writing, students reveal their perceptions, attitudes, coping skills, and problem-solving strategies. Story writing tasks can be structured to encourage students to explore the decision making process and identify behavioral alternatives and consequences (Dehouske, 1982, p. 11).

In writing for therapeutic benefit, there is no concern with any particular format. Concern is focused exclusively on content. The written forms may include poetry, stories, essays, books, diary and journal entries, scripts for cartoons, and so on. The special educator wishing to use writing as a therapeutic intervention must encourage the children to write original and creative materials. The emphasis is on the affective content of the children's efforts. The teacher may wish to present the students with story situations and incomplete stories to be completed from a personal perspective.

The spoken work.   Although many children are not developmentally or emotionally prepared to enter formal verbal psychotherapy, they frequently enjoy and profit from verbal communication. Their communication takes the form of group storytelling sessions and informal conversations and discussions.

Newcomer (1980) suggests that the therapeutic benefit of storytelling is greatest if children create original materials to tell the group. The teacher helps the children create stories and cast themselves as characters in the stories. The stories may be acted out by the children, with the affective aspects emphasized.

Bibliotherapy.   Bibliotherapy is an indirect intervention that uses the interaction between the reader and literature for therapeutic purposes. This interaction can be used with children and youth with behavior disorders to encourage them to fulfill their needs, relieve pressures, and improve mental and emotional well-being (Russell & Russell, 1979).

For bibliotherapy to be effective, children must be able to read, motivated to read, and exposed to appropriate reading materials. Literature must be selected by the special educator and child that focuses on children's needs, is at the appropriate level, is real, and accurately represents the characters in the story (Cianciolo, 1965).

Hoagland (1972) indicates that bibliotherapy is a three-phase process. First, the children must identify themselves in the literature—they must perceive themselves as a part of the story or as a character. Second, children must become emotionally involved in the story and the problem it presents. Finally, they must arrive at a greater understanding of themselves and their problems by identifying with the characters or situations in the story.

Learning activities used to facilitate bibliotherapy include writing a summary of the book for discussion; dramatization, role playing, or presenting skits or puppet shows on the message in the literature; and making artworks that represent characters and situations in literature.

Although bibliotherapy emphasizes written literature, these techniques can be applied to a variety of media, including video recordings, films, cartoons, poetry, or audio tapes.

OBJECTIVE FIVE: *To discuss the self-control curriculum.*

One of the most significant occurrences in the education of children and youth with behavior disorders in recent years has been the renewed emphasis on the self-control curriculum, or affective education. This approach emphasizes helping children focus on increasing their awareness and understanding of personal emotions, values, and attitudes through educational activities (Epanchin & Monson, 1982). Through affective education, children become increasingly aware of the relationship between self and others, and improve their interpersonal problem-solving skills.

Perhaps the social skills curriculum most compatible with the psychoeducational framework and especially Redl's fourth management alternative, prevention, is the "Psychoeducational Curriculum for the Prevention of Behavioral and Learning Problems" (commonly referred to as the "Self-Control Curriculum") by Fagen, Long, and Stevens (1975).

This curriculum is based on the assumption that the common denominator for disruptive behaviors of children is a lack of self-control. To function effectively, children must develop the capacity to control their behavior, even when they are frustrated. Self-control is defined as "one's capacity to direct and regulate personal action (behavior) flexibly and realistically in a given situation" (Fagen & Long, 1976). An important objective of the curriculum is the reduction of students' anxiety over loss of control, by increasing skills and confidence in regulating impulsive behavior.

Skillful self-control depends on the integration of eight skill clusters. These skill clusters, in turn, are composed of several specific skills. These clusters and their skills are presented in Figure 9-2. In the curriculum, the learning of each specific skill is accomplished through a variety of learning activities. Through growth in the eight skill clusters, the authors predict growth in the student's capacity to direct and regulate their personal action in given situations. Activities that make up the curriculum include games, role playing lessons, and discussion. Activities are implemented in small

FIGURE 9-2   The Self-Control Curriculum: Overview of Curriculum Areas and Units

Area	Curriculum Unit
Selection	1. Focusing and concentration 2. Mastering figure-ground discrimination 3. Mastering distractions and interference 4. Processing complex patterns
Storage	1. Developing visual memory 2. Developing auditory memory
Sequencing and ordering	1. Developing time orientation 2. Developing auditory-visual sequencing 3. Developing sequential planning
Anticipating consequences	1. Developing alternatives 2. Evaluating consequences
Appreciating feelings	1. Identifying feelings 2. Developing positive feelings 3. Managing feelings 4. Reinterpreting feeling events
Managing frustration	1. Accepting feelings of frustration 2. Building coping resources 3. Tolerating frustration
Inhibition and delay	1. Controlling action 2. Developing goals
Relaxation	1. Developing body relaxation 2. Developing thought relaxation 3. Developing movement relaxation

S.A. Fagen, N.J. Long, & D.J. Stevens, *Teaching Children Self-Control: Preventing Emotional and Learning Problems in the Elementary School* (Columbus, OH: C.E. Merrill, 1975), p. 77. Reprinted by permission of the publisher.

developmental steps and include positive feedback. Short, regular training sessions are advised.

Morse (1979) indicated that the self-control curriculum advocates inserting a cognitive pause between the impulse and its expression. Training in self-control assists students by teaching them to use cognitive processes to balance their behavioral options in terms of their experiences and goals.

SUMMARY

In this chapter, the psychoeducational framework was introduced. Specific psychodynamic–psychoeducational interventions including counseling, surface-management techniques, expressive media, and affective education were presented.

The breadth and depth of the psychodynamic interventions available to the special educator cannot be presented in a single chapter. Although evaluative research evidence is scant, these interventions appear to be limited only by the needs and desires of the child or young person and the initiative of the special educator. Each year, new and creative intervention techniques are reported in the professional and popular literature. The recent trend toward prevention of behavior problems through the self-control curriculum will continue to impact on the education of children and youths with behavior disorders.

REVIEW QUESTIONS

1. Review the material on the psychodynamic perspective presented in Chapter 1. Discuss the relationship between that material and the information in this chapter.

2. Using the professional literature, locate and discuss other interventions based in the expressive arts. Can the expressive arts make a significant contribution to a therapeutic program? Why? How?

APPLICATION ACTIVITY

The following are several incidents that may require the special educator to employ surface-management interventions. Decide if you would tolerate the behavior, permit the behavior, or intervene. If you choose to intervene, indicate which technique or techniques may be appropriate.

Incident	Permit, Tolerate, or Intervene	Technique (if you choose to intervene)
Michael breaks his pencil during the spelling test; he leaves his seat to sharpen it.		
Amelia is frustrated with her long-division worksheet; she crumples the paper and throws it in the trash.		
LaKeesha and Joel push each other in the lunch line.		
Marvin taps his pencil while he is thinking.		
LouAnn brings her doll to class daily and combs its hair, rocks it, and talks to it.		

Incident	Permit, Tolerate, or Intervene	Technique (if you choose to intervene)
Four of the six members of the "Wild Bunch" reading group are no longer attending to the Word Bingo game.		
Alonzo stops in the line on the way back from physical education to get a drink.		
Linda is about ready to give up on the grammar worksheet; she is bouncing her eraser on her desk and kicking at the wall.		
James and Joshua are talking in the back of the room during another group's reading instruction.		
Julio says, "Big deal!" under his breath when you ask him to rewrite an essay.		

10

Behavioral Interventions

This chapter is a discussion of behavior management from the social learning and behavior modification perspective. The principles of behavior modification and the steps in the behavior change process are introduced. Several behavioral interventions for application with children and youths with behavior disorders are presented. Each intervention is explained and exemplified. The use of behavior modification techniques in the process of self-management is reviewed. The chapter concludes with a discussion of a continuum of behavioral interventions, their purposes, and applications.

OBJECTIVES

After completing this chapter, you will be able to—

1. Describe the principles of behavior modification;
2. Apply the behavior change process to selected behaviors of children and youths with behavior disorders;
3. Describe and apply selected behavior modification interventions;
4. Identify the procedures for training students in cognitive behavior modification for self-management;
5. Identify a continuum of behavioral interventions ranging from the least to the most restrictive.

A CASE FOR CONSIDERATION

"It's time for lunch, folks. Line up by the door," said Ms. Martinez. The usual mad scramble for the first position in line ensued. The journey to the cafeteria was noisy and disorganized. Julia, as usual, forgot her lunch and had to return to the room. Michael pushed into Juan, spilling the contents of his lunch tray. By the time all of the eight children with behavior disorders were seated at their lunch table, all eyes in the cafeteria were upon them. Ms. Martinez decided it was time to start applying some behavioral techniques to manage the behaviors of her hungry class.

After three weeks, a very different lunchtime routine was observed. After saying "Line up at the door," Ms. Martinez added, "I like the way Lucinda and Ben lined up. Good job. Lucinda may lead the line and Ben may turn out the lights." The other students quieted and stood by the door. "This is a good, quiet line. Nice work," said Ms. Martinez. Julia, noticing the small sign by the door that said, *"Do you have your lunch?"* returned to the shelf for her brown bag. "People who walk quietly to the lunchroom earn points," said Ms. Martinez, marker in hand. As the students reached the lunch line itself, Ms. Martinez placed a slash mark on a point card for each quiet child. "Remember the rule about lines. Keep your hands to yourself, and no pushing. People who follow the line rules may have points when they are seated." After the students were seated, Ms. Martinez again placed slash marks on the students' cards.

Ms. Martinez applied behavioral principles to modify the behavior of her students. Through planning and positive reinforcement, lunchtime was no longer a dreaded daily battle. In this chapter, the use of similar programs to manage students' behaviors is discussed.

OBJECTIVE ONE: To describe the principles of behavior modification.

The special educator with a behavior modification perspective sees the behavior disorders of children and youths as problems of learning. The inappropriate behaviors exhibited are assumed to be learned from the environment. The individual has either not learned the behaviors required to successfully work in the environment or has learned inappropriate or nonproductive behaviors.

The special educator with a behavior modification perspective is concerned with *what* an individual does, not *why* the individual exhibits specific behaviors. The cause of the behavior is assumed to exist outside of the individual in the environment. To change a behavior, termed a "target" behavior, the special educator manipulates the consequence the individual's behavior has on the environment (Walker & Shea, 1984).

Principles of Reinforcement

To the special educator with the behavior modification perspective, the learning of both appropriate and inappropriate behaviors is primarily dependent on the systematic application of the principles of reinforcement. These principles are applicable to all the behavior management interventions presented in this chapter. They must be consistently and appropriately applied in the behavior change process:

Principle 1: Reinforcement depends on the exhibition of the target behavior.
Principle 2: The target behavior is reinforced immediately after it is exhibited.
Principle 3: During the early stages of the behavior change process, the target behavior is reinforced each time it is exhibited.
Principle 4: When the target behavior reaches a satisfactory rate, it is reinforced intermittently.
Principle 5: Social reinforcers are always applied with tangible reinforcers.

Consequences of Behavior

Behavioral consequences have a direct influence on the behavior an individual exhibits. Behavior can be changed (increased or decreased, initiated or eliminated) by the systematic manipulation of consequences. The four possible consequences of behavior are: positive reinforcement, negative reinforcement, extinction, and punishment.

Figure 10-1 presents several examples of appropriate and inappropriate behavior, the consequences of that behavior, the probable effect of the consequences on the repetition of the behavior in the future, and the classification of the behavior.

Positive reinforcement. In positive reinforcement, a reward is presented after the target behavior is exhibited. The consequence is pleasurable to the individual and thus tends to increase the frequency with which the target behavior is exhibited in the future. (See the cases of Charles, Manuel, and Chantelle in Figure 10-1.)

Negative reinforcement. Negative reinforcement is the removal of an already-operating aversive stimulus (negative reinforcers). As a consequence of the removal of the negative reinforcer, behavior is strengthened. (See the case of Marguerite in Figure 10-1.) Axelrod (1977) describes negative reinforcement in the classroom setting as "an operation in which a student performs a desired behavior and the teacher removes something he dislikes, that is, perceived as unpleasant" (p. 8). For example, when the student works diligently on a classroom assignment, the teacher excuses the student from homework that is perceived as unpleasant by the student.

FIGURE 10-1　Behavior: Consequences, Probable Effect, and
　　　　　　　　 Classification

BEHAVIOR	CONSEQUENCES	EFFECT ON THE BEHAVIOR IN THE FUTURE	CLASSIFICATION
Charles empties the trash.	Parents praise Charles.	Charles will continue to empty the trash.	Positive reinforcement
Manuel brushes his teeth after meals.	Manuel receives a nickel each time.	Manuel's toothbrushing behavior will increase.	Positive reinforcement
Elizabeth empties the dishwasher.	Elizabeth is ignored.	Elizabeth no longer empties the dishwasher.	Extinction
Chantelle works quietly in her seat.	Teacher praises Chantelle.	Chantelle will continue to work quietly in her seat.	Positive reinforcement
Kyle sits with his feet on the sofa.	Kyle is spanked when he has his feet on the sofa.	Kyle will not sit with his feet on the sofa.	Punishment
Marguerite complains that the other girls laugh at her, and she refuses to go to school.	Marguerite's parents allow her to stay home from school.	Marguerite's school-attending behavior will decrease.	Negative reinforcement
John complains of headaches at homework time.	John is allowed to go to bed without completing his homework.	John will have "headaches" whenever it is homework time.	Negative reinforcement
Elmer puts Elsie's pigtails in the paint pot.	Ms. Walker administers the paddle to Elmer's posterior.	Elmer will not put Elsie's pigtails in the paint pot.	Punishment

Extinction.　Extinction is the removal of a reinforcer that sustains or increases a target behavior. Unplanned and unsystematic extinction interventions are frequently applied. For example, we tend to ignore the many inappropriate behaviors exhibited by others with the hope that the behavior will decrease in frequency. (See the case of Elizabeth in Figure 10-1.)

Punishment.   Punishment is the presentation of an aversive stimulus as the consequence of a target behavior. Although frequently used, punishment is perhaps the least effective behavior modification intervention. Punishment tends to suppress inappropriate behaviors rather than extinguish them. This suppression is of short duration, and frequently the behavior recurs in the absence of the punishment and/or punisher (McDaniel, 1980). (See the cases of Kyle and Elmer in Figure 10-1.)

Effects of consequences.   Before continuing the chapter, a thorough understanding of the various consequences presented in Figure 10-1 is needed. The basic difference between punishment and extinction is the effect on the target behavior. Punishment, in most cases, suppresses but does not eliminate the behavior. Extinction, properly applied, eliminates the behavior over time. Positive reinforcement increases a behavior, whereas punishment and extinction decrease it. Negative reinforcement may either increase or decrease a behavior, depending on the target behavior.

Generalization and Discrimination

Two concepts basic to an understanding of learning are generalization and discrimination.

Generalization is the process by which a behavior reinforced in the presence of one stimulus will be exhibited in the presence of another stimulus. This process is important because if generalization did not occur, each response would have to be learned by the individual in each specific situation in which it is to be applied. Instead, the individual generalizes responses; that is, applies concepts learned in one situation to many and varied situations. For example, as children, we learn honesty, respect for authority, and computational skills, which we generalize to the completion of our state and federal tax returns.

Stokes and Baer (1978) described nine techniques designed to assess or to program for generalization. These techniques, applied after a behavior change takes place, include:

1. *Train and hope*—it is hoped that some generalization occur, but generalization is not actively pursued.
2. *Sequential modification*—generalization is assessed, and if absent or deficient, systematic, sequential modification in every nongeneralized condition is pursued.
3. *Introduce to natural maintaining contingencies*—the transfer of behavioral control from the teacher to natural contingencies that can be expected to operate in the environment.

4. *Train sufficient exemplars*-more and more exemplars are taught until generalization is sufficient.

5. *Train loosely*—little control over stimuli presented is used during teaching, so as to maximize sampling of the relevant dimensions of the behavior.

6. *Use indiscriminate contingencies*—generalization may be observed if intermittent schedules are used or indiscriminate contingencies are applied.

7. *Program common stimuli*—generalization will supposedly occur if there are sufficient stimulus components occurring in common in both teaching and generalization settings.

8. *Mediate generalization*—establishing behaviors that will be used for other problems as well.

9. *Train to generalize.*

Stokes and Baer also make several suggestions regarding the assistance of students in generalizing behaviors. Natural contingencies are an advantage to generalization. In addition, training more exemplars may help children and youths with behavior disorders to generalize. Reinforcing generalization and self-reports of the target behavior also assists in generalization. It is important to remember that just because a student behaves in one way in one situation does not mean that generalization of that behavior to other settings has occurred.

Through the process of *discrimination*, individuals learn to act one way in one situation and another way in a different one. Without the ability to discriminate, we would generalize behaviors to a variety of situations in which they would be inappropriate. We learn discrimination by means of differential reinforcement: a behavior is reinforced in the presence of one stimulus, but the same behavior is not reinforced in the presence of another stimulus.

OBJECTIVE TWO: *To apply the behavior-change process to selected behaviors of children and youth with behavior disorders.*

Steps in the Behavior-Change Process

The five steps in the behavior-change process are (1) selecting the target behavior, (2) collecting and recording baseline data, (3) identifying reinforcers (4) implementing interventions and collecting and recording intervention data, and (5) evaluating the effect of the intervention.

Selecting the target behavior.   The first step in the behavior change process is the identification of the behavior to be changed. In the vast majority of human situations, it is not difficult to select one or more behaviors exhibited by an individual that appear inappropriate to some other individual under certain circumstances. When making decisions in selecting target behaviors, the following variables should be considered:

the number of behaviors potentially needing change; their frequency, duration, and intensity; and the type of behavior.

It is generally recommended that the special educator just beginning to use behavior modification techniques not attempt to change more than one or two behaviors simultaneously.

In the target behavior selection step, potential behaviors are ranked in order of priority with regard to their significance to the individual in the specific environment in which he or she is functioning. The special educator progresses through the priority list from the most to the least significant behavior.

The need for and probable effectiveness of an intervention in a target behavior is in large part determined by the behavior's frequency, duration, intensity, and type. These variables bear on whether a behavioral intervention is appropriate or even necessary, on the intervention to be applied, on the probable course of the behavior change process, and on the probable results of the intervention. More specifically, some behaviors respond effectively and efficiently to behavior modification techniques; others do not. Some behaviors must be changed for the sake of the individual's well-being; others are relatively innocuous and do not require change. The special educator must use professional judgment, common sense, and experience when selecting target behaviors. Responsible professionals cannot modify a behavior simply for the satisfaction of modifying it or merely to make an individual conform for the sake of conforming.

After selecting a target behavior, the special educator considers the direction of the behavior change process. There are two basic directions a behavior may follow as a consequence of intervention: it may increase or decrease.

A target behavior must be observable and measurable. It must be directly observable by the special educator in the environment in which it occurs. If it is observable, then it can be measured; that is, counted. Thus we can determine how often and how long it occurs in a given time period.

Collecting and recording baseline data.   Information collected before any intervention is implemented to change the behavior is called baseline data. Baseline data are very important because they provide the foundation on which the behavior change process is established. These data are used to determine the effectiveness of the intervention during the implementation and evaluation steps.

In addition, during intervention, reinforcement is initiated at a level of performance immediately above or below the baseline level, depending on whether the behavior is being increased or decreased. In this manner, the special educator is assured that the target behavior will be reinforced frequently and that the intervention will have meaning to the child or young person.

To obtain meaningful baseline data, the special educator engages in two activities: counting and charting the target behavior. Counting the behavior means enumerating the number of times a behavior occurs in a given period of time. Charting it means preparing a visual display of the behavior in graphic form.

These two processes are of great importance in the behavior change process. When the practitioner knows the rate or average duration of the occurrences of a behavior in a time frame, he or she can select a potentially efficient reinforcement schedule before implementing the intervention. Equally important is the application of baseline data to the implementation and evaluation phases. By comparing baseline data with intervention data, the effectiveness of the intervention can be evaluated. Judgments can be made regarding the responsiveness of the target behavior to interventions; that is, is the behavior increasing or decreasing, as projected? Data-collection techniques are presented in Chapter 6.

Identifying reinforcers.   A behavioral intervention is only as effective as its reinforcers. Regardless of the intervention applied, if the exhibition of the target behavior is not reinforced with a reward acceptable to the individual exhibiting the behavior, the probability of the individual's continuing to exhibit that behavior is reduced.

A reinforcer must be reinforcing to the individual. The only effective test of a specific reinforcer for the individual is to *try it.*

The two most effective means of selecting reinforcers for an individual are (1) observing the child to determine the reinforcers he or she selects when given the opportunity, and (2) asking the child what is preferred.

There are a variety of aids available in the literature to assist special educators in the difficult task of selecting effective reinforcers for children and youths with behavior disorders. These include the "Children's Reinforcement Survey Schedule" (Cautela, 1977), "Methods for Identifying Potential Reinforcers for Children" (Blackham & Silberham, 1975), and the "Target Behavior Kit" (Kroth, 1972).

According to Raschke (1979), students' performance rates accelerated under self-selected reinforcers, as opposed to teacher-selected reinforcers. As a consequence of this research, Raschke (1981) published a procedure for designing reinforcement surveys that permit the child or youth to choose rewards. This procedure is designed to be responsive to the needs and interests of the individual children and teacher in a specific instructional setting. To develop a survey, the special educator follows four simple steps: selects content items, designs a survey inventory, administers the inventory, and summarizes the results.

The content of the inventory reflects not only the child's likes and dislikes but what is practical and possible in the specific special education setting. To assist in the selection of the survey's content, the special educator is encouraged to consult several lists of potential reinforcers in the literature.

The survey itself may take one of several forms: an open-ended, multiple-choice, or rank-order format. Examples of the open-ended and multiple-choice formats are presented in Figures 10-2 and 10-3 respectively.

FIGURE 10-2 Reinforcement Assessment: Open-Ended Format

1. If I had 10 minutes free time during this class, I would most like to ____________
2. My favorite type of activity that I wish we would do more often in this class is ____________
3. My favorite seating arrangement in this class is ____________
4. My favorite place to sit in this class is ____________
5. My favorite way to learn new information in this class is ____________
6. My favorite instructional equipment to use in this classroom is ____________
7. The special jobs I like to help the teacher with the most in this class are ____________
8. If I could change one class rule for 1 hour in this class, the rule I would change would be ____________
9. If I were to choose two students in this classroom to do a fun activity with, I would select ____________
10. If I went to the store and had 50 cents to spend on whatever I wanted, I would buy ____________
11. The person in this school I like most to praise me when I do good work is ____________
12. In this class, I feel proudest of myself when ____________
13. The thing that motivates me the most to do well in this classroom is ____________
14. The nicest thing that has ever happened to me in this class for doing good work is ____________
15. The best reward in this class that the teacher could give me for good work is ____________

From D. Raschke, "Designing Reinforcement Surveys—Let the Student Choose the Reward," *Teaching Exceptional Children, 14*(3), 92-96.

FIGURE 10-3 Reinforcement Assessment: Multiple-Choice Format

1. The way I best like to learn about something new in this class is:

   a. Lecture
   b. Books
   c. Pamphlets
   d. Films
   e. Tapes
   f. Language master
   g. Small-group work
   h. Guest speaker

2. My favorite writing tool to use in this class is:

   a. Magic Markers
   b. Felt pens
   c. Colored pencils
   d. Colored chalk

3. My favorite seating arrangement in this class is:

   a. Desks in rows
   b. Chairs at tables
   c. Desks randomly scattered
   d. Study carrels randomly scattered

4. The special job I like to help the teacher with the most in this class is:

   a. Handing out papers
   b. Putting away supplies
   c. Decorating a bulletin board
   d. Running the filmstrip projector
   e. Writing the assignment on the chalkboard
   f. Straightening up cupboards and bookcases

5. The best privilege I could earn in this class for good work would be to:

   a. Sit anywhere I want in the class
   b. Help the teacher grade papers
   c. Put an assignment on the chalkboard
   d. Give the class announcements
   e. Pick a partner to work with

6. When I do well in this class, I like it most when the teacher:

   a. Smiles at me
   b. Informs the class of my good work
   c. Writes a note on my paper
   d. Tells me privately in words
   e. Draws a big happy face on my paper
   f. Puts my good work on the bulletin board

7. When I do good work in this class, I would most like to earn:

a. Free time
b. Praise from the teacher
c. A favorite activity with a friend
d. A favorite activity with the teacher
e. Good work displayed on a bulletin board

8. My favorite free-time activity in this class is:

a. Playing checkers or a card game
b. Listening to the radio or playing records
c. Working a puzzle or doing a craft activity
d. Visiting with a friend
e. Reading a favorite book
f. Playing a computer game

9. The nicest thing that could happen to me for doing good work in this class would be:

a. Receiving an award in front of the class
b. Receiving an A+ on a project
c. A phone call to my parents describing my good work
d. Having my work displayed in the hallway
e. Earning free time for the whole class

10. The best tangible reward I could earn in this class would be a:

a. Gold star
b. Happy gram
c. Good work badge
d. Certificate of achievement
e. Scratch 'n sniff sticker
f. Spacemen stamp

11. If I had 50 cents to buy anything I wanted, I would buy:

a. A yo-yo
b. A frisbee
c. A poster
d. Some silly putty
e. A comic book

12. Something really different I would work hard for in this class would be:

a. A warm fuzzy
b. A monster tattoo
c. Some space dust
d. A creepy spider
e. Some monster teeth
f. A vampire fingernail
g. A squirt ring

From D. Raschke, "Designing Reinforcement Surveys—Let the Student Choose the Reward," *Teaching Exceptional Children, 14*(3), 92-96. Copyright 1981 by the Council for Exceptional Children. Reprinted by permission.

The administration of the survey should include specific instructions that emphasize that there are no right or wrong answers and stress the confidentiality of responses. Using the information obtained from the completed inventories, special educators can develop individual and group preference lists.

The following points concerning the use of reinforcers should be remembered:

1. The strength of a reinforcer can only be determined by using it. What is reinforcing to one individual is not necessarily reinforcing to another.
2. Even the most powerful reinforcer loses its effectiveness and must be replaced if satiation occurs.
3. Observing the effects of reinforcers and searching for new ones is a continuing process.
4. The goal of behavioral interventions is an individual who responds to naturally occurring social reinforcement. The special educator cannot rely on tangible reinforcers only, but should always present social with tangible reinforcers.

Implementing interventions and collecting and recording intervention data. In this step of the behavior change process, the special educator selects a behavioral intervention for implementation. The most effective behavioral interventions for use with children and youth with behavior disorders are discussed in detail in the next section of this chapter.

Next, the special educator selects one or more schedules of reinforcement to be applied during the behavior change process. A schedule of reinforcement is the pattern with which the reinforcer is presented or not presented in response to the exhibition of a target behavior. The schedule used has a significant effect on the behavior change process.

The five most common types of reinforcement schedules are continuous (C), fixed ratio (FR), variable ratio (VR), fixed interval (FI), and variable interval (VI). The primary distinctions among these schedules are the timing and frequency of reinforcement (Gardner, 1978).

A continuous schedule of reinforcement requires the presentation of the reinforcer immediately after each occurrence of the target behavior or after each time period during which the behavior was exhibited. This schedule is useful, at least initially, during the behavior change process. Its application will frequently change the behavior rapidly. However, it is not recommended for long-term use because individuals tend to satiate on a continuous schedule and gains are lost. A schemata of a continuous schedule of reinforcement is presented in Figure 10-4.

The ratio schedules (FR and VR) focus on the completion of a specific number of tasks before a reinforcer is presented to the individual. The interval schedules, FI and VI, depend on the exhibition of specific

FIGURE 10-4 Continuous Reinforcement

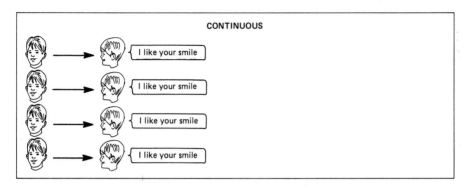

From W.I. Gardner, *Learning and Behavior Characteristics of Exceptional Children and Youth: A Humanistic Behavioral Approach* (Boston: Allyn & Bacon, 1978). Used by permission.

behaviors for a definite period of time before a reward is presented to the individual.

When a fixed ratio schedule is applied, the reinforcer is presented after a specific number of occurrences of the behavior. This schedule results in a high rate of response. It is most appropriately applied during the beginning phase of the behavior change process (See Figure 10-5).

Variable ratio schedules are used to sustain a high level of response after an acceptable frequency has been attained by means of a fixed ratio schedule. Under the variable ratio schedule, the ratio of the reinforcement presentations varies (See Figure 10-6).

FIGURE 10-5

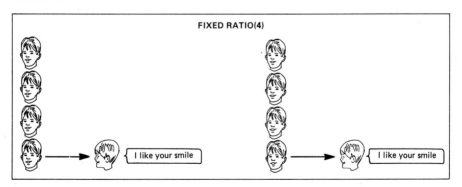

From W.I. Gardner, *Learning and Behavior Characteristics of Exceptional Children and Youth: A Humanistic Behavioral Approach* (Boston: Allyn & Bacon, 1978). Used by permission.

FIGURE 10-6

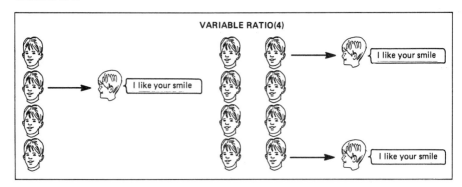

From W.I. Gardner, *Learning and Behavior Characteristics of Exceptional Children and Youth: A Humanistic Behavioral Approach* (Boston: Allyn & Bacon, 1978). Used by permission.

When a fixed interval schedule of reinforcement is being applied, a specified period of time must elapse before a reward is presented to the individual. The reward is presented immediately after the first response after the specified time period has elapsed. It has been found that the longer the time interval between reinforcements, the less frequent the level of performance. (See Figure 10-7).

A variable interval schedule is similar to a variable ratio schedule. However, the presentation of the reinforcer is based on a behavioral-response mean. In this case, the individual whose behavior is being changed is not aware of when the reward will be given. However, he or she does know that a reward will be given for exhibiting the target behavior (see Figure 10-8). The special educator should be careful when changing from a fixed to variable schedule. If this is done too early or too late in the behavior change process, the newly acquired behavior may be extinguished.

FIGURE 10-7   Fixed Interval Schedule

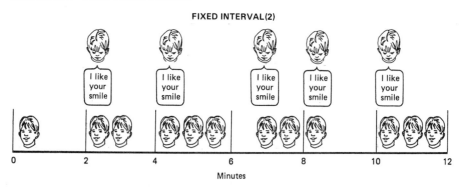

From W.I. Gardner, *Learning and Behavior Characteristics of Exceptional Children and Youth: A Humanistic Behavioral Approach* (Boston: Allyn & Bacon, 1978). Used by permission.

FIGURE 10-8 Variable Interval Schedule

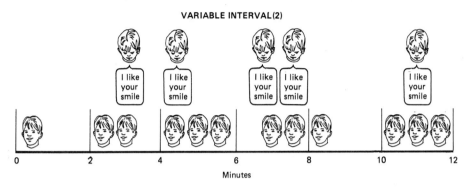

From W.I. Gardner, *Learning and Behavior Characteristics of Exceptional Children and Youth: A Humanistic Behavioral Approach* (Boston: Allyn & Bacon, 1978). Used by permission.

The schedule selected for use varies with the behavior being changed. If the concern is to keep an individual on-task for a period of time, an interval schedule is appropriate. If the behavior is concerned with the completion of a specific number of tasks, a ratio schedule is applied.

Concurrent with the implementation of an intervention, the special educator collects data on its effectiveness. This is accomplished by means of counting and charting, as discussed previously concerning baseline data. The most important characteristics of the effective implementation of an intervention are consistency and persistence. It is essential that the reinforcer be presented as a consequence of the target behavior in accordance with the schedule of reinforcement. Behaviors do not, generally, change overnight; therefore, the special educator is urged to persist in the application of the interventions for a minimum of two weeks.

Evaluating the effect of the intervention. Intervention data provide the special educator with a yardstick for the evaluation of changes in the target behavior. By collecting and charting intervention data daily, the special educator can evaluate the effectiveness of the intervention throughout the behavior change process by comparing them with the baseline data.

If the behavior is changing in the desired direction, the special educator may proceed with the behavior change program as planned. However, if the behavior is not changing as projected, the special educator reevaluates the behavior change program: that is, the reinforcer, the intervention, and the schedule of reinforcement.

OBJECTIVE THREE: *To describe and apply selected behavioral interventions.*

By applying the principles of behavior modification and the steps in the behavior change process presented in the previous sections, behaviorists have developed many behavior change interventions. Several of those found to be effective by special educators serving children and youths with behavior disorders are discussed in this section. These include positive reinforcement, extinction, punishment, reinforcement of incompatible behaviors, shaping, contingency contracting, time-out, token economy, modeling, and desensitization.

Positive reinforcement.   Positive reinforcement is known by several names, such as positive attention, approval, social reinforcement, and rewarding. Here, it is defined as the process of rewarding an appropriate behavior to increase the probability that it will recur. The advantages of positive reinforcement are that it is responsive to the child's natural need for attention and approval and decreases the probability that the child will exhibit inappropriate behavior.

Two guidelines should be used when applying positive reinforcement. First, when students are initially learning a new behavior, they must be rewarded each time it occurs. Second, once the behavior is established at a satisfactory level of frequency, students are rewarded intermittently.

Public reinforcement may be unwelcome by some children, so the special educator should be careful to ascertain if the child is embarrassed by positive reinforcement in the presence of peers, teachers, and others. Finally, the special educator must be observant to determine if the reinforcers being used are in fact positively reinforcing for the child.

Extinction.   As noted earlier, the discontinuation or withholding of the reinforcer of a target behavior that has been previously reinforcing it is called extinction. Extinction is also known as systematic ignoring.

When consistently and persistently applied, extinction results in the gradual decrease and elimination of the target behavior. Behaviors that are ignored become nonfunctional and consequently stop. Extinction is an effective means of eliminating annoying and nonproductive behavior. Because it is a benign intervention, it generally avoids the potential for conflict between special educator and child. Among the behaviors responsive to this intervention are whining, tattling, mild tantrums, demands for attention, and the like. It may also be used to decrease inappropriate language, derogatory comments, meaningless questions, and annoying affectations and fads. The key to applying extinction effectively is learning how to ignore the target behavior and then doing so with consistency.

Some behaviors simply should not be ignored. They are either too significant to the child's functioning or too dangerous to the child, others, or property to be ignored. In many cases, when extinction is initially applied, an "extinction burst" occurs, in that the behavior being ignored increases in frequency for a brief period of time before it decreases. However, if the intervention is continued in response to the target behavior, it will decrease over time.

Punishment.   Punishment is imposed on individuals to decrease or eliminate inappropriate behaviors. As noted previously, punishment is the presentation of an aversive stimulus as a consequence of an inappropriate behavior. Punishment may be accomplished by adding an aversive stimulus—that is, spanking, shouting, assigning additional work, and the like—or by taking away privileges, such as free time, dessert, and television.

Punishment may be physical, psychological, or a combination of both. The punisher may use paddling or spanking (physical) or a derogatory statement (psychological) as a consequence of the target behavior.

The short-term effectiveness of punishment is difficult to dispute (Wood, 1978). Punishment does effectively attain for the punisher his or her immediate objective: to stop the inappropriate behavior. However, there are several reasons for avoiding punishment (Clarizio & Yelon, 1976; Wood & Lakin, 1978):

1. Punishment does not eliminate the inappropriate behavior; it merely suppresses it.
2. Punishment does not provide the child or young person with a model of acceptable behavior.
3. Aggression by the punisher presents the child with an inappropriate model.
4. The emotional results of punishment may be fear, tension, stress, or withdrawal, which may further immobilize a child.
5. Punishment may increase the child's frustration, which may result in further deviation.

In addition, the special educator should recognize that punishment may result in physical or emotional harm to the child.

From the perception of the punished child or young person, punishment is frequently associated with the punisher rather than with the inappropriate behavior. As a result, the child's reaction to punishment may be dislike and avoidance of the punisher rather than changed behavior. A variety of behavior management interventions presented in this text are more effective than punishment, which is of questionable value to both the child and special educator. It is not recommended for application in the special-education program for behavior-disordered children and youth. "All reasonable positive alternatives should have been considered, if not actually tried, before the decision is made to use an aversive procedure" (Wood, 1978, p. 120).

If punishment is used, the special educator must adhere to the following guidelines:

1. Specify and communicate the punishable target behaviors to the students by means of discussions and agreed-on "rules of behavior," which are posted and reviewed frequently.
2. Provide models of acceptable behavior that the students can imitate.
3. Punish the child immediately after the punishable behavior is exhibited.
4. Be consistent in the application of punishment. If the behavior is punishable one day, it is punishable the next.
5. Be fair in the use of punishment. What is punishable for one child is generally punishable for another. The only exceptions are when punishment is not imposed on specific children for therapeutic purposes.
6. Impose the punishment impersonally. Do not punish a child when you are emotionally involved, angry, or otherwise out of control.

The authors of this text are irrevocably opposed to the use of physical and psychological punishment of children and youths with behavior disorders, whether it be paddling, slapping, spanking, the use of electric shock, or derogatory comments. There are more human behavior management interventions possible.

When punishment must be implemented as a behavior management intervention, two forms are preferred: loss of privileges and reprimands.

Unlike the vast majority of interventions discussed in this text, loss of privileges is a negative behavior management intervention, although its results may be positive. Loss of privileges is also known as deprivation of privileges; response cost; and aversive natural, logical, artificial, and arbitrary consequences of behaviors. When loss of privileges is applied, a portion of the child's positive reinforcers is taken away following the exhibition of the target behavior. A specific portion of either present or future privileges may be taken.

This intervention is most effective when the privilege the child loses is a natural or logical consequence of the target behavior. For example, if a child refuses to work on assignments during class time, the privilege of free time is lost, or if a child is late for the school bus, he or she misses it. It is not always possible to impose natural consequences; frequently, therefore, special educators must impose artificial ones. In an artificial consequence, the relationship between the privilege lost and the behavior exhibited is arbitrary. The relationship exists only because the teacher decides it will exist. This artificial relationship must be explained or demonstrated to the child or youth.

Another form of punishment is the reprimand. To be reprimanded is to be scolded, "yelled at," "bawled out," or otherwise verbally chastised for exhibiting an inappropriate target behavior. Reprimands are useful when a child is engaging in behavior that is potentially harmful to him- or herself, others, and property, and necessitates immediate action.

It is suggested that reprimands be used selectively in response to specific behaviors. The reprimand should include a statement of an appropriate alternative to the inappropriate behavior. Appropriate behaviors should be positively reinforced.

Reinforcement of incompatible behaviors. Occasionally, in the special education setting, it is effective to decrease the frequency of inappropriate target behaviors by systematically reinforcing a behavior that is in opposition to or incompatible with that behavior.

The effectiveness of this intervention depends on the selection of the pairs of incompatible behaviors. For example:

> A child or young person cannot be seated and standing at the same time. Rather than focusing interventions on standing (inappropriate behavior), the special educator reinforces sitting (the incompatible behavior). In this case, the inappropriate behavior, standing, is ignored; sitting is positively reinforced.
>
> A child cannot be talking and silent at the same time. The special educator using this intervention reinforces silence and ignores talking.
>
> A child cannot be on-task (attending to work) and off-task (not attending to work) simultaneously. The special educator positively reinforces on-task and ignores off-task behavior.

This technique is applicable to a number of behaviors exhibited by children and youth with behavior disorders. If applied with consistency over a period of time, it can be a very effective intervention.

Shaping. Shaping is the reinforcement of successive approximations of behaviors leading to the appropriate target behavior. It is primarily applied to establish behavior not previously exhibited by the individual or very infrequently exhibited.

Shaping is accomplished by the consistent, systematic, and immediate reinforcement of approximations of the target behavior. Just as the sculptor shapes and molds an object of art from clay, the special educator shapes and molds a "new" behavior from an undifferentiated behavior response (Neisworth, Deno, & Jenkins, 1969). Shaping can be applied to both behaviors and academic problems.

During shaping, the special educator only reinforces those behavioral manifestations that approximate the target behavior. Only those approximations closest to the target behavior are reinforced. Never reinforce lower-level approximations; to do so would be to reinforce a behavior that is the reverse of the proposed direction of change.

Shaping is similar to climbing a ladder; that is, one rung is mounted at a time while one foot is still firmly placed on the previous rung. The child is reinforced for climbing each rung on the ascent to the top of the ladder. The child is only reinforced when he or she ascends to the highest rung to which he or she is capable of climbing at a particular point in the shaping process. The child is never reinforced for climbing to a rung lower than that to which he or she is capable.

Contingency contracting. A contract is a verbal or written agreement between two or more individuals or groups that stipulates the responsibilities of each concerning a specified item or activity. Contingency contracting is defined by Becker (1979) as arranging conditions in such a way that the child is allowed to do something he or she wants to do after completing something you want that individual to do.

Contingency contracting is based on Premack's (1959) principle: A behavior that has a high rate of occurrence can be used to increase a behavior with a low rate of occurrence. This concept is best exemplified by an *XY* statement: *If you do x, then you can do or get y.* Some sample verbal contracts are:

> "If you eat your peas, then you can have some ice cream."
> "If you do ninety percent of your class assignments this week, then you may attend the class party and movie on Friday afternoon."
> "If you complete your workbook assignment, then you may have ten minutes of free time."

Two examples of written contracts in the appropriate form are presented in Figures 10-9 and 10-10. The first is useful with elementary-school-age children, the second with older children.

Walker and Shea (1984) suggest that:

1. The contract must be negotiated and freely agreed to by all persons involved.
2. The contract must include the agreed-upon achievement or production level.
3. The reinforcer must be consistently presented to the child or youth in accordance with the terms of the contract.
4. The contract must include a date on which it can be reviewed and renegotiated.

Contracts can be used effectively to change a broad range of behaviors. They have been found very effective with older children and youth with behavior disorders.

Time-out. Time-out, or "time away from positive reinforcement" (Powell & Powell, 1982), is the removal of a child or youth from an apparently reinforcing setting to a presumably nonreinforcing one for a specified and limited period of time. Such removal can effectively decrease an inappropriate target behavior.

FIGURE 10-9 Contract for Elementary-School Students

SPEEDING
ALONG...

> I, Cathy Smith will be able to answer addition facts (0-5) by Friday, December 10. I will reach this goal by practicing my flash cards with Sarah 10 minutes a day. When I reach this goal I will earn a sticker page.

Student   Teacher   Date

Renegotiation Date

FIGURE 10-10 Contract Appropriate for Secondary-School Students

CONTRACT

The following contract has been mutually agreed upon by John Daniels (student) and Mr. Quantrall (teacher).

John Daniels will complete the self-instructional packet on filling out a job application by Monday, November 11, homeroom period. He will receive at least a 90% on each of the activities in the packet.

If this packet is completed as described above, Mr. Quantrell and John will agree upon a "day off" during which time John will use his resource room time assisting coach Matthias with the Junior High basketball team.

This contract will be reviewed by both John and Mr. Quantrell on November 1.

Signed _____
John Daniels

_____
Michael Quantrell

According to Lewellyn (1980) there are three levels of time-out: observational, exclusionary, and seclusionary. Rutherford and Neel (1978) noted five kinds: ignoring, contingent observation, removal of materials, reduction of response-maintenance stimuli, exclusion, and seclusion. Ignoring or extinction has been discussed previously, and is not reviewed here.

Observational time-out or contingent observation is an intervention in which the child is withdrawn from a reinforcing environment by being placed on the perimeter of the environment, where he or she may hear and see the activity but not participate. During observational time-out, the child can observe the appropriate behavior as it occurs among the members of the group from which he or she has been removed. Removal of materials is a form of time-out during which materials a child is using inappropriately are removed. Reduction of response-maintenance stimuli is a time-out intervention that involves the reduction or elimination of stimuli in the environment necessary for a response, such as turning out the lights when a child responds inappropriately.

Exclusionary time-out is an intervention in which the child leaves the reinforcing environment for a presumed nonreinforcing environment yet remains in the classroom. In this case, there may be a private, out-of-the-way area of the room to which the child retires for a period of time. In seclusionary time-out, the child leaves the reinforcing environment and retires to a time-out room or an isolated area generally not in the classroom.

The effectiveness of time-out depends on several factors: the child, the special educator's application of the intervention, the child's understanding of the rules of time-out, the characteristics of the time-out area, the duration of the time-out period, and the evaluation of the effectiveness of the intervention.

The teacher must know the child's or young person's reactions to isolation or time-out. For acting-out, aggressive, group-oriented children, time-out is often an effective intervention. These children typically want to be with their peers and involved in group activities. For withdrawn, passive, solitary children, however, time-out is contraindicated. These children may be quite content to be left in "their own little worlds" while in time-out. Time-out is never used with a fearful child; it would only exacerbate the child's problem. In addition, time-out should not be used as a punishment for failure to do academic work unless such failure is due to the child's inappropriate behavior.

To be effective, time-out must be applied with consistency over a period of time. Frequently, special educators are inconsistent in their application of time-out; as a result, the child becomes confused and the behavior is unwittingly reinforced.

In most classroom settings, it is not necessary to construct or install a time-out room, although this practice is followed in many special-education settings serving severely behavior-disordered students. A chair in an out-of-the-way corner of the classroom is frequently adequate. Time-out areas can be constructed using room dividers, screens, filing cabinets, or book-cases.

The time-out area must be safe and properly lighted and ventilated. A chair is placed in the time-out area for the child. However, young children may prefer to sit on the floor. A monitor's chair is located outside the area.

If time-out is to be effective, the child must learn what behaviors are inappropriate and the consequences for exhibiting those behaviors. The rules of behavior should be discussed with the students and posted in the classroom for periodic review.

Time-out is ineffective if a child is required to remain outside the group for a lengthy period. A child should not spend more than four or five minutes in time-out.

For purposes of evaluation, the teacher or aide maintains a time-out log. A sample log form is presented in Figure 10-11. This log includes the time the child enters and leaves the time-out area, behavior and activity immediately before and after time-out, and any unusual incidents that occurred during it. The log is posted on the outside of the time-out area. The teacher evaluates the overall effectiveness of the intervention by analyzing the log, which provides clues as to why the intervention is effective or ineffective with a particular child.

The time-out intervention does not include lecturing, reprimanding, and/or scolding a child before, during, or after the time-out period. All explanations should be brief and concise. It is essential that the time-out intervention include reinforcing the child's appropriate behavior. It is also recommended that the child return to the task that was interrupted by time-out. If returned to the task, the child learns that time-out cannot be used to avoid assignment.

Because of recent controversy with regard to the use and abuse of time-out in special education programs, seclusionary time-out should be avoided except in the most carefully controlled situations. Evaluations should be carefully conducted, parent permission should be obtained, and the interventions written into the child's IEP.

Token economy. The token economy is undoubtedly the most versatile and widely used of the behavioral interventions. It is an exchange system that provides the individual or group whose behavior is being changed with nearly immediate feedback cues on the appropriateness of their behavior. These cues, or tokens, are at a later time exchanged for backup reinforcers. The token economy intervention may be combined with the cost-response intervention, discussed previously. In this case, the student loses tokens for specific inappropriate behaviors.

FIGURE 10-11   Time-Out Log Form

DATE/TIME In/Out	BEFORE	DURING	AFTER	COMMENTS	INITIALS
10-28-86 9:15 9:19	Biting, hitting	Kept screaming "I'm sorry"	Returned quietly	Upset	P.H.
10-30-86	Kicked student	Knocked on door	Returned to Math	Screamed "I hate Matthew" on the way to time out	P.H.

Name: _____

The tokens are usually valueless to the students initially. However, their value becomes apparent to the students when they learn that they can be exchanged (traded) for backup reinforcers (items and activities).

When developing a token economy, the special educator must first select a target behavior or behaviors. These behaviors must be discussed and clarified with the group. After selecting a token, a menu of backup reinforcers is developed and posted in the classroom. Time must be provided for exchange of tokens. As the school year progresses, the educator must frequently revise the reward menu and backup reinforcers to avoid satiation.

The properly managed token economy is effective because individuals are only competing with themselves and the reinforcer menu provides a variety of desirable reinforcers.

Modeling.   Modeling is providing behavior after which the child or young person is to pattern his or her behavior. During the intervention, the individual is systematically reinforced for imitating the model. Modeling is also known as observational learning, identification, vicarious learning, contagion, and social learning (Bandura, 1969).

According to Clarizio and Yelon (1976), exposure to a model has three potential effects on the individual. First, the child may acquire a target behavior from the model that was not previously a part of his or her behavioral repertoire. Second, the child may inhibit inappropriate target behaviors for which the model is punished or otherwise discouraged. Finally, the child's elicited approximations of the model's behavior are reinforced. These elicited behaviors are not necessarily "new" ones. They may be previously learned but dormant.

Special educators planning to use modeling interventions should consider whether the child is developmentally capable of imitating a model. The model must also be acceptable, and someone whom the child will imitate. Modeling can be used with effect to increase appropriate and decrease inappropriate target behaviors.

Desensitization. The process of systematically reducing a learned fear is called desensitization (Wolpe, 1961). This behavioral intervention was developed by Wolpe in the 1950s and 1960s, and has been used to reduce fears and anxiety related to public speaking, school attendance, participation in groups, swimming, animals, flying, test taking, and similar behaviors. Although the special educator cannot apply systematic desensitization on the basis of the information provided here, its general principles can be used in special education programs.

The principles of desensitization can be applied by a special educator under the following conditions:

1. The special educator must have a positive relationship with the student. The student must trust and feel free to express feelings to the special educator.
2. The special educator must construct a hierarchy of anxiety-evoking stimuli; that is, a hierarchy of stimuli on a continuum from the least to the most anxiety-evoking stimulus surrounding the individual's fear.
3. The special educator must have sufficient time to accompany the individual as he or she progresses through the hierarchy.

The special educator must recognize that desensitization is time-consuming. Consistency and patience are essential. It is frequently necessary to repeat some of the specific anxiety-evoking stimuli several times to reduce their effect on the child.

Deffenbacher and Kemper (1974) applied systematic desensitization in a program to reduce test-taking anxiety in twenty-eight junior-high-school students (twelve girls and sixteen boys). All students had been referred to the program by a counselor, parent, or teacher. The hierarchy of test-taking anxiety-evoking stimuli used with the students included:

You are attending a regular class session.

You hear about someone who has a test.

You are studying at home. You are reading a normal assignment.

You are in class. The teacher announces a major exam in two weeks.

You are at home studying. You are beginning to review and study for a test that is a week away.

You are at home studying, and you are studying for the important test. It is now Tuesday and three days before the test on Friday.

You are at home studying and preparing for the upcoming exam. It is now Wednesday, two days before the test on Friday.

It is Thursday night, the night before the exam on Friday. You are talking with another student about the exam tomorrow.

It is the night before the exam, and you are home studying for it.

It is the day of the exam, and you have one hour left to study.

It is the day of the exam. You have been studying. You are now walking on your way to the test.

You are standing outside the test room talking with other students about the upcoming test.

You are sitting in the testing room waiting for the test to be passed out.

You are leaving the exam room, you are talking with other students about the test. Many of their answers do not agree with yours.

You are sitting in the classroom waiting for the graded test to be passed back by the teacher.

It's right before the test, and you hear a student ask a possible test question which you cannot answer.

You are taking the important test. While trying to think of an answer, you notice everyone around you writing rapidly.

While taking the test, you come to a question you are unable to answer. You draw a blank.

You are in the important exam. The teacher announces thirty minutes remaining but you have an hour's work left.

You are in the important exam. The teacher announces fifteen minutes remaining but you have an hour's work left. (Deffenbacher & Kemper, 1974, p. 219.)

This desensitization program consisted of eight sessions (one per week) with groups of two to five students. According to Deffenbacher and Kemper, the intervention effectively reduced test-taking anxiety in the junior high school students.

OBJECTIVE FOUR: *To identify procedures for students to use cognitive behavior modification for self-management.*

Cognitive behavior modification is "the selective, purposeful combination of principles and procedures from diverse areas into training regimens or interventions, the purpose of which is to instate, modify, or extinguish cognitions, feelings, and/or behaviors" (Harris, 1982, p. 5). Though there are several procedures that may be used when applying cognitive behavior modification, these interventions appear to have five common attributes (Lloyd, 1980). Self-treatment, be it self-control, self-verbalization, self-monitoring, or self-reinforcement, is one common attribute. Verbalization is a second component. The third commonality among the procedures is the identification of a series of steps through which students proceed in order to solve problems. Fourth, the primary means of instruction in cognitive behavior modification is modeling. Finally, a great deal of the application of cognitive behavior modification has been to delaying impulsive responding and to developing and evaluating alternative ways of responding. In cognitive behavior modification, changes in cognitions are brought about through self-instruction (Hall, 1980). Unlike other behavioral interventions, which may be nonverbal, cognitive behavior modification relies heavily on verbal communication to change behavior.

There are two kinds of cognitive behavior-modification interventions: self-instructional training, aimed at verbally mediated self-control; and problem-solving training. These are described next.

Self-instructional training. The components of self-instructional training include modeling, shaping, prompting, and social reinforcement (Harris, 1982). Students are trained through six basic steps (Kendall, 1977):

1. The teacher models the task while talking out loud as the student observes.
2. The student performs the task, making statements out loud for self-instruction.
3. The teacher models the task while whispering the self-instructions.
4. The student performs the task, whispering self-instructions.
5. The teacher uses covert self-instructions with pauses and behavioral signs of thinking.
6. The student performs the task using covert self-instructions.

Harris (1982) indicates that self-instructional training has the advantage of having students play an important, collaborative role in their own training. As students continue in their training, the special educator gradually fades supports, so that students are generating and answering questions on their own. This technique also can occur across tasks and settings, providing students with a skill that is applicable to the demands of coping in the community.

Self-instructional training has been used to increase attending and reflective learning styles, to develop self-regulation and management skills, to develop social skills and control of aggression and behavioral problems, and to develop academic skills.

Problem-solving training.   The second common cognitive behavior-modification intervention is problem-solving training. Meichenbaum (1980) indicates that cognitive techniques for problem solving assist students to learn how to learn, and increase their generalization of behaviors and ability to try new strategies. Through cognitive behavior modification, students can learn (a) self-interrogation and self-checking, (b) breaking problems into manageable tasks, and (c) assessing strategies within the student's abilities to match those that are appropriate to the task.

There are several considerations in using cognitive behavior-modification techniques with children and youth with behavior disorders. The special educator must be aware of the characteristics of each student when applying these procedures. Cognitive behavior modification is a verbal technique. Thus, students must have adequate language development to participate in these interventions. Kendall (1977) indicated that less-capable students may need pretraining in the use of self-instructions, attending, and copying a model. Limited memory may also affect the student's ability to apply these techniques.

OBJECTIVE FIVE: *To use group-oriented contingencies in the classroom.*

Special educators should apply social reinforcers whenever applying other contingencies on the behavior of children and youth with behavior disorders. Activity reinforcers and privileges are naturally occurring reinforcers that may be readily applied with social reinforcers, rather than relying on tangible items. Barrish, Saunders, and Wolf (1969) describe a technique designed to reduce disruptive classroom behavior through a game involving competition for privileges that occur naturally in the classroom. This group-contingency program involved dividing students into two teams, in which disruptive behavior by a member resulted in possible loss of privileges for every member of the team

In this study of the "Good Behavior Game," two target behaviors, out of seat and talking out, were selected for a fourth-grade classroom of twenty-four students. The game was introduced by the teacher as a game that would be played during specific periods of the day. Students were informed that the class was divided into two teams, and when a team or teams won the game, that team (or teams) would receive privileges. Rules were described to the students to delineate the two target behaviors. The teacher then explained that whenever a rule was broken, that team would receive a mark on the chalkboard. If a team had the fewer marks or if neither team received more than five marks, the team(s) would get to (a) wear victory tags, (b) put a star next to each member's name on a winner's chart, (c) line up first for lunch, and (d) take part in a special free-time period at the end of the day, during which the losing team would continue to work. The teacher also indicated that if a team or teams had no more than twenty marks in a week, it would get a week-long privilege of going to recess four minutes early.

Through a multiple baseline and reversal design, the "Good Behavior Game" was demonstrated to significantly decrease the target behaviors. However, the application of these group contingencies was not without problems. Special projects for the free-time period required planning by the teacher. In addition, two students were consistently found to cause their teams to receive "marks." When these two students refused to play the game, "marks" were allotted to them individually rather than to the group.

Care must be taken when applying group contingencies. When selecting target behaviors, the special educator must be sure that all the students are able to comply with the rules. Plans must be made for those students who refuse to play the game and sabotage their teams' efforts. The "Good Behavior Game" may augment other behavior-management programs, but it is not the panacea for classroom management of children and youth with behavior disorders.

OBJECTIVE SIX: *To identify a continuum of interventions ranging from least to most restrictive.*

Public Law 94-142 requires that students be educated in the least restrictive environment in which they can succeed. This component of the law should be applied not only to student placement, but to the interventions used with students while they are receiving services in that placement. The special educator is accountable for using the least-restrictive behavior-management interventions that will ensure student success.

Interventions vary in restrictiveness according to their impact on the student and variation from the normal, everyday classroom interaction. The continuum of interventions presented in Figure 10-12 (based on Lewellyn, 1980), arranges interventions as they increase in restrictiveness from normal classroom behavior management interventions and physical impact on the student.

The first of the interventions, which involves reinforcement of appropriate behavior, occurs throughout the school day in regular and special education. Students are reinforced for "being good," "working hard," and "behaving." The next step on the continuum, in which specific behaviors are reinforced, is slightly more restrictive. In this step, students are reinforced for individual, specific behaviors that are made apparent to them and consequently to their classmates. Students may be reinforced for not talking, keeping their hands to themselves, or completing specific tasks. The next step, in which students receive reinforcement for incompatible alternatives, is yet more restrictive. In this step, more planning and management is required. The special educator must develop an alternative to the target behavior and specifically reinforce that behavior.

The two subsequent steps in the continuum are yet more restrictive. Extinction, or systematic ignoring, is more restrictive than the positive interventions discussed earlier, because it involves a restriction in the interaction that typically occurs between teacher and student. Though it is perceived as being benign, it is more restrictive than the interventions previously discussed above because it is less "normal"; students in classrooms are usually attended to by teachers. The next step, stimulus change, is even less "normal." In this intervention, rather than dealing with the target behavior, the special educator arranges conditions so that the target behavior cannot occur. For example, the student who chews pencils is given a ball-point pen with which to write, because it is hard and not "chewable." The decision to avoid the occurrence of a behavior rather than dealing with the behavior is more restrictive for the student.

Nonexclusionary time-out is the next phase on this continuum. This intervention is restrictive in that it prevents the student from participating fully in his or her educational program. The next group of interventions are so restrictive that they should receive administrative and parental approval before implementation. They could have possible negative side effects on the student, the class, and the special educator. Physical restraint,

FIGURE 10-12   Continuum of Behavioral Interventions

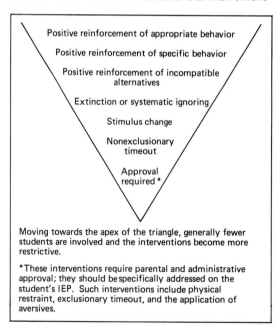

Positive reinforcement of appropriate behavior

Positive reinforcement of specific behavior

Positive reinforcement of incompatible alternatives

Extinction or systematic ignoring

Stimulus change

Nonexclusionary timeout

Approval required *

Moving towards the apex of the triangle, generally fewer students are involved and the interventions become more restrictive.

*These interventions require parental and administrative approval; they should be specifically addressed on the student's IEP. Such interventions include physical restraint, exclusionary timeout, and the application of aversives.

(Adapted from Lewellyn, 1980.)

exclusionary time-out, and the application of aversives are only warranted when the student demonstrates behaviors dangerous to him- or herself and others.

This continuum provides a structure for selecting behavioral interventions. Special educators are urged to try a less restrictive intervention and apply it consistently and persistently for at least two weeks before moving down the continuum to a more restrictive one. Through the consistent application of interventions, more restrictive ones may be unnecessary. The special educator is accountable for documenting the effects of all behavioral interventions and should have adequate data to justify educational decisions.

This particular continuum is only an example. Special educators are urged to survey interventions available for application in their work setting and arrange them on a continuum from the least to the most restrictive of the students' personal freedom to function normally. This continuum is then applied by the educator to aid in the selection and implementation of behavior management interventions.

SUMMARY

In this chapter, interventions from the behavioral perspective were discussed. The principles of behavior modification and the application of the behavior change process were presented. A continuum of interventions was presented, with guidelines for the implementation of individual behavioral techniques. Two unique applications of behavioral techniques, cognitive behavior modification and group-oriented contingencies, were also discussed.

REVIEW QUESTIONS

1. Review the material on the behavioral perspective in Chapter 1. Relate that material to the behavioral interventions presented in this chapter.
2. Discuss the significance of the principles of reinforcement in the special education program for a child or youth with behavior disorders.
3. Using the professional literature, locate, analyze, and discuss additional behavioral interventions not presented in this chapter.
4. List advantages and disadvantages of applying group contingencies. What are some of the considerations of using group consequences? Are there any advantages? Disadvantages?
5. Discuss the problem-solving strategies that the special educator may teach to children and youth with behavior disorders through cognitive behavior modification procedures.

6. Review the continuum of interventions presented in Objective Six. Do you agree with this continuum? How would you rank the interventions discussed in this chapter in terms of their restrictiveness toward the student and/or normalization?

APPLICATION ACTIVITIES

1. Select a student with whom you are familiar (or one from Appendix B). Identify the procedures, materials, strategies, and activities you would complete in each of the following phases of the behavior-change process.

Selecting a Target Behavior

Procedures:
Materials:
Strategies:
Activities:
Possible target behaviors:

Collecting and Recording Baseline Data

Procedures:
Materials:
Strategies:
Activities:
Possible data-collection techniques:

Identifying Reinforcers

Procedures:
Materials:
Strategies:
Activities:
Possible reinforcers:

Implementing Interventions and Collecting and Recording Intervention Data

Procedures:
Materials:
Strategies:
Activities:
Possible interventions:

Evaluating

Procedures:
Materials:
Strategies:

Activities:

Criteria for evaluating program:

2. Review the steps used in teaching students self-instruction. Select a school-related activity or task. Describe the verbal and body language you would provide for the student in each of the six steps listed:
   a. Performing the task while talking out loud as student observes
   b. Student performs task
   c. Teacher models task performance while whispering abbreviated form of verbalizations
   d. Student performs the task, whispering to himself or herself
   e. Teacher performs the task, using covert self-instructions, with pauses and behavioral signs of thinking
   f. Student performs the task, using covert instruction

   What are some activities or tasks that seem appropriate for using cognitive behabior modification techniques? What seem inappropriate?

11

Environmental and Biophysical Interventions

INTRODUCTION

This chapter concludes the discussion of behavior management interventions for application with children and youth with behavior disorders. Three important topics are presented: (a) environmental and (b) biophysical interventions and (c) guidelines for the ethical management of behavior.

The chapter begins with a discussion of the environmental framework from which a variety of interventions are derived. These include, among others, group composition and processes, the instructional environment, class meetings, and milieu therapy. Three examples of the application of the environmental perspective in a special-education setting with children and youth with behavior disorders are discussed: Project Re-ed, Developmental Therapy, and the Engineered Classroom. The section concludes with a discussion of an ecological interview strategy helpful to special educators working with others (parents, teachers) who are directly serving children and youth with behavior disorders.

The next section focuses attention on the biophysical framework and the interventions derived from it. Among the interventions reviewed are several preventive and curative strategies, genetic counseling, nutrition, diet, medication, and occupational and physical therapy. A detailed discussion of the special educator's role in biophysical interventions is presented. The chapter concludes with the presentation of guidelines for the ethical management of behavior. In this section, the principles of normalization, fairness, and respect for the dignity and worth of the individual are presented.

OBJECTIVES

After completing this chapter, you will be able to—

1. Discuss the environmental framework;
2. Describe the application of several behavior management interventions derived from the environmental perspective;
3. Simulate an ecological interview;
4. Discuss the biophysical framework;
5. Describe the application of several behavior management interventions derived from the biophysical perspective;
6. Discuss the special educator's role in biophysical interventions;
7. Discuss guidelines for the ethical management of behavior.

A CASE FOR CONSIDERATION

The six children, ten through twelve years old, sat cross-legged on the floor with their teacher and the classroom aide. Mr. Nolan said, "Margaret, would you please begin the pow-wow today? What is your goal?" Margaret thought for a moment, then said, "My goal is to start my work the first time I'm told." Mr. Nolan reiterated, "Your goal is to follow directions?" Margaret nodded in agreement. Mr. Nolan continued, "Do you think you're achieving your goal?" Margaret answered, "I did a good job on my goal yesterday. When you gave out folders and said to get to work, I did it right away. When Ms. Barb told me to put away the earphones and get to my reading group, I did." "Congratulations, Margaret," Mr. Nolan said. "Are you ready for a new goal?" "Sure," said Margaret; "I'd like the new goal of being able to work with Maria on some projects." "Let's see how we can say that, Margaret. Do you want to work on cooperating with other students?" Margaret nodded.

Mr. Nolan wrote Margaret's new goal on the chalkboard. "I think that's a good goal, Margaret. We will all help you work on it." Turning to the next student, he said, "Luis, what would you like to say to Margaret about the way she's working on her goals?" Luis said, "I think it's neat the way Margaret finished up her goal about doing what you all say. Margaret, I'd like to work on some projects with you." "Thank you, Luis," Mr. Nolan stated. "It's your turn, now. What goal have you been working on?"

Mr. Nolan is using a strategy employed in some environmental interventions, the class meeting or "pow-wow." This group intervention is employed to help children learn to manage their own behaviors.

OBJECTIVE ONE: To discuss the environmental framework.

The terms *environmental* and *ecological* are often used interchangeably in the literature (Swap, Prieto, & Harth, 1982). In this discussion, the authors have chosen, quite arbitrarily, to use the term *environmental*. *Ecological* will be used only when the relationship between the child and his or her specific environment is discussed. This word choice is also based on our wish to differentiate the model presented in Chapter 2 from the present discussion.

In varying degrees, the interventions derived from the environmental perspective view the child's or young person's behavior problems as a consequence of the environment in which he or she is functioning or the relationship between the child and that environment. More specifically, rather than seeing the child as disturbed, the special educator applying the environmental perspective believes that the child's problem is a consequence of the interaction between the child and the environment (Hobbs, 1966; Swap, 1974).

The environmental framework is based on several assumptions about children or youth with behavior disorders, their environments, and the interaction between the child or youth and the environment (Swap, Prieto, & Harth, 1982). First, the disturbance is assumed to be a consequence of either the environment's effect on the child or the interactions between the child and the environment. To be effective, environmental interventions must in some way change the ecological system. A third assumption is that environmental interventions are chosen from several theoretical perspectives. Careful evaluation of these interventions is essential in that unanticipated consequences may occur. Finally, it is assumed that each interaction between the child and setting is unique.

OBJECTIVE TWO: To describe the application of behavior management interventions derived from the environmental perspective.

According to Rhodes and Gibbins (1972) and Wagner (1972), environmental interventions may be classified into four groups: excitor-centered, respondent-centered, excitor-respondent centered, and exchange- or interface-centered. Classification is based on the primary target of the intervention; that is, the child or youth, the environment, the child and environment, or the relationship or interface between the child and the environment. There is, admittedly, overlapping among these groups. Although the intervention may be focused on one or two elements of the total system—child, environment, or interface—it is assumed that it will impact on the total system.

Excitor- or child-centered interventions aim their changes almost exclusively at the child. Among the interventions classified in this group are (a) remediation interventions, such as social adaptation and skill and academic training; (b) natural community interventions; (c) school-community interventions, such as school mental health programs; (d) artificial community interventions, such as specialized communities, camps, and residential centers; and (e) artificial group interventions.

Respondent- or environment-centered interventions aim their change effect primarily at the environment in which the child or youth is functioning. Among the interventions classified in this group are (a) the architectural and physical character of the environment; (b) time, space, and artifacts; (c) scale; (d) shape; (e) privacy; (f) personal space; (g) usability; (h) staff personnel. Also included in this group are interventions aimed primarily at changing the family and school environments.

The third group, excitor-respondent or child-environment interventions, are aimed at changing both the child or youth and the environment in an effort to facilitate functioning. Among the interventions classified in this group are (a) community street-club activities and (b) modification in the child-school relationship, as in Project Re-ed, which is discussed later in this chapter.

The final group of environmental interventions, interface interventions, are aimed at the relationship between the child and the specific environment in which he or she is functioning. These interventions aim to (a) train students in behavior modification techniques, which they apply in school with teachers and peers, and (b) assess and modify the specific problem interface in which the child is functioning ineffectively.

It is both impractical and impossible to report in this chapter all the environmental interventions in the literature. Consequently, a few examples from each group are presented. Those selected are judged by the authors to be most pertinent to the special educator.

Group Processes

A number of highly potent behavior management interventions are closely associated with groups. In these interventions, group processes are used therapeutically to help children and youth with behavior disorders function effectively. Some behavior management interventions that can be considered group-process interventions are discussed in Chapter Nine under the heading Counseling Techniques and in Chapter Ten as behavioral interventions.

Anderson and Marrone (1979) described the use of therapeutic discussion groups in public school classes for emotionally disturbed students.

As a result of twelve years of experience with over six thousand children, they concluded " . . . we cannot imagine a program for emotionally handicapped students that would not fit the proven, cost effective methodology of therapeutic discussion groups in the classroom" (p. 15).

After a period of experimentation during which students were involved in individual therapy, therapeutic discussion groups, or no therapeutic treatment, it was concluded that the group model benefited the children and teachers in several ways. Teachers benefited by receiving support from doing team work with mental health professionals. In addition, they received training in psychodynamic theory and techniques that enhanced their understanding of students' behavior. The group structured time for communication and affective education, as well as increasing the opportunity for early intervention with children with potential problems. Through the group, appropriate student behavior could be reinforced, and empathy, concern, and caring were encouraged. The goal of the therapeutic discussion groups was to change behavior. Group techniques were applied successfully with psychotic, passive-aggressive, and depressed children.

Weekly group sessions of thirty to sixty minutes are conducted with the psychologist or psychiatrist, teacher, aide, and social worker. Meeting length varies with the age of the children and their needs. Pre-and postmeeting sessions are conducted by the mental-health consultant with the special educator to discuss concerns, needs, and child's behaviors, as well as to evaluate the session. Group sessions are a standard part of each student's program and are conducted in a circle in the classroom.

Anderson and Marrone suggest the following group-process guidelines:

1. Children may speak on any topic. Physical aggression and obscene language are considered inappropriate.
2. Confidentiality is stressed.
3. Discussion may be initiated or facilitated by centering on a specific student interest, need, positive behavior, or similar topic.
4. After several weekly meetings resulting in an increased understanding by the team of the students' needs, the following therapeutic progression is applied:
   a. Help the student recognize his or her ineffective behavior.
   b. Help the student explore and recognize the feelings behind the ineffective behaviors.
   c. Identify the source of the feelings.
   d. Connect these feelings with the students' actions and their consequences.
   e. Facilitate the student's commitment to change.
   f. Plan alternatives with the student.
   g. Support the student's efforts to change.
   h. Recognize the new behavior and encourage it.

There are several prerequisites for the successful implementation of discussion groups in the public schools. Anderson and Marrone maintain that a belief in the use of therapeutic discussion groups and administrative support is essential. In addition, the program must have a competent mental-health consultant (psychiatrist, clinical psychologist, caseworker, counselor) who accepts the team concept.

The Instructional Environment

The instructional environment has a significant impact on the functioning of children and youth with behavior disorders. Instructional aspects of the environment have been discussed in Chapter 5. In this section, several variables that facilitate many of the behavioral interventions explored in this text and instructional methods used by the special educator are discussed. The special educator should ensure that—

the environment is a comfortable setting, in which the child or young person feels free to function;

unnecessary physical barriers are removed to maximize communication;

students are provided with a private area that is theirs and theirs alone;

the environment is interesting.

Group Meetings

Meetings as behavior management interventions can be a part of the daily routine. Class meetings may deal with students' normal problems of living and learning in a group setting. Over a period of time, the members of the class learn, with guidance, to seek solutions to their problems through verbal transactions with peers and the special educator rather than by means of physical and/or verbal confrontation or withdrawal. If properly guided, group members grow in understanding of themselves and others. They learn to conceptualize problems from another person's point of view.

Group meetings can help children and youths with behavior disorders to set goals for themselves. In addition, through group meetings, students may learn to provide support for one another and develop new coping skills.

Harth and Morris (1976) discussed the goal-setting meeting or the "pow-wow." Such a meeting, conducted by the special educator, is used to help children and youth with behavior disorders set goals for themselves. Goal setting is seen as the first step in a child's effort to gain self-control. In the meeting, the child is given an opportunity to (a) become aware of his or her behavior, (b) verbalize it, and (c) make a public commitment to change the behavior with the assistance of peers and teachers.

The goal-setting meeting is scheduled as the first activity of the first day of school each week. Children and teacher sit in a circle in the classroom. Each child is requested to present his or her behavior goal for the week. The teacher encourages the children to establish goals that are challenging but realistic. New children are helped to establish their goals by the special educator and peers.

Each child's goal is recorded and posted on a chart in the classroom. These goals and the child's progress are evaluated at the next weekly session.

Morris (1982) describes several advantages to using the pow-wow. It requires each student to determine a personal behavioral goal and think about what events bring about certain behaviors. It provides a stimulus to students to become more observant about what is going on around them. When students are asked to indicate whether or not an individual has attained a goal, they must be able to give specific instances to support their opinions; to do so, they must observe others. Morris maintains that the pow-wow improves the self-image of many children, and may be the only time during the day when students have the opportunity to hear positive statements about themselves.

The steps involved in setting up the pow-wow are outlined in Figure 11-1.

Group meetings may also be used to encourage students to support one another in their efforts to achieve self-management. Virden (1984) describes a support group to train students to become independent and insightful helpers for their peers.

Virden's group meetings are student centered and controlled. Two meetings are scheduled daily. During the meeting, students and teacher sit in a tight circle to form a community. The group leader reviews or "thinks through" the day with the students, and coping problems the students had are discussed. A "problem list," including such behaviors as hurting self, others, and property, lying, being disrespectful, making others look foolish, and so on may be used to facilitate the discussion of coping difficulties. After the members of the group have shared the problems they have encountered during the day as a group, the members decide which problems need attention. At this time, members offer suggestions for dealing with specific problems of individual members. As part of the group process, students are urged to maintain daily journals to increase awareness of their coping problems.

Through the peer-support group process, students are helped to avoid "but games"—offering excuses for behavior—and "getting-back games"—seeking revenge or denigrating others. Ideally, a feeling of trust and positive behavioral expectations is shared by all members of the group and the special educator.

Media may be a useful adjunct to group meetings. Elias (1979) used video tapes of different coping situations as the focus of group meetings designed to help students develop constructive strategies and skills applicable to actual problem situations. Video tapes depicting children between the ages of eight and twelve years working through common problem

FIGURE 11-1   Steps Involved in Setting Up the Pow-Wow

1. Seat students in a circle.
2. Explain that this is a pow-wow and that each member will set a personal behavioral goal to be attained by the next pow-wow.
3. (For first pow-wow only.) Starting with child on your left, make a statement such as follows, to each child in turn:
   "If we had done this before, you would now tell us whether or not you'd met your goal, and then we would ask the others if they thought you had. Since this is the first time we are doing this, you should set a goal for next time."
   Explain goals, giving examples as necessary. (Go to step 8.)
   (For second and all following pow-wows.) Have child on your left restate his or her goal (read it if child does not remember it).
4. Ask child to answer yes or no as to whether the goal was met.
5. Ask each person whether the goal was met. (If no, elicit specific instance. If none can be given, then it is assumed that child met the goal.)
6. After completing circle, ask child again whether goal was met.
7. Ask child to make new goal.
8. Ask each person in the circle if the goal seems appropriate. (If no, elicit reason.)
9. Ask child if he or she wants to keep goal or change it in light of comments. (If child wants to change, do so. If not, keep goal.)
10. Write goal on large piece of paper next to child's name.
11. Ask each person for ways to help meet the goal.
12. Ask each person to make one positive comment about the child who just finished making goal.
13. Go to next child and proceed with steps 3–12.
14. After last child is finished, post goals in clear sight.

From R. Harth & S.M. Morris, *"Group Processes for Behavior Change", Teaching Exceptional Children, 8* (4), 136-39. Copyright 1976 by The Council for Exceptional Children. Reprinted by permission.

situations such as peer pressure, learning how to express feelings, and understanding parents were viewed and discussed by the group. According to Elias, group members exhibited an increase in overall positive behaviors, a decrease in social isolation, and greater popularity than students who did not participate in group discussions. This group demonstrates that the viewing and discussion of prosocial television may be useful in training students to think through various behavioral alternatives and their consequences.

The meeting formats discussed here are designed to find realistic solutions to the real problems of children and youth with behavior disorders. As a behavior management intervention, the meeting has significant potential as a preventive and remedial technique when applied consistently and appropriately.

Milieu Therapy

Milieu therapy is essentially a clinical concept; although it varies in ease of application, it can be applied in any setting in which children or youth with behavior disorders function. In varying degrees, this environmental intervention can be applied in a residential, day-school, special classroom, regular classroom, or camp setting. It is most easily applied in the residential or camp setting, because in these environments the special educator can generally exercise more control over the environment than in a day school or special or regular class.

Milieu implies the total environment in which a child lives—everything that is done to, with, for, or by an individual in the place where he or she finds himself (Long, Morse, & Newman, 1980).

According to Redl (1959), a milieu is not "good" or "bad" in itself; its effects on an individual or group depend on the needs in interaction with the milieu. Redl further indicated that no single aspect of the environment is more important than any other. The importance of the various discrete aspects of the environment is dependent on the needs of the individual or group functioning in that particular setting.

Since it is not possible, a priori, to design with certitude a therapeutic milieu for a child or youth with behavior disorders, milieu therapy is a continuous process conducted throughout the child or youth's placement in a particular setting. Individual educators and the entire staff in the setting must be constantly alert to the impact of the milieu on the individual and adjust it when feasible, to facilitate the rehabilitation process. Although these adjustments may appear simple when written, such environmental manipulations are difficult tasks, requiring personnel who are observant and sensitive to the needs of the individual and group.

Redl (1959) identified several critical elements in the milieu. The social structures must be explored in terms of the roles and functions of various individuals and groups within it. The values and standards that are unconsciously and consciously communicated should also be explored. The environmental routines, rituals, and behavior limits should be evaluated as to whether they are facilitating or frustrating individual and group program goals.

In exploring the milieu, Redl suggested that the impact of the natural group processes be evaluated, as well as the impact of the individual's behavior. Personnel attitudes and feelings and overt behavior should be explored. The activities, performances, space, equipment, time, and props all should be assessed as to their appropriateness in meeting the needs of the students. The effects of both the outside and nonimmediate environment should be explored. Finally, the behavioral limits and program responsiveness should be evaluated as to their therapeutic effects.

The therapeutic milieu in any setting, residential or day school, must be continuously monitored, discussed, evaluated, and manipulated for the benefit of the child or young person. The special educator has a primary function in the total therapeutic process of adjusting to fit the students' needs the environment for which he or she is responsible. The educator serves in this function as a consequence of training and close continuous association with the students with behavior disorders.

Project Re-Ed. Project Re-Ed is a cooperative program of George Peabody College for Teachers and the states of Tennessee and North Carolina. During the last two decades, the Re-Ed model has been replicated, in whole and in part, in many areas of the country. The purpose of the program was to "develop and evaluate the effectiveness and feasibility of residential schools for disturbed children, schools . . . staffed by carefully selected teachers backed by consultants from the mental health professions (Hobbs, 1964, p. 1).

Project Re-Ed operated schools in Tennessee and North Carolina. Each school served forty children, aged six to twelve years. Children admitted to Re-Ed are unable to benefit from day-care programs in their home communities. The duration of residential treatment ranged from two months to two years, but was generally four to six months. To remain involved with their families and local communities, the children lived at the Re-Ed facilities from Sunday afternoon to Friday afternoon and at home on weekends.

The children were grouped by age into classes of eight. Two trained teacher-counselors were responsible for each group of children, one during the school day, the other during the afternoon, evening, and nighttime hours. As a team, the teacher-counselors were responsible for their group's therapeutic program twenty-four hours a day. The teacher-counselors were assisted by psychiatrists, psychologists, and social workers, as well as aides, volunteers, and specialized teachers of art, music, crafts, and physical education.

In the Re-Ed program, heavy emphasis was placed on formal school work, individualized to meet the needs of each child. This emphasis is based "on the conviction that school represents one of the most important concerns of the child, the other being his family" (Hobbs, 1964, p. 13).

In addition to school and residential services, the project provided a camping program, a teacher-counselor training program, and consultation and training services for the child's family and local school staff.

The objective of the reeducation process was to help the child, family, school, and community achieve sufficient reorganization with respect to the requirements of each from the other to make the whole system work in a reasonably satisfactory fashion, without undue stress. These limited goals were sought by—

1. restoring the child's trust in adults, and developing social competencies and self-confidence;
2. providing the child with an appropriate academic program;
3. drawing upon resources in the child's home community, especially by giving assistance to the family;
4. assisting the staff of the child's regular school to modify the program for the child's success;
5. increasing the child's social acceptability;
6. assisting the child in developing self-control;
7. facilitating the child's sense of belonging in the home community.

Weinstein (1969) studied the home and school adjustment of 250 students at two Re-Ed schools (Wright and Cumberland) before and after participation in the programs. The students' adjustment was evaluated from the perceptions of parents, the referring agency, and local school personnel. Several questionnaires, checklists, rating scales, and interview techniques were used to collect pre- and post-Re-Ed data on each child.

Referring-agency personnel reported that the majority of the students were moderately to greatly improved as a result of the Re-Ed intervention. Parents reported that after the Re-Ed experience, their children exhibited fewer symptoms, were more socially competent, and were more in agreement with parental'standards of behavior. In addition, parents saw the child as more relaxed, less aggressive, and more dominant after the intervention. The referring teachers viewed the students as less disruptive, harder working, more willing to confront challenges, and relating more appropriately with peers. Cumberland School students were found by the teachers to be academically adequate; Wright School students were not. In general, students lacked the academic skills expected for their age and grade.

Developmental Therapy.   Developmental therapy (Wood, 1975a) is a comprehensive environmental approach to the treatment of severely emotionally disturbed and behavior disordered children and youth. It has been used in the classroom setting with youngsters aged three to fourteen years. Developmental therapy was developed by the staff of the Rutland Center in Athens, Georgia.

> Developmental therapy is designed for special education teachers, mental health workers, pre-school teachers, parents, and paraprofessionals using the therapeutic classroom setting with five to eight children in a group. It is a treatment process which (a) does not isolate the disturbed child from the mainstream of normal experiences; (b) uses normal changes in development as a means to guide and expedite the therapeutic process; and (c) has an evaluation system as an integral part of the curriculum.

By using the goals established for each area of the developmental therapy curriculum and by following the treatment sequences outlined by the developmental objectives, a teacher can facilitate the social and emotional growth of a child. When a child learns successful, pleasure-producing responses, pathological and nonconstructive behaviors will no longer be necessary. With developmental therapy, the teacher assists the child in assimilating experiences designed to encourage the mastery of developmental milestones. Interpersonal techniques and educational activities are used as the vehicles for this process (Wood, 1975a, p. 3).

The practitioner who desires to implement the developmental-therapy strategy in the classroom should accept its underlying assumptions:

1. Emotional and behavioral problems in young children occur concurrently with normal functioning, and may be difficult to differentiate.
2. Physical and psychological development follow a specific sequence.
3. Behavioral change is an individual process, and occurs relative to the environment, experiences, and biological constituents.
4. Pleasurable experiences are necessary for the development of self-knowledge and self-confidence.
5. Children learn through experiences.

The developmental therapy curriculum includes four areas of learning: (1) behavior (the physical adaptive responses the child makes toward the environment, (2) communication (verbal and nonverbal interpersonal processes), (3) socialization (behaviors that lead toward group experiences), and (4) preacademics (readiness and basic learning skills).

As a child successfully engages in the four curriculum areas, he or she progresses through a sequence of steps, or developmental therapy stages. These stages are (1) responding to the environment with pleasure, (2) responding to the environment with success, (3) learning skills for successful group participation, (4) investing in group processes, and (5) applying individual and group skills in new situations.

As the child moves through these stages, several important teaching-learning variables are modified to facilitate the therapeutic process. These variables are the teacher's role, techniques, and interventions, and the environment and experiences. In addition, the therapeutic goals for each curriculum area vary as the child progresses through the five stages of developmental therapy.

Materials by Wood and her associates are available that discuss several facets of developmental therapy, including the theory (Wood, 1975b); curriculum objectives, instructional materials, program activities, classroom design, parent training and involvement, and treatment effectiveness (Wood, 1975a); music (Purvis & Samet, 1976); art (Williams & Wood,

1977); and developmental therapy for young children with autistic characteristics (Bachrach, Mosley, Swindle, & Wood, 1978).

The validity of developmental therapy was explored in a study of thirty-three subjects by Center (1981). The study examined the assumption in the model that there is a close relationship between the child's problems as reported by the Referral Form Checklist (RFCL) (Wood, 1975) and the child's Developmental Therapy Objectives Rating Form (DTORF). No statistically significant relationship was found between problem variables and developmental deficits. The results of this study have limited generalization, owing to sampling limitations.

Kaufman, Paget, and Wood (1981) studied the effectiveness of developmental therapy in reducing the severe problem behaviors of children and maintaining their reduction over time. Referral Form Checklist (RFCL) scores were used as the data base for this study. Children's scores on the RFCL obtained immediately prior to admission were compared with their scores immediately after treatment and approximately two years after treatment.

Sampling difficulties resulted in nonrandom samples. The scores of thirty-seven children were studied between admission and the end of treatment; thirty-six between admission and two years after treatment. The scores of children in the sample were studied at all three points in time.

The results of the study demonstrated that the children show a large, statistically significant decrease in severe problem behaviors as reported by parents on the RFCL as a result of the developmental-therapy experience both immediately after and approximately two years after treatment.

Hewett's Developmental Strategy.   Hewett's developmental strategy for educating children with inappropriate behaviors is presented in *The Emotionally Disturbed Child in the Classroom* (Hewett, 1968; Hewett & Taylor, 1980). In these works, Hewett presents both a theory of exceptionality and a strategy for the treatment of emotionally disturbed children:

> The emotionally disturbed child is a socialization failure. Underlying all of the specialized terms and complex diagnostic labels used to describe him is the implication that his behavior, for whatever reason, is maladaptive according to the expectations of the society in which he lives. The term socialization is used . . . to refer to the process by which these expectations are learned and met by members of a society during the course of their development from infancy to adulthood. At each age level, certain behavior capabilities, knowledge, belief, and customs must be acquired if successful adaptation to the environment is to occur. As an individual's behavior deviates from what is expected for his age, sex, and status it is maladaptive and he may experience serious difficulties in getting along (p. 3).

To help special educators know not only where they are going during the instructional process but also how to get there, Hewett and Taylor

(1980) described six levels of learning competencies through which children should progress:

Attention: making contact with the environment.
Response: participating in the environment verbally and motorically.
Order: following routines.
Exploratory: becoming accurate and thorough explorers of the environment.
Social: gaining the approval and avoiding the disapproval of others.
Mastery: learning skills related to academics and independent functioning.

The student's progress through the tasks associated with each of the levels of learning competencies is facilitated by the teacher, through manipulating three variables: (1) curriculum (learning tasks) (2) conditions (selection and arrangement of learner expectations), and (3) consequences (the selection and provision of reinforcement). Hewett and Taylor indicate that

the process of assigning a task the child needs to learn, is ready to learn, and can be successful learning; selecting conditions which are appropriate; and providing meaningful consequences can be conceived of as the orchestration of success leading to harmony in the classroom (p. 122).

Materials are available on the assessment and placement of children on the learning hierarchy (Hewett & Taylor, 1980), on educational activities associated with each level of the hierarchy (Hewett, 1968; Hewett and Forness, 1984; Hewett and Taylor, 1980), on classroom design (Hewett, 1968), and on parental involvement (Hewett & Taylor, 1980).

OBJECTIVE THREE: *To simulate an ecological interview.*

The special educator frequently finds it necessary to consult with others (parents and teachers) who are in direct contact with the child or youth with behavior disorders. Under these circumstances, the special educator must obtain information on the child's functioning and environments before decisions can be made with regard to potentially effective interventions. The most effective way to obtain such information is to observe the child or young person in the environment causing concern. Observation, however, is sometimes impossible because of the remoteness of the environment and scheduling conflicts. The special educator must then rely on interviews to acquire the needed information.

By means of an ecological interview, the special educator can obtain information on the unique characteristics of the child, the school or home, and the relationship between the child and the environment.

"Ecological assessment is justified only if it leads to ecological intervention" (Hardin, 1978, p. 20). Several protocols for ecological assessment have been developed and used with children and youth with behavioral and learning problems (Gallagher, 1979; Hardin, 1978; Wahler & Cormier, 1970). The ecological interview strategy developed by Wahler and Cormier is discussed in Chapter 3. Rather than repeating this description or discussing other protocols, the authors have chosen to discuss several variables to be included in the development of an ecological interview format.

When developing an ecological interview format, the special educator should consider environmental and student conditions (Gallagher, 1979). An interview strategy that explores these two conditions permits the special educator to make decisions on the basis of objective information from persons who can directly observe the child functioning in the environment. In an initial interview, descriptions of the behaviors of concern and the environments in which the behaviors are exhibited are obtained (Wahler & Cormier, 1970). Variables to be discussed in this initial interview are presented in Figure 11-2.

From such descriptive information, an observation checklist is developed. The checklist stresses both time and place. Through direct observation by the special educator or directed observation by another person in the environment, the frequency and duration of the behaviors of concern are counted and tallied. Information may also be recorded on the antecedents and consequences of the behavior. An effort is made to place equal emphasis on both appropriate and inappropriate behaviors. A sample observation form is presented in Figure 11-3.

On the basis of the observer's data, the special educator can suggest potentially effective interventions. At this junction in the process, the special educator and parent or teacher begin the behavior-change process, as presented in Chapter Nine.

Special educators should also consider self-reports in ecological assessment. Safran and Safran (1984) described a self-monitoring mood chart for use with eight- to twelve-year-old children with behavior disorders. Words and pictures arranged on a five-point scale were provided for students to increase the teachers' awareness of the students' affect (Figure 11-4). This self-report, paired with a checklist for morning events completed by parents (Figure 11-5), provides the special educator with insight into the relationship between morning events at home and initial mood in school.

OBJECTIVE FOUR: To describe the biophysical frame of reference.

In this section, several biophysical interventions about which educators should have knowledge are discussed. These include several preven-

FIGURE 11-2   Variables for Consideration in Ecological Interviews

Environmental conditions within the school

Classroom atmosphere
   Background noise
Teacher expectations and limits
Mode and pacing of presentations
   Visual materials enhance or distract?
   Auditory materials enhance or distract?
   Time constraints
Scope and sequence of skills taught
Teacher-student relationships
   Teacher physical proximity
Peer relationships

Environmental conditions within the home

Parent expectancies
Parent awareness of child's needs
Parent-child relationships
Sibling relationships
Parent acceptance

Conditions unique to the student

Response to tasks or demands
   Attempts tasks
   Responds thoughtfully or impulsively
   Needs prompting
   Perseverance
   Avoidance behaviors
   Refusal
   Destructiveness
   Hostility or belligerence
   Anxious or relaxed

Self-report

(Adapted from Gallagher, 1979; Hardin, 1978)

tive and curative techniques, such as genetic counseling, nutrition, megavitamin therapy, general and specialized physical examinations, and medication. In the majority of these interventions the educator plays an important supportive role to the physician and other medical personnel.

FIGURE 11-3   Example of Child-Behavior Checklist

	FOLLOWS DIRECTIONS	COMMUNITY BEHAVIORS KEEPS HANDS TO SELF	USES APPROPRIATE LANGUAGE
In own yard			
In neighbor's yard			
Shopping			
In playground/park			
In church			
In car			

The biophysical frame of reference implies that the source of the child's or young person's behavior disorder is an organic defect. There are two known causes of biophysical defects in unborn and newborn children: environment and heredity. Environmental factors of special importance to the health of the child are direct maternal ones (metabolic disorders, age, and number and frequency of pregnancies) and those that affect the mother during pregnancy (diseases and infections, drugs, tobacco, diet, and injuries). The larger environment itself may affect the child's physical well-being as a consequence of pollution, radiation, toxic wastes, and the like.

Heredity, or the transmission of the characteristics or traits of the parents to their children, is a factor in birth defects. Hereditary characteristics are transmitted from parents to children by chromosomes. The inherited characteristics of a child are determined by the composition of the gene-carrying chromosomes from the parents and the manner in which they combine at the time of conception.

It is generally agreed in the literature that birth defects are best reduced or controlled by preventive techniques rather than curative techniques. Among the curative interventions available to the physician are chemical regulation, corrective surgery, and rehabilitation through training.

Chemical regulation includes interventions such as medication and diet. Corrective surgery is frequently effective in reducing the effects of cleft lip and palate and some visual, auditory, and speech problems.

FIGURE 11-4   Self-Monitoring Mood Chart

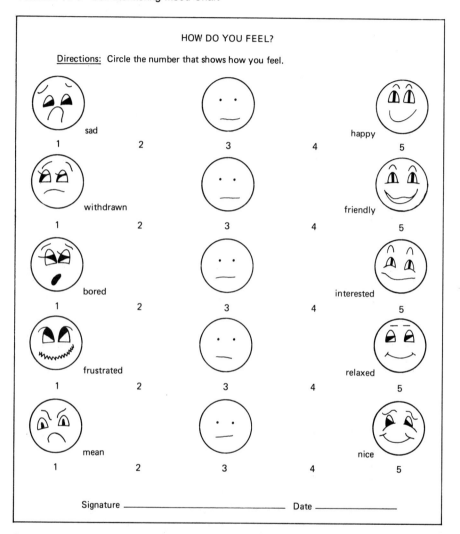

Rehabilitation and training services, including special education, have a significant, positive impact on the lives of individuals with mental, visual, auditory, learning, or behavioral impairments. Preventive interventions include prenatal care and genetic counseling. Several preventive and curative interventions are discussed in the following section.

FIGURE 11-5   Checklist for Morning Events

MORNING EVENTS	EASILY	SOME DIFFICULTY	GREAT DIFFICULTY
Waking			
Grooming			
Dressing			
Breakfasting			
Interacting with siblings			
Leaving the house			

(From Safran & Safran, 1984, p. 174.)

OBJECTIVE FIVE: *To describe the application of several preventive and curative biophysical interventions.*

Genetic Counseling

Genetic counseling involves providing an estimate of the probability of occurrence (or recurrence) of a disease or defect in a particular individual (Kameya, 1972). The major goal of genetic counseling is the prevention of birth defects.

Although the genetic counselor cannot predict the exact occurrence of a defective child, the probability of the occurrence of disabilities in the offspring of specific parents and parents-to-be can be predicted. The genetic counselor only provides the parents with medical information on the probability that a defective child will be born. The ultimate decision to give birth to or abort the unborn child is the parents' (Shaw, 1974).

Prenatal Care

Prenatal care involves a variety of examinations and interventions designed to ensure that the unborn child develops normally in a healthy environment. By means of careful prenatal care, the parents and physician can not only determine the growth and developmental patterns of the unborn child but are in a position to intervene if there are indications of problems. Prenatal care includes consideration of the mother's diet, exercise, and personal hygiene, as well as the emotional status of both parents.

Postnatal Care

Postnatal care is essential for the continued health and well-being of all children. Children should receive physical examinations at least once a year. Conscientious health care permits the family physician and parents to guide the child through the developmental stages and to recognize and intervene if problems arise. Postnatal care includes appropriate vision, hearing, and dental care.

Nutrition

The precise relationship between specific nutrients and behavior disorders in children and youths is unknown. However, an important relationship between these factors in all probability does exist. Research has demonstrated the relationships between several nutrients and specific physical disorders. Knapczyk (1979) cited three major types of diet-related conditions that are associated with behavior disorders in school-age children. These include hypoglycemia, vitamin/mineral deficiencies, and allergies. The student with hypoglycemia may become either lethargic and appear unmotivated and withdrawn or hyperactive and inattentive. Vitamin/mineral deficiencies have been related to hyperactive behaviors. Various specific foods and food additives have been related to allergic reactions in children (Knapczyk, 1979).

In his review of the research literature on child nutrition, Kameya writes (1972):

> While the results of some of these studies may be ambiguous because of confounding variables, they are strongly suggestive that malnutrition is one of the primary factors in the retardation of physical and mental development. Moreover, the social and economic concomitants of malnutrition are not subject to change within one generation. Preventive medicine and applied nutrition could, on the other hand, bring immediate and palpable results—especially in underdeveloped countries, and also in the rural and ghetto areas of this nation (P. 149).

Diet

Lately, there has been considerable publicity about the effects of diet control on the hyperactive behaviors of children. Feingold (1973, 1975) hypothesized that naturally occurring salicylates and artificial food additives may cause the hyperkinetic syndrome in children who have a genetically determined predisposition.

Elimination of these substances from a child's diet would eliminate the symptoms of the hyperkinetic syndrome. Feingold claims that 48 percent of his patients were effectively treated by the diet he proposed and that symptoms can be reversed within a few hours if the diet is broken. Cook and Woodhill (1976) supported Feingold's claim in a clinical study of fifteen hyperkinetic children, but cautioned against the generalization of their finding because the sample was limited and the study did not meet rigorous research standards. In Brenner's (1977) study of fifty-nine children, approximately one third of the children able to tolerate the diet showed marked improvement as reported by parents and physicians.

Weiss, Williams, Margen, Abrams, Citron, Cox, McKillen, and Ogar (1980) conducted a challenge study of twenty-two children with regard to behavioral responses to artificial food colors. Twenty of the twenty-two children displayed no convincing evidence of sensitivity to the color challenge as reported by parents. Swanson and Kinsbourne (1980) studied the effects of food dyes on children's laboratory learning performance. Twenty children were classified as hyperactive; the same number were not. Both groups were challenged with food dyes. The performance of the hyperactive children was impaired on the days they received food dyes. Performance of the nonhyperactive children was not affected.

In a review of the pertinent empirical investigations with regard to the Feingold diet, Baker (1980) concluded that the differential results reported by Feingold, parents, and others using the diet may be due to variables other than the eliminated substances. He found that in properly controlled studies, the positive effects of the diet evaporated.

Medical Examinations

Medical examinations may be performed to exclude the possibility of diseases involving bodily systems that could account for the behavior or learning disorders (Millichap, 1975). Neurological examinations are performed to determine the probability of neurological malfunctioning. This examination includes an evaluation of the individual's gait, coordination, muscular power and tone, handedness, sensory perception, speech, vision, and hearing.

Medication

Although behavior-modifying medications have been prescribed for children and youth with behavior disorders since the late 1930s (Wilson & Sherrets, 1979), the treatment-evaluation process remains complicated (Baldwin, 1973). The physician must not only be concerned with the individual child's personal status, but must evaluate the child's environment, potentially biased evaluations of those associated with the child, and the actual and potential effects of other interventions being applied, such as special education.

Several reviews have been published (Baldwin, 1973; Gadow, 1979;

Renshaw, 1974) describing the use of medication with children, particularly in the treatment of hyperactivity. These reviews are summarized in the following paragraphs:

Central-nervous-system stimulants. Stimulants are prescribed for their calming effect on prepubertal children of both sexes. This is called a paradoxical effect. Although at this time the specific reasons for this effect are unknown, stimulants have a calming and quieting effect on some children, whereas they generally stimulate an adult. Trade names of stimulants include Ritalin, Dexedrine, and Cylert.

The sought-for positive effects of the stimulants are (a) increased controlled physical activity; (b) increased goal directedness; (c) decreased impulsivity and disruptions; (d) decreased distractibility; (e) increased attending; (f) improved performance, cognition, and perception; (g) improved motor coordination; (h) improved cooperation; (i) decreased negative and increased positive behavior.

Stimulants have several possible side effects. Students may experience nausea, loss of appetite, and weight loss. There may be a disruption in sleep patterns, with insomnia or infrequent drowsiness both observed. Nervousness, depression, and crying are also noted. When the stimulant is first introduced, severe shaking and fear may be observed.

Antianxiety and antipsychotic drugs. These drugs are prescribed for their calming effects; some individuals may return to a more acceptable mode of functioning as a result of these medications. Trade names include Mellaril, Thorazine, Librium, Miltown, and Equanil. Mellaril and Thorazine are the most frequently prescribed tranquilizers for children.

Desired positive effects of tranquilizers are increased calmness and improved behavior and social functioning. Possible negative effects include nausea, drowsiness, dry mouth and nasal congestion, nervousness, rashes, increased appetite, and weight gain.

Anticonvulsants and Antihistamines. Anticonvulsants are used to treat children whose behavior and learning problems are complicated by seizures. Trade names for these medications include Dilantin, Mysoline, and Valproic Acid.

Antihistamines are used to counteract the effects of various allergies. Trade names include Benadryl, Vistaril, and Phenergan. According to Renshaw (1974), these medications are exceptionally safe. They are often prescribed for their sedative effects on children in pain and at nighttime.

Though medication can have a beneficial effect on children and youth, it cannot make up for "lost" years of learning. Medication does not provide the discipline, love, or structure needed by children and youth with behavior disorders. Medication cannot reverse essential deficits such as mental retardation and cerebral palsy (Renshaw, 1974).

OBJECTIVE SIX: *To discuss the special educator's role in biophysical interventions.*

The special educator plays an important supportive role to the medical personnel in the application of biophysical interventions. This supportive role includes (a) referral, (b) collaboration with and reporting of observations, (c) modification of classroom structure and curricular content to meet the needs of the child or young person, (d) obtaining permission to administer medication, and (e) safeguarding medication and administering it to the child or young person in school.

Referral.   The special educator is not qualified to refer a child directly to a physician or to suggest the prescribing of medication. However, special educators may inform parents of a child's behavior problems. The school may initiate contact with medical personnel on behalf of a particular child, with parental consent. It is suggested that an educator not directly involved with the child in the school serve as a contact person and intermediary between the teacher and parents during the referral process (Report of the Conference on the Use of Stimulant Drugs, 1971).

Collaboration with and reporting of observations to the physician.   A primary role of the special educator in biophysical interventions is the provision of current and objective feedback to the physician on the observable effects of the medication on the child's behavior and learning (Wilson & Sherrets, 1979). The majority of the present-day symptom-control medications are experimental substances, whose effects on a particular child cannot be predicted exactly. Thus, feedback to the prescribing physican will assist in efforts to maximize the positive effects of medication on the child. Because special educators are trained observers and are with the child throughout the day, they are in an excellent position to observe the effects of the medication and report, through proper channels, to the physician.

Modification of classroom structure an curricular content.   During the biophysical treatment process, especially in the beginning weeks, the child's behavior and learning styles may change significantly. Consequently, it may be necessary to modify both classroom structure and curricular content to respond to the child's needs. Classroom structure may have to be increased or decreased to permit the child to adjust to "new" behaviors and interests. The curriculum may have to be changed to allow the child to learn the knowledge and skills neglected by earlier, less successful programming.

Obtaining permission to dispense medication.   The special educator must obtain permission to dispense medication in the school when medical personnel (a physician and/or nurse) are not available during the day (Courtnage, Stainback, & Stainback, 1982). A child should not be dismissed from school because medical personnel are not immediately available to administer medication. Educators may dispense medication with proper permission. Courtnage and associates (1982) suggest the development of a school policy on medication in an effort to improve services and minimize personnel liability. A permission form based on their suggestions for the administration of medication is presented in Figure 11-6.

FIGURE 11-6 Authorization for the Administration of Medication

```
Name of Student _____ Birthdate _____

Address _____ Phone _____

School _____ Grade _____ Teacher _____

Part I—Physician's Statement
     1. Name/type of medication _____
     2. Dosage/amount to be given _____
     3. Frequency/times to be administered _____
     4. Duration (week, month, indefinite, etc.) _____
     5. Anticipated reaction to medication (Symptoms, side
        effects, etc.) _____
_____
Physician's signature _____ Date signed _____

Address                        Phone

Part II—Parent's Request/Approval
  I hereby request and give my permission for the above-
named school to administer the medication prescribed on
this form to my child.
_____
Parent's signature _____ Date signed _____

Part III—Designated Person(s) Administering Drugs
  I have agreed to administer the medication as requested
by the parents and in accordance with directions listed
above by the physician.
_____
Signature of Person(s) _____ Date _____
administering medication

Copies to: Physician
           Parents
           School
```

Safeguarding and administering medication. When medication is dispensed in the school, the following guidelines should be followed:

1. Permission forms should be obtained and filed in the child's record folder.
2. Medications should be stored in a central location, in a locked cabinet. A refrigerator may be necessary for some medications.
3. Medications must be properly labeled with the child's and physician's names. The label should include directions for use.
4. Medications should be logged in and out of the school. Medication should be inventoried daily. One professional member of the school's staff should be appointed to inventory medication and function as a contact person in all communications with parents, physicians, and other medical personnel related to medication.
5. A responsible adult must be present when the child takes medication.
6. A log, to be completed each time a child takes medication, should be affixed to the wall in the medication area or in the child's individual file. A sample form is presented in Figure 11-7. The completed forms should be retained.

OBJECTIVE SEVEN: *To discuss guidelines for the ethical management of behavior.*

Many behavior management interventions have been discussed in chapters 8–11. Each of these interventions can, under the proper circumstances, effectively modify the behavior of children and youths.

Paramount to the effective application of any intervention by special educators is appropriate training and experience under professional supervision. Readers are urged to study carefully the literature on the interventions of interest by utilizing the chapter references. They are also encouraged to consult with appropriately trained and certified specialists.

Behavior-management interventions should be used only for the benefit of the child or young person. They should never be used primarily for the benefit of the child's teacher, peers, or parents.

In 1969, Allen proposed three principles to govern the selection and application of behavior management interventions with exceptional individuals. These principles are discussed next as guidelines for the ethical application of behavior management interventions. They are the principles of normalization, fairness, and respect for the dignity and worth of the individual.

Principle of normalization.   "To let the handicapped person obtain an existence as close to the normal as is possible" (Nirje, 1967, cited in Allen, 1969, p. 7).

When applying this principle, the special educator must use as a point of reference the child's real environment (including the behaviors of the children and adults within that environment). This principle requires an

FIGURE 11-7 Individual Student-Medication Log

Name of student _____ Birthdate _____

Date	Time	Medication/ dosage	Person dispensing medication	Notes

understanding of the similarities and differences between various groups and subgroups in society. The educator must base decisions on knowledge of the individual child's growth and development pattern as well as the child's needs, interests, strengths, exceptionalities, and potential.

During the decision-making process, the special educator must respond to the following question: Will the application of this intervention facilitate the child's movement toward the normally anticipated and observed behavior in this environment (that environment in which the child is functioning or will function in the future), or will it simply eliminate the child (and thus, the behavior) as an inconvenience or annoyance to others in the environment, such as the teacher, peers, administrators, and parents? The special educator is always required to use the least restrictive intervention needed to attain the purpose for intervening.

Principle of fairness.   Fairness or due process of law

> requires that in decision-making affecting one's life, liberty, or vital interests, the elements of due process will be observed, including the right to notice, to a fair hearing, to representation by counsel, to present evidence and to cross-examine witnesses testifying against one (Allen, 1969, p. 82).

Although this principle is phrased in legal terminology, it can be translated for special educators' use: "Is this technique fair to the child as an individual?"

Interventions may not be applied arbitrarily, without evidence that the child or young person is, in fact, exhibiting the inappropriate behavior. Also, interventions are sometimes used that serve to prohibit the child from finding success in school. Unfairness is evidenced when a teacher refuses to use a technique that is obviously needed by a child or young person for successful functioning in school. For example, educators may not use tangible or token reinforcers because they "do not believe in them" even though observation of the child proves that the child only responds to such reinforcers.

Other examples of unfairness are the refusal to attempt systematically to change a child's behavior, arbitrary placement in special programs without attempting in-class interventions, and unwillingness to provide needed services or request assistance from others. When the principle of fairness is fully implemented, decisions are made exclusively from the point of view of the child's welfare.

Principle of respect for the dignity and worth of the individual.   This refers to "one's right to be treated as a human being, and not as an animal or statistic" (Allen, 1969, p. 83).

In our actions toward children and youths with behavior disorders, we must demonstrate respect for them as human beings. When interventions are evaluated from the perspective of this principle, we find that some common practices—such as the use of physical and psychological punishments, isolation, physical restraint, and electric shocks—violate it.

These techniques have been used and remain in use in some educational settings. They are applied by individuals who justify their use as a means to attain their end. They have been justified as the "only way" to accomplish a particular end or objective.

The Council for Exceptional Children's Delegate Assembly (1983) has adopted standards for the ethical application of behavior-management interventions. These standards for the managements of behavior are:

> 1.2.1 Special education professionals participate with other professionals and with parents in an interdisciplinary effort in the management of behavior. Professionals:
> 1.2.1.1 Apply only those disciplinary methods and behavioral procedures which they have been instructed to use and which do not undermine the dignity of the individual or the basic human right of exceptional persons (such as corporal punishment).
> 1.2.1.2 Clearly specify the goals and objectives for behavior management practices in the exceptional person's Individualized Education Program.
> 1.2.1.3 Conform to policies, statutes, and rules established by state/ provincial and local agencies relating to judicious application of disciplinary methods and behavioral procedures.
> 1.2.1.4 Take adequate measures to discourage, prevent, and intervene when a collegue's behavior is perceived as being detrimental to exceptional persons.
> 1.2.1.5 Refrain from aversive techniques unless repeated trials of other methods have failed and then only after consultation with parents and appropriate agency officials (p. 9).

Each special educator must have a clearly defined ethical system to guide his or her work with children and youth with behavior disorders. This system should incorporate the principles of normalization, fairness, and respect for the dignity and worth of the individual. One simply cannot operate ethically on the principle of "any means to attain an end."

SUMMARY

In this chapter, environmental and biophysical interventions were presented. Each framework and the interventions it generates were discussed. In addition, the use of an ecological interview to individualize programming was presented and the special educator's role in biophysical interventions was described.

The chapter concluded with ethical guidelines for the application of behavior-management interventions. These guidelines should be followed when applying any intervention described in chapters 8–11.

REVIEW QUESTIONS

1. Review the material on the environmental perspective in Chapter 1. Relate that material to the environmental interventions described in this chapter.
2. Using the professional literature, locate, analyze, and discuss additional environmental interventions applicable in programs for children and youths with behavior disorders not presented in this chapter.
3. What are the most significant of the biophysical interventions in this chapter from the perspective of the educator? Why?
4. What is the purpose of medication? Who is responsible for prescribing it? Why? Who is responsible for administering it? Why?
5. What is the educator's role in biophysical interventions? Although limited, the educator's role is significant. Why?
6. Discuss the compatibility (or incompatibility) of the environmental and biophysical interventions reviewed in this chapter. Is a synthesis possible?
7. Discuss the significance of each of the following principles as they relate to children and youth, parents, teachers, and schools in a democratic society: the principle of normalization, the principle of fairness, and the principle of respect for the dignity and worth of the individual. What other principles should be applied to determine the ethical acceptability of a treatment program for a child or youth with behavior disorders?

APPLICATION ACTIVITIES

1. The ecological interview assists the special educator to obtain information on the child's functioning and environment before making decisions with regard to potentially effective interventions. Select a child with whom you are familiar (or a case from Appendix B). Address each of the following variables and develop an ecological interview format to address the needs of the child.

Environmental Conditions (School)

What information do you need regarding:
atmosphere
stimuli
physical arrangement
interpersonal relationships
time

Environmental Conditions (Home)

What information do you need regarding:
atmosphere

demands and expectations
physical information
interpersonal relationships

Conditions Unique to the Child

What information do you need regarding:
approach to work, demands, expectations, limits
response to individuals in the environment

What behaviors are of concern?

Complete the following observation for use with the child.

SITUATIONS   **BEHAVIORS**

2. Evaluate each of the following behaviors in terms of the ethical guidelines of normalization, fairness, and respect for human dignity.

	NORMALIZATION	FAIRNESS	RESPECT
1. Joey hit the bus driver, who responded by hugging him and telling him it was okay.			
2. Luisa is put in the corner during math class for the entire period each day she forgets her homework.			
3. Matthew's mouth is washed out with soap for cursing.			
4. Diana's second-grade teacher makes her wear a diaper pinned over her clothing, because she wets her pants.			
5. Ms. Skelton refuses to use tangible reinforcers, because "students shouldn't work for bribes."			

12

Parental Involvement

The diagnosis of an exceptionality in one of its members is traumatic for any family (Barsch, 1968; Love, 1970). This unexpected turn of events has a dramatic effect on the exceptional individual's mother, father, brothers, and sisters. It modifies their personal behavior and, consequently, the manner in which they relate to one another. Also affected is the manner in which the family, as a social unit, and its individual members interact with friends, relatives, and others outside of the family (Buscaglia, 1975; Chinn, Winn, & Walters, 1978; Rossi, 1985).

Although the initial effects of the diagnosis of exceptionality are felt primarily by the parents, they are soon transmitted to all family members. This appears to be true regardless of whether the exceptionality is diagnosed at the child's birth or later in life. Unfortunately, there is relatively little empirical research reported on a family's initial reactions to an exceptionality or on the emotional states through which the family and its individual members pass before adjusting to it.

Parents, special educators, physicians, and counselors, however, report a variety of emotional reactions by parents to such a diagnosis (Hoff, 1978; Seligman, 1979). Among these are shock, disbelief, rejection, guilt, shame, fear, withdrawal, isolation, and frustration (McDowell, 1976). Such reactions appear to be a normal response to a traumatic event. It is believed that these emotional states must be "worked through" before the fact of the exceptionality is accepted (Prescott & Iselin, 1978). There may be a need for individual and family counseling during this period of adjustment;

however, appropriate counseling services, for all practical purposes, are not universally available.

Once the family members, especially the parents, have accepted the child's exceptionality, they begin the process of finding practical assistance for themselves and the child. At this time, parents and professionals come together and begin to work cooperatively to help the exceptional child realize his or her full potential.

This chapter describes a model for parent–special educator involvement designed to facilitate positive and productive cooperation for the benefit of the child or youth with behavior disorders. Several activities in which parents and special educators can become involved to assist the child are discussed. The chapter also includes discussions of the need and desirability of parental involvement, its ecological basis, and reasons some parents are not involved and/or are less than positively involved in parent–special educator activities.

OBJECTIVES

After completing this chapter, you will be able to—

1. Discuss the need for and desirability of parental involvement in the education of children and youth with behavior disorders;
2. Describe the ecological basis for parent–special educator involvement programs;
3. Discuss the parent–special educator involvement model and its components;
4. Implement several parent–special educator involvement activities;
5. Discuss several reasons some parents and special educators are unable to become involved in cooperative activities.

A CASE FOR CONSIDERATION

"Mary Elizabeth doesn't do anything I ask her to do, Ms. Stuart." Mrs. Ioka had requested a conference with Ms. Stuart, her daughter's special education teacher, because of persistent noncompliance. "Her bed's never made, she never does her job of taking out the garbage, and when I ask her to keep an eye on her seven-year-old sister, she has even left her alone in the house and gone out by herself. I punish her, make her stay in her room, and take away dessert, but she just doesn't seem to care."

Ms. Stuart replied, "So Mary Elizabeth doesn't seem to follow through on her jobs, and taking things away doesn't seem to help."

"Right," replied Mrs. Ioka. "She just says things like, "So what!" or "Big deal," whenever I punish her. She has to start helping out. She's fourteen, and just lies around or goes out walking alone."

"Well, Mrs. Ioka, we're using a technique here at school with Mary Elizabeth that seems to get her working. It's called a token economy."

"Token economy?"

"Right. What we can do is sit down with Mary Elizabeth and determine what kinds of things she'd like to work for at home. Are there certain things she really likes?"

"She likes not to do her chores. But she also likes records. Going out for pizza with her brother Keith on Friday nights is also a big deal."

"Good. Then we have some options. What things do you really want Mary Elizabeth to do?"

"I want her to make her bed. She should take out the garbage, too—that's her job. She also is supposed to set the table for dinner, but I always have to do it when I get home from work."

"So we have three jobs to start with. When we meet with Mary Elizabeth, we'll decide how many points doing each of those jobs without being reminded is going to be worth. Then we'll put a price on records and going out for pizza. Maybe we can also have her buy a 'day off' with her points."

"I bet she'd like that, Ms. Stuart. She doesn't like to do any chores," said Mrs. Ioka.

"We'll need to try this system for two weeks. If she doesn't do the job without any reminders, no points. As soon as she has enough points, she can 'buy' her treat."

"I'll try anything," said Mrs. Ioka. "Mary Elizabeth just has to start doing her part."

In this case, Mrs. Ioka and Mrs. Stuart cooperatively planned a program to change the inappropriate behaviors Mary Elizabeth was exhibiting at home. Both parent and professional contributed and shared information about the child's behavior. The special educator knew a technique that had been successful in the past with the student. The parent knew what her daughter liked and disliked. Together, they developed a cooperative program to help a child with a behavior problem.

OBJECTIVE ONE: To discuss the need for and desirability of parental involvement in the education of the child or youth with behavior disorders.

Although mandated by Public Law 94-142, among some special educators there remains skepticism concerning the need for and desirability of school-sponsored education and training for parents of exceptional children. We agree with the assertion of Clements and Alexander (1975) that:

> It is unnecessary to revisit the already proven axiom that parents are effective change agents in the lives of exceptional children. It is, perhaps, equally as extravagant to indulge in outlining the boundaries of social and academic learning and perpetuate the pseudoissue of who governs which set of con-

structs when, in reality, these are shared and interactive responsibilities. We must instead face an important issue in the third quarter of the twentieth century: parents are moving both physically and intellectually back into the mainstream of American education (p. 1).

The question that special educators must address, then, is not whether parent education is needed or desirable but how to most effectively and efficiently conduct parent–special educator cooperative activities for the benefit of children and youth with behavior disorders. The special educator is the person primarily responsible for organizing these activities.

Gardner (1974) maintains that joint home-school endeavors are more effective in meeting the needs of children with behavior disorders than school endeavors only. Parents, he contends, need assistance in recognizing that their interactions with their children may exacerbate the behavior problem. Gardner maintains that parents need information, guidance, and support provided through specific, concrete, and practical suggestions about how they can best promote the optimal adjustment for their child.

Educational programs for children and youths with behavior disorders frequently stress the need for parental involvement (Susser, 1974; Wood, 1975a). Success in the classroom will be lasting only if there is a twenty-four-hour-a-day follow-through and consistency of approach between school and home (Susser, 1974).

Parents are also aware of their need for education and training. In their writings, parents of exceptional children describe a need for assistance through meaningful education and training (Stigen, 1976). Parents suggest that there is a need for sensitive, practical assistance in the conduct of their roles as primary therapists for their children, and point out the apparent lack of training and sensitivity of professionals toward parents of exceptional children.

As a result of an extensive review of the literature, Shea and Bauer (1985) concluded:

1. There is a need for education and training for parents of exceptional children.
2. Such programs are desirable because they not only respond to the needs of parents but have a significant positive effect on the child.
3. The special educator, a specialist in instructional processes and behavior management, is the logical professional to coordinate parent programs.
4. There should be consistency between the approaches used in the home and school if the child is to derive maximum benefit from the efforts of both parent and special educator.
5. Parent programs should be practical, concrete, specific, and meaningful to the parents.

OBJECTIVE TWO: *To describe the ecological basis for parent–special educator involvement.*

The ecological contexts that affect the child or youth with behavior disorders are described in detail in Chapter 2. The ecological framework stresses that the understanding of human development and behavior requires examining the context of interactions in many settings (Bronfenbrenner, 1977). The mesosystem, the interrelations among major settings containing the developing child at a particular point in his or her life, includes both home and school. To effectively respond to student needs, the special educator must involve those in the mesosystem (parents, guardians, siblings, or surrogate parents) in the child's education and management program).

Bronfenbrenner contends that an ecological approach invites consideration of the joint impact of two or more settings on their elements. School and home jointly impact on the child or young person with behavior disorders. Subsystems that may become apparent include parent-child, parent-special educator-child, special educator-child, sibling-child, sibling-parent-child, and so on. As Bronfenbrenner suggests, the design of ecological experiments involving a person in more than one setting should take into account the possible subsystems and effects that exist, or could exist, across settings. Consequently, programming should take these subsystems into account. Those to be considered when studying the ecological systems in which the child or youth with behavior disorders functions include:

nature and requirements of the parents' work
neighborhood, health, and welfare services
relations between school and community
informal social networks
patterns of recreation and social life
growth of single-parent families
delegation of child care to specialists outside of the home
existence and character of an explicit national policy on children and families

By analyzing the child or young person with behavior disorders and his or her parent or parents and family with reference to these contexts, the special educator can develop individualized parent education-and-training programs to meet the unique needs of each parent and child.

OBJECTIVE THREE: *To describe the parent–special educator involvement model and its components.*

The parent–special educator involvement model presented in this section is a school-based service delivery system applied to facilitate the individualization of parent education and involvement activities designed to assist the child or youth with behavior disorders realize his or her full potential. The model is a prescriptive teaching methodology or procedural framework that parallels processes mandated by Public Law 94-142 for Individualized Education Programs. It is predicated on the belief that each parent is a unique individual with unique needs. Consequently, it is designed to respond to the individual abilities, needs, and wishes of the participating parent. In addition, the model recognizes the individuality of each participating child and special educator. Finally, the model is sensitive to variations among the contexts in which parents, special educators, and children function.

Parent–special educator involvement is not designed for, nor may it be applied with, parents suffering from severe personal social-emotional conflicts, psychopathologies, or marital difficulties. It is not a form of psychotherapy, as important as such treatment may be to a particular parent. Special educators and other professionals applying the model must recognize and accept the fact that some parents are unable to benefit their children through this and similar programs. Parents in need of assistance for complex psychopathologies, personal social-emotional conflicts, and marital difficulties must be referred to appropriately qualified and certified therapists, counselors, or social-service professionals.

In addition, the effectiveness of the model, as with any model, is limited by the interest, willingness, and ability of the parents and special educator participating in the program.

The Model

The parent–special educator involvement model includes five phases: (1) intake and assessment, (2) selection of goals and objectives, (3) planning and implementing of activities, (4) evaluation of activities, and (5) termination/review. These phases are discussed in the remainder of this section and summarized on the flow chart in Figure 12-1.

Phase 1: Intake and assessment.   Intake and assessment consist of one or more conferences between the parent(s) and special educator. The goals of these conferences are—

1. to establish a positive interpersonal relationship;
2. to communicate assessment information and a description of the child's special and regular educational program;
3. to ascertain the parents' perceptions of the child or youth and his or her behavior disorders, special needs, and prognosis;
4. to determine the parents' needs, desires, interests, and competencies relative to their child's special needs and their parenting functions; and
5. to facilitate the introduction of the parents into the involvement program.

FIGURE 12-1 The Parent-Teacher Involvement Model

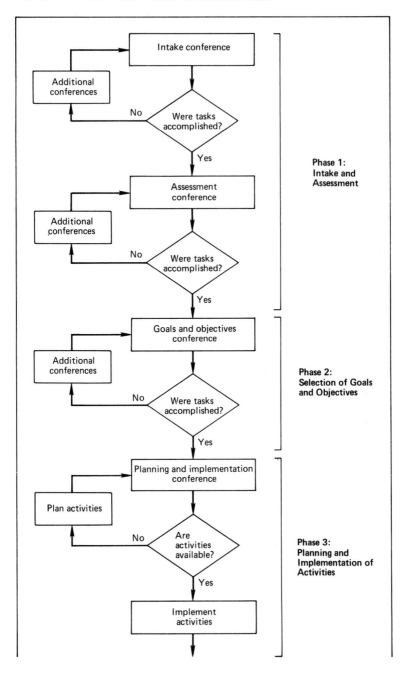

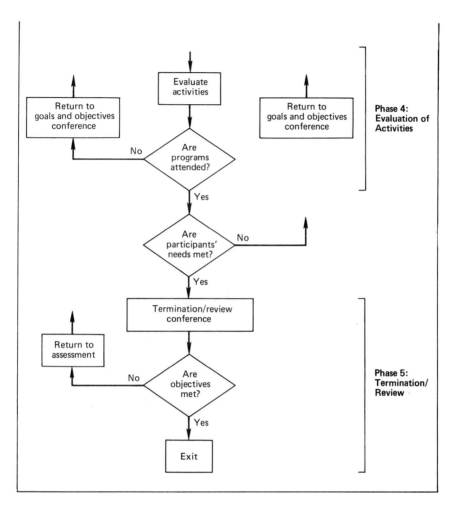

From T.M. Shea & A.M. Bauer, *Parents and Teachers of Exceptional Students: A Handbook for Involvement* (Boston: Allyn & Bacon, 1985). Used by permission.

Intake conferences are conducted to enable the parent and special educator to begin establishing a positive interpersonal relationship. Such a relationship is essential to the success of parent–special educator involvement. Also, during intake, the child's special- and regular-education programs are carefully reviewed with the parents. The child's IEP may also be reviewed at this time.

Assessment conferences focus primarily on the parents' perception of the child and his or her behavior disorder. The conference provides the special educator an opportunity to ascertain the parents' capacity to attend to the child's problem and their understanding of the child's behavior disorder as it was presented during intake. The parents assess the child and his or her behavior disorder from their perspective, and the special educator and parents assess the parents' interest in, willingness to partake in, readiness, capacity, and need for a parent-teacher involvement program. The conference is terminated only when parents and teacher agree that the tasks have been accomplished.

Although these conferences rely primarily on interview techniques for assessment, various formal and informal checklists and inventories may be used to supplement the interview. A brief review of several checklists and inventories is presented in Appendix B.

The intake and assessment phase is terminated when the parents and special educator agree they have sufficient information and understanding to enter Phase 2 of the model. If adequate information is not available to both parents and teacher or if consensus has not been reached, Phase 1 activities are continued.

Phase 2: Selection of goals and objectives.   In Phase 2, selection of goals and objectives, parents and special educator synthesize the assessment data accumulated during Phase 1. Phase 2 tasks are usually accomplished in one conference, which clarifies the unmet needs of parents and special educator with regard to the child or youth with behavior disorders.

These unmet needs are translated by the parents and special educator into program goals and objectives. Goals are global targets of the involvement program and state the desired outcomes of the yet-to-be-determined activities. Objectives are precise, specific, and limited statements of the desired results of activities and state the behavior knowledge, or skill the parent, special educator, or child will exhibit at the conclusion of an activity, the conditions under which the new behavior will be exhibited, and the criteria for acceptable performance of the new behavior.

Program objectives must be determined before the parents and special educator enter the next phase of the model. Objectives are selected independent of program availability. If a program is not available in response to a specific objective, then an appropriate activity is designed in response to that objective.

Frequently, parents and teachers select more objectives than can be attained during the time available for collaboration. Therefore, objectives are organized in order of priority. Which objectives are to be given first priority, second priority, and so on must be agreed on. It is prudent to include at least one of the parents' and one of the special educator's high-priority objectives among those selected for immediate implementation.

Phase 3: Selection and implementation of activities.   Phase 3 contains one or more activities-selection conferences and the implementation of those activities agreed upon. During the activities selection conferences, parents and special educator translate objectives into involvement activities. These desired activities are compared with those available in the school and community. If appropriate activity programs are not available, the parents and special educator plan a suitable activity or select a viable alternative from those available.

Although not limited to these, the parents and special educator may choose one or more of the activities presented in the next section of this chapter. These are organized into four groupings: written and telephone communication; conferences; groups; and home, school, and community activities. They range on a rough continuum from minimum to maximum involvement on the part of the parents and special educator. For example, telephone communications require limited involvement; while a home, school, and community activity may require extensive involvement.

The criteria applied for placement on the continuum are (a) the intensity of personal involvement required of parents and special educator for success, (b) the openness of the communications between parents and special educator, (c) the degree of personal content possible in the activity, and (d) the duration and frequency of participation. During planning and prior to implementation, parents and special educator agree on the time, place, and circumstances of conducting the activity. This phase is concluded with the implementation of the activities.

Phase 4: Evaluation of activities. The activity-evaluation phase focuses on the effectiveness and efficiency of the activities implemented. It includes both process and content evaluations. Data collected during the evaluation enable both the special educator and parents to determine if they are participating as agreed in the activity and if the necessary activities are offered.

Phase 5: Termination/review. The final phase of the parent–special educator involvement model is a termination/review conference. Generally, the involvement process is terminated only when the parent or special educator leaves the school or community or when the child or youth graduates from school or is assigned to another program or classroom. However, parent and special educator confer at least annually to review and, if necessary, to modify their involvement program. This is done in response to the ever-changing needs of the child, parents, and special educator. The child's annual Individualized Education Program conference may be an appropriate and convenient time to review the parent–special educator involvement.

The program-development form. To facilitate parent–special educator involvement, a program development form such as presented in Figure 12-2 is helpful.

FIGURE 12-2 Program Development Form

Parent's Names ———— Teacher ———— Date ————

I Assessment	II Goals and Objectives	III Activities	IV Evaluation
A. List the assessment techniques used to obtain the data synthesized in IB.	A. List the goals, by priority, derived from the assessment process and mutually agreed on by parents and teacher.	List the activities designed by parents and teacher to meet the objectives in IIB.	A. Process: List the procedures parents and teacher will use to evaluate the processes for carrying out the activities in III.
B. List the needs mutually agreed upon using the assessment techniques in 1A.	B. List the objectives derived from the goals in IIA.		B. Content: List the procedures parents and teachers will use to evaluate the content of the activities in III.

From T.M. Shea & A.M. Bauer, *Parents and Teachers of Exceptional Students: A Handbook for Involvement* (Boston: Allyn & Bacon, 1985). Used by permission.

The special educator completes the program development form as he or she progresses with the parent through the phases of the model. In Column I, Section A of the form, the special educator lists the techniques selected to assess the parents' needs. Assessment techniques may include formal and informal scales, inventories, tests, and interviews. After administering the assessment instruments, the special educator lists the needs of the parents in Column I, Section B. These needs are discussed fully with the parent.

By studying the needs in Column I, Section B and discussing them with the parents, program goals are selected. The mutually agreed-upon goals are listed by priority in Column II, Section A. The goals are translated into specific, mutually agreed-upon objectives, which are listed in Section B of Column II.

In Column III, the special educator records the activities in which the parent and special educator will engage to attain their objectives. In Column IV, the process (Section A) and content (Section B) evaluation techniques to be applied to ascertain the effectiveness of the activities presented in Column III are specified.

OBJECTIVE FOUR: *To implement several parent–special educator involvement activities.*

In this section, a broad range of parent–special educator involvement activities are presented. They are organized into four groups: written and telephone communication; individual conferences; groups; and school, home, and community activities.

The parents' and special educator's ability to implement the activities described here is dependent on the reliability of the assessment procedures used to determine the parents' needs, the time the parents and special educator have available for collaboration, the special educator's level of expertise and skills in a particular activity, and the resources available to facilitate conducting the activity.

Written and Telephone Communication

Written and telephone communications are appropriate for parents who are unable to participate in more extensive activities. They require minimal personal commitment and time on the part of both special educator and parent. Consequently, in all probability, they will have limited impact on the behaviors of the child, parents, and teacher.

Written and telephone contact are impersonal in nature; thus, the probability of establishing positive working relationships between the parents and special educator is reduced. Although of potentially limited impact, such activities can facilitate the parent-education-and-training program and should be available as a normal part of the special education program.

Report cards. The traditional report card, with its "A, B, C" grading is of limited value to the parents of children and youth with behavior disorders. This appears to be true whether the grading system is alphabetical, numerical, satisfactory-unsatisfactory, or pass-fail. Other report-card formats may be more beneficial for the parents in reviewing the specific tasks the child can or cannot complete with competency. When parents are in a position to note their child's strengths and weaknesses, they will often attempt to supplement his or her educational program at home. A portion of a report-card format that may provide more specific information to the parent of a child with behavior disorders is presented in Figure 12-3.

FIGURE 12-3 Pupil-Progress Report

Dear *Mrs. Frangini* :

This report on ___*Joseph*___'s progress will be sent to you at the end of each nine weeks of school unless it is felt that a conference may be more beneficial to discuss your child. Please feel free to discuss this report with me.

Your interest and support in your child's educational program is appreciated.

Name _____

For nine weeks ending: *March 17, 1986*

I. Individualized Educational Plan Objectives being implemented during these nine weeks

Objectives:	Comments:
A. Keeps hands to self throughout school day	A. Has not been aggressive since March 1
B. Decrease inappropriate language	B. About 3 infractions a day
C. Completes 3 tasks in one hour independently	C. Needs verbal reminder to keep working
D. Make positive comments about others during group	D. Needs models and verbal cues

II. Classroom behavior and social skills:

5 - Almost all of the time

4 - Most of the time

3 - Some of the time

2 - With teacher help and assistance
1 - Has much difficulty in this area

	In the Special Education Program		In the Regular Education Program	
	Last Report	Present	Last Report	Present
Follows classroom rules	3	4	2	3
Completes assignments	1	2	2	2
Responsibile for materials	3	3	2	3
Controls own behavior	4	4	3	4
Asks for help when needed	4	5	2	2
Cooperates when others are working	3	4	3	4
Stays in seat	3	3	3	3
Demonstrates self-control	3	4	3	4
Accepts constructive criticism	3	4	2	3
Respects property of others	2	3	2	3
Cooperates during group activities	4	5	3	3
Follows rules in lunchroom	2	4	4	4
Follows rules on bus	3	3	3	3

Special Educator comments: Joseph is working on controlling his behavior. He rarely strikes out physically but still needs help controlling his language. Mrs. Nolan

Regular Educator comments:
Joseph needs more supervision than my other students but is not a real distraction. Ms. Stuart

Parent signature and comments:
Looks good to me! Johanna Franzini

Daily reports.   The reports and grades issued periodically by schools probably influences students' performance positively. This effect, however, is probably also short-lived. More frequent feedback on students' academic and behavioral performance is likely to inspire continued positive performance—a proposition that has encouraged several investigators to explore the use of daily report cards (Dickerson, Spellman, Larsen, & Tyler, 1973; Edlund, 1969; Kroth, 1975; Kroth, Whelan, & Stables, 1970; Powell, 1980). The daily report card has several advantages. It is an efficient method of coordinating and monitoring training, and, assuming the special educator obtains the parents' commitment to it, a forum for two-way communication.

"Passport" to positive parent-teacher communications.   Methods for increasing cooperation between parents and special educators in their efforts to assist a child during the remediation process in school are frequently sought, but they are elusive. The "passport" (Runge, Walker, & Shea, 1975) is a potentially effective technique for increasing and maintaining parent–special educator cooperation.

The "passport" itself is an ordinary spiral notebook that the child carries about daily, both to and from home and to and from the classrooms in which the child is instructed. It is a medium for communication among parents, special teachers, regular teachers, teachers' aides, and others, concerning the child's remediation and behavior.

At the beginning of the school year or when enrolling in the special-education program, "passport" procedures are explained to the child, who learns that he or she will be rewarded for carrying the notebook.

The child is rewarded by means of points for appropriate efforts, accomplishments, and behavior. Points are also awarded at home for appropriate behavior and home-study activities. If the child does not carry the notebook, he or she cannot be awarded points. The accumulated points are exchanged on a periodic basis for tangible rewards.

Notes, notices, and letters.   Notes, notices, and letters can be of assistance in the special educator's efforts to notify parents of concerns such a schedule changes, field trips, attendance, and so on. Letters and notes sent to parents can include invitations to conferences and activities, letters of welcome, thank-you notes, and so on.

Caution should be exercised in sending notes to parents. All notes should be clear, concise, positive in tone, and written in the parents' primary language. A poorly composed, negative note can result in unwarranted and unnecessary punishment of a child or youth.

Notes and notices can be of value when used in conjunction with an individual parent-teacher conference or with parent-teacher group activities. Rutherford and Edgar (1979) recommend notes and letters for four purposes: to praise the student's general academic performance and behavior; to informally and positively address specific academic and behavior problems; to informally evaluate the child's performance; and to provide a structured performance evaluation as a supplement to the periodic report card.

Kaplan and Hoffman (1981) and Kaplan, Kohfeldt, and Sturla (1974) developed a variety of formats for awards, glad notes, and certificates for special educators to duplicate and send to parents, either as part of a systematic communication program or as periodic reinforcers (Figure 12-4).

Telephone contact.   Positive, periodic, and consistent telephone contact between the parents and special educator have a significant impact on the child's instructional performance and behavior. However, as in the case of notes and notices, negative and inconsistent telephone contact can have an unwarranted negative effect on the student.

Special educators must exercise great caution not to burden the already busy parents with classroom and school behavior-management problems. It is impossible in most cases for parents to control a child's school behavior from home unless severe punishments are imposed. Telephone contact is of considerable assistance to the special educator to

FIGURE 12-4   Behavior and Achievement Award

encourage parents to attend meetings, conferences, and the like. Such contacts demonstrate the special educator's personal interest in the child and parents.

Newsletters.   Newsletters can provide information on long- and short-range program plans, explain instructional methods, and report on activities and events (Granowsky et al., 1977). They are a good way to maintain regular contact with parents, especially those unable to participate in group meetings (Liddle, Rockwell, & Sacadat, 1967), and may be an integral part of a program designed to communicate both with and to parents (Fedderson, 1972). Cooke and Cooke (1974), Cory (1974), and England (1977) view the newsletter primarily as a technique for communicating information to parents. A newsletter may be weekly, biweekly, or monthly, depending on classroom needs, personnel, time, and materials. However, it should be distributed regularly. Parents usually read newsletters "on the run." Thus, they should not exceed four to six typewritten pages, should be written in common language, and be positive and personal.

Special educators can supplement their contributions to the newsletter by soliciting contributions from other staff members, parents, and children. Children's and parents' contributions increase the newsletter's readership because parents enjoy this type of personal material. Every child in a class should contribute an article or drawing to the newsletter sometime during the year. Newsletters may contain general news of the class, announcements, learning activities, recognition of volunteers, program descriptions, and question-and-answer columns.

Parents may be willing to help prepare and distribute newsletters—often writing articles, typing manuscripts, or duplicating. Newsletters can be sent home with the children, distributed at parent meetings, or mailed.

Parent–Special Educator Conferences

The parent–special educator conference is an "individualized, personalized meeting between two or three significant persons in the child's life with the purpose of accelerating his or her growth" (Kroth & Simpson, 1977, p. 2). The approach to a given conference depends on its purpose and content (Barsch, 1968). This section presents several types of conferences useful to parents and special educators of children and youth with behavior disorders: progress-report, problem-solving, behavior management training, and Individualized Education Program meetings.

Individual-parent–special educator conferences should be included in the education-and-training program of each child's parents. They are offered in addition to other involvement activities. If the parents are able to participate in their child's program at a minimal level only, they should be encouraged to attend conferences. If parent conferences are properly prepared and conducted, they can have a significant impact on both the special educator's and the parents' understanding of the child and program.

Progress-report conferences. The progress-report conference serves two important purposes. First, it is an opportunity for the parents to systematically give to and receive from the special educator information about the child relative to school and home activities, behavior, and achievements. Second, it is an opportunity for the special educator to systematically evaluate the child's educational program and to give to and receive from the parents information relative to their child's home and school activities, behaviors, and achievements. It is an opportunity for the special educator, on the basis of his or her evaluations and information received from the parents, to modify the child's educational program as necessary.

The individual-parent–special educator conference is conducted at a mutually agreed-on time at a mutually covenient location. The conference is child- and program-centered. It is a verbal report card. As such, it is an occasion to review and explain for the parents their child's progress in various curricular, cocurricular, and behavioral areas.

The conference is, in many cases, a "show and tell" session. The special educator can show the parents their child's work and the instructional materials used in the program and demonstrate various items of instructional equipment. In many cases, the parents will respond positively to the teacher's invitations to "try out" the materials and equipment.

A conference report is written in advance of the session. The report is prepared using an outline similar to that in Figure 12-5. The process of preparing the report enables the special educator to focus attention on the child's program and progress. Progress-report conferences are special educator-controlled. During the session, the special educator reviews the report and responds to the parents' questions. The report may include questions the special educator wishes to discuss with the parents.

Problem-solving conferences. Conferences to plan and carry out solutions to academic and behavior problems, problem-solving conferences, are frequently useful to both parents and special educators. According to Kroth (1972a, 1975), the successful problem-solving conference considers in detail the environment in which the problem occurs, the nature of the problem, conference preplanning, conference timing, required data and information, needs of parents and special educators for reinforcement, and provisions for training parents to solve the problems. Parents and special educators must recognize that the child may have a problem in one environment but not in another. They must determine if the problem is primarily exhibited at home, in school, in the community, or in several contexts.

FIGURE 12-5   Outline for Preconference Report

A. Social behavior (in the classroom, during recess, on field trips, on the bus)

1. Self-control (in large and small groups, during activities)
2. Affective behavior (enthusiasm, leadership, followership, obedience, responsibility, reactions to rewards and discipline)
3. Group participation (in the classroom, during recess, on field trips, during activities)
4. Social amenities (manners, courtesies, respect for others and their property)

B. Communications

1. Modes of communication (speaking, conversing, eye contact, reading, writing, spelling, music, gestures)
2. Listening (responsiveness, direction following, stories, music)
3. Language activities (awareness, receptive language, expressive language, language development, verbal communication of experiences)
4. Language skills (speech, spontaneous language, words, sentences)

C. Basic knowledge

1. Information (name, age, address, siblings, parents, friends, places, things, colors, shapes, letters, numbers)
2. Reading (or readiness)
3. Spelling
4. Arithmetic
5. Social studies (current events)
6. Art (second and third dimensional)
7. Music
8. Sensory-motor skills (recreation, physical education)
9. Perception (auditory, visual, tactile)

D. Self-care, practical and work skills

1. Work tools (paste, paper, pencil, blocks, puzzles, knife, spoon, fork, scissors, saw, hammer, cutting torch, level)
2. School chores and duties (hanging up clothes, serving table, setting table, cleaning, washing)
3. Bathroom and grooming (toilet training, cleaning hands and face)
4. Body use (awareness, climbing, walking, running, moving self and objects)

Parents and special educators can structure their cooperation during a problem-solving conference by setting goals, selecting potential interventions, carrying out those interventions, and providing feedback.

Behavior management training conferences. Training conferences teach parents how to design, carry out, and evaluate home and home-school behavior management interventions. The literature amply documents that training in the principles and practices of behavior management helps parents change their children's behavior (Berkowitz & Graziano, 1972; Schopler & Reichler, 1971).

Preferably, both parents attend training conferences to ensure that they consistently use the same management interventions at home. With the special educator using the same techniques at school, the child has the security of consistent expectations through the day.

Following a structured conference procedure in the early stages of training is helpful to both parents and special educator. Several structured training procedures are available in the literature. One such procedure, using the psycho-situational assessment interview as a medium of training, is discussed next (Walker & Shea, 1984).

The psycho-situational assessment interview (Bersoff & Grieger, 1971) is a behavioral intervention technique that can be applied productively with parents. It can serve as a useful aid in determining the parents' assessment of the child's behavior and in training. The purpose of the strategy is to analyze the inappropriate behavior manifested by the individual and to uncover the antecedents and consequences that elicit, reinforce, and sustain it. This information contributes to decisions concerning interventions to modify the behavior.

The four major tasks to be accomplished during the interview are (1) defining the behavior, (2) explicating specific situations in which the behavior occurs (3) uncovering the contingencies that seemingly sustain the behavior, and (4) detecting any irrational ideas that make it difficult for the parents to objectively understand, accept, and modify the behavior.

The psycho-situational interview may be a single session or a series of sessions. If the interviewer is only concerned with obtaining data in an effort to design an intervention that excludes parent participation, one session may be sufficient. However, the strategy frequently can be applied to an ongoing intervention program that includes both the special educator and parents.

The special educator may suggest that the parents keep a log of the child's behavior (an example of a simple log is presented in Figure 12-6.) Explain fully how the log should be used. The special educator should complete the top portion of the form, describing the target behavior. The parents write the day or date of the behavior's first occurrence each day in

FIGURE 12-6 Behavior Log Form

Target behavior _____

Observer's name _____ Child observed _____

Day or Date	Time		Antecedents	Consequences	Applied interventions	Comments
	Begins	Ends				

From T. M. Shea & A. M. Bauer, *Parents and Teachers of Exceptional Students: A Handbook for Involvement* (Boston: Allyn & Bacon, 1985). Used by permission.

the far left column. They then note the time the behavior begins and ends for each occurrence that day. If the behavior ends quickly, they note the time only in the "Begins" column. Each time the behavior occurs, parents note its antecedents and consequences in the appropriate column. In the "Applied interventions" column, they note what they or someone else did to change the child's behavior. Finally, in the "Comments" column, parents make any·additional observations about the behavioral incident.

Individualized Education Program meeting. The Individualized Education Program mandated by Public Law 94-142 is central to providing effective education and related services to children and youth with behavior disorders. The law reaffirmed the legitimate and crucial role of parents in the education of their children, requiring that parents be active participants in the development, approval, and evaluation of their children's Individualized Education Program. Specifically, parents participate with professionals in the assessment, planning, approval, placement, and evaluation processes. Parents may also participate actively in implementing their children's education and related service program.

The IEP itself and the IEP meeting are both unfamiliar to many parents. Thus, to avoid the inefficient use of time at an IEP meeting, the special educator should prepare the parents to participate productively and positively. Several authors have urged that parents receive at least the following information prior to the meeting (Bauer, 1981; Lusthaus & Lusthaus, 1979; Winslow, 1977):

> adequate notice of the meeting
>
> an opportunity prior to the meeting to review the child's educational records with a professional familiar with it
>
> an agenda stating the IEP meeting's objectives, discussion topics, and any questions to be addressed to the parents
>
> a list of the people to attend the meeting and descriptions of their functions and positions
>
> information on obtaining an independent or supplemental assessment of their child, if they so desire
>
> information on who may accompany the parents to the meeting (child, attorney, interpreter)
>
> a list of the information or materials they may wish to bring (records, test results, reports, observational data, and so on)

Before the meeting, parents should talk to their child about school, teachers, and peers. They may wish to invite the child to attend the meeting (Gillespie & Turnbull, 1983). Parents who have never attended an IEP meeting may benefit from talking with more experienced parents. They may wish to visit their child's placement and talk with the special educator. Parents should prepare a list of questions they wish answered at the meeting and clarify their short-term and long-term expectations for their child.

During the meeting, parents should feel free to make comments, ask questions, and offer recommendations. Thus, professionals in attendance should be approachable, listen to parents' ideas, and communicate a sense of unity. Parents must be sure they have a complete understanding of the child's program, as presented during the meeting.

At the end of the meeting, parents should either receive or arrange to receive a copy of their child's IEP. Parents' responsibilities do not end with the meeting, for they should monitor implementation of the child's IEP as well, continuing to meet and otherwise communicate with those persons directly responsible for service to the child.

Groups

Special educators frequently use groups to foster communication with parents. Carefully designed group activities can have value for the participants, with ultimate benefit to the child or youth with behavior disorders. When arranging groups, the special educator should have a clear idea of their purpose and plan accordingly. This section discusses the general issues of planning and conducting large and small parent–special educator involvement groups.

Group activities demand more planning and preparation and often greater personal involvement by parents and special educators than do written and telephone communications and parent–special educator conferences. Personal involvement varies with group purpose; that is, a social-emotional support group requires greater commitment than a large group designed to transmit information.

Groups are organized for three basic purposes: to transmit information; to teach and learn instructional, behavior-management, or interpersonal communication skills; and to provide social-emotional support.

Both large and small groups are effective for transmitting information. However, a small group is preferable for exchanging personal or highly specific information. Small groups are best for social-emotional support. Either-size group can be used effectively for training and instruction with a limited instructor-to-parent ratio.

Group processes and procedures vary with the purpose of the group. Structured processes are appropriate for instruction and information exchange. Less structure is more appropriate in support groups. Participants in large groups are usually passive recipients. Small-group participants, however, can actively engage in discussion, problem solving, and the exploration of feelings. Frequently, it is necessary for a few participants to plan, organize, and conduct activities for the entire membership of a large group. On the other hand, small groups encourage shared control.

Large group planning.   Careful, systematic planning is crucial to successful large group activities (Croft, 1979). Kroth (1975) suggested organizing a parents' advisory committee to work with the special educator in planning and publicizing group activities. This small, representative committee plans and conducts three or four meetings annually. Its objectives are:

> To identify potential members and assess their needs and interests
> To establish general and specific meeting objectives
> To design or select methods of attaining the group's objectives
> To determine criteria and measurements to evaluate meetings' effectiveness.

Potential members' needs and interests can be determined by a survey questionnaire, an orientation meeting, or in preliminary small group sessions of representatives of potential members. Objectives of the meetings should be clearly stated in terms of what the participants will know or be able to do at the end of the activity. Activities are the "highways and signposts" members use to reach the objectives. Activities may include lectures, discussions, panels, social events, visits, film viewings, reading assignments, workshops, work projects, and so on. At the conclusion of the meetings, tests, checklists, rating scales, and other techniques are applied to evaluate the programs.

Conducting large group meetings. Planning and preparation are of tle value if the meeting is at an inconvenient time, poorly publicized, inaccessible, disorganized, or inhospitable. Several authors have suggested guidelines for conducting a large-group meeting (Bailard & Strang, 1964; Karnes & Zehrbach, 1972, Kroth, 1975). Their suggestions are summarized here:

> Participants should receive proper notification of the meeting via bulletin, newsletter, written invitation, or personal telephone communication.
> Meetings should begin and end on time.
> Meeting sites should be appropriate for the group's purpose and size.
> Necessary transportation and child-care services should be provided.
> All communication during the meeting must emphasize that parents and special educators are equals.
> Meeting content should be appropriate and understandable.
> An informal, friendly atmosphere should be established.
> Time should be available for questions, comments, and discussion.
> The meeting should be evaluated, using a form similar to that in Figure 12-7.

Small group planning. Small group programs can be effective for a variety of informational, instructional, and social-emotional purposes. Once it has been established that small group activities may be desirable, planners must consider many of the same factors as for a large group: goals and objectives, physical setting, meeting time, length and frequency, group

FIGURE 12-7   Meeting-Evaluation Form

Meeting Topic ————————————————— Date —————

Check the response that best reflects your feelings about
this meeting.

The topic of this meeting was

———— very important to me

———— somewhat important to me

———— unimportant to me

The information was

———— very useful to me

———— useful to me

———— not useful to me

The presenter was

———— very good

———— good

———— fair

———— poor

The materials handed out or used were

———— very good

———— good

———— fair

———— poor

Would you like more information on this topic?   Yes   No

Comments ———————————————————————————

Thank you for letting us know how you feel.

Your advisory committee

size, program, attendance, materials and equipment, refreshments,
leader's qualifications, transportation, and child-care services (Dinkmeyer
& McKay, 1976).

Facilities should be appropriate for the group size, private, and free
of physical barriers, which may inhibit the easy flow of communication.
Generally, evenings are the best meeting time. However, parents not
employed outside the home may prefer to meet during the day. Meetings
should be no more than two hours in length nor conducted more frequently than once each week or less frequently than once each month.

The size of the group should be determined in advance. It should not
exceed a ratio of twelve parents to one leader if this will inhibit communication. The members of the group should have similar interests and con-

cerns. If must be determined if attendance will be mandatory or permissive. Attendance rules are usually determined by the purpose of the group and the nature of the program, such as whether the material presented is cumulative in nature.

Planning lessons or the program sequence is an important part in preparing for training, instructional, and information groups. The leader should distribute outlines, agendas, materials, and texts to the members to alert them to the content and sequence of the program.

Conducting a small group meeting. Karnes and Zehrbach (1972) suggest the following guidelines for conducting small-group meetings:

> The content should be a direct response to the concerns expressed by the members. It should be challenging, yet easily understood.
>
> Members should share responsibilities for planning and conducting meetings.
>
> Members should prepare for the meetings by reading articles, parts of books, reviewing tapes, films, and video tapes, and digesting information in other ways.
>
> Meetings should be responsive to the members' individual social, emotional, and intellectual needs.
>
> The atmosphere should further meeting goals, and be relaxed and informal
>
> Teachers should participate and facilitate, but not dominate, the meeting.
>
> Members should be supportive of new members and reluctant participants.

Small group leaders have many responsibilities before, during, and after the meeting. These include preparing themselves through study, preparing the setting and necessary materials, establishing the session tone, facilitating activities, resolving problems, and evaluating the meetings.

Small group leaders can select from a range of directive and nondirective leadership techniques (Kroth, 1975). Directive techniques, which assume that parents need help to make effective decisions about their children, are generally most appropriate for information and training meetings. Nondirective techniques are more appropriate for small groups designed to provide social-emotional support. The nondirective leader is primarily responsible for setting an atmosphere conducive to discussion. Nondirective techniques assume parents are capable of free choice about themselves and the child or youth with behavior disorders and will make effective decisions if given the opportunity.

Selected Meeting Models

Special educators without skills in planning, conducting, and evaluating large and small groups can select specific group models to fulfill their purposes. This section presents models for informative group meetings and for communication, problem-solving, discussion, and training groups.

No single model will respond to all parents' needs. Consequently, special educators must use professional judgment in matching group processes to parents' needs, strengths, personal characteristics, and cultures.

Informational meetings.   Informational meetings are effective when special educators wish to inform parents collectively about some aspect of their children's special education program (Hymes, 1974; Kelly, 1974). Kelly suggested that academic programs, special remedial and experimental programs, contemporary school-community concerns (sex education, drugs, alcohol abuse), and behavior management are all appropriate themes for such meetings. Hymes included program objectives, instructional methods and materials, and facilities and equipment in this list. Kroth (1972a, 1975) added classroom activities and their rationale, class and school schedules, the testing program, specialized training, and community services.

Bailard and Strang (1964) suggested that teachers hold a meeting to review the role and functions of the school staff, including principal, regular education teacher, special education teacher, program supervisor, counselor, psychologist, social worker, and others. In some cases, special educators may want to call a series of informational meetings devoted to various aspects of a single theme. If the meeting theme is not in the special educator's areas of expertise, a community or school professional with the needed knowledge and experience should be available to contribute to the meeting.

The open house is an annual event in most special education programs. Its goals are to describe for parents the objectives of the special-education programs and related services and to familiarize them with the accompanying instructional methods and materials (Jacobson, 1974). Generally held in the fall, the open house is an excellent opportunity to introduce parents to the parent-teacher involvement program. It is helpful if other professionals and paraprofessionals associated with the program attend the open house to describe their roles in the program

The open house is an opportunity to display students' academic work, artwork, texts, workbooks, and other instructional materials. The special-education teacher may wish to describe the classroom program briefly, including subject matter, psychomotor and physical education activities, and affective-education programs. Parents will probably be interested in the behavior-management techniques applied in the program as well. Parents' questions and comments should be invited.

"Worry Workshops for Parents" (Downing, 1974) require greater personal commitment than do open houses. Designed to both educate and counsel parents, worry workshops emphasize interpersonal interactions, self-exploration, and individual counseling. They link parents to school counseling programs, offering an eclectic mixture of parent-education mini-courses and individual and family counseling services.

Workshop planning begins with an assessment of community and school needs and resources. Mental health clinics, drug-abuse centers, social welfare agencies, vocational-rehabilitation offices, and public health departments often act as instructional, counseling, therapy, and referral resources. In addition, these agencies help publicize the workshops.

As part of the worry workshop, counseling service is available during school hours, afternoons, and two evenings a week. Individual counseling sessions are essential to the program as a means of serving parents uncomfortable in a group setting or those wishing to discuss personal and highly specific concerns. In general, counseling services focus on the child's learning and the parents' contributions to the child's learning.

Parent-education offerings emphasize interpersonal relations that influence a child's learning. The mini-courses run for three or four weeks, with groups meeting once a week for two or three hours. A counselor or school psychologist leads the groups, with other professionals contributing as resource people.

Problem-solving groups.   Rutherford and Edgar (1979) developed a problem-solving process model that provides logical and sequential procedures generally applicable to most problems, conceptual frameworks, and intervention strategies. A four-step process provides a structure for facilitating group activities: defining the problem, identifying probable solutions, implementing a solution, and evaluating the results.

In the first step, the group describes the problem and specifies its parameters, determining the people, times, and settings related to the problem and reaching consensus on the desired outcome of the problem-solving process. At this stage, the group considers who owns the problem: the child, the parent, the teachers, or a combination of these people.

The second step, identifying probable solutions, calls for the group to prepare a plan for solving the problem. Group members consider the who, what, when, how, and how many of the proposed solution, paying special attention to the parents' and special educator's roles.

The third step is to carry out the proposed solution as planned. During this stage, the parents and special educator, as well as the child, need reinforcement for their efforts and successes. Changing a child's behavior may require that the parents and teachers change their personal behavior. Frequently, a positive change in the child's behavior is sufficiently rewarding to sustain their efforts. However, when change is slow, the parents and special educator become frustrated and discouraged and may discontinue their efforts. To avoid this consequence, an external reinforcement program may be necessary, whereby parents and teacher reinforce one another through periodic conferences, notes, or telephone calls.

The final step in the problem-solving process, evaluation, is a continuous process, which takes place throughout the implementation of the solution. The group assesses the impact of the intervention on the problem, and the efficiency and consistency of parents' and special educator's efforts. Collecting and graphing observational data on the frequency, percent, or duration of the behavior are helpful in evaluating the solution's effectiveness. Observations can ascertain the efficiency and consistency of interventions. The parents and teacher may want to observe one another's efforts and discuss their observations.

Discussion groups.   In 1978, Shea described a model for parent–special educator discussion groups. These groups have as their objectives to communicate practical information to parents, help parents solve problems related to their child, and provide a setting for support and understanding. The groups are parent-centered and focus on an agreed-upon informational topic and on parents' immediate practical concerns and problems.

The first part of each session is devoted to a ten-minute presentation, by the special educator or a parent, of a topic announced at the previous session. Thus, members have had an opportunity to read or simply think about the subject before the meeting. After the presentation, group members discuss the topic and relate it to their concerns and circumstances. The group can select discussion topics in several ways. It can adopt a topic from a text on parenting, child development, behavior management, or exceptionality. Or the special educator can present the members with a list of ten to fifteen topics, which they rank in order of preference.

In the second part of the meeting, the parents and teacher discuss a variety of situations and problems of current interest to parents, such as laws governing services for children and youth with behavior disorders, physicians, treatments and medication, the qualities needed to be an effective parent, sex education, and punishment.

Training for the IEP process.   The vast majority of parents of exceptional children would profit greatly from training in the IEP process. Katz et al. (1980) designed an adult-education course to help parents improve their effectiveness in the IEP meeting. The course includes three two-hour training modules or lessons. Modules include "Parents' Role and Rights Under Public Law 94-142," the parents' role in evaluating and observing their exceptional children, and preparing for the IEP meeting itself.

School, Home, and Community Activities

Today, many parents are volunteering their services in classrooms and schools. Others, unable to go to school, exhibit interest in their children's education by contributing time and effort to committee work and home-teaching programs. This section discusses a variety of activities to involve parents and help them be effective in classroom, school, home, and community services for children and youth with behavior disorders. Among the roles of parents discussed are as paraprofessionals, aides, instructors, volunteers, and home teachers.

Parents as paraprofessionals. Parents can improve their behavior-management and instructional skills in a variety of classroom and school functions. While improving their personal competencies, parents can also be instrumental in improving classroom and school services for children and youth with behavior disorders.

In addition to serving as aides in the classroom, parents of exceptional children can go on field trips, to parties and special events and work as library, clerical, lunchroom or cafeteria, and playground and physical-education aides. They can help various specialized personnel also, such as music and art teachers, physical and occupational therapists, psychologists and counselors, social workers, and others.

Parents as instructors. With minimal guidance, parents can become effective instructors. They can prepare and conduct brief lessons or more extended mini-courses related to their occupations, hobbies, and other interests. Hicks (1977), for example, invited parents to teach half-hour lessons, including discussions of occupations, avocations, travel, and special interests. On occasion, the children visited the parent's home or workplace a part of the lesson.

Parents as volunteers. Parent volunteers can contribute significantly to the quality of the services offered to exceptional children. Along with teachers and paraprofessionals, they can become an integral part of the child's educational team. The special education parent volunteer works under the direct supervision of a professional teacher, therapist, administrator, or other qualified staff person, and occasionally under a teacher's assistant. Volunteers generally work on task-specific activities. For example, they may check a child's home or class assignments, assist during field trips and special events, serve as a companion or guide for a child, reinforce acceptable behavior and work, or prepare instructional materials and equipment (Greer, 1978).

Volunteers should participate in a brief preservice training program, as well as in on-the-job training. Preservice training workshops introduce volunteers to special education, school, and classroom processes and procedures, and spell out their roles and functions. The training emphasizes the importance of confidentiality and attendance and offers an opportunity to discuss the program with experienced volunteers and to visit the classroom to observe and discuss the program with the teacher. On-the-job training is a continuous process, in which volunteers learn the specific activities for which they will be responsible.

The prudent special educator matches tasks with the volunteers' abilities, interests, and special skills. A questionnaire completed by potential volunteers during recruitment or preservice training can help teachers assign tasks and develop schedules. Individual interviews can supplement questionnaire data.

Figure 12-8 lists a broad range of activities in which parent volunteers may participate.

FIGURE 12-8   Parent-Volunteer Activities

Room Parents Can:

Recruit and schedule volunteers
Help in preservice and inservice training
Oversee classroom committees
Coordinate parties, field trips, special events, student performances, and parent meetings

During School Hours, Parent Volunteers Can:

Design and construct bulletin boards
Research, organize, and supervise field trips
Supervise cafeteria, playground, halls
Locate resources needed by the professional staff
Assist in the library, audiovisual center, equipment room, school office
Serve as interpreter for non-English-speaking parents
Coordinate all-school special events

After School Hours, Parent Volunteers Can:

Create and construct learning materials
Conduct and supervise tutoring
Care for equipment, materials, physical facilities
Meet with other parents
Serve on school committees

In the Home and Community, Parent Volunteers Can:

Coordinate and supervise special events
Locate community resources useful to the school
Organize and conduct fund-raising activities
Serve as members and officers in community organizations
Lobby at the local, regional, state, and federal level for schools and children

(From Shea & Bauer, 1985.)

Parents on committees.   Parent participation as chairpersons or members of classroom and school committees can contribute significantly to the child's education. Through committee work, parents not only contribute to the classroom and school but also receive indirect training in serving exceptional children's needs. They develop appreciation for staffing concerns, curriculum development, fiscal exigencies, materials, and equipment needs, and other demands of instructional programming.

An advisory committee, for example, can serve as a liaison between school, home, and community, functioning as a permanent parent-to-parent communications committee to announce meetings, special events, legislative happenings, personnel changes, and so on. The school or classroom advisory committee can assume responsibility, in cooperation with the professional staff, for organizing and directing several ad hoc or temporary committees.

Parents as home-based teachers.   In recent years, special educators have increasingly advocated home programs for exceptional children. Programs to train parents as home-based teachers vary greatly in structure, content, and skill requirements. Programs may simply teach parents how to monitor their children's work on teacher-assigned projects, or they may train parents to teach highly specific readiness skills and academic knowledge to supplement or reinforce school instruction. The program content may emphasize parent-child interpersonal interactions or may focus on instruction in specific skills.

Parents may become involved in supervising home-study projects for the children. However, the amount of homework assigned each day should be limited. Parents can establish a study time and area that is convenient for both parent and child. Parents may reinforce children's efforts and accuracy.

Vantour and Stewart-Kurker (1980) developed a lending library to motivate parents and children in home-study programs. They rewrote the instructions in commercially available instructional materials to make them easy to use for parents and children at home. Teachers wrote prescriptions to specify the book, cards, games, and other materials the child should take home from the library. The system allowed teachers to coordinate library materials with classroom lessons.

The parent-resource center.   Establishing a parent-resource center is an effective way to meet the informational and social-emotional needs of the parents of exceptional children (Edmister, 1977; Karnes & Franke, 1978). The center's staff should select materials and equipment carefully to respond to the parent users' needs. Borrowers can use materials at the center or borrow them for the home or classroom. The center can also provide important services to parents, exceptional children, and teachers, serving as a facility for individual study, small-group meetings, conferences, informal discussions, and social activities.

OBJECTIVE FIVE: *To discuss several reasons some parents and special educators are unable to become involved in cooperative activities.*

Although many parents recognize a need for and welcome professional support in efforts to help their children, some parents and special educators do not cooperate in the education of the children and youth with behavior disorders for whom they are responsible. Consequently, both lose their most valuable ally in the effort to help the child.

Morrison (1978) suggested two basic reasons for the lack of effective cooperation between parents and teachers. First, no real effort is made in most schools to implement effective parent-involvement programs. Second, there is a lack of enthusiasm by teachers and other educators to make parent programs work, perhaps because of the fear of "outside influences" in the classroom.

Several situational factors may influence parents' lack of involvement (MacMillan & Turnbull, 1983). The more severe the child's disability, the greater the demands on the parents. For some parents, the school day is their only respite; thus, they seek to remain uninvolved. Family factors—such as whether it is a one-parent family, the availability of family support, whether both parents work, and the availability of child care—and other factors make it impossible for some parents to become involved.

Lee (1980) listed several failings of parent programs, which many parents view as insurmountable barriers to participation:

> Inconvenient meeting times and locations
>
> Inadequate parental input in program planning
>
> Unwarranted assumptions about knowledge and skills the parents need to participate productively in activities
>
> Inadequate feedback on parents' efforts and a lack of follow-up to meetings or workshops
>
> Parents' feelings of inadequacy as a consequence of professionals' domination
>
> Lack of skill, time, and materials for parents to implement the suggestions of professionals
>
> Feelings of competition between parent and special educator for child's attention and affection
>
> Parents' lack of enthusiasm as a consequence of previous failures in collaboration
>
> Lack of responsiveness to parents' "real" needs on the part of special educators and programs

Special educators frequently live, work, and recreate in a subculture different from the parents whose children they serve. As professionals who must be able to work with parents from many subcultures, special educators must make every effort to understand each parent and his or her life circumstances.

According to Chinn (1979), the parents of culturally diverse children have several reasons for choosing noninvolvement. They may feel the school has reneged on its commitment to help them succeed. Minority parents' involvement with schools and special education may have been unpleasant (Marion, 1981). Those minority parents who do participate in involvement activities may do so with suspicion. They may see special education as a "dumping ground" for children and youth unable to learn and for "troublemakers." They may believe that special educators view minority children as inferior.

Special educators, too, have reasons for not encouraging parent involvement. They may feel that parents don't care, don't accept their child's problem, or don't have the training to be involved. In addition, special educators may oversimplify the issue by equating parental involvement in educational programs with their involvement with the exceptional child (MacMillan & Turnbull, 1983). Parents' decisions not to be involved in their child's educational program does not mean they are not involved with the child at home. These authors assert that parents have the right to choose not to be involved in educational programs when they determine that noninvolvement is beneficial to them, the child, or the family. Parents forced into involvement against their better judgment may become frustrated, be absent from work or from their families for extended times, have decreased free time, or become an inordinate drain on the school staff. Decisions about the degree of involvement should grow out of individual preferences rather than generalized expectations.

SUMMARY

In this chapter, a model for involving parents in the education of their child with behavior disorders was presented. A discussion of the need for and desirability of parental involvement was followed by the presentation of the ecological perspective on parent involvement.

The chapter provided a variety of activities that the special educator may select cooperatively with parents to meet the needs of their students. In conclusion, several reasons for noninvolvement in cooperative activities were presented.

REVIEW QUESTIONS

1. Why is the training and education of parents of children and youth with behavior disorders not only desirable but necessary?
2. What is the parent–special educator involvement model? What are its purposes? Its limitations?

3. Analyze and discuss the model presented in Figure 12-1. What are the strengths and weaknesses of the model? How could it be improved?

4. Why is a positive, productive interpersonal relationship between teacher and parent(s) critical to the success of parental involvement?

5. What are some of the variables in the ecological subsystems that should be taken into account when planning parental involvement? Why?

6. What are some of the reasons parents state for not participating in parent education? How can these be overcome?

7. What is the psycho-situational interview technique? For what purposes can it be applied?

APPLICATION ACTIVITY

Select one of the class lists provided in Appendix B (or a class with which you are familiar). For the parents of each of the students on the list, prepare the following materials as part of a plan for initiating a parent–special educator involvement program:

A welcome letter
An invitation to parent-involvement intake and assessment conferences
An agenda for a parent-involvement intake conference
A list of possible topics for informational meetings
An evaluation form for informational meetings.

13

Secondary School Students with Behavior Disorders

Until recently, programs for secondary school students with behavior disorders were generally neglected (Heller, 1981). In a survey of the fifty states, the District of Columbia, Puerto Rico, and American Samoa, Hirshoren and Heller (1979) found considerable variation in the kinds of behavior problems exhibited by students served in secondary school programs. They also found three major service patterns at the secondary-school level: special classes, resource rooms, and vocational programs. Hirshoren and Heller contend that there is a broadening effort to elaborate and extend these for secondary school students with behavior disorders.

In this chapter, the unique problems of the adolescent with behavior disorders are described. Programming goals and current program options available for this group of students are reviewed. In addition, the competencies needed by students for successful integration into the community upon leaving school are discussed.

OBJECTIVES

After completing this chapter, you will be able to—

1. Describe several problems unique to adolescents with behavior disorders;
2. Describe the goals of programming for secondary school students with behavior disorders;

3. Describe the program options currently available to secondary school students with behavior disorders;

4. Describe several model programs for secondary school students with behavior disorders;

5. Describe the ecological-assessment process applicable in secondary-school programs for students with behavior disorders;

6. Discriminate between the career and vocational competencies needed by secondary students.

A CASE FOR CONSIDERATION

"I just don't understand why you're not trying to teach him to read," said Mr. Martinez. "You learn to read in school. You don't learn how to push a broom."

The Individualized Education Program team was discussing goals and objectives for seventeen-year-old Javier. It was true that Javier was reading at the 2.5 grade level. His survival reading skills were more efficient, but overall, reading remained a major difficulty for him.

"I'm sorry you feel that way, Mr. Martinez," replied Ms. Stuart, the resource room teacher. "We strongly feel that the little time Javier has left in school needs to be used as effectively as possible. To assure his success and to prepare him to enter the adult community, we feel we should provide Javier with vocational training rather than continuing to work only on reading and other academic skills."

"Javier will still be in a reading class," interjected Mr. Nolan, the vocational education instructor. "He has to be able to read job sheets, directions for doing various maintenance tasks, and work schedules. We will work on reading job applications and advertisements. However, we'll be working on what he needs to read instead of general reading."

Ms. Stuart looked toward the end of the table, where Javier was sitting, gently tapping his fingers on the table. "Javier," she said, "I'm sorry we seem to be excluding you from the discussion. We've been talking as if you were not here! How do you feel about your school program?"

"I want to get out of here and get a job," said Javier. "I can't read. I never could. I don't like to, and I don't think I'll ever read any more than I have to." He looked toward his father, and said, "Pop, if I haven't learned to read yet, what makes you think I ever will? What I need to know is how to get and keep a job."

Discussions of educational goals and objectives for adolescents with behavior disorders frequently take this direction. After several years of remediation, a shift occurs during the secondary-school years to help the student learn survival and vocational skills. Parents, who are more comfortable with the traditional role of the school, frequently feel that special educators are not meeting their obligations as teachers if they do not teach the basic academic skills. This chapter focuses on the problems of adolescents with behavior disorders, what to teach them, and what programs should be available to them.

OBJECTIVE ONE: *To describe several problems unique to adolescents with behavior disorders.*

Adolescence is a difficult period for all young persons. For the 0.005 percent to 6.5 percent (Hirshoren & Heller, 1979) of the secondary school population with behavior disorders, adolescence is particularly difficult. Secondary school students with behavior disorders are not readily accepted by their peers. They lack social experience and possess a limited repertoire of social skills. Their decision-making skills are inadequate, and they often make the same "mistakes" repeatedly (Silverman, Zigmond, & Sansone, 1981).

The prevalence of behavior disorders among secondary school students is estimated to be between 2 and 12 percent (Grosenick & Huntze, 1980). However, only 12 percent of the states reported serving more than 1 percent of the secondary school population in programs for such students.

This lack of programming at the secondary school level is a result of several factors. First, the school organization at the secondary level is departmentalized, and students who do not fit the existing structure are often either poorly served or excluded from school. In addition, special education is an unwelcome variant in many secondary schools (Heller, 1981). The organization and requirements of the secondary school—moving from class to class, adjusting to the behaviors of several teachers, navigating large physical plants, and so on—tend to exacerbate the problems of students with behavior disorders (Silverman, Zigmond, & Sansone, 1981).

The limited availability of secondary school programs is also a result of a lack of college and university training programs for teachers of adolescents with behavior disorders. Although teachers of students with behavior disorders are frequently certified to instruct students from kindergarten to twelfth grade, little real training is provided specifically for teaching adolescents. As a result, teachers are certified but not trained to work in the secondary school (Heller, 1981; Cegelka & Phillips, 1978). Adolescents with behavior disorders are frequently placed in job-training programs without regard for the appropriateness of these programs to meet their unique needs and the competency of the teachers to work effectively with them (Heller, 1981).

Most special education programs are designed to provide remediation to young children (Cegelka & Phillips, 1978). Older students are often unable to profit from such programs (Heller, 1981), and neither vocational education nor special education personnel appear to be motivated to provide needed services to adolescents with behavior disorders (Cegelka & Phillips, 1978).

According to Epstein, Cullinan, and Rosemier (1983), secondary school students identified as behavior disordered are readily differentiated by regular education teachers on the Behavior Problem Checklist from their nonidentified peers. Though no significant differences were found for sex, the adolescents with behavior disorders demonstrated more inappropriate behaviors than their nonidentified peers. Significantly greater problems are noted in conduct disorders and personality problems as measured by the Behavior Problem Checklist.

Rezmierski and Rezmierski (1979) describe four negative conditions inherent in secondary school programs for students with behavior disorders. First, there is a "slippage of hope," a diminishing belief that these students will succeed in school and gain the skills needed to be successful adults. The second negative condition is a "stacking of experiences"; that is, by the time the student reaches secondary school, the number and variety of educational, social, physical, and emotional experiences are so great that it is extremely difficult to understand behavior patterns. Third, there is the shifting of power in adolescent programs, so that as students become older, they are more mobile and assertive, and consequently more difficult to manage. They are physically larger and more threatening. Thus, previously successful control techniques become inappropriate and in some cases dangerous. Finally, Rezmierski and Rezmierski suggest that special educators serving secondary school students have difficulty maintaining social-emotional distance from their students' problems and behaviors. The extreme behavior problems of these students make it difficult for the teachers to remain emotionally neutral. This is compounded by the closeness in age of students and educators.

Some adolescents with behavior disorders are successful after graduation from secondary school. Leone (1984) studied the status of eighteen adolescents two to four years after they had successfully completed a residential day-treatment program. He found that in spite of substantial deficits in academics, only four of the eighteen students were unemployed or not in a job-training program. Only one student had returned to the program for additional treatment. Leone suggests that the program provided these students with coping strategies that enabled them to deal with the interpersonal difficulties that had caused their earlier problems. He did, however, suggest that alternative explanations of the success of these students should be seriously considered; that is, they might simply have matured and abandoned certain inappropriate behaviors. Of course, a third alternative is that the students' behavior problems were initially transitory in nature or misdiagnosed.

Adolescents with behavior disorders may demonstrate severe problem patterns that must be responded to immediately if irrevocable harm to the student and others is to be avoided. Among these problem patterns are suicide, dropping out of school, conflicts with the justice system, and mental illness.

Suicide. Suicide is the third leading cause of death among individuals between the ages of fifteen and twenty-four years (Bryan & Herjanic, 1980). If they are to help the severely depressed or potentially suicidal adolescent, special educators must be alert to the following behavior (Bryan & Herjanic, 1980):

1. Expressions of low self-esteem and hopelessness. Student appears sad, tearful, and withdrawn.
2. Unusual shifts in behavior; that is, sudden hostility and destructiveness, irritability, and loss of interest in activities.
3. Disturbed sleep patterns—insomnia or early awakening. The student, on the other hand, may spend an abnormally lengthy period of time just lying in bed or sleeping, or may use substances to induce sleep.
4. Changes in eating habits; that is, either a loss of appetite or an unusual increase in food intake.
5. Complaints of headaches, stomachaches, muscle aches, or tiredness without apparent physical cause.
6. Changes in school behavior—such as refusing to attend, not completing assignments, shortened attention span, daydreaming, and loss of memory.
7. Changes in energy level, including listlessness, boredom, and dejection.
8. Changes in appearance such as slowed gait, poor posture, neglect of personal appearance, daydreaming, and slowed speech.
9. Reverting to age-inappropriate behaviors such as whining, bedwetting, dependence, and fearfulness.
10. Verbal expressions of a wish to die or kill oneself and an inordinate concern with death or dying.

When an adolescent consistently exhibits one or more of these behaviors, the special educator should be kind and understanding and alert the appropriate authorities. The special educator's concern should be shared with parents or guardians and school authorities, with the recommendation that immediate assistance be given to the student.

School dropouts. According to Douglas (1969), school dropouts are characterized by:

1. Consistent low school achievement
2. Low socioeconomic status, including a cultural background that does not regard school highly
3. Consistent poor reading achievement
4. Poor verbal learning skills
5. A lack of interest in co-curricular activities and a failure to perceive oneself as a member of the school community
6. A record of antisocial behavior
7. Self-selected peers who are socioeconomically similar, poor school achievers, and, perhaps, in difficulty with the justice system
8. Poor attitude toward school and teachers
9. A record of poor school attendance

A careful reading of these characteristics suggests that there is a significant similarity between students classified as dropouts and those identified as behavior-disordered.

Difficulties with the justice system.   Morgan (1979), in his survey of 204 state correctional facilities, found that 42.1 percent of the children committed to such institutions had some type of handicapping conditions. Of the total committed, 16.2 percent were identified as emotionally handicapped.

Keilitz and Miller (1980) offered three explanations for the disproportionate prevalence of handicapping conditions among juvenile offenders. First, "the school failure rationale," which leads the offenders to perceive themselves as socially unattractive to peers and adults. This negative self-perception leads to absenteeism, suspension, dropping out, and delinquent behavior. Second, the "susceptibility rationale," which argues that the behavioral characteristics of children and youths with learning and behavior disorders (impulsiveness, inappropriate response to social cues, and a limited ability to perceive the consequences of one's actions) make these students more susceptible to becoming juvenile offenders. The final explanation is "differential treatment." Keilitz and Miller suggest that students with poor school peformance are viewed differently by the justice system, and consequently treated more severely.

Mental illness.   As is true of mentally ill adults, adolescents with mental illness are frequently caught in the "revolving door" of treatment and care in psychiatric facilities. Bloom and Hopewell (1982) conducted a follow-up study of thirty-three adolescents discharged from a psychiatric hospital. Forty-three percent were reinstitutionalized within six months of discharge. In the successful group, 54 percent were enrolled in public school. Several factors bearing on readmission emerged from this study. Students' reinstitutionalization rates increased with the length of the original hospitalization. Adolescents' reinstitutionalization rates were similar to those of adult psychiatric patients. It was found that successful educational placement was critical to maintaining students in the community. In addition, the presence of at least one biological parent in the home improved the likelihood of an adolescent's successful reintegration into the community.

OBJECTIVE TWO: *To describe the goals of programming for secondary school students with behavior disorders.*

Cegelka and Phillips (1978) stated that "the imminence of the secondary student's adulthood requires that the quality of his total life adjustment be of paramount concern to those persons involved in developing the IEP and designing the educational experiences" (p. 86). In secondary school, teaching to address the needs of the contexts in which the student is currently functioning and will be required to function in the future is essential.

Special educators assigned to secondary schools face a dual challenge with regard to effectively serving adolescents with behavior disorders. First, they must continue programs to remediate the adolescents' specific learning and behavior problems. Second, they must design programs responsive to adolescent life needs (Marsh, Gearheart, & Gearheart, 1978).

McDowell and Brown (1978), however, maintain that by secondary school, the time for remediation is past. They contend that functional life skills must be taught. In a controversial statement, they assert that acquiring a high-school diploma may not be an appropriate goal for some students with behavior disorders. Rather, they suggest that an appropriate program for this population includes training in social skills and self-control, functional academics, vocational curriculum and training, and placement in work-study programs.

The major educational goals for adolescents with behavior disorders that emerged from our review of the literature (Francescani, 1982; Knoblock, 1979; Cegelka & Phillips, 1978; Marsh, Gearheart, & Gearheart, 1978; McDowell & Brown, 1978; Rusch, 1979) are: (a) survival skills, (b) self-management, and (c) vocational training.

Survival skills. Rusch (1979) describe survival skills as "those behaviors that, when acquired, increase the likelihood of successful competitive employment in any vocational setting" (p. 143). He contends that special educators cannot develop lists of survival skills in isolation. The survival skills taught to adolescents must be corroborated by potential consumers and relevant to the contexts in which the student will function. Rather than working from a preordained list of objectives, Rusch suggests identifying the specific skills needed for success in future contexts and then teaching these to students. Reading, mathematics, and other academic subjects would be designed to respond to students' needs in the future contexts.

McDowell and Brown (1978) stress the application of students' life experiences in teaching survival skills, because such experiences are relevant to their everyday needs. Basic academic skills are taught through topics such as money management, filling out job applications, reading bus schedules, obtaining a driver's license, and home management. Though the term *relevance* has almost become trite in the field of special education, Knoblock (1979) provided some thoughts on the importance of a relevant survival curriculum for adolescents with behavior disorders. His comments can guide special educators in efforts to develop appropriate goals, objectives, and activities for students:

Students being taught a relevant curriculum feel more capable of solving their problems.

The importance of working with people must be stressed in the curriculum.

Students see the value placed on developing verbal and nonverbal interpersonal skills.

Life interests become the basis of school experiences.

Students recognize that there aren't always "right answers" when making life decisions.

Communication (Francescani, 1982) is an often-neglected skill when compared to other skills more obviously interrelated to basic learning such as, reading and mathematics. Yet secondary school-age students with behavior disorders have difficulties in both conversing and listening. In conversing, instruction is needed to assist students to choose topical content and organize it; use an appropriate voice including intensity, pitch, and language patterns; and use effective nonverbal communication. In listening, students need help developing their skills in asking questions to clarify content, paraphrasing, and giving feedback.

An additional survival skill needed by adolescents is the ability to find and use appropriate community agencies. This skill will allow them to overcome reliance on others to facilitate their efforts and ensure their success. Knowing who to call for what kinds of assistance is an invaluable tool for the adolescent with behavior disorders.

Self-management.   Behavior management is as important in the secondary school as it is on any other educational level (McDowell & Brown, 1978). However, because these students will soon be faced with few extrinsic behavioral controls, self-management training becomes essential. Students need to be able to manage their own behaviors. Training should be provided in problem-solving and appropriate behavioral interaction (Francescani, 1982). Stress-reduction techniques can help adolescents to cope with difficulties in the contexts in which they function or will function.

Vocational training.   McDowell and Brown (1978) discuss several objectives for vocational training for secondary school students with behavior disorders. They state that the goal of a vocational-training program for this population is to help the students learn competencies that allow them to enter the world of work and function successfully. The vocational-training objectives recommended by McDowell and Brown include—

Skill training in the basic competencies needed for employment;

Evaluating skill performance and work-related attitudes, and providing occupational guidance based on student interests and vocational strengths and weaknesses;

Training in job-related safety skills;

Developing positive feelings toward self and work;

Training in the satisfactory performance of assigned work and making related adjustments in social attitude;

Orienting students to relevant community employment;

Maintaining students in the program;

Developing an awareness of the responsibilities of adulthood.

This review of the three major goals of programming for secondary-school students with behavior disorders suggests that limited, single-option programs cannot meet the diverse needs of this population effectively. A secondary curriculum must be provided, which ensures that the knowledge and skills being taught are appropriate to current and future contexts in which the students function.

OBJECTIVE THREE: *To describe the program options currently available to secondary school students with behavior disorders*

Public schools are the major service provider for adolescents with behavior disorders. The public schools serve 75 to 95 percent of those adolescents classified as behavior-disordered (Grosenick & Huntze, 1980). In a national needs assessment conducted by Grosenick and Huntze, seven program options available to secondary students with behavior disorders were found: (1) self-contained classes, (2) resource room programs, (3) crisis-teacher/teacher-consultant/diagnostic-teacher services, (4) special schools, (5) out-of-district placements, (6) homebound services, and (7) career and/or vocational education.

In a survey of 222 junior and senior high school teachers of students with behavior disorders, Schmid, Algozzine, Maher, and Wells (1984) found that 59 percent of those surveyed were assigned to resource rooms. Twenty-eight percent worked in self-contained classes. The findings of Schmid and associates contrast sharply with those reported by Hirshoren and Heller (1979), who surveyed the special education directors in the fifty states, the District of Columbia, American Samoa, and Puerto Rico. The latter's survey results generally agreed with the findings of Grosenick and Huntze (1980), that the most frequent service available to secondary school students with behavior disorders is the self-contained special class. The services least frequently provided were crisis intervention and psychotherapy. In fact, Hirshoren and Heller found that services tended to be limited to the special class, resource room, and vocational education.

Wiederholt and McNutt (1979) discuss two educational alternatives, remedial and compensatory education, that can be implemented to replace special classes and resource rooms. They describe the goal of remedial education as identifying and remediating student deficits, with total remediation as an ultimate, though often unrealistic, goal. Wiederholt and McNutt state that remedial education has three strengths. First, it encourages the identification of the skills students must learn to function effectively. It focuses on remediating students' deficits rather than ignoring them. Finally, remedial education provides an option to students who, owing to severe deficits, are unable to cope with regular education. Remedial education, however, has weaknesses. It fails to focus on the many contexts in which the student lives and must function. It fractionalizes the student program, so that instruction is composed of bits and pieces that may not be easily combined into a comprehensive whole. Finally, it lacks the basic research needed to validate it as a realistic alternative for secondary students with behavior disorders.

Compensatory education, the second option discussed by Wiederholt and McNutt, is implemented to help students circumvent their deficits. Its purpose is to give students assistance and support to earn a high-school diploma. In compensatory education, students may be taught the same subject matter taught to regular education students, but using different methods and instructional materials. In addition, testing procedures may be modified to respond to each student's most effective mode of learning. Changes may be made in the instructional format.

Wiederholt and McNutt discuss the strengths and weaknesses of compensatory education. On the positive side, it enables students to earn the high-school diploma required by employers and for admission to post-secondary educational programs. However, a high-school diploma may be irrelevant for many of these students. In compensatory education, the modifications in normal programs and requirements may be so great that the diploma loses its meaning. Finally, the regular education offered through the vehicle of compensatory education simply may not provide students with the life skills they need to function.

The special class.   Hirshoren and Heller (1979) and Grosenick and Huntze (1980) report that the special class is the service most frequently provided secondary students with behavior disorders. The maximum number of students assigned to self-contained classrooms ranges from eight to fifteen (Hirshoren & Heller, 1979).

Guetzloe and Cline (1981) argue that the special class should not be a terminal placement for secondary school students with behavior disorders. They suggest that these students be gradually and systematically integrated into the regular school program. They further urge the integration of students with behavior disorders into school group-work experiences with token pay. If the students succeed at this level, paid group experiences under a special educator's supervision should be provided. As a final step in integration from a self-contained program, they propose a continuum of placements in structured, supervised part-time work with gradual increases in social demands. Applying this or a similar continuum of services assures that the secondary student with behavior disorders does not remain in the "holding pattern" of the self-contained classroom.

The resource room. The goal of the resource room for students with behavior disorders at the secondary school level is to "involve the student in learning within the structure of the regular class, to help the student maintain himself within this structure, and to enable the student to profit from it" (Connor & Muldoon, 1967). The resource room services enable the adolescent to meet the demands of responsible interaction with the adults and peers encountered in daily school life.

Adamson (1983) suggests fifteen direct and fifteen indirect services for secondary students with behavior disorders. The direct services are offered to the student in the resource room, while the indirect ones are offered primarily to the regular teacher serving the secondary school student. These services, provided by resource room personnel, are presented in Figure 13-1.

Vocational education. Wiederholt and McNutt (1979) state that the purpose of vocational education is to provide the training students require to ensure gainful employment as skilled and semiskilled technicians. The advantages of vocational education include preparing students with behavior disorders for the world of work by instructing them in marketable skills. It is also a viable alternative to the traditional college-preparatory track found in most schools. Finally, vocational education provides apprenticeship opportunities from which adolescents with behavior disorders profit.

Vocational education does have disadvantages. It is not always possible, in a vocational-education program, to accommodate the broad range of the individual differences found among secondary school students with behavior disorders. In addition, the training provided in the program is sometimes too restrictive, in that students are trained for specific occupations rather than in broadly applicable vocational skills. The affective development and social skills training needed by students with behavior disorders are frequently not included in vocational education.

In conclusion, all three of the services (special class, resource room, and vocational education) discussed here should be available to secondary students with behavior disorders. However, Schmid, Algozzine, Maher, and Wells (1984) found that 38 percent of the 167 secondary school teachers of students with behavior disorders they surveyed reported having little or no time for remediation. Thirty-two percent reported focusing teaching time on remediation of basic skills, 31 percent on counseling, and 43 percent on modifying inappropriate behavior.

FIGURE 13-1 Resource-Room Services for Secondary-School Students

Direct Services

Teaching school survival skills

Developing behavior and performance contracts

Monitoring student progress and providing feedback

Role-playing potential problems that may be encountered in the mainstream context

Teaching problem-solving skills

Providing consequences for misbehavior

Anticipating and monitoring regular education assignments

Providing rewards and incentives

Providing regular educators, parents, and students with feedback by means of progress reports

Assisting students in time management

Providing crisis intervention

Providing training in appropriate social behavior

Providing training in the negotiating skills needed to function in regular education

Applying precision teaching techniques

Instructing students in the use of study aids, such as calculators and tape recorders

Indirect Services

Modifying and substituting assignments

Modifying grading procedures

Providing lower-level materials for content areas

Providing task-analysis assistance to regular educators

Sharing instructional ideas with regular educators

Developing instructional plans

Brainstorming instructional and behavioral alternatives to real problems encountered by regular educators

Problem solving

Cofacilitating group meetings

Observing and providing feedback to regular educators with regard to student functioning

Developing learning centers, modules, or packets

Arranging "buddy" support systems to facilitate regular education functioning

Arranging for peer tutoring

Increasing awareness of regular educators and students

Providing crisis intervention

(Adapted from Adamson, 1983.)

Although federal law mandates appropriate programs for secondary students with behavior disorders, Grosenick and Huntze (1980) found several mechanisms being used by school personnel to avoid serving these students. They indicated that in-school suspensions, continuous suspensions, shortened school days, homebound instruction, alternative-school placement, and ignored truancy are used to remove or avoid programming for secondary school students with behavior disorders. Barnette and Parker (1982) contend that suspension and expulsion are frequently applied in efforts to control students. Temporary removal, they maintain, can cause inconsistent programming and irreparable harm to students. The courts have ruled that suspension is a change in placement and can only be implemented if there is an official modification of the student's Individualized Education Plan and with the parents' consent. Students can only be suspended when they present a danger to themselves or others.

OBJECTIVE FOUR: *To describe several model programs designed for secondary school students with behavior disorders.*

Although secondary school students with behavior disorders are served primarily in public school programs, the format, structure, and content of available programs vary greatly. In this section, the School Survival Skills Curriculum (Silverman, Zigmond, & Sansone, 1981), the Personal Adjustment Level System (Eskey & Hauser, 1984), the Self-Improvement Level Systems (Breman, Ruppert, & Cohen, 1984), and the Social Skills Model (McGinnis, 1984) are presented. These programs are designed for the mildly and moderately behaviorally disordered. For secondary students with severe behavior disorders, the Independent Living Skills Inventory (Vogelsberg, Anderson, Berger, Haselden, Mitwell, Schmidt, Skowron, Ulett, & Wilcox, 1980) and the On-Campus Program (Vetter-Zemitzsch, Bernstein, Johnston, Larson, Simon, & Smith, 1984) are presented.

The School Survival Skills Curriculum.   The goals of the School Survival Skills Curriculum (Silverman, Zigmond, & Sansone, 1981) are to prepare students to function effectively in the secondary school and in other environments in which they may find themselves in the future. To meet these goals, three educational strands are employed: (1) behavior control, in which students learn to control their behavior and environment, (2) teacher-pleasing behavior, in which students learn behavior patterns that usually lead to increased positive regard by the teacher for the student and (3) study skills, in which students learn strategies to compensate for deficiencies in basic skills. The objectives of these strands are presented in Figure 13-2.

FIGURE 13-2   School Survival Skills

Behavior-Control Strand

Students will be able to—

identify the behaviors they exhibit in specific school settings;

verbalize the effects of their behaviors on others;

recognize that the consequences they experience are the result of their behaviors;

identify options to habitual behaviors exhibited in specific school settings that result in negative consequences;

identify and substitute an option to a habitual behavior that results in negative consequences in a positive setting;

practice substituting more profitable behavior options in context;

generalize their awareness and knowledge of the effects of the options to other settings.

Teacher-Pleasing Behavior

Students will be able to—

identify overt and covert rules in each classroom;

identify the behaviors they demonstrate that meet (or fail to meet) the requirements of each classroom;

identify appropriate behaviors in various classrooms;

substitute more profitable behaviors in contrived settings;

contract to substitute a more profitable behavior in the mainstream setting;

generalize teacher-pleasing behaviors to other settings;

Study Skills

Students will be able to—

organize assignments for the efficient use of study time;

follow oral and written directions in the regular classroom;

listen to lectures and identify central themes and facts that support that theme;

locate needed information in a text;

take organized notes from a text;

use lecture and reading notes to study for different types of tests;

apply strategies to take different types of tests.

From R. Silverman, N. Zigmond, & J. Sanson, (1981) "Teaching Coping Skills to Adolescents with Learning Problems," *Focus on Exceptional Children, 13* (6), 1-20. Used by permission.

The student's program is based on assessment information obtained by the special educator from a variety of sources, including school records; interviewing personnel, parents, and the student; and observation of the student in regular education. This information is used to develop both individual and group profiles of survival-skill needs.

No formal empirical research has been done on this program; however, students completing it report improved interaction with peers and adults, better grades, and fewer altercations with authority figures. Their teachers report that students are better prepared, more involved, and less abrasive.

The Personal Adjustment and Self-Improvement Level systems.   The Personal Adjustment Level System (PALS) (Eskey & Hauser, 1984) and the Self-Improvement Level System (Breman, Ruppert, & Cohen, 1984) were developed to stabilize school attendance and increase appropriate behavior. The programs aim to improve self-esteem, responsibility, and decision-making and problem-solving skills. Students are also prepared for the world of work.

In these systems, students progress through five levels designed to facilitate intrinsic motivation, appropriate behavior, and increased academic achievement. The levels approach is employed to give students a feeling of accomplishment and motivation to return to regular education.

Weekly small group and individual counseling sessions are an integral component of the levels system. In addition, students are required to participate in various classroom activities such as study-skills seminars, values-clarification exercises, and substance-abuse seminars. Parental involvement in individual conferences, home programs, and group nights are valuable components.

Besides the contingencies enforced at specific levels, there are several general requirements of students. Students who do not wish to attend group counseling sessions, for example, may not progress beyond Day 1 of their present level; or, after conferring with the regular and special educators, students who violate agreed-upon behavior standards may be removed from regular education classes. The PALS curriculum levels, requirements, and incentives are described in Figure 13-3.

The Social Skills Model.   McGinnis (1984) describes a structured learning approach designed to teach students what to do as well as what not to do. This five-step model provides a structure for the planned, direct, and systematic teaching of prosocial skills. The model is unique in that it includes ongoing assessment of program effectiveness.

The first phase of the program is preassessment. Potential students are selected as a result of peer, teacher, and parent reports. Preassessment

FIGURE 13-3 Personal Adjustment Levels System (PALS)

Level 0
Requirements

    maintain appropriate classroom behavior

    attend class from second through sixth period

    arrive on time, bring materials

    sleeping in class is not permitted

    abusive or vulgar language is not permitted

    students may not leave the room without permission

    visitors are permitted with teacher's permission only

    comply with all school rules

    attend weekly group-therapy meetings

    negotiate behavioral contracts with the teacher

    present weekly assignments at specified times

    submit journals for review at specified times

    failure to comply with policies involves loss of days from level, loss of privileges, in-school suspension, out-of-school suspension, intervention from the dean, and home intervention

Level 1
Requirements

    goal-setting conferences with social worker

    IEP conference with teacher

    demonstrate knowledge of school rules, PALS rules, and routine

    maintain a daily journal

    record assignments

    participate in weekly group-therapy meetings

    demonstrate appropriate behavior 70 percent of the time

    complete 65 percent of assignments

    participate in required class activities

    document "helping others" on a weekly basis

    attend 20 consecutive days

    demonstrate progress on 60 percent of IEP goals

    contained for all classes except physical education

Incentives:

    in-school field trips

    one cafeteria pass a week

    one off-campus lunch with teacher

Level 2
Requirements

    All Level 1 requirements concerning log, conference, weekly group therapy, helping others, participation in activities remain in force

    complete 75 percent of assignments

    demonstrate appropriate behavior 75 percent of the time

    attend 30 consecutive days

demonstrate progress on 75 percent of IEP goals

must be passing 80 percent of classes to continue to Level 3

Incentives:

bonus days

food privileges

two cafeteria passes per week

two off-campus lunches with teacher

in-school field trips

Level 3
Requirements

All Level 1 and 2 requirements concerning log, conference, weekly group therapy, helping others, participating in activities remain in force

complete 85 percent of assignments

demonstrate appropriate behavior 90 percent of the time

attend 60 consecutive days

demonstrate progress on 90 percent of IEP goals

must pass all classes

Incentives:

three cafeteria passes a week

four off-campus lunches with teacher

food privileges

in-school field trips

off-campus field trips

bonus days

Level 4
Requirements

100 percent attendance

complete 90 percent of assignments

contract for group-therapy meeting

appropriate behavior 90 percent of the time

in regular education for all classes

passing all classes

progress on all IEP goals

meet with teacher on daily or weekly check-in basis

meet with social worker to discuss progress and review goals

Level 5
Requirements (regular class)

students are only monitored. After 15 days, a meeting is called to determine new placement.

From M. Eskey and S. Hauser, *PALS* (Personal Adjustment Level System), 1984; 1985 (Hinsdale, IL: Hinsdale Township High School). Used by permission.

is followed by direct observation of the student to determine the specific skills he or she needs to function successfully. The next phase of the program is developing an instructional plan to teach the student the needed skills. During this phase, the time of instruction is scheduled with consideration given to the peers who may facilitate the student's progress. Group rules are established, and individual skills are introduced by the special educator. During the program, the level of instructional support and artificial-reinforcement systems are gradually faded.

A structured learning approach is applied during the third stage of the Social Skills Program. The student's specific skills and skill levels are assessed. Modeling, role-playing, and performance feedback are applied by the special educator to insure learning. "Homework" is assigned to facilitate the transfer of training. In the first stage of Homework, the student thinks of situations within the classroom in which he or she could practice the skill being presented. In the second stage of Homework, the student is given "red flags"; that is, he or she is placed in contrived situations to assess how effectively the newly learned skills are applied. Successful performance in the contrived situations allows the student to progress to a level during which behaviors are self-recorded on a series of prepared sheets. The final Homework stage involves fading the self-recording system to a simple three-by-five-card reminder.

The fourth phase of the Social Skills Model focuses on the generalization to various contexts of the prosocial skills the students have learned. Students are helped to apply their new skills in different settings, and with different materials and personnel. At this time, they are instructed in self-reinforcement and those specific skills needed for effectively functioning.

The last phase of the model is postteaching assessment. By assessing the effectiveness of the program, the special educator can continue to develop the skills needed to teach students prosocial skills.

Independent Living Skills Inventory.   The Independent Living Skills Inventory (Vogelsberg & associates, 1980) is an assessment instrument employed as the basis of a functional curriculum designed to help students complete a transition from dependent to independent living. The inventory assesses the skills needed to select, set up, and survive in an apartment. The Inventory also includes a suggested training model.

Each of the areas of the Independent Living Skills Inventory is potentially a separate curriculum. The inventory is outlined in Figure 13-4. It is used to develop training priorities for each student. Once a deficit has been identified, a plan for skill acquisition is developed. By completing the inventory and then teaching the necessary skills, students with severe behavior disorders can acquire the specific skills they need for living independently.

Because of the comprehensiveness of the inventory, considerable time must be devoted to learning all the skills needed for independent

FIGURE 13-4 The Independent Living Skills Inventory

I. Selecting an independent living situation
   a. Information is gathered about the individual
   b. Legal concerns, including using community-service personnel, parents, and guardians as supports
   c. Financial considerations, including assisting in the development of a format to calculate how much money is coming in and how much will be spent on a monthly basis
   d. Where and how to look for an apartment
   e. Environmental considerations, including public transportation, proximity to support services, recreational facilities
   f. Physical setting, if accessibility is an issue
   g. Landlord considerations, including reputation and responsibilities
   h. Finalizing, factors to consider once a final decision to rent or lease an apartment is made

II. Setting up an independent living situation
   a. Initial preparation, including arranging for utilities, cleaning
   b. Materials inventory, including cleaning, kitchen, bathroom, bedroom, living room, and general-maintenance materials
   c. Obtaining and storing needed materials

III. Surviving in an independent living situation
   a. Scheduling, to train students what needs to be done each day, over a week, over a month, and over a year
      1. Daily schedule checklist, skills ranging from arising to alarm clock to bathing and preparing the next day's lunch in the evening
      2. Weekly calendar, to delineate chores, leisure-time activities, and personal activities, including grocery shopping, bill payment, leisure-time activities, and so on
      3. Monthly calendar, including, for example, rent payment, upcoming social activities, and doctor's appointments
      4. Yearly calendar, dates that are transferred to the monthly calendar at the beginning of each month, including, for example, lease renewal, doctor or dentist appointment, insurance payments
      5. Expenses, a means of calculating the balance between monthly income and monthly expenses
   b. Specific skills room by room, including the food-management, clothing-management, and maintenance skills
   c. Transportation, using public transportation
   d. Safety skills
   e. Money-management skills, including using a checking account, savings account, charge cards, and lay-away plans
   f. Communication, being able to initiate, sustain, and terminate telephone, mail, personal notes, and direct social interaction
   g. Leisure time
   h. Miscellaneous, such as problem-solving skills

From R. T. Vogelsberg et al., "Programming for Apartment Living: A Description and Rationale of an Independent Living Inventory," *Journal of the Association for the Severely Handicapped* (1980), *5*, 38-54. Used by permission.

living. Students may need to start skill training early in their secondary school career. This time requirement is a disadvantage, since it may remove the students further from the mainstream of regular education.

On-Campus Program. Vetter-Zemitzsch and associates (1984) describe an "on-campus program" for secondary school students with serious behavior disorders. It is based on the premise that the most appropriate place to serve these adolescents is in the high school. Ideally, in the on-campus-program students spend one semester in a self-contained class, one semester partially mainstreamed, and a final semester fully mainstreamed with support. Psychotherapeutic and educational interventions are applied through special educators, vocational coordinators, social workers, clinical psychologists, and program aides.

The On-Campus Program curriculum primarily means career and vocational training. Among the interventions included are:

Family conferences. School and home efforts are coordinated to support the student and establish limits.

Problem-solving conferences. Conferences are fairly brief (ten to fifteen minutes), and usually involve a student, special educator, counselor or administrator, and, at times, regular classroom staff. In problem-solving conferences, the "S-C-A-N" model is applied. Students are taught to state the problem in their own words (S), clarify the part they played in the problem as well as the behavior of the other person (C), ask for suggestions for alternative solutions to the problem behavior (A), and, finally, negotiate a plan of action (N).

Behavioral contracts, developed in both family- and school-focused conferences.

Behavior point systems, in which students are reinforced for being on time, in their seats for the entire period, working the entire period, using appropriate language, and demonstrating appropriate behavior.

Group counseling, to enhance personal problem-solving skills, elicit peer feedback on interpersonal style, and explore affective and cognitive reasons for the behavior.

Crisis intervention, during which a calm, supportive therapist encourages the student to talk about the immediate events that precipitated a crisis.

Though there are little empirical data to support this program, the average daily attendance of students involved rose 47 percent. In addition, more students passed their regular education classes during participation in the On-Campus Program than prior to its implementation.

OBJECTIVE FIVE: *To describe the ecological-assessment process applicable in secondary school programs for students with behavior disorders.*

Secondary school students with behavior disorders need programs that address the demands of their daily living roles as concerned citizens, purchasers or spenders, learners, and investors (Clark, 1980). In order to address these demands, the special educator performs an ecological assessment to determine the actual demands of the contexts in which the students are functioning. Before initiating an ecological assessment, the special educator responds to several broad questions related to the student and program (Brolin & D'Alonzo, 1979):

> Should the program be job-centered or life-centered?
>
> Should career needs be addressed separately or permeate the program?
>
> Is the special educator, regular educator, or vocational educator ultimately responsible for the student's skill development?
>
> What is the impact on present and future mainstreaming efforts of responding to the student's career needs?
>
> Does addressing needs determined through ecological assessment result in the abandonment of the student's current program?
>
> What training and preparation are needed by those educators responsible for meeting the career needs of these students?

Schumaker, Pederson, Hazel, and Meyen (1983) presented a model for the evaluation of a social curriculum for mildly handicapped adolescents. With modification, this model appears appropriate for selecting objectives and activities for the ecological assessment of secondary students with behavior disorders.

Five considerations should be addressed when performing an ecological assessment. First, does the objective and/or activity promote social and career competence? Teaching such competence is a complex task. Not only are individual skills complex, but frequently these must be synchronized and coordinated to ensure success. In addition, the student must be motivated to achieve goals. The initial step in the ecological assessment of career needs, then, is determining whether or not the tentatively selected objectives and/or activities will motivate students to increase their skills.

The second consideration when conducting an ecological assessment of career needs is to determine whether the objective and/or activity accommodates the learning, social, and behavioral characteristics of the student. In view of the contexts in which the adolescent presently functions and will function, the special educator must address the following questions:

> Do this objective and activity address the student's academic and cognitive skills?
>
> Do they provide for the discrimination of social cues and the acquisition of problem-solving skills?
>
> Do they provide for the student's success?

Do they provide the student with strategies for coping in the environment? Do they address the generalization of behavior to other contexts in which the student may find himself or herself? Do they facilitate self-motivation?

A third consideration in the ecological assessment of career needs is whether or not the objectives and/or activities actually address students' deficits. Students with behavior disorders often have such extensive instructional needs that "practicing" skills they already possess is an ineffective use of instructional time. Thus, caution should be exercised to address only students' deficits.

The fourth consideration in ecological assessment is whether the student is to be given training in context as well as skills. In general, if students are to be helped to develop discrimination skills and appropriate behaviors, they must be assessed in the contexts in which they are to function.

Finally, consideration is given to the appropriateness of the instructional methodologies. Schumaker and associates suggest a three-phase program. First, there should be an awareness phase, during which the new skill is described and the student is provided with a rationale for its use. Practice, a second phase, includes both verbal and behavioral rehearsal. The final phase is the application or generalization of the skill in the applied context.

After determining the current and possible future contexts for each student, the special educator reviews the student's tentative program in view of the five considerations. In this way, the proposed program will be appropriate to the needs of the adolescent. The reader is urged to review the additional information on Wahler and Cormier's (1970) system of ecological assessment presented in Chapter 3.

OBJECTIVE SIX: *To discriminate between the career and vocational competencies needed by secondary school students.*

Grosenick and Huntze (1980) state that although there is considerable discussion of vocational programs for secondary school students with behavior disorders, relatively few students are actually served in such programs. They found that overall, only approximately 2 percent of all handicapped secondary school students participate in vocational education, and the number of students with behavior disorders in the program is miniscule.

Educators frequently confuse career and vocational education. Hoyt (1977) suggests that vocational education is a much narrower concept than career education. Whereas vocational education focuses on the competencies needed for specific employment, career education includes a range of skills needed for employment, such as job seeking, decision making, and appropriate work skills and behavior.

Vocational training.   Vocational competencies focus on work-related skills. Brolin (1976) suggests six such competencies needed by secondary school students. Three of them are more appropriately classified as career competencies:

Demonstrating work habits appropriate to a specific job market
Obtaining specific and saleable entry-level occupational skills
Developing adequate manual skills and physical stamina to compete in the labor market

Competencies that Brolin classifies as both career and vocational in nature are:

Exploring occupational possibilities
Selecting and planning occupational choices
Seeking, securing, and keeping jobs compatible with personal attitude, interests, and needs

Career education.   The focus of career education contrasts sharply with that of vocational education. Clark (1980) describes career education as:

that formal and informal attempt to make one ready for the course of one's life. This course will involve various roles (family member, neighbor, citizen, and worker), various environments (home, neighborhood, and community), and innumerable events (home living, mobility, consumer activities, interpersonal interactions, and work activities) (p. 11).

Brolin and Alonzo (1979) describe career education as a total educational concept, bringing meaning to the curriculum for secondary students, and providing career awareness, career exploration, instruction in decision making, and skills development. In view of the needs of secondary students with behavior disorders, this total educational approach appears more appropiate for youth with behavior disorders than specific vocational training. Career education is life education, as demonstrated by Brolin and Kokaska's (1982) Life-Centered Career Education Model. The model demonstrates the broad range of skills that are a part of the career-education program. The curriculum areas and major competencies covered in the model are presented in Figure 13-5.

FIGURE 13-5   Life-Centered Career-Education Competencies

Daily Living Skills

home financial management
home selection, management, and maintenance
personal care
child care and family living
food purchasing and preparation
clothing purchasing and care
involvement in civic activities
utilization of recreational and leisure facilities
mobility in the community

Personal Social Skills

self-awareness
self-confidence
socially responsible behavior
interpersonal skills
independence
problem solving
communication skills

Occupational Guidance and Preparation

knowledge and exploration of occupational possibilities
selection and planning of occupational choices
appropriate work habits and behaviors
physical-manual skills
specific occupational skills
seeking, securing, and maintaining employment

(adapted from Brolin & Kokaska, 1982)

SUMMARY

In this chapter, programming for secondary school students with behavior disorders is discussed. Several problems unique to adolescents with behavior disorders—such as suicide, leaving school, and mental illness—are reviewed. The organizational patterns and specific settings indigenous to the secondary school and that may exacerbate the deviant behaviors of adolescents were discussed. The goals of programming for secondary school students with behavior disorders are presented, and several program options are discussed. To provide the reader with information regarding the state of the art of programs for this population, five program models were presented. The chapter concluded with a discussion of the ecologcal assessment of adolescents and a comparison of vocational and career education.

REVIEW QUESTIONS

1. Describe some characters of the organization of the secondary school that may exacerbate the problems of adolescents with behavior disorders.
2. Identify the social service agencies in your community that provide support to adolescents who have attempted suicide and to their families. Are there "hotline" services available? Support groups? S.O.S. (Survivors of Suicides) chapters?
3. Contrast the needs of secondary school students with behavior disorders for basic academic skill remediation to instruction in functional skills. What are the advantages and disadvantages of each approach?
4. Through contact with the local education agency, identify the program options available to secondary students with behavior disorders in the local school district. What are the policies concerning suspension and expulsion of students with behavior disorders?
5. Review Adamson's options for resource room services. Describe one instructional objective that could be realized through the implementation of each of the direct and indirect service options listed.
6. Describe the advantages and disadvantages of employing a level system with adolescents with behavior disorders.
7. Search the literature for program models for adolescents with behavior disorders that were not discussed in this chapter.
8. Compare and contrast the goals of vocational and career education. Does one subsume the other?

APPLICATION ACTIVITIES

To determine whether instructional objectives, activities, and interventions are appropriate for an adolescent with behavior disorders, the special educator must consider the criteria expressed in the following questions (adapted from Schumaker & associates, 1983):

1. Does the objective, activity, or intervention actively promote social and career competence?
2. Does the objective, activity, or intervention accommodate the characteristics of the student?
3. Does the objective, activity, or intervention address a deficit?
4. Does the objective, activity, or intervention provide for training in context as well as skill training?
5. Does the activity employ methodology demonstrated to be effective?

Review the following objectives, activities, and interventions. Rate them on criteria listed. Determine whether each objective is appropriate for the student briefly described in the left-hand column.

	Promote Competence	Accommodate Characteristics	Address Deficits	Context	Methods
John practices clerical skills by sorting zip-coded index cards into a 3-by-5 file.					
Mary runs the cafeteria dishwasher independently; when staff members are absent, she "practices" this skill.					
Michael is removed from vocational-training class for three days whenever he arrives without materials.					
Louisa, who has a severe attention problem, is given a 45-minute job at the drill press.					
Elizabeth is trained in meal preparation through a workbook; because of her behavior, she is refused use of the home-economics room.					

Appendix A

Screening Instruments for Behavior Disorders

Several screening instruments for the identification of children and youth at high risk for behavior disorders are described in this appendix. The list is selective, and the instruments presented vary with regard to their validity, reliability, and ease of administration. They should be evaluated with reference to Lambert and Bower's criteria for acceptable screening techniques (see Objective 2 in Chapter 3). In addition, the literature, especially the research literature on the instruments, must be studied before a prudent decision can be made with regard to the usefulness of a technique.

THE SCALES OF INDEPENDENT BEHAVIOR

BRUININKS, R. H., WEATHERMAN, R. F., WOODCOCK, R. W., & HILL, B. K. (1984). *The Scales of Independent Behavior.* Allen, TX: DLM Teaching Resources.

The Scales of Independent Behavior are standardized nationally for a population ranging from infants to adults over forty years of age. They offer a variety of options in administration, including (a) a full battery to assess the individual's mastery of 226 items (administration time one hour); (b) a short form containing 32 items (ten- to fifteen-minute administration time); (c) an early development scale for children from birth to two and a half years; (d) a four-cluster option that organizes adaptive behavior into motor skills, social-interaction and communication skills, personal-living skills, and community living skills scales; (e) an interview format and a report format; and (f) a problem behavior scale, which measures serious and often difficult-to-define behaviors.

Items are rated on a Likert-type scale of 0 (never or rarely, even if asked), 1 (does, but not well, or about one fourth of the time, or may need to be asked), 2 (does fairly well, or about three fourths of the time, or may need to be asked), and 3 (does very well, always or almost always, without being asked). The Scales of Independent Behavior provide age scores, percentile ranks, standard scores, stanines, and normal curve equivalents. In addition, they provide instructional functioning scores of instructional ranges, relative-performance indexes, and functioning levels. Microcomputer scoring is available.

DENVER DEVELOPMENTAL SCREENING TEST MANUAL (REVISED)

FRANKENBURG, W. K., DODDS, J. B., & FANDAL, A. W. (1970). *Denver Developmental Screening Test Manual (Revised)*. Denver: University of Colorado Medical Center.

The Denver Developmental Screening Test (DDST) is used with children from birth to six years of age. It was designed and standardized to meet the need for a simple, useful tool to assist in the early identification of developmental problems. Specialized training is not required to administer or score this test, and specialized equipment and materials needed to administer the instrument are minimal.

The test is composed of 105 items in four categories: a) personal social skills, b) fine motor and adaptive skills, c) language skills, and d) gross motor skills. Items are scored as pass, failure, refusal, or no opportunity. Some items are scored on the report of parents. The number of items administered to a specific child varies with age and performance. In scoring, the tester is encouraged to note the child's behavior.

PUPIL BEHAVIOR RATING SCALE

LAMBERT, N. M., BOWER, E. M., & HARTSOUGH, C. S. (1979). *Pupil Behavior Rating Scale*. Monterey, CA: Publishers Test Service.

The Pupil Behavior Rating Scale is a teacher-observation screening instrument for students in kindergarten through seventh grade that assesses three dimensions of affective behavior: classroom adaptation, interpersonal skills, and intrapersonal behavior.

Peer rating and self-rating instruments are also provided. Peer ratings are evaluated by asking, "Who could this be?" Pictures are used for children in the lower grades (K through third), and a "school play" is used for children in the higher grades (fourth through seventh). Self-ratings for children from kindergarten to grade three are attained through a picture-game format. For children in grades three through seven, the school play is again used.

BEHAVIOR EVALUATION SCALE

McCarney, S. B., Leigh, J. E. & Cornbleet, J. (1983). *Behavior Evaluation Scale.* Columbia, MO: Educational Services.

The Behavior Evaluation Scale (BES) is a fifty-two item scale that is designed for use with students from kindergarten through twelfth grade. Ten to twenty minutes are required for its administration. Items are evaluated using a scale ranging from 1 (never or not observed) to 7 (continuously throughout the day). The scale is completed by the classroom teacher and other school personnel providing direct services. It is advantageous for one month of observation to precede completion of the scale. The items on the scale are weighted according to the relative severity of the behaviors. A behavior quotient, or global index of the student's behavior, is computed. Individual scores in the areas of learning problems, interpersonal difficulties, inappropriate behavior, unhappiness and depression, and physical symptoms and fears are plotted on a profile for instructional use.

BEHAVIOR PROBLEM CHECKLIST

Quay, H. C., & Peterson, D. R. (1967) *Behavior Problem Checklist.* Champaign, IL: University of Illinois.

The Behavior Problem Checklist measures four problem behavior dimensions: conduct disorders (psychopathy, unsocialized aggression), personality disorders, inadequacy and immaturity, and subcultural delinquency. Normative data, including studies of reliability and interrater reliability, are reported in the manual.

The checklist is completed by persons familiar with the child or young person, including parents and teachers. The rating system allows the rater to differentiate between behavior observed, behavior observed but mild, and behavior observed and severe.

VINELAND ADAPTIVE BEHAVIOR SCALES

Sparrow, S. S., Balla, D. A., & Cicchetti, D. V. (1984). *Vineland Adaptive Behavior Scales.* Circle Pines, MN: American Guidance Service.

The Vineland Adaptive Behavior Scales is a 1984 revision of the Vineland Social Maturity Scale. Three versions are available, including an interview edition survey format, interview edition expanded format, and a classroom edition. The survey and expanded forms assess individuals from birth to eighteen years eleven months, and the classroom edition is appropriate for students from three to twelve years eleven months. Four domains of behavior—communication, daily living skills, socialization, and motor skills—are assessed. In addition, an optional maladaptive behavior scale is included to measure inappropriate behavior that may interfere with functioning. As well as adaptive levels and age equivalents, a graphic presentation of standard scores and bands of error is used in scoring.

DEVEREUX CHILD BEHAVIOR RATING SCALE

DEVEREUX ADOLESCENT BEHAVIOR RATING SCALE

DEVEREUX ELEMENTARY SCHOOL BEHAVIOR RATING SCALE

SPIVACK, G., & SPOTTS, J. (1966). *Devereux Child Behavior Rating Scale.* Devon, PA: The Devereux Foundation.

SPIVACK, G., SPOTTS, J., & HAIMES, P. E. (1967). *Devereux Adolescent Behavior Rating Scale.* Devon, PA: The Devereux Foundation.

SPIVACK, G., & SWIFT, M. (1967). *Devereux Elementary School Behavior Rating Scale.* Devon, PA: Devereux Foundation.

The Devereux Child Behavior Rating Scale is designed to describe and evaluate the behavior disorders of children, primarily in "real life" situations. The instrument is useful for students eight to twelve years of age, and is completed by individuals familiar with the child's behavior in a home-type situation.

The instrument includes ninety-seven items rated on scales ranging from five to nine choices. Raw scores and standard scores are provided for seventeen behavior factors: distractibility, poor self-care, pathological use of senses, emotional detachment, social isolation, poor coordination and body tone, incontinence, messiness, inadequate independence, unresponsiveness to stimulation, proneness to emotional upset, need for adult contact, anxious-fearful ideation, impulse ideation, inability to delay, social aggression, and unethical behavior.

The Devereux Elementary School Behavior Rating Scale is designed for use by elementary-school teachers to identify and measure behaviors that may be interfering with learning. It may also be used as a screening instrument and to assess behavior changes over time. The scale focuses on overt behaviors and is useful for students in kindergarten through sixth grade. It is completed by the teacher who rates each item on either a five- or seven-point scale.

The completed instrument provides raw and standard scores for eleven behavior factors: classroom disturbance, impatience, disrespect and defiance, placing blame, achievement anxiety, reliance on external circumstances, comprehension, inattention with withdrawal, irrelevant responsiveness, creative initiative, and need for closeness to teacher. Three additional items are concerned with inability to change, slowness, and quitting before completing a task.

The Devereux Adolescent Behavior Rating Scale (DAB) is designed to measure the deviant behavior of adolescents. It can be administered by teachers or others familiar with the student.

The DAB is composed of eighty-four statements about behavior; these are rated on either a five-point or an eight-point scale. These statements are clustered into twelve behavior factors and three rational clusters, plus eleven additional items. Raw and standard scores can be derived for all factors and clusters. The behaviors measured are unethicalness, defiance-resistive behavior, domineering-sadistic behavior, heterosexual interest, hyperactivity, poor emotional control, need for approval and dependency, emotional distance, physical inferiority and timidity, schizoid behavior and withdrawal, bizarre speech and cognition, and bizarre actions. The rational clusters in the DAB include inability to delay, paranoid thinking, and anxious self-blame.

The DAB can be used for screening and treatment evaluation.

Appendix B

Individual Case Study and Group Data for Application Activities

INTRODUCTION

The information in this appendix may be used by the reader to complete several of the Application Activities presented in the text. Students from two special education programs are described: a resource room and a self-contained special class. In addition to descriptions of the students, information is provided regarding program level, number of students in the group, the referring teacher, grade level, availability of support staff, and schedule contraints.

RESOURCE ROOM FOR STUDENTS WITH BEHAVIOR DISORDERS

Level: Intermediate grades
Number of students served daily: 14
Teacher: Ms. Keith
Support staff: None
Schedule constraints:

The school principal has requested that you meet at least once a week with each of the three teachers whose students you serve. He also asks that you assist Ms. Rookie, a new teacher, in managing the behavior of some of her students.

Lunch: Fourth grade—11:30–12:15
Fifth grade—11:45–12:30
Sixth grade—12:00–12:45
Recess: Fourth grade—9:45–10:00
Fifth grade—10:00–10:15
Sixth grade—10:00–10:15

Students from Mrs. Smith's Class, Fourth Grade

John

Academic: at grade level in all areas except reading; word recognition, 2.5; reading comprehension, 2.3; uses no phonics or work attack skills; relies on picture cues; "spaces out" during reading instruction in the room; Mrs. Smith wants him "out of the room when trying to teach reading to the other students," 10:00–10:40.

Social: prefers to play alone; some specific interests (dinosaurs, electricity)

Language: receives speech therapy on Tuesdays and Thursdays at 11:15–11:35 for articulation problems; rarely verbalizes in class

Behavioral concerns: has difficulty attending to tasks; "spaces out" during class; completes few tasks; spends free time looking at pictures in encyclopedias and science books

Mary

Academic: receives consultative services for learning disabilities

Behavioral concerns: great deal of difficulty attending to task; does not comply with class rules; uses inappropriate language during large group activities; will ask to use the rest room and remain there during assemblies, large group activities, content-area classes, etc.

Clare

Academic: reading comprehension is below the norms of the test. Mrs. Smith reports that she "refuses to work with someone as low as Clare. She should be somewhere else, like a special room," and wants her out of the room for reading, 10:00–10:40

Social: immature; cries when confronted by Mrs. Smith over work completion or behavior issues

Behavioral concerns: cries easily; is tall and obese, large for her age, prefers to play with younger children, but is physically rough with them

Louise

Academic: near grade level in all areas

Behavioral concerns: was withdrawn during parents' divorce and referred for services, continues to come to resource room daily for point sheet for initiating social approaches with other students, asking the teacher for help, and speaking during group activities and discussions

Todd

Academic: able to perform well above grade level

Behavioral concerns: refuses to do "that busy-baby work"; crumples up worksheets he feels are "stupid" and throws them at teacher and other students; spends half day in resource room (morning academic instructional time) working independently at his own level in mathematics and language arts; returns to classroom for afternoon content-area subjects—science, health, social studies; complies during the afternoon as long as he is interested

Social: intolerant of others; refers to the slower students as "morons" and "dummies"

Jennifer

Academic: great deal of difficulty in math; uses her fingers or marks on worksheets when computing; Mrs. Smith will not accept any paper with "chicken scratching" on it and has stopped giving her any mathematics work in the classroom

Behavioral concerns: frequently absent, complaining of stomachaches, headaches, pains; when given assignments, begins the task but attempts to return it before it is completed

Dwayne

Academic: does not complete independent work in the classroom; will not practice skills or skill worksheets such as multiplication tables, and is falling further and further behind in mathematics

Behavioral concerns: enjoys reading and participates well in reading group; says, "Math is dumb. I want to be a lawyer, and they don't do math"; refuses to complete math assignments; reads during mathematics class; on one occasion threw the mathematics book toward the teacher

Michael

Academic: reverses numbers when taking dictation in mathematics and consistently fails dictated math tests; easily frustrated; Mrs. Smith reports that she doesn't have time to give him the test in a 1:1 setting and sends tests to resource room with Michael whenever his group is being tested

Behavioral concerns: Mrs. Smith and Michael "don't hit it off"; he refers to her as "Granny Smith" and in one "discussion" concerning a mathematics worksheet scratched her arm while trying to grab the paper from her

Other concerns: John, Mary, and Clare are unable to use the current social studies book Mrs. Smith has selected. Mrs. Smith indicated that she does not have time to search out materials just for them, and that she would prefer that they come to the resource room for social studies, from 2:15 to 3:00.

Students from Mrs. Niceteacher's Class, Fifth Grade

Jill

Academics: two grades below grade level in reading, at grade level in all other areas

Behavioral concerns: Jill's behavior is so disruptive during reading class (talking out, pushing and shoving other students in the group, destroying materials) that Mrs. Niceteacher has requested that she come to the resource room from 9:00 to 9:45. Mrs. Niceteacher has agreed to set aside time for her to work individually with Jill, if she is given the appropriate materials

Mark

Academic: Mark has a specific problem in making inferences from what he reads

Behavioral concerns: Mark is not attentive during reading (spins the book, writes on his desk and hand, and grabs other students' materials); attentional difficulties are not as severe in other subject areas

Leon

Academic: word recognition and reading comprehension are both far below grade level; Leon has recently been retested and is being considered for a change in placement to educable mentally handicapped; needs further assessment

Behavioral: Leon is withdrawn in class; frequently says, "I don't know." Mrs. Niceteacher feels that Leon truly "does not know," and wants help in developing successful activities for him

Kristin

Behavioral concerns: "[I] hate school and teachers and all the dumb stuff they make you do"; refuses to speak to Mrs. Niceteacher for several consecutive days; hides in the rest room during resource-room time; far below grade level in all areas; Mrs. Niceteacher claims she has not completed a single assignment or made one positive statement during group activities

Students from Mr. Henson's Class, Sixth Grade

Greg

Behavioral concerns: Greg is currently under psychiatric care; extremely withdrawn; does not attend to activities in the classroom; has been referred for self-contained special class placement several times but his parents refuse the placement and are currently pursuing the disagreement in the courts. Mr. Henson requests that he come to the resource room from 1:30 to 2:15, when the other students are having math class, as it is very difficult to involve him during this time because of the large amount of independent work done in class. When not involved, will abuse himself (picks at the skin on his fingers, pokes himself with pencil, etc.)

Barb

Academic: Barb has not yet learned her multiplication tables and spells poorly; she refuses to study such tasks, indicating that they are "boring."

Behavioral concerns: attempts to "forget" to come to the resource room, but Mr. Henson polices her schedule. She wants to use the same books as the other students, and will "borrow" their materials and replace them with her "special" books, worksheets, etc.

SELF-CONTAINED CLASSROOM

Level: Primary School Students with Behavior Disorders
Number of Students: 7
Teacher: Ms. Stuart
Support staff: Paraprofessional 9:00–11:30 A.M., 1:00–2:00 P.M.
Schedule constraints:
    Recess: 10:00–10:15
    Lunch: 11:15–12:00

Mark

Mark, seven years old, is at first-grade level in mathematics and language arts. His self-help skills are poor, due to his fine-motor problems; he is unable to button small buttons, buckle a belt, or tie shoes. He is very verbal, but has difficulty sequencing when relating experiences. Fine-motor academic skills are poor. He uses a stencil to produce shapes, has an incorrect pencil grasp, and cannot cut along a line. He frequently bumps into objects and is unable to ride a large tricycle, jump on two feet, or balance on one foot. Mark becomes frustrated with motor tasks and refuses to attempt them. He interacts well with adults but poorly with peers. He has been diagnosed as having an "attention deficit disorder" by a neurologist; his mother feels he is learning-disabled and misplaced. Mark is distractible, has difficulty completing tasks, and is frequently out of his seat.

Susie

Susie, six years old, recognizes her colors, writes her first name, and is demonstrating readiness to begin reading instruction. She can rote count, but owing to problems in attention, makes frequent errors in counting objects. Susie wets her pants when not reminded to use the toilet or when playing or excited. She has difficulty following complex instructions. Susie is frequently "on top of" the teacher during group activities; when the teacher or aide ignores her behavior, she grabs her face. Susie requires frequent extrinsic rewards to attend to and complete tasks.

Patricia

Patricia, eight years old, is at grade level in reading and mathematics, and appears to be ready to begin attending regular second grade part time. When Patricia completes her work, she leaves her seat and takes materials from the teacher's desk and shelves. When told to put them down, she gives the teacher or aide eye contact and then tears or crumples the item or materials. When reprimanded, she curses at teacher, aide, and students.

Sally

Sally, six years old, has just been placed in the room after two unsuccessful years in kindergarten. She participated in few activities, cried frequently. Her behavior is immature (eating all foods with a spoon or fingers, asking for Mommy, bringing in toys suitable for much younger children), yet her cognitive skills seem to be at grade level. Sally volunteers little verbal information, and reacts to unpleasant situations by crying and sucking her thumb. She does not participate with the group, and requires external rewards to complete tasks, stay in her seat, and remain with the group.

Joel

Joel, eight years old, is one grade level behind in mathematics and language arts. He requires an "invitation" to participate in group activities. He does not follow directions, and when told to perform an activity, says in a firm voice, "Make me." He uses inappropriate language, and grabs the teacher or aide when he has a request. Joel is frequently out of his seat, and attends to tasks for no more than five minutes.

Lawrence

Lawrence, eight years old, is near grade level in academic areas. He only expresses needs by responding affirmatively or negatively to the questions of others. Lawrence attends language therapy; the therapist feels his language problem is elective. Lawrence requires constant external rewards to complete tasks, stay in his seat, or demonstrate the skills that the teacher "knows" he knows. Lawrence works well in a one-on-one situation, but "spaces out" during group activities. He remains physically close to the teacher or other adults on the playground.

Tyler

Tyler, nine years old, is currently being phased into a third-grade classroom, where he spends most of the afternoon. He continues to have difficulties with task completion, and a point sheet is used in the special and regular classrooms to increase his task completion. When frustrated in the regular classroom, he asks if he can "go back" to the special class. He does not interact with the other students in third grade, who are still a bit afraid of him because of his reputation for being aggressive. He must receive mathematics and language-arts instruction in the morning in the special class. He is approximately at grade level.

References

The numbers in brackets at the end of each citation represent the chapter(s) in which the citation occurs. An asterisk designates suggested reading.

ADAMSON, D. R. (1983). Linking two worlds. Serving resource students at the secondary level. *Teaching Exceptional Students, 15* (2), 70–76. [13]

ALGOZZINE, B. (1980). The disturbing child: A matter of opinion. *Behavioral Disorders, 5* (2), 112–15. [1,2]

ALGOZZINE, B., MERCER, D. C., & COUNTERMINE, T. (1977). The effects of labels and behavior on teacher expectations. *Exceptional Children, 44* (2), 131–32. [1]

*ALGOZZINE, R., SCHMID, R., & CONNORS, R. (1978) Toward an acceptable definition of emotional disturbance. *Behavioral Disorders, 4* (1), 48–52. [1]

ALLEN, J.I. (1980). Jogging can modify disruptive behaviors. *Teaching Exceptional Children 12* (2), 66–70. [9]

ALLEN, R. C. (1969). *Legal Rights of the Disabled and Disadvantaged.* Washington, D.C.: U. S. Department of Health, Education and Welfare, National Citizens Conference on Rehabilitation of the Disabled and Disadvantaged. [11]

ALVIN, J. (1965). *Music for the Handicapped Child.* London: Oxford University Press. [9]

ANDERSON, N., & MARRONE, R. T. (1979). Therapeutic discussion groups in public school classes for emotionally disturbed children. *Focus on Exceptional Children, 12* (1), 1–15. [11]

*APTER, S. (1977). Applications of ecological theory toward a community special education model. *Exceptional Children, 43,* 366–73. [2, 5, 7]

AXELROD, S. (1977). *Behavioral Modification for the Classroom Teacher.* New York: McGraw-Hill. [10]

AXLINE, V. M. (1947). *Play Therapy.* Boston: Houghton Mifflin. [1, 9]

AYRES, A. J. (1979). *Sensory Integration and the Child.* Los Angeles: Western Psychological Services. [1]

BACHRACH, A., MOSLEY, A. R., SWINDLE, F. C., & WOOD, M.M. (1978). *Developmental Therapy for Young Children with Autistic Characteristics.* Baltimore: University Park Press. [11]

BAILARD, V., & STRANG, R. (1964). *Parent-Teacher Conferences.* New York: McGraw-Hill. [12]

BAILEY, J. S., WOLF, M. M., & PHILLIPS, E. L. (1970). Home based reinforcement and the modification of pre-delinquents' classroom behavior. *Journal of Applied Behavior Analysis, 3,* 223–33. [7]

BAKER, E. M., & STULLKEN, E. H. (1938). American research studies concerning the "behavior" type of exceptional child. *Journal of Exceptional Children, 4,* 36–45. [1]

BAKER, R. W. (1980). The treatment of behavior disorders with medication. In S. G. Sapir & A. C. Nitzberg (eds.), *Children with Learning Problems.* New York: Brunner/Mazel, Inc. [11]

BALDWIN, R. W. (1973). The treatment of behavior disorders with medication. In S. G. Sapir & A. C. Nitzberg (eds.), *Children with Learning Problems.* New York: Brunner/Mazel, Inc. [11]

BANDURA, A. (1969). *Principles of Behavior Modification.* New York: Holt, Rinehart & Winston. [10]

BANDURA, A. (1973). *Aggression: A Social Learning Analysis.* Englewood Cliffs, NJ: Prentice-Hall. [2]

BARNETTE, S. M., & PARKER, L. G. (1982). Suspension and expulsion of the emotionally handicapped: issues and practices. *Behavioral Disorders, 7* (3), 173–79. [13]

BARRISH, H., SAUNDERS, M., & WOLF, M. (1969). Good behavior game: Effects on individual contingencies for group consequences on disruptive behavior in a classroom. *Journal of Applied Behavior Analysis, 2,* 119–124. [10]

BARSCH, R. H. (1968). *The Parent of the Handicapped Child.* Springfield, IL: Charles C. Thomas. [12]

BARTON, E. J., & ASCIONE, F. R. (1984). Direct observation. In T. H. Ollendick & M. Herson (eds.), *Child Behavioral Assessment: Principles and Procedures.* New York: Pergamon Press. [3]

BARUCH, D. W. (1952). *One Little Boy.* New York: Dell. [1, 9]

BAUER, A. M. (1980). *Head Teacher's Handbook.* St. Louis: Special School District of St. Louis County, Missouri. [6]

BAUER, A. M. (1981). Program for parents of severely handicapped student—A plan. Edwardsville, IL: Southern Illinois University. [12]

BECKER, W. C. (1979). Introduction. In L. Homme, A. P. Csanyi, M. A. Gonzales, & J. R. Recks (eds.), *How to Use Contingency-Contracting in the Classroom.* Champaign, IL: Research Press. [10]

BEEZ, W. V. (1972). Influence of biased psychological reports on teacher behavior and pupil performances. In A. Morrison & D. McIntyre (eds.), *The Social Psychology of Teaching.* New York: Penguin Books. [8]

*BELL, J. P. (1979). Our needs and other ecological concerns: A teacher's personal view of working with "secondary school-aged seriously emotionally disturbed children." *Behavioral Disorders, 4* (3), 168–72. [4, 6]

BELSKY, J. (1980). Child maltreatment: An ecological integration. *American Psychologist, 35,* 320–35. [2]

BENSON, D., & CESSNA, K. (1980). *Guideline Handbook for Educational and Related Services for SIEBD Students.* Denver: Colorado Department of Education. [3, 4]

BERKOWITZ, B. P., & GRAZIANO, A. M. (1972). Training parents as behavior therapists: A review. *Behavior Research and Therapy, 10* (4), 297–317. [12]

BERKOWITZ, P. H., & ROTHMAN, E. P. (1960). *The Disturbed child: Recognition and Psychoeducational Therapy in the classroom.* New York: New York University Press. [7, 9]

BERKOWITZ, P. H., & ROTHMAN, E. P. (1967). *Public Education for Disturbed Children in New York City.* Springfield, IL: Charles C. Thomas, 1967. [7, 9]

BERSOFF, D. N., & GRIEGER, R. N. (1971). An interview model for the psychosituational assessment of children's behavior. *American Journal of Orthopsychiatry, 41* (3), 483–93. [12]

BETTLEHEIM, B. (1950). *Love Is Not Enough.* New York: The Free Press. [1]

BIRLESON, P. (1980). The validity of depressive disorder in childhood and development of a self-rating scale: A research report, *Journal of Child Psychology and Psychiatry, 22, 73–88. [3]*

BLACKHAM, G. J., & SILBERMAN, A. (1975). *Modification of Child and Adolescent Behavior.* Belmont, CA: Wadsworth. [10]

BLOOM, R. B., & HOPEWELL, L. R. (1982). Psychiatric hospitalization of adolescents and successful mainstream re-entry. *Exceptional Children, 48* (4), 352–57. [13]

BORNSTEIN, P. H., BORNSTEIN, M. T., & DAWSON, B. (1984). Integrated assessment and treatment. In T. H. Ollendick & M. Herson (eds.), *Child Behavioral Assessment: Principles and Procedures.* New York: Pergamon Press. [3]

BOWER, E. M. (1960). *Early Identification of Emotionally Handicapped Children in School.* Springfield, IL: Charles C. Thomas, 1960. [3]

BOWER, E. M. (1961). *The Education of Emotionally Handicapped Children: A Report to the California Legislature. Sacramento: California State Department of Education. [1]*

BOWER, E. M. (1980). Slicing the mystique of prevention with Occam's razor. In N. Long, W. Morse, & R. Newman (eds.), *Conflict in the Classroom* (4th ed.). Belmont, CA: Wadsworth. [3]

BREMAN, N., RUPPERT, B., & COHEN, S. (1984). *Self-Improvement Level System.* Hinsdale, IL: Hinsdale Central High School. [13]

BRENNER, A. (1977). A study of the efficacy of the Feingold diet on hyperkinetic children. *Clinical Pediatrics, 16,* 652–56. [11]

BROLIN, D. (1976). *Vocational Preparation of Retarded Citizens.* Columbus, OH: Charles E. Merrill. [13]

*BROLIN, D. E., & D'ALANZO, B. J. (1979). Critical issues in career education for handicapped students. *Exceptional Children,* 45, 246–53. [13]

BROLIN, D., & KOKASKA, C. (1982). Cited in Brolin, D. (1982). *Vocational Preparation of Persons with Handicaps* (2nd ed.). Columbus, OH: Charles E. Merrill. [13]

BRONFENBRENNER, U. (1977). Toward an experimental ecology of human development. *American Psychologist, 32,* 513–31. [2, 12]

BRONFENBRENNER, U. (1979). *The Ecology of Human Development.* Cambridge, MA: Harvard University Press. [2]

BROPHY, J., & EVERTSON, S. M. (1976). *Learning from Teaching: A Developmental Perspective.* Boston: Allyn & Bacon. [2]

*BROWN, F., HOLVOET, J., GUESS, D., & MULLIGAN, M. (1980). The individualized curriculum sequencing model (III). Small group instruction. *Journal of the Association for the Severely Handicapped, 5,* 352–67. [6]

BROWN, L., NIETUPSKI, J., & HAMRE-NIETUPSKI, S. (1976). The criterion of ultimate functioning and public school services for severely handicapped children. In M. A. Thomas (ed.), *Hey, Don't Forget About Me!* Reston, VA: Council for Exceptional Children, 2–15. [5]

*BROWN, V. (1984). Teaching independent student behaviors to behaviorally disordered youth. In J. Grosenick, S. Huntze, E. McGinnis, & C. Smith (eds.), *Social/Affective Interventions in Behavior Disorders.* Des Moines: Iowa Department of Public Instruction. [4]

*BROWN, W. (1982). Classroom climate: Possible effects of special needs on the mainstream. *Journal for Special Educators, 19* (2), 20–27. [4]

BRYAN, D. P. AND HERJANIC, B. (1980). Depression and suicide among adolescents and young adults with selective handicapping conditions. *Exceptional Education Quarterly, 1* (2), 57–66. [13]

*BUSCAGLIA, L. (ED.). (1975). *The Disabled and Their Parents: A Counseling Challenge.* Thorofare, NJ: Charles B. Slack. [12]

CANTRELL, R. P., CANTRELL, M. L., HUDDLESTON, C. M., & WOOLRIDGE, R. L. (1969). Contingency contracting with school children. *Journal of Applied Behavior Analysis, 2,* 215–20. [7]

*CARROLL, A. W. (1974). The classroom as an ecosystem. *Focus on Exceptional Children, 6* (4), 1–11. [2, 7]

CAUTELA, J. R. (1977). *Behavioral Analysis Forms for Clinical Intervention.* Champaign, IL: Research Press, Inc. [10]

CEGELKA, P. T., & PHILLIPS, M. W. (1978). Individualized education programming at the secondary level. *Teaching Exceptional Children, 10* (3), 84–87. [13]

CENTER, D. B. (1981). The relationship of behavior problems to developmental deficits in children with behavior disorders. *Behavioral Disorders, 6* (3), 135–38. [11]

CHENEY, C., & MORSE, W. C. (1972). Psychodynamic interventions in emotional disturbance. In W.C. Rhodes and M.L. Tracy (eds.), *A Study of Child Variance, Vol. II: Interventions.* Ann Arbor: University of Michigan Press. [9]

CHETKOW, B. H. (1964). Discipline problems in camp. *Recreation, 57* (3), 136–37. [8]

*CHINN, P. C. (1979). The exceptional minority child: Issues and some answers. *Exceptional Children, 45* (7), 532–36. [12]

CHINN, P. C., WINN, J., & WALTERS, R. H. (1978). *Two-Way Talking with Parents of Special Children: A Process of Positive Communication.* St. Louis: C. V. Mosby. [12]

CHRISTIE, L. S., MCKENZIE, H. S., & BURDETT, C. S. (1972). The consulting teacher approach to special education: Inservice training for regular classroom teachers. *Focus on Exceptional Children, 4* (5), 1–12. [4]

CIANCIOLO, P. J. (1965). Children's literature can affect coping behavior. *Personnel and Guidance Journal, 43* (9), 897–903. [9]

CLARIZIO, H. F., & MCCOY, G. F. (1976). *Behavior Disorders in Children* (2nd ed.). New York: T. Y. Crowell, Inc. [1, 3, 10]

CLARIZIO, H. F. & YELON, S. L. 1976). Learning theory approaches to classroom management: Rationale and intervention techniques. *Journal of Special Education, 1,* 267–74. [10]

CLARK, G. (1980). Career preparation for handicapped adolescents: A matter of appropriate education. *Exceptional Education Quarterly, 1* (2), 11–18. [13]

CLEMENTS, D. H. (1985). *Computers in Early and Primary Education.* Englewood Cliffs, NJ: Prentice-Hall. [6]

CLEMENTS, J. E., & ALEXANDER, R. N. (1975). Parent-training: Bringing it all back home. *Focus on Exceptional Children, 7* (5), 1–12. [12]

COHEN, R., POLSGROVE, L., RIETH, H., & HEINEN, J. (1981). The effects of self-monitoring, public graphing, and token reinforcement on the social behaviors of underachieving children. *Education and Treatment of Children, 4* (2), 125–38. [3]

COHEN, S. B., ALBERTO, P. A., & TROUTMAN, A. (1979). Selecting and developing educational materials: An inquiry model. *Teaching Exceptional Children, 12* (1), 7–11. [6]

COMBS, A. W., AVILA, A. D., & PURKEY, W. W. (1978). *Helping Relationships: Basic Concepts for the Helping Professions* (2nd ed.). Boston: Allyn & Bacon. [7]

CONNOR, E. M., & MULDOON, J. F. (1967). Resource programming for emotionally disturbed teenagers. *Exceptional Children, 33,* 261–65. [13]

CONOLEY, J. C., APTER, S. J., & CONOLEY, C. W. (1981). Teacher consultation and the resource teacher: Increasing services to seriously disturbed children. In F. H. Wood (ed.), *Perspectives for a New Decade: Education's Responsibility for Seriously Disturbed and*

Behaviorally Disordered Children and Youth. Reston, VA: Council for Exceptional Children. [4]

Cook, J. H. (1972). *The Effects of Small Group Counseling on the Classroom Behavior of Sociometrically Underchosen Adolescents.* Unpublished doctoral dissertation, University of Georgia. [9]

Cook, P. S., & Woodhill, J. M. (1976). The Feingold dietary treatment of the hyperkinetic syndrome. *Medical Journal of Australia, 2,* 85–89. [11]

Cooke, S., & Cooke, T. (1974). Parent training for early education of the handicapped. *Reading Improvement, 11* (3), 62–64. [12]

Cory, C. T. (1974). Two generations of volunteers: Parents. *Learning. 3* (2), 76–79. [12]

Cosper, M. R., & Erickson, M. T. (1984). Relationships among observed classroom behavior and three types of teacher ratings. *Behavioral Disorders, 9* (3), 189–94. [3]

*Council for Exceptional Children Delegate Assembly (1983). Code of ethics and standards for professional practice. *Exceptional Children, 50* (3), 8–12.

Courtnage, L., Stainback, W., & Stainback, S. (1982). Managing prescription drugs in school. *Teaching Exceptional Children, 15* (1) 5–10. [11]

Creekmore, N. N., & Maden, A. J. (1981). The use of sociodrama as a therapeutic technique with behavior disordered children. *Behavior Disorders, 7* (1), 28–33. [9]

Croft, D. J. (1979). *Parents and Teachers: A Resource Handbook for Home, School, and Community Relations.* Belmont, CA: Wadsworth. [12]

Cruickshank, W. (1967). *the Brain-Injured Child in Home, School, and Community.* Syracuse, NY: Syracuse University Press. [7]

Cruickshank, W., Bentzen, R. F., Ratzeburg, F., & Tannhauser, M. (1961). *A Teaching Method for Brain-Injured and Hyperactive Children.* Syracuse, NY: Syracuse University Press. [7]

*Cullinan, D., & Epstein, M. H. (1982). Administrative definitions of behavior disorders: Status and directions. In F. H. Wood and K. C. Lakin (eds.), *Disturbing, Disordered or Disturbed? Perspectives on the Definition of Problem Behavior in Educational Settings.* Reston, VA: Council for Exceptional Children. [1]

Cullinan, D., Epstein, M. H., & Kauffman, J. (1984). Teacher's ratings of students' behaviors: What constitutes behavior disorders in school? *Behavioral Disorders, 10* (1), 9–19. [2]

Curran, T. J., & Algozzine, B. (1980). Ecological disturbance: A test of the matching hypothesis. *Behavioral Disorders, 5,* 169–74. [2]

D'Alonzo, B. (1974). Puppets fill the classroom with imagination. *Teaching Exceptional Children, 6* (3), 141–44. [9]

David, D., & Newcomer, P. L. (1980). Art and music therapy. In P. L. Newcomer, *Understanding and Teaching Emotionally Disturbed Children.* Boston: Allyn & Bacon, 391–408. [9]

Deffenbacher, J. & Kemper, C. (1974). Systematic desensitization of test anxiety in junior high students. *The School Counselor, 21,* 216–22. [10]

Dehouske, E. J. (1982). Story writing as a problem solving vehicle. *Teaching Exceptional Children, 15* (1), 11–17. [9]

Delacato, C. (1966). *Neurological Organization and Reading.* Springfield, IL: Charles C. Thomas. [1]

DeMagistris, R. J., & Imber, S. C. (1980). The effects of life space interviewing on the academic and social performance of behavior disordered children. *Behavior Disorders, 6* (1), 12–25. [9]

Deno, E. (1970). Special education as developmental capital. *Exceptional Children, 37* (3), 229–37. [4]

Deno, S. L., Mirkin, P. K., & Wesson, C. (1984). How to write effective data-based IEP's. *Teaching Exceptional Children, 16* (2), 99–105. [5]

DESCHLER, D. D., & GRAHAM, S. (1980). Tape recording education materials for secondary handicapped students. *Teaching Exceptional Children, 12* (2), 52–54. [6]

DEXTER, B. (1980). Classroom forum. *Focus on Exceptional Children, 12* (8), 11–12. [6]

Diagnostic and Statistical Manual of Mental Disorders (3rd ed.). (1980). Washington, D.C.: American Psychiatric Association. [1]

DICKERSON, D., SPELLMAN, C. R., LARSEN, S., & TYLER, L. (1973). Let the cards do the talking—A teacher-parent communication program. *Teaching Exceptional Children, 4* (4), 170–78. [12]

DINKMEYER, D., & McKAY, G. D. (1976). *Systematic Training for Effective Parenting: Leader's Manual.* Circle Pines, MN: American Guidance Service. [12]

*DONNELLAN, A. M. (1984). The criterion of the least dangerous assumption. *Behavioral Disorders, 9* (2), 141–150. [4, 5, 6]

DOUGLAS, H. R. (1969). An effective junior high school program for reducing the number of dropouts. *Contemporary Education, 41,* 34–37. [13]

DOWNING, C. J. (1974). Worry workshop for parents. *Elementary School Guidance and Counseling, 9* (2), 124–31. [12]

DREIKURS, R., & CASSEL, P. (1972). *Discipline Without Tears.* New York: Hawthorn Books. [8]

DREIKURS, R., & GREY, L. (1968). *Logical Consequences: A New Approach To Discipline.* New York: Hawthorn Books. [8]

DUERKSEN, G. L. (1981). Music for exceptional students. *Focus on Exceptional Children, 14* (4), 1–11. [9]

DUNSING, J., & KEPHART, N. (1965). Motor generalization in space and time. In J. Hellmuth (ed.), *Learning Disorders* (Vol. 1). Seattle, WA: Special Child Publications. [1]

EDELBROCK, C. (1984). Developmental considerations. In T.H. Ollendick & M. Hersen (eds.), *Child Behavioral Assessment: Principles and Procedures,* New York: Pergamon Press, 20–37. [1]

EDLUND, C. V. (1969). Rewards at home to promote desirable school behavior. *Teaching Exceptional Children, 1* (4), 121–27. [12]

*EDMISTER, P. (1977). Establishing a parent resource center. *Childhood Education, 54* (Nov.–Dec.), 62–66. [12]

EDWARDS, L. L. (1980). Curriculum modification as a strategy for helping regular classroom behavior disordered students. *Focus on Exceptional Children, 12* (8), 1–11. [5]

ELIAS, M. J. (1979). Helping emotionally disturbed children through prosocial television. *Exceptional Children, 46* (3), 217–18. [11]

ELMAN, N. M., & GINSBERG, J. (1981). *The Resource Room Primer.* Englewood Cliffs, NJ: Prentice-Hall. [4]

*ENGELMAN, S. (1982). Dear Ziggy. *Direct Instruction News, 1* (3), 9.[6]

*ENGLAND, D. W. (1977). Hearing from the teacher when nothing is wrong. *English Journal, 66* (6), 42–45. [12]

*ENGLERT, C. S. (1984). Measuring teacher effectiveness from the teacher's point of view. *Focus on Exceptional Children, 17* (2), 1–14. [6]

EPANCHIN, B. C., & MONSON, L. B. (1982). Affective education. In J. L. Paul & B. C. Epanchin (eds.), *Emotional Disturbance in Children: Theories and Methods for Teachers.* Columbus, OH: Charles E. Merrill Publishing Co. [9]

*EPSTEIN, M. H., CULLINAN, D., & ROSEMIER, R. A. (1983). Behavior problems of behaviorally disordered and normal adolescents. *Behavioral Disorders, 8* (3), 171–75. [13]

EPSTEIN, M. H., CULLINAN, D., & SABATINO, D. (1977). State definitions of behavior disorders. *Journal of Special Education, 11,* 417–25. [1]

ESKEY, M., & HAUSER, S. (1984). *Pals (Personal Adjustment Level System).* Hinsdale, IL: Hinsdale South High School. [13]

FABRY, B. D., & CONE, J. D. (1980). Autographing: A one-step approach to collecting and graphing data. *Education and Treatment of Children, 3,* 361–68. [5]

*FAGEN, S. A., & LONG, N. J. (1976). Teaching children self-control: A new responsibility for teachers. *Focus on Exceptional Children, 7* (8), 1–10. [9]

*FAGEN, S. A., LONG, N. J., & STEVENS, D. J. (1975). *Teaching Children Self-Control: Preventing Emotional and Learning Problems in the Elementary School.* Columbus, OH: Charles E. Merrill. [9]

FALVEY, M., FERRARA-PARRISH, P., JOHNSON, F., PUMPIAN, I., SCHROEDER, J., & BROWN, L. (1979). Curricular strategies for generating comprehensive, longitudinal and chronological age-appropriate functional individual vocational plans for severely handicapped adolescents and young adults. In L. Brown, M. Falvey, D. Baumgart, I. Pumpian, J. Schroeder, and L. Gruenewald (eds.), *Strategies for Teaching Chronological Age-Appropriate Functional Skills to Adolescent and Young Adult Severely Handicapped Students* (Vol. 9, part 1). Madison, WI: Madison Metropolitan School District. [5]

FEDDERSON, J., JR. (1972). Establishing an effective parent-teacher communication system. *Childhood Education, 49* (2), 75–80. [12]

Federal Register. (AUGUST 23, 1977). *42* (163), 42, 478. [1, 3, 4, 13]

Federal Register. (JANUARY 19, 1981). *46* (12), 5460–5474. [3]

FELDMAN, D., KINNISON, L., JAY, R., & HARTH, R. (1983). The effects of differential labeling on professional concepts and attitudes towards the emotionally disturbed/behaviorally disordered. *Behavioral Disorders, 8* (3), 191–97. [1]

FEINGOLD, B. F. (1973). Food additives and child development. *Hospital Practice, 8,* 11. [11]

FEINGOLD, B. F. (1975). *Why Your Child is Hyperactive.* New York: Random House. [11]

FENTON, K. S., YOSHIDA, R. K., MAXWELL, J. P., & KAUFMAN, M. J. (1979). Recognition of team goals: An essential step toward rational decision making. *Exceptional Children, 45,* 638–44. [4]

FEROLO, M., ROTATORI, A. F., & FOX, R. (1984). Increasing visual attention by music therapy programming for sensory stimulation with profoundly retarded children. *ICEC Quarterly, 33* (2), 17–21. [9]

FEROLO, M. A., ROTATORI, A., MACKLIN, F., & FOX, R. (1983). The successful use of behavior modification in music therapy with severely/profoundly retarded people. *ICEC Quarterly, 3* (2), 30–34. [9]

*FEUERSTEIN, R. (1980). *Instrumental Enrichment.* Baltimore: University Park Press. [7]

FINCH, A. J., DEARDORFF, P. A., & MONTGOMERY, L. E. (1974). Individually tailored behavioral rating scales: A possible alternative. *Journal of Abnormal Child Psychology, 2,* 209–17. [3]

FINCH, A. J., & MONTGOMERY, L. E. (1973). Reflection impulsivity and information seeking in emotionally disturbed children. *Journal of Abnormal Child Psychology, 1,* 358–62. [1]

*FITZGERALD, G. E. (1982). Practical approaches for documenting behavioral progress of behaviorally disordered students. Monograph #6. Des Moines, IA: Drake University. [5]

FLORIDA DEPARTMENT OF EDUCATION. (1979a). *A Resource Manual for the Development and Evaluation of Special Programs for Exceptional Students.* Vol. II-E: *Emotionally Handicapped.* Tallahassee: Florida Department of Education. [3]

FLORIDA DEPARTMENT OF EDUCATION. (1979b). *State Board of Education Rule 6A-6.3016.* Tallahassee, Florida. [1, 3]

FORNESS, S. R. (1981). Concepts of learning and behavior disorders: Implications for research and practice. *Exceptional Children, 48,* 56–64. [2, 7]

FORNESS, S. R., & CANTWELL, D. P. (1982). *DSM III:* Psychiatric diagnoses and special education categories. *Journal of Special Education, 16,* 49–65. [1]

FRANCESCANI, C. (1982). MARC: An affective curriculum for emotionally disturbed adolescents. *Teaching Exceptional Children, 14* (6), 217–22. [13]

FREUD, S. (1933). *New Introductory Lectures on Psychoanalysis.* New York: W. W. Norton & Co., Inc. [1]

FREUD, S. (1949). *An Outline of Psychoanalysis.* New York: W. W. Norton & Co., Inc. [1]

*FRITH, G. H. (1981). "Advocate" vs. "Professional employee": A question of priorities for special educators. *Exceptional Children, 47* (7), 486–92. [4]

FROSTIG, M. (1968). *Education for Children with Learning Disabilities* (Vol. 1). New York: Grune & Stratton. [1]

GADOW, K. (1979). *Children on Medication: A Primer for School Personnel.* Reston, VA: Council for Exceptional Children. [11]

GALLAGHER, P. A. (1979). *Teaching Students with Behavior Disorders; Techniques for Classroom Instruction.* Denver: Love. [4, 6, 11]

GARDNER, W. I. (1974). *Children with Learning and Behavior Problems: A Behavior Management Approach.* Boston: Allyn & Bacon. [12]

GARDNER, W. I. (1978). *Children with Learning and Behavior Problems.* Boston: Allyn & Bacon. [10, 12]

*GATLIN, H. (1980). Dialectics and family interaction. *Human Development, 23* 245–53. [2]

GEARHEART, B. R. (1977). *Learning Disabilities: Educational Strategies* (2nd ed.). St. Louis: C. V. Mosby. [7]

GETMAN, G. N. (1963). *The Physiology of Readiness Experiment.* Minneapolis, MN: Programs to Accelerate School Success. [1]

GILBERT, G. M. (1957). A survey of "referral problems" in metropolitan child guidance centers. *Journal of Clinical Psychology, 13,* 37–42. [1]

GILHOOL, T. K. (1973). Education: An unalienable right. *Exceptional Children, 39* 597–609. [1]

GILLESPIE, E. B., & TURNBULL, A. P. (1983). It's my IEP! Involving students in the planning process. *Teaching Exceptional Children, 16* (1), 26–29 [12]

GINOTT, H. (1959). The theory and practice of therapeutic intervention in child treatment. *Journal of Consulting Psychology, 23,* 160–66 [9]

GLASSER, W. (1965). *Reality Therapy: A New Approach to Psychiatry.* New York: Harper & Row. [1, 9]

GLASSER, W. (1969). *Schools Without Failure.* New York: Harper & Row. [9]

GLICK, B. H. (1968). *The Investigation of Changes in Self-Concept, Social Self-Esteem and Academic Self-Responsibility of Emotionally Disturbed Boys who Participate in Open-Ended Classroom Meetings.* Unpublished doctoral dissertation, Syracuse University. [9]

GOOD, T. L. (1983). Classroom research: A decade of progress. *Educational Psychologist, 18,* 127–44. [6]

GOODMAN, L. (1978). Meeting children's needs through materials modification. *Teaching Exceptional Children, 10* (3), 92–94. [6]

GRANWOSKY, A., ET AL. (1977). How to put parents on your classroom team. *Instructor, 87* (4), 54–62. [12]

GREER, J. V. (1978). Utilizing paraprofessionals and volunteers in special education. *Focus on Exceptional Children, 10* (8), 1–15. [6, 12]

*GROSENICK, J. K., & HUNTZE, S. L. (1979). *National Needs Analysis in Behavior Disorders: A Model for a Comprehensive Needs Analysis in Behavior Disorders.* Columbia, MO: Department of Special Education, University of Missouri. [1]

*GROSENICK, J. K., & HUNTZE, S. L. (1980). *National Needs Analysis in Behavior Disorders: Adolescent Behavior Disorders.* Columbia, MO: Special Education Department, University of Missouri. [13]

GROSENICK, J. K., HUNTZE, S. L., KOCHAN, B., PETERSON, R. L., ROBERTSHAW, C. S., & WOOD, F. (1982). *National Needs Analysis in Behavior Disorders Working Paper: Psychotherapy as a Related Service.* Columbia, MO: Department of Special Education, University of Missouri. [4]

GROSS, A. M. (1984). Behavioral interviewing. In T. H. Ollendick & M. Hersen (eds.), *Child Behavioral Assessment: Principles and Procedures.* New York: Pergamon Press. [3]

GRUMLEY, L. (1984). *Day Treatment Program Agreement.* Jeffersonville, IN: Clark County Special Education Cooperative. [8]

*GUESS, D., HORNER, D., UTLEY, B., HOLVOET, J., MAXON, D., TUCKER, D., & WARREN, S. (1978). A functional curriculum sequencing model for teaching the severely handicapped. *AAESPH Review, 3,* 202–15. [5]

*GUESS, D., & NOONAN, M. J. (1982). Curricula and instructional procedures for severely handicapped students. *Focus on Exceptional Children, 14* (5), 1–12. [5]

GUETZLOE, E., & CLINE, R. (1981). Adolescents with severe behavior disorders in the regular secondary school. In F. H. Wood (ed.), *Perspective for a New Decade: Education's Responsibility for Seriously Disturbed and Behaviorally Disordered Children and Youth.* Reston, VA: CEC. [13]

HALL, R. J. (1980). Cognitive behavior modification and information-processing skills of exceptional children. *Exceptional Education Quarterly, 1,* 8–15. [10]

HALLAHAN, D., & KAUFFMAN, J. (1982). *Exceptional Children.* Englewood Cliffs, NJ: Prentice-Hall. [2]

*HARDIN, V. B. (1982). Ecological assessment and intervention for learning disabled students. *Learning Disabilities Quarterly, 1* (2), 15–20. [7, 11]

HARING, N. G., LIBERTY, K. A., & WHITE, O. R. (1980). Rules for data-based strategy decisions in instructional programs: current research and instructional implications. In W. Sailor, B. Wilcox, and L. Brown (eds.), *Methods of Instruction for Severely Handicapped Students.* Baltimore: Paul H. Brookes. [5]

*HARING, N. G., & PHILLIPS, E. L. (1962). *Educating Emotionally Disturbed Children.* New York: McGraw-Hill. [7]

HARRIS, K. R. (1982). Cognitive behavior modification: Application with exceptional children. *Focus on Exceptional Children, 15* 1–16. [10]

HARTH, R. (1982) The Feuerstein perspective on the modification of cognitive performance. *Focus on Exceptional Children, 15* (3), 1–12. [7]

HARTH, R., & GLAVIN, J. P. (1971). Validity of teacher rating as a sub-test for screening emotionally disturbed children. *Exceptional Children, 37* (8), 605–6. [3]

HARTH, R., & MORRIS, S. M. (1976). Group processes for behavior change. *Teaching Exceptional Children, 8* (4), 136–39. [11]

HAWES, R. M. (1970). *Reality Therapy in the Classroom.* Unpublished doctoral dissertation, University of the Pacific. [9]

HAYNES, S. N., & WILSON, C. C. (1979). *Behavioral Assessment.* San Francisco: Jossey-Bass. [3]

HELLER, H. W. (1981). Secondary education for handicapped students: In search of a solution. *Exceptional Children, 47* (8), 582–83. [13]

HELTON, G. B. (1984). Guidelines for assessment in special education. *Focus on Exceptional Children, 16* (9), 1–16. [3]

*HERON, T. E., & CATERA, R. (1980). Teacher consultation: A functional approach. *School Psychology Review, 9,* 283–89. [4]

HEWETT, F. M. (1968). *The Emotionally Disturbed Child in the Classroom: A Developmental Strategy for Educating Children with Maladaptive Behaviors.* Boston: Allyn & Bacon. [1, 11]

HEWETT, F. M., & FORNESS, S. R. (1984). *Education of Exceptional Learners.* Boston: Allyn & Bacon. [11]

HEWETT, F. M., & TAYLOR, F. D. (1980). *The Emotionally Disturbed Child in the Classroom: The Orchestration of Success.* Boston: Allyn & Bacon. [1, 11]

HIBBEN, J., & SCHEER, R. (1982). Music and movement for special needs children. *Teaching Exceptional Children, 14* (5), 171–76. [9]

*HICKS, J. (1977). Parent's Day. *Early Years, 8* (2) 53–54.

HILDRETH, G. (1928). A survey of problem pupils. *Journal of Educational Research, 19,* 1–14. [1]

*HIRSHOREN, A., & HELLER, O. (1979). Programs for adolescents with behavior disorders. The state of the art. *Journal of Special Education. 13,* 275–81. [13]

HOAGLAND, J. (1972). Bibliotherapy: Aiding children in personality development. *Elementary English, 15,* 390–94. [9]

HOBBS, N. (1964). Mental health's third revolution. *American Journal of Orthopsychiatry, 34,* 822–33. [11]

HOBBS, N. (1966). Helping disturbed children: Psychological and ecological strategies. *American Psychologist, 21* (12), 1105–15. [1, 2, 11]

HOFF, L. E. (1978). *People in Crisis.* Menlo Park, CA: Addison Wesley. [12]

HOLLAND, R. (1970). An analysis of the decision making process in special education. *Exceptional Children, 46* (7), 551–54. [3, 4]

*HOLVOET, J., GUESS, D., MULLIGAN, M., & BROWN, F. (1980). The individualized curriculum sequencing model (II): A teaching strategy for severely handicapped students. *Journal of the Association for the Severely Handicapped, 5,* 325–36. [5]

*HOMME, L., CSANYI, A. P., GONZALES, M. A., & RECHS, J. R. (1970). *How to Use Contingency Contracting in the Classroom.* Champaign, IL: Research Press. [7, 10]

HOPS, H., & LEWIN, L. (1984). Peer sociometric forms. In T. H. Ollendick & M. Hersen (eds.), *Child Behavioral Assessment: Principles and Procedures.* New York: Pergamon Press. [3]

HOYT, K.·B. (1977). *A primer for Career Education.* Washington, D.C.: U. S. Government Printing Office. [13]

HUNTZE, S. L., & GROSENICK, J. K. (1980). *National Needs Analysis in Behavior Disorders: Human Resource Issues in Behavior Disorders.* Columbia, MO: Department of Special Education, University of Missouri. [1, 4]

*HYMES, J. L., JR. (1974). *Effective Home School Relations.* Sierra Madre, CA: Southern California Association for the Education of Young Children. [12]

*JACOBSON, I. (1974) A plan for open house. *The Pointer, 19* (1), 74–75. [12]

JOHNSON, L. V., & BANY, M. A. (1970). *Classroom Management: Theory and Skill Training.* New York: Macmillan. [8]

JOHNSON, S., WAHL, G., MARTIN, S. & JOHANSSON, S. (1973). How deviant is the normal child: A behavioral analysis of the preschool child and his family. *Advances in Behavior Therapy, 4,* 37–54. [1]

JOINT COMMISSION ON MENTAL HEALTH OF CHILDREN. (1969). *Crisis in Child Mental Health.* New York: Harper & Row. [1]

*JOYCE, B., & WEIL, M. (1980). *Models of Teaching.* Englewood Cliffs, NJ: Prentice Hall. [7]

KAMEYA, L. I. (1972). Behavioral interventions in emotional disturbance. In W. C. Rhodes and M. I. Tracy (eds.), A *Study of Child Variance.* Vol. II: *Interventions.* Ann Arbor: University of Michigan Press, 195–252. [1, 11]

*KAPLAN, P. G., & HOFFMAN, A. G. (1981). *It's Positively Groovy.* Denver: Love. [12]

*KAPLAN, P. G., KOHFELDT, J., & STURLA, K. (1974). *It's Positively Fun: Techniques for Managing Learning Environments.* Denver: Love. [12]

*KARNES, M. B., & FRANKE, B. (1978). *Family Involvement.* Urbana, IL: Institution for Child Behavior and Development, University of Illinois. [12]

*KARNES, M. B., & ZEHRBACH, R. (1972). Flexibility in getting parents involved in the school. *Teaching Exceptional Children, 5* [1], 6–19 [12]

*KARRAKER, R. J. (1972). Increasing academic performance through home-managed contingency programs. *Journal of School Psychology, 10,* 173–79. [7]

KATZ, S., BORFTEN, D., BRASILE, M., MEISNER, M., & PARKER, C. (1980). Helping parents become effective partners: The IEP process. *The Pointer, 25* (1), 35–45. [12]

KAUFMAN, J.M. (1976). Nineteenth century views of children's behavior disorders. *Journal of Special Education, 10,* 335-49. [1]

KAUFFMAN, J. M. (1981). *Characteristics of children's behavior disorders* (2nd ed.). Columbus, OH: Charles C. Merrill. [1]

KAUFFMAN, J. M. (1982). An historical perspective on disordered behavior and an alternative conceptualization of exceptionality. In F. H. Wood and K. C. Lakin (eds.), *Disturbing, disordered or disturbed: Perspectives on the definition of problem behaviors in education settings.* Reston, VA: Council for Exceptional Children. [2, 7]

KAUFFMAN, J. M. (1985). *Characteristics of children's behavior disorders* (3rd ed). Columbus, OH: Charles C. Merrill. [1]

KAUFMAN, A. S., PAGET, K. D. & WOOD, M. M. (1981). Effectiveness of developmental therapy for severely emotionally disturbed children. In F. H. Wood (ed.), *Perspectives for a new decade: Education's responsibility for serious disturbed and behaviorally disordered children and youth.* Reston, VA: Council for Exceptional Children, 176–88. [11]

KAUFMAN, A. S. & REYNOLDS, C. R. (1984). Intellectual and academic assessment. In T. H. Ollendick & M. Herson (eds.), *Child behavioral assessment: Principles and procedures.* New York: Pergamon Press. [3]

KAVALE, K., & HIRSHOREN, A. (1980). Public school and university teacher training programs for behaviorally disordered children: Are they compatible? *Behavioral Disorders, 5* (3), 151–55. [1, 2]

*KEILITZ, L., & MILLER, S. L. (1980). Handicapped adolescents and young adults in the justice system. *Exceptional Education Quarterly, 1* (2), 117–26. [13]

*KELLY, E. J. (1974). *Parent-Teacher Interaction: A Special Educational Perspective.* Seattle: Special Child Publications. [12]

KENDALL, P. C. (1977). On the efficacious use of verbal self-instructional procedures with children. *Cognitive Therapy and Research, 1,* 331–41. [10]

*KERR, M. M., & NELSON, C. M. (1983). *Strategies for Managing Behavior Problems in the Classroom.* Columbus, OH: Charles E. Merrill. [4, 5, 6, 7]

KNAPCZYK, D. R. (1979). Diet control in the management of behavior disorders. *Behavioral Disorders, 5* (1), 2–9. [11]

*KNOBLOCK, P. (1979). Educational alternatives for adolescents labeled emotionally disturbed. In D. Cullinan & M. H. Epstein (eds.), *Special Education for Adolescents.* Columbus, OH: Charles E. Merrill. [13]

KNOBLOCK, P. (1983). *Teaching emotionally disturbed children.* New York: Houghton-Mifflin. [1]

KOHLFELDT, J. (1976). Blueprints for construction: Teacher-made or teacher-adapted materials. *Focus on Exceptional Children, 8,* 1–14. [6]

KOPPITZ, E. M. (1977). Strategies for diagnosis and identification of children with behavior and learning problems. *Behavioral Disorders, 2* (3), 136–40. [3]

*KROTH, R. L. (1972a). Facilitating educational program by improving parent conferences. *Focus on Exceptional Children, 4* (7), 1–9. [12]

KROTH, R. L., (1972b). *Target behavior kit.* Olathe, KA: Select-Ed, Inc. [10]

*KROTH, R. L. (1975). *Communication with parents of exceptional children: Improving parent-teacher relationships.* Denver: Love. [12]

KROTH, R. L. & SIMPSON, R. (1977). *Parent conferences as a teaching strategy.* Denver: Love. [12]

KROTH, R. L., WHELAN, R. J. & STABLES, J. M. (1970). Teacher application of behavior principles in home and classroom environments. *Focus on Exceptional Children, 1* (3), 1–9. [12]

*KURDEK, L. A. (1981). An integrative perspective on children's divorce adjustment. *American Psychologist, 36* (8), 856–66. [2]

LAMBERT, N. M., & BOWER, E. M. (1961a) *A Process for In-School Screening of Children with Emotional Handicaps: Manual for School Administrators and Teachers.* Sacramento: California Department of Education. [1, 3]

LAMBERT, N. M., & BOWER, E. M. (1961b). *A Process for In-School Screening of Children with Emotional Handicaps: Technical Report for School Administrators and Teachers.* Sacramento: California State Department of Education. [3]

*LAMBIE, R. A. (1980). A systematic approach for changing materials, instruction, and assignments to meet individual needs. *Focus on Exceptional Children, 13* (1), 1–16. [6]

LAMENT, M. M. (1978). Reaching the exceptional student through music in the elementary classroom. *Teaching Exceptional Children, 11* (1), 32–35. [9]

LANE, B., BONIC, J., & WALLGREN-BONIC, N. (1983). The group walk-talk: A therapeutic challenge for secondary students with social-emotional problems. *Teaching Exceptional Children, 16* (1), 12–17. [9]

*LARSON, S. C., & POPLIN, M. S. (1980). *Methods for Educating the Handicapped: An Individualized Education Program Approach.* Boston: Allyn & Bacon. [5]

*LEE, B. (1980). Materials developed for parent involvement. Springdale School, Special School District of St. Louis County, Mo. [12]

*LEONE, P. (1984). Descriptive follow-up of behaviorally disordered adolescents. *Behavioral Disorders, 9* (3), 207–14. [1, 9, 13]

LEVINSON, C. (1982). Remediating a passive aggressive emotionally disturbed pre-adolescent boy through writing: A comprehensive psychodynamic structured approach. *The Pointer, 26* (2), 23–27. [9]

LEWELLYN, A. (1980). *The Use of Quiet Rooms and other Time-Out Procedures in Public School.* Mattoon, IL: Eastern Illinois Area Special Education. [10]

*LIDDLE, G. B., ROCKWELL, R. E., AND SACADAT, E. (1967). *Educational Improvement for the Disadvantaged in an Elementary Setting.* Springfield, IL: Charles C. Thomas. [12]

*LILLY, M. S., & GIVENS-OGLE, L. B. (1981). Teacher consultation: Present, past and future. *Behavioral Disorders, 6,* 73–77. [4]

LIPTON, M. A., DiMASCIO, A., & KILLAM, K. (1978). Introduction and historical overview. In M. A. Lipton, A. DiMascio, & K. Killam (eds.), *Psychopharmacology: A Generation of Progress.* New York: Raven Press. [1]

LLOYD, J. (1980). Academic instruction and cognitive behavior modification: The need for attack stategies training. *Exceptional Education Quarterly, 1,* 53–63. [10]

LONG, K. A. (1983). Emotionally disturbed children as an underdetected and underserved public school population: Reasons and recommendations. *Behavioral Disorders, 9* (1), 46–54. [1, 2]

LONG, N. J., MORSE, W. C., & NEWMAN, R. G. (1980). *Conflict In the Classroom (4th ed.).* Belmont, CA: Wadsworth. [3, 9, 11]

*LOVE, H. D. (1970). *Parental Attitudes Toward Exceptional Children.* Springfield, IL: Charles C. Thomas. [12]

*LUND, K. A., SCHNAPS, L., & BIJOU, S. W. (1983). Let's take another look at record keeping. *Teaching Exceptional Children, 15* (3), 155–59. [5]

*LUSTHAUS, C., & LUSTHAUS, E. (1979). When is a child ready for mainstreaming? *The Exceptional Parent, 9* (5), R2–R4. [12]

*LYON, S. & LYON, G. (1980). Team functioning and staff development: A role release approach to providing integrated educational services to severely handicapped students. *Journal of the Association for the Severely Handicapped, 5,* 250–63. [4]

MAES, W. R. (1966). The identification of emotionally disturbed elementary school children. *Exceptional Children, 32,* 697–09. [3]

MANDELL, C. J., & GOLD, V. (1984). *Teaching Handicapped Students.* Minneapolis: West. [3, 6]

*MANLEY, S. C., & LEVY, S. (1981). the IEP organizer: A strategy for turning IEP's into daily lesson plans. *Teaching Exceptional Children, 14* (2), 70–71. [6]

MARCUS, S. D., FOX, D., & BROWN, D. (1982). Identifying school children with behavior disorders. *Community Mental Health Journal, 18* (4), 249–56. [3]

*MARION, R. L. (1981). *Educators, Parents, and Exceptional Children.* Rockville, MD: Aspen Systems Corp. [12]

MARMOR, J., & PUMPIAN-MINDLIN, E. (1950). Toward an integrative conception of mental disorders. *Journal of Nervous and Mental Disease, 3,* 19–29. [2]

MARONEY, S. (1983). Terminology and definitions in the education of emotionally disturbed/ behaviorally disordered students. *1983 Survey of Consultants.* Reston, VA: Council for Children with Behavioral Disorders. [1]

*MARSH, G. E., GEARHEART, C. K., & GEARHEART, B. R. (1978). *The Learning Disabled Adolescent: Program Alternatives in The Secondary School.* St. Louis: C. V. Mosby. [13]

*MASH, E. J. (1979). What is behavioral asssessment? *Behavioral Assessment, 1,* 23–29. [3]

*McCORMICK, L., & GOLDMAN, R. (1979). The transdisciplinary model: Implication for service delivery and personnel preparation for the severely and profoundly handicapped. *AAESPH Review, 4,* 152–61. [4]

McDANIEL, T. (1980). Corporal punishment and teacher liability: Questions teachers ask. *The Clearing House, 54,* 10–13. [10]

*McDowell, R. L. (1976). Parent counseling: The state of the art. *Journal of Learning Disabilities, 9* (10), 614–19. [12]

*McDowell, R. L., & Brown, G. B. (1978). The emotionally disturbed adolescent: Development of program alternatives in secondary education. *Focus on Exceptional Children, 10,* 1–15. [4, 13]

MacFarlane, J., Allen, L. , & Honzik, M. A. (1954). *A Developmental Study of the Behavior Problems of Normal Children Between Twenty-one Months and Fourteen Years.* Berkeley: University of California Press. [1]

*McGinnis, E. (1984). Teaching social skills to behaviorally disordered youth. In J. Grosenick, S. Huntze, E. McGinnis, & C. Smith (eds.), *Social/Affective Interventions in Behavior Disorders.* Des Moines: Iowa Department of Public Instruction. [13]

*McGinnis, E., Kiraly, J., & Smith, C. R. (1984). The types of data used in identifying public school students as behaviorally disordered. *Behavioral Disorders, 9* (4), 239–46. [1, 3]

McMahon, R. J. (1984). Behavioral checklists and rating scales. In T. H. Ollendick & M. Hersen (eds.), *Child Behavioral Assessment: Principles and Procedures.* New York: Pergamon Press. [3]

*MacMillan, D. L., and Turnbull, A. P. (1983). Parent involvement with special education: Respecting individual differences. *Education and Training of the Mentally Retarded, 18,* 4–9. [12]

Meichenbaum, D. (1980). Cognitive behavior modification: A promise yet unfulfilled. *Exceptional Education Quarterly, 1,* 83–88. [10]

Michel, D. E. (1976) *Music Therapy: An Introduction to Therapy and Special Education Through Music.* Springfield, IL: Charles C. Thomas. [9]

Millichap, J. G. (1975). *The Hyperactive Child with Minimal Brain Dysfunction.* Chicago: Yearbook Medical Publishers, Inc. [11]

Minner, S. (1981). Using photography as an adjunctive and creative approach. *Teaching Exceptional Children, 13* (4), 145–47. [9]

*Minner, S., Knutson, R., & Minner, J. (1981). Involving regular teachers in IEP meetings. *The Pointer, 25* (8), 19–21. [4]

*Montgomery, M. D. (1978). The special educator as consultant: Some strategies. *Teaching Exceptional Children, 10,* 110–12. [4]

Moreno, J. L. (1946). *Psychodrama.* Beacon, NY: Beacon House. [9]

Morgan, D. I. (1979). Prevalence and type of handicapping conditions found in juvenile correctional institutions: A national survey. *Journal of Special Education, 13,* 283–95.

Morris, S. M. (1982). A classroom process for behavior change. *The Pointer, 26* (3), 25–28. [11]

*Morrison, G. S. (1978). *Parent Involvement in the Home, School, and Community.* Columbus, OH: Charles E. Merrill. [12]

Morrow, L. W., & Presswood, S. (1984) The effects of a self-control technique on eliminating stereotypic behavior in a multiply-handicapped institutionalized adolescent. *Behavioral Disorders, 9* (4), 247–53. [1]

Morse, W. C. (1965). The crisis teacher. In N. Long, W. C. Morse, and R. Newman (eds.), *Conflict in the Classroom* (1st ed.). Belmont, CA: Wadsworth. [1]

*Morse, W. C. (1976). The helping teacher/crisis teacher concept. *Focus on Exceptional Children, 8* (4), 1–11. [4]

Morse, W. C. (1979). Self-control: The Fagen-Long curriculum. *Behavioral Disorders, 4,* 83–91, [9]

Morse, W. C. (1980). Worksheet in life space interviewing. In N. J. Long, W. C. Morse, & R. G. Newman (eds.), *Conflict in the Classroom (4th ed.).* Belmont, CA: Wadsworth. [9]

Morse, W. C., Cutler, R. L., & Fink, A. H. (1964). *Public School Classes for the Emotionally Handicapped: A Research Analysis.* Reston, VA: Council for Exceptional Children. [1, 7]

*Mour, S. (1977). Teacher behaviors and ecological balance. *Behavioral Disorders, 3* (1), 55–58. [2]

MOUSTAKAS, C. E. (1953). *Children in Play Therapy.* New York: McGraw-Hill. [9]

MUNROE, R. L. (1955). *Schools of Psychoanalytic Thought: An Exposition, Critique, and Attempt at Integration.* New York: Holt, Rinehart, and Winston.[1]

NECCO, E., WILSON, C., & SCHEIDMANTEL, J. (1982). Affective learning through drama. *Teaching Exceptional Children, 15* (1), 22–24. [9]

NEEL, R. S. (1984). Teaching social routines to behaviorally disordered youth. In J. Grosenick, S. Huntze, E. McGinnis, & C. Smith (eds.), *Social/Affective Interventions in Behavior Disorders.* Des Moines: Iowa Department of Public Instruction. [8]

NEISWORTH, J. T., DENO, S. L., & JENKINS, J. R. (1969). *Student Motivation and Classroom Management: A Behavioristic Approach.* Newark, DE: Behavior Technics. [10]

NELSON, C. M., & GREENOUGH, K. N. (1983). The case for noncategorical educational programming for behaviorally disordered children and youth. In J. Grosenick, S. Huntze, & C. R. Smith (eds.), *Noncategorical VS. Categorical Issues in Programming for Behaviorally Disordered Children and Youth.* Columbia, MO: University of Missouri. [3]

*NELSON, C. M., & STEVENS, K. B. (1981). An accountable consultation model for mainstreaming behaviorally disordered children. *Behavioral Disorders, 7,* 82–92. [4]

NELSON, R. O., & HAYES, S. C. (1979). Some current dimensions of behavioral assessment. *Behavioral Assessment, 1,* 1–16. [3]

NEWCOMER, P. L. (1980). *Understanding and Teaching Emotionally Disturbed Children.* Boston: Allyn & Bacon. [9]

*NEWMAN, R. (1982). A primer on subgroups. *The Pointer, 26* (3), 16–24. [8]

NICHOLS, P. (1984). Down the up staircase: The teacher as therapist. In J. Grosenick, S. Huntze, E. McGinnis, and C. Smith (eds.), *Social/Affective Interventions in Behavioral Disorders.* Des Moines: State of Iowa Department of Public Instruction. [9]

NIRJE, B. (1967). The normalization principle and its human management inplications. In R. Kugel and W. Wolfensberger (eds.), *Changing Patterns in Residential Services for the Mentally Retarded.* Washington, D.C.: President's Committee on Mental Retardation. [11]

*NOIE, D. (1983). Occupational and physical therapy as related services. *Teaching Exceptional Children, 15* (2), 105–7. [4]

OLLENDICK, T. H., & HERSEN, M. (1984). An overview of child behavioral assessment. In T. H. Ollendick & M. Hersen (eds.), *Child Behavioral Assessment: Principles and Procedures.* New York: Pergamon Press. [3]

OLSON, J., ALGOZZINE, B., & SCHMID, R. E. (1980). Mild, moderate, and severe behavioral handicaps: An empty distinction? *Behavioral Disorders, 5,* 96–101. [1]

PACQUIN, M. (1978). The effects of pupil self-graphing on academic performance. *Education and Treatment of Children, 1 (2), 5–16. [3]*

*PANTIEL, M., & PETERSEN, B. (1984). *Kids, Teachers, and Computers.* Englewood Cliffs: Prentice-Hall. [6]

PARSONS, T. (1951). *The Social System.* New York: The Free Press. [1]

PAUL, J. L., & EPANCHIN, B. C. (1982). *Emotional Disturbance in Children.* Columbus, OH: Charles E. Merrill. [1, 2, 3, 4]

PETER, L. J. (1965). *Prescriptive Teaching.* New York: McGraw-Hill. [9]

PETERSON, D. R. (1961). Behavior problems of middle childhood. *Journal of Consulting Psychology, 25,* 205–209. [2]

PETERSON, D. R. (1964). An empirical approach to the classification of disturbed children. *Journal of Clinical Psychology, 29,* 326–37. [2]

PETERSON, D. R., BECKER, W. C., SHOEMAKER, D. J., LURIA, Z., & HELLMER, L. A. (1961). Child behavior problems and parental attitudes. *Child Development, 32,* 151–62. [2]

PETERSON, D. R., QUAY, H. C., & CAMERSON, G. R. (1959). Personality and background factors in juvenile delinquency as inferred from questionnaire responses. *Journal of Consulting Psychology, 23,* 395–99. [2]

*POPLIN, M. S. (1979). The science of curriculum development applied to special education and the IEP. *Focus on Exceptional Children, 11,* 1–16. [5]

*POWELL, T. H. (1980). Improving home-school communication: sharing daily reports. *The Exceptional Parent, 10* (5), S24–S26. [12]

POWELL, T. H., & POWELL, I. Q. (1982). Guidelines for implementing timeout procedures. *The Pointer, 26,* 18–21. [10]

PREMACK, D. (1959). Reinforcement theory. In D. LeVine (ed.), *Nebraska Symposium on Motivation: 1965.* Lincoln: University of Nebraska Press. [10]

*PRESCOTT, M. R., & ISELIN, K. L. W. (1978). Counseling parents of a disabled child. *Elementary School Guidance and Counseling, 12,* 170–77. [12]

*PRIETO, A. G., & RUTHERFORD, R. B. (1977). An ecological assessment technique for behaviorally disordered and learning disabled children. *Behavioral Disorders, 2* (3), 169–75. [3]

PUGACH, M. C. (1982). Regular classroom teacher involvement in the development and utilization of IEP's. *Exceptional Children, 48,* 371–74. [3]

*PURKEY, W. W., & NOVAK, J. M. (1984). *Inviting School Success.* Belmont, CA: Wadsworth. [7]

PURVIS, J. & SAMET, S. (1976). *Music in developmental therapy.* Baltimore: University Park Press. [9, 11]

QUAY, H. C. (1964). Dimensions of personality in delinquent boys as inferred from the factor analysis of case history data. *Child Development, 35,* 479–84. [2]

QUAY, H. C. (1966). Personality patterns in preadolescent delinquent boys. *Educational and Psychological Measurement, 26,* 99–110. [2]

QUAY, H. C. (1975). Classification in the treatment of delinquency and antisocial behavior. In N. Hobbs (ed.), *Issues in the classification of children (Vol. 1).* San Francisco: Jossey-Bass.

QUAY, H. C. (1977). Measuring dimensions of deviant behavior: The behavior problem checklist. *Journal of Abnormal Child Psychology, 5,* 277–87. [2, 3]

QUAY, H. C. (1978). Behavior disorders in the classroom. *Journal of Research and Development in Education, 11,* 8–17. [1, 2]

QUAY, H. C. (1979). Classification. In H. C. Quay & J. S. Werry (eds.), *Psychopathological disorders of childhood* (2nd ed.). New York: Wiley. [2]

RASCHKE, D. (1979). The relationship of internal-external control and operant reinforcement procedures with learning and behavior disordered children. Unpublished doctoral dissertation, University of Wisconsin. [10]

RASCHKE, D. (1981). Designing reinforcement surveys—let the students choose the reward. *Teaching Exceptional Children, 14,* 92–96. [10]

RATHS, L. E., HARMIN, M., & SIMON, S. B. (1966). *Values and Teaching.* Columbus, OH: Charles E. Merrill. [9]

*REDL, F. (1959). The concept of the life space interview. *American Journal of Orthopsychiatry, 29* 1–18. [9, 11]

REDL, F. (1965). Foreword. In N. J. Long, W. C. Morse, and R. G. Newman (eds)., *Conflict in the Classroom: The Education of Emotionally Disturbed Children.* Belmont, CA: Wadsworth. [1]

REDL. F., & WINEMAN, D. (1951). *Children who Hate.* New York: The Free Press. [1]

REDL, F., & WINEMAN, D. (1952). *Controls from Within.* New York: The Free Press. [1]

REILLY, M. J., IMBER, S. C., & CREMINS, J. (1978). *The Effects of Life Space Interviews on Social Behaviors of Junior High School Needs Students.* Paper presented at the 56th International Council for Exceptional Children, Kansas City. [9]

REINERT, H. R. (1972). The emotionally disturbed. In B. R. Gearheart (ed.), *Education of the Exceptional Child.* San Francisco: Intext Educational Publishers. [1]

RENSHAW, D. C. (1974). *The Hyperactive Child.* Chicago: Nelson-Hall. [11]

REPORT OF THE CONFERENCE ON THE USE OF STIMULANT DRUGS IN THE TREATMENT OF BEHAVIORALLY DISORDERED YOUNG SCHOOL CHILDREN. (1971). *Journal of Learning Disabilities, 4,* 523–30. [11]

REYNOLDS, C. R., & RICHMOND, B. O. (1978). What I think and feel: A revised measure of children's manifest anxiety. *Journal of Abnormal Child Psychology, 6,* 271–80. [3]

REZMIERSKI, V., & REZMIERSKI, L. (1979). The institution special education program: A working program and its message to teacher training. *Behavioral Disorders, 4* (3), 173–82. [13]

RHODES, W. C. (1972). Overview of interventions. In W. C. Rhodes and M. L. Tracy (eds.), *A Study of Child Variance:* (Vol. 2) *Interventions.* Ann Arbor: University of Michigan Press. [1, 8]

RHODES, W. C., & GIBBINS, S. (1972). Community programming for the behaviorally deviant child. In H. C. Quay & J. F. Werry (eds.), *Psychopathologcial Disorders of Childhood.* New York: Wiley. [11]

RHODES, W. C., & PAUL, J. L. (1978). *Emotionally Disturbed and Deviant Children: New Views and Approaches.* Englewood Cliffs, NJ: Prentice-Hall. [1]

RICH, H. L. (1978). A matching model for educating the emotionally disturbed and behaviorally disordered. *Focus on Exceptional Children, 10* (3), 1–11. [2]

RIEGEL, K. F. (1975). Toward a dialectical theory of development. *Human Development, 18,* 50–64. [2]

RIMLAND, B. (1969). Psychogenesis vs. biogenesis: The issues and evidence. In S. C. Plog & R. G. Edgerton (eds.), *Changing Perspectives in Mental Illness.* New York: Holt, Rinehart & Winston. [1]

ROBERTS, T. B. (1975). *Four Psychologies Applied To Education: Freudian—Behavioral—Humanistic—Transpersonal.* Cambridge, MA: Schenkman Publishing Co. [1]

ROSENSHINE, B. (1977). Review of teaching variables and student achievement. In G. D. Borich & K. S. Fenton (eds.), *The Appraisal of Teaching: Concepts and Process.* Menlo Park, CA: Addison Wesley. [6]

ROSENSHINE, B. (1980). How time is spent in elementary classrooms. In C. Denham & A. Lieberman (eds.), *Time to Learn.* Washington, D.C.: National Institute of Education. [6]

ROSENTHAL, D. (ED.). (1963). *The Genain Quadruplets: A Case Study and Theoretical Analysis of Heredity and Environment in Schizophrenia.* New York: Basic Books. [1]

ROSENTHAL, R., & JACOBSON, L. (1966). Teacher's expectancies: Determinants of pupils' IQ gains. *Psychological Reports, 19,* 115–18. [8]

ROSSI, A. S. (1975). Transition to parenthood. In F. Winch & G. B. Spanler (eds.), *Selected Studies in Marriage and the Family.* New York: Holt, Rinehart & Winston. [12]

ROTER, M. J. (1981). Music, a therapeutic intervention for emotionally disturbed youth. In F. H. Wood (ed.), *Perspectives for a New Decade: Education's Responsibility for Seriously Disturbed and Behaviorally Disordered Children and Youth.* Reston, VA: Council for Exceptional Children, 154–62. [9]

RUBENSTEIN, F. A. (1948). Childhood mental disease in America. A review of the literature prior to 1900. *American Journal of Orthopsychiatry, 18,* 314–21. [1]

RUBIN, R., & BALOW, B. (1971). Learning and behavior disorders: A longitudinal study. *Exceptional Children, 38,* 293–98. [8]

*RUNGE, A., WALKER, J., & SHEA, T. M. (1975). A passport to positive parent-teacher communications. *Teaching Exceptional Children, 7* (3), 91–92. [12]

RUSCH, F. R. (1979). Toward the validation of social/vocational survival skills. *Mental Retardation, 17,* 143–45. [13]

RUSS, D. F. (1972). A review of learning and behavior theory as it relates to emotional disturbance in children. In W. C. Rhodes & M. L. Tracy (eds.), *A Study of Child Variance* (Vol. I). Ann Arbor: University of Michigan Press. [1]

RUSSELL, A. E., & RUSSELL, W. A. (1979). Using bibliotherapy with emotionally disturbed children. *Teaching Exceptional Children. 11,* 168–69. [9]

RUTHERFORD, R. B., & EDGAR, E. (1979). *Teachers and Parents: A Guide to Interaction and Cooperation* (abridged ed.). Boston: Allyn & Bacon. [12]

*RUTHERFORD, R. B., & NEEL, R. (1978). The role of punishment with behaviorally disordered children. *Monograph in Behavior Disorders.* Tempe, AZ: Arizona State University. [10]

RUTTER, M. L. (1980). Raised lead levels and impaired cognitive/behavioral functioning: A review of the evidence. *Developmental Medicine and Child Neurology, 22,* Supplement 42. [1]

RUTTER, M. L., TIZARD, J., & WHITMORE, K. (1970). *Education Health, and Behavior.* New York: Wiley. [1]

SAFRAN, S., & SAFRAN, J. (1984). The self-monitoring mood chart: measuring affect in the classroom. *Teaching Exceptional Children, 16* (3), 172–75. [11]

SAILOR, W., & GUESS, D. (1983). *Severely Handicapped Students: An Instructional Design.* Boston: Houghton Mifflin. [5]

SALEND, S. J., & VIGILIANTI, D. (1982). Preparing secondary students for the mainstream. *Teaching Exceptional Children, 14* (4), 137–40. [4]

SANKAR, D. V. (1979). Plasma levels of folates, riboflavin, Vitamin B6 and ascorbate in severely disturbed children. *Journal of Autism and Developmental Disorders, 8,* 73–82. [1]

SARASON, I. G., GLASER, E. M., & FARGO, G. A. (1972). *Reinforcing Productive Classroom Behavior.* New York: Behavioral Publications. [1]

SCHEAF, W. A. (1972) The effects of paired learning and Glasser-type discussions on two determinants of academic achievement and on reading achievement of male delinquents. Unpublished doctoral dissertation, Case Western Reserve University. [9]

*SCHMID, R., ALGOZZINE, B., MAHER, M., & WELLS, D. (1984). Teaching emotionally disturbed adolescents: A study of selected teacher and teaching characteristics. *Behavioral Disorders, 9* (2), 105–12. [13]

SCHOPLER, E., & REICHLER, R. J. (1971). Parents as cotherapists in the treatment of psychotic children. *Journal of Autism and Childhood Schizophrenia, 1,* 87–102. [12]

SCHROEDER, S. R., & SCHROEDER, C. (1982). Organic factors. In J. L. Paul & B. Epanchin (eds). *Emotional Disturbance in Children.* Columbus, OH: Charles E. Merrill. [1]

*SCHUMAKER, J. B., PEDERSON, C. S., HAZEL, J. S., & MEYEN E. L. (1983). Social skills curricula for mildly handicapped adolescents: A review. *Focus on Exceptional Children, 16* (4), 1–16. [13]

SCOTT, L. C., & GOETZ, E. M. (1980). Issues in the collection of in-class data by teachers. *Education and Treatment of Children, 3,* 365–71. [5]

SCOTT, M. (1980). Ecological theory and methods for research in special education. *Journal of Special Education, 4,* 279–94. [2]

*SELIGMAN, M. (1979). *Strategies for Helping Parents of Exceptional Children.* New York: Free Press. [12]

SHAPIRO, E. S. (1984). Self-monitoring procedures. In T. H. Ollendick & M. Hersen (eds)., *Child Behavioral Assessment: Principles and Procedures.* New York: Pergamon Press. [3]

SHAW, C. R. (1974). *The Psychiatric Disorders of Childhood.* New York: Appleton-Century-Crofts. [11]

SHEA, T. M. (1968). *Cooperative Assessment-Remediation Center for Emotionally Handicapped Children.* Carbondale: Southern Illinois University, Department of Special Education. [3]

SHEA, T. M. (1978). *Teaching Children and Youth with Behavior Disorders.* St. Louis: C. V. Mosby. [8, 12]

*SHEA, T. M., & BAUER, A. M. (1985). *Parents and Teachers of Exceptional Children: A Handbook for Involvement.* Boston: Allyn & Bacon. [12]

SHEARN, D. F., & RANDOLPH, D. L. (1978). Effects of reality therapy methods applied in the classroom. *Psychology in the Schools, 15,* 79–83. [9]

*SILVERMAN, R., ZIGMOND, N. & SANSONE, J. (1981). Teaching coping skills to adolescents with learning problems. *Focus on Exceptional Children, 13* (6), 1–20. [13]

SLOWITSCHEK, C. E., LEWIS, B. L., SHORES, R. E., & EZZELL, D. L. (1980). Procedures for analyzing student performance data to generate hypotheses for the purpose of educational decision making. *Behavioral Disorders, 5* (3), 136–50. [5]

SMITH, C. R., FRANK, A. R., & SNIDER, B. C. F. (1984). School psychologsts' and teachers' perceptions of data used in the identification of behaviorally disordered students. *Behavioral Disorders, 10* (1), 27–32. [3]

*SMITH, C. R., & McGINNIS, E. (1982). Professional and ethical issues related to teaching behaviorally impaired students. In R. Peterson and J. Rosell (eds.), *Professional and Ethical Issues Related to Teaching Behaviorally Impaired Students.* Lincoln, NE: Nebraska University. [2, 7, 8]

SOLOMON, J. (1951). Therapeutic uses of play. In H. H. Anderson & G. L. Anderson (eds.), *An Introduction To Projective Techniques.* Englewood Cliffs, NJ: Prentice-Hall. [9]

*SPEECE, D. L., & MANDELL, C. J. (1980). An analysis of resource room support services for regular teachers. *Learning Disability Quarterly, 3,* 49–53. [4]

STAINBACK, S., & STAINBACK, W. (1980). Some trends in the education of children labelled behaviorally disordered. *Behavioral Disorders, 5* (4), 240–49. [3]

STENNETT, R. G. (1966). Emotional handicaps in the elementary years: phase or disease? *American Journal of Orthopsychiatry, 36,* 444–49. [1]

STIGEN, G. (1976). *Heartaches and Handicaps: An Irreverent Survival Manual.* Palo Alto, CA: Parents' Science and Behavior Books. [12]

STOKES, T. R., & BAER, D. M. (1978). An implicit technology of generalization. *Journal of Applied Behavior Analysis, 10,* 341–67. [10]

STRAIN, P. S., SAINTO, D., & MAHEADY, L. (1984). Toward a functional assessment of severely handicapped learners. *Educational Psychologist, 19* (3), 180–87. [3]

STRAUSS, A. A., & LEHTINEN, L. (1947) *Psychopathology and Education of the Brain-Injured Child.* New York: Grune & Stratton, Inc. [7]

*SUSSER, P. (1974). Parents are partners. *The Exceptional Parent, 4* (3), 41–47. [12]

SWANSON, J. M., & KINSBOURNE, M. (1980). Food dyes impair performance of hyperactive children on a laboratory learning test. *Science, 207* (28), 1485–86. [11]

*SWAP, S. M. (1974). Disturbing classrooms: A developmental and ecological view. *Exceptional Children, 41,* 163–71. [2, 11]

SWAP, S. M., PRIETO, A. G., & HARTH, R. (1982). Ecological perspectives of the emotionally disturbed child. In R. L. McDowell, G. W. Adamson, & F. W. Wood (eds.), *Teaching Emotionally Disturbed Children.* Boston: Little, Brown. [11]

SYDNEY, J., & MINNER, S. (1983). The influence of sibling information on the placement recommendation of special class teachers. *Behavioral Disorders, 9* (1), 43–45. [4]

*THIAGARAJAN, S. (1976). Designing instructional games for handicapped learners. *Focus on Exceptional Children, 7,* 1–11. [6]

THOMAS, A., & CHESS, S. (1977). *Temperament and Development.* New York: Brunner/Mazel. [1]

THOMAS, E. D., & MARSHALL, M. J. (1977). Clinical evaluation and coordination of services: An ecological model. *Exceptional Children, 44* 16–22. [2]

THORNDIKE, E. L. (1932). *The Fundamentals of Learning.* New York: Teacher's College Press. [1]

THURMAN, S. K. (1977). Congruence of behavioral ecologies: A model for special education programming. *Journal of Special Education, 11,* 329–33. [2]

THURSBY, D. D. (1977). Everyone's a star. *Teaching Exceptional Children, 9* (3), 77–78. [9]

*TYMITZ-WOLF, B. (1982). Guidelines for assessing IEP goals and objectives. *Teaching Exceptional Children, 14* (5), 198–200. [5]

*TYMITZ-WOLF, B. (1984). An analysis of EMR children and worries about mainstreaming. *Education and Training of the Mentally Retarded, 19,* 157/-67. [4]

*VANTOUR, J. A. C., & STEWART-KURKER (1980). A library for exceptional children promotes home-school cooperation. *Teaching Exceptional Children, 13* (1), 4–7. [12]

*VETTER-ZEMITZSCH, A., BERSTEIN, R., JOHNSTON, J., LARSON, C., SIMON D., & SMITH, A. (1984). The on-campus program: A systematic/behavioral approach to behavior disorders in high school. *Focus on Exceptional Children, 16* (6), 1–8. [13]

VIRDEN, T. (1984). Supportive peer groups: A behavior mangement program for children. In J. Grosenick, S. Huntze, E. McGinnis, & C. Smith (eds.), *Social/Affective Interventions in Behavior Disorders.* Des Moines: Iowa Department of Public Instruction. [11]

*VOGELSBERG, R. T., ANDERSON, J., BERGER, P., HASELDEN, T., MITWELL, S., SCHMIDT, C., SKOWRON, A., ULETT, D., & WILCOX, B. (1980). Programming for apartment living: A description and rationale of an independent living inventory. *Journal of the Association for the Severely Handicapped, 5* (1), 38–54. [13]

WAGNER, M. (1972). Environmental interventions in emotional disturbance. In W. C. Rhodes & M. L. Tracy (eds.), *A Study of Child Variance.* (Vol. II:) *Interventions.* Ann Arbor: University of Michigan Press. [1, 11]

*WAHLER, R. G., & CORMIER, W. H. (1970). The ecological interview. A first step in outpatient child behavior therapy. *Journal of Behavioral Therapy and Experimental Psychology, 1,* 279–89. [3, 11, 13]

*WALKER, J., & SHEA, T. M. (1984). *Behavior Management: A Practical Approach for Educators.* St. Louis: C. V. Mosby. [1, 6, 10, 12]

WEBER, W. A. (1977). Classrooms management. In J. M. Cooper (ed.), *Teaching Skills: A Handbook.* Lexington, MA: D. C. Heath and Company. [8]

*WEHMAN, P., & MCLAUGHLIN, P. J. (1981). *Program Development in Special Education.* New York: McGraw-Hill. [4]

WEINSTEIN, L. (1969). Project re-ed schools for emotionally disturbed children: Effectiveness as viewed by referring agencies, parents, and teachers. *Exceptional Children, 35* (9) 703–11. [11]

WEISS, B., WILLIAMS, J. H., MARGEN, S., ABRAMS, B., CITRON, L. J., COX, C., McKIBBEN, J., & OGAR, D. (1980). Behavioral responses to artificial food colors. *Science, 207* (28), 1487–88.[11]

WERRY, J., & QUAY, H. (1971). The prevalence of behavior symptoms in younger elementary school children. *American Journal of Orthopsychiatry, 41* (1), 136–43. [1]

WHELAN, R. J., DeSAMAN, L. M., & FORTMEYER, D. J. (1984). Oh! Those wonderful feelings (the relationship between pupil affect and achievement). *Focus on Exceptional Children, 16* (8), 1–8. [2]

WHITE, M. A. (1961). Evaluating psychological problems of school children. *Exceptional Children, 28,* 75–78. [3]

WICKMAN, E. K. (1928). *Children's Behavior and Teacher's Attitudes.* New York: Commonwealth Fund. [1]

*WIEDERHOLT, J. L., HAMMILL, D. D., & BROWN, V. (1978). *The Resource Teacher: A Guide to Effective Practice.* Boston: Allyn & Bacon. [4]

*WIEDERHOLT, J. L., & McNUTT, G. (1979). Assessment and instructional planning: A conceptual framework. In D. Cullinan & M. H. Epstein (eds.), *Special Education for Adolescents.* Columbus, OH: Charles E. Merrill. [13]

WILLIAMS, G. H., & WOOD, M. M. (1977). *Developmental Art Therapy.* Baltimore: University Park Press. [9, 11]

WILSON, E. O. (1975). *Sociobiology: The New Synthesis.* Cambridge, MA: Harvard University Press. [1]

WILSON, J. E., & SHERRETS, S. D. (1979). A review of past and current pharmacological interventions in the treatment of emotionally disturbed children and adolescents. *Behavioral Disorders, 5* (1), 60–69. [11]

*WINSLOW. L. (1977). Parent participation. In S. Torres (ed.), *A Primer on Individualized Education Programs for Handicapped Children.* Reston, VA: The Foundation for Exceptional Children. [12]

*WITT, J. C., ELLIOTT, S. N., & MARTENS, B. K. (1984). Acceptability of behavioral interventions used in the classroom: The influence of the amount of teacher time, severity of behavior problem, and type of intervention. *Behavioral Disorders, 9* (2), 95–104. [4, 5]

WOLPE, J. (1961). The systematic desensitization treatment of a neurosis. *Journal of Nervous and Mental Disease, 132,* 189–203. [10]

WOOD, F. H. (1978). Punishment and special education: Some concluding comments. In F. H. Wood and K. C. Lakin (eds.), *Punishment and Aversive Stimulation in Special Education: Legal, Theoretical and Practical Issues in Their Use with Emotionally Disturbed Children and Youth.* Minneapolis: University of Minnesota. [8, 10]

*WOOD, F. H. (1981). The influence of personal, social, and political factors on the labeling of students. In F. H. Wood (ed.), *Perspectives for a New Decade: Education's Responsibility for Seriously Disturbed and Behaviorally Disordered Children and Youth.* Reston, VA: Council for Exceptional Children.

*WOOD, F. H. (1981). The influence of personal, social, and political factors on the labeling of students. In F. H. Wood (ed.), *Perspectives for a New Decade: Education's Responsibility for Seriously Disturbed and Behaviorally Disordered Children and Youth.* Reston, VA: Council for Exceptional Children. [1]

WOOD, F. H., & LAKIN, K. C. (1978). The legal status and use of corporal punishment and other aversive procedures in schools. In F. H. Wood and K. C. Lakin (eds.), *Punishment and Aversive Stimulation in Special Education: Legal, Theoretical and Practical Issues in Their Use with Emotionally Disturbed Children and Youth.* Minneapolis: University of Minnesota. [10]

WOOD, M. M. (1975a). *Developmental Therapy: A Textbook for Teachers as Therapists for Emotionally Disturbed Young Children.* Baltimore: University Park Press. [11, 12]

WOOD, M. M. (1975b). A developmental curriculum for social and emotional growth. In L. Lillie (ed.), *Early Childhood Curriculum: An Individualized Approach.* Palo Alto, CA: Science Research Associates, Inc. [11]

WOOD, M. M. (1976). Foreword. In J. Purvis and S. Samet (eds.), *Music in Developmental Therapy.* Baltimore: University Park Press, vii–viii. [9]

*YAMAMOTO, K. (1969). *Teaching: Essays and Readings.* Boston: Houghton Mifflin Co. [7]

YSSELDYKE, J., ALGOZZINE, B., & ALLEN, D. (1982). Participation of regular education teachers in special education teaching decision making. *Exceptional Children, 48,* 365–66. [3]

*YSSELDYKE, J. E., REGAN, R., THURLOW, M. & SCHWARTZ, S. (1981). Current assessment practices: The "cattle dip approach." *Diagnostique, 7* (2), 16–27. [3]

Index